D0559716

A HISTORY OF SCOTTISH
CONGREGATIONALISM

A HISTORY OF SCOTTISH CONGREGATIONALISM

Harry Escott

GLASGOW

The Congregational Union of Scotland

217 WEST GEORGE STREET, C.2

First published 1960

DEDICATION

TO

Robert Kinniburgh, James Ross, Fergus Ferguson, G. L. S. Thompson, and John T. Hornsby, departmental historians of Congregationalism in Scotland, upon whose sure foundations I have builded, this the first complete history of the Congregational Churches and their Union is respectfully dedicated.

Printed in Great Britain at
The University Press
Aberdeen

PREFACE

ALTHOUGH the writer is indebted, and deeply, to the printed works of Kinniburgh, Ferguson and Ross in presenting this book to the public, it is for the most part a *new* work. Its architecture at least is entirely new.

To particularise. The story of seventeenth and mid-eighteenth-century Congregational Independency, sketched in Dr. Ross's book, is here more fully and simply re-told in the light of recent research in this field. One has been privileged, for instance, to survey the life and teaching of John Glas in the meridian light that J. T. Hornsby has thrown into this dark corner of our annals. Wholly new chapters are supplied on the contributions of David Dale and the Bereans to eighteenth-century Independency. In regard to the Haldane Revival, the most momentous and romantic episode of the entire story, it was thought best to set it against the background of the politics and culture of the French Revolutionary era, as these affected the social life of Scotland. If any success has been achieved in this part of our task, the praise is due to G. L. S. Thompson's researches into the *Origins of Congregationalism in Scotland*, upon which one has freely and gratefully drawn.

Dr. Ross's excellent book, as he himself confessed in its preface, confined itself in the main to an exploration of the *origins of* Congregationalism. A somewhat bigger aim characterises the present work. It attempts to deal more fully with the evolution of Congregationalism both in its C.U. and E.U. traditions. For example, it traces the revolt from Calvinism, too narrowly regarded by our denominational historians from the Evangelical Unionist angle, as a more ubiquitous phenomenon. Actually the revolt from the theology of the *Westminster Confession* was precipitated by non-theological factors in the social life of the nation, and it was in fact active within the churches of the Congregational Union perhaps before, but certainly contemporaneously with, James Morison's historic embodiment of it.

Much more is written in this book than in any of its predecessors about the Liberal Era in nineteenth-century Congregationalism. An appraisement long overdue is offered of the life and

v

labours of John Hunter, our chief exponent of theological liberalism, whose emancipating work was done mainly in the impinging
spheres of hymnology and liturgy.

The whole of part six, 'Our Day and Age', and almost the like
of part seven, 'A Chronicle of the Churches', have not appeared in
public before. And naturally it is with shyness that they do so now
with such suddenness. For it would be strange indeed if the
writer were not to intrude his own views in such inchoate pages, as
these in the nature of the case must be. And more than surprising
would it be, too, if all his conclusions were representative of an
official interpretation of the events.

Anyone who essays to write about the origins of Scottish
Congregationalism must perforce build upon James Ross's foundation. This has been done in the present work, and sometimes
Ross's massive masonry has been broken up only to be reared
again in a renewed form or in another place. But time has
revealed one or two little fissures in the factual rock. First, Dr.
Ross's contention that the earliest Reformed churches in Scotland
were Congregationalist in character and intention seems to us both
historically and psychologically untenable, for reasons that will be
put forth fully in the following narrative. Second, he errs we
believe, along with his brother historians, in according such a
prominent place to Robert and James Haldane in the genesis of
the Congregational movement, as to hide the supreme rôle played
by that great and modest man Greville Ewing in the architecture
of an important religious denomination. The present work
corrects these defects in the historical survey of its great predecessor.

It must be said, however, that one has never found it difficult
to hold with James Ross that Congregationalism (after its seven-
teenth-century experiments), even in this Presbyterian citadel of
the north has a lineage and character essentially Scottish. There is,
without a shadow of a doubt, such an ecclesiastical *genre* and social
phenomenon as *Scottish* Congregationalism for the historian to
trace and evaluate. The belief that this is so, along with the conviction, strengthened by the circumstances of our time, that we
need to re-explore our spiritual roots for guidance and inspiration
alike, is the *raison d'être* of this book.

It is not unnatural that in an uprooted age like the present
the writing and reading of history, particularly denominational
religious history, should be regarded as a waste of a man's precious

time. Life is too brief and contemporary problems too urgent, it is argued sometimes, to justify the expenditure of time and energy upon what are considered merely academic or antiquarian pursuits. Like Nietzsche modern men and women believe, perhaps, that history tends to render them unfit for life, paralysing their activity by awakening a nostalgia for ancient bygone policies and pieties. This is exactly the criticism we expect to hear, when this book goes out in search of readers.

It is commonly thought that the toil of the religious historian is profitless, as it results only in the exhumation of skeletons all dust and bones to be classified later in some ivory tower, and labelled. Surely, you ask, far from history being a source of inspiration and guidance for the present business of living, is it not in reality an academic escape from its stinging immediacy? The seven years of research and writing that the present historian has spent amidst the business and worries of a city pastorate constitute a more convincing argument against such a view than any amount of uncostly protestation. The fact that this book is now completed is proof enough (to the writer at any rate) that the purpose of historical study is to reach the warm moist roots of things—those values and virtues, principles and ideals, which far from desiccating life, preserve its freshness and ensure its development. Rightly conceived the writing of history is more like a resurrection than an excavation: the aim of the historian is not to embalm the past but to enliven it, and through it to enlighten the present. Of his scraps and pieces, his reminiscences, records, researches (as one historian has so aptly said), the true historian may say with Mark Antony in the market-place, 'You are not wood, you are not stones, but men'.

In this age without the consciousness of roots, the writing and study of history, under God's good hand, may be part of our preservation. As churchmen a knowledge of God's ways with our fathers, and the measure of their walk with Him may save us from much foolish wandering, and fill our drooping spirits, as well, with a great hope. It is periodically necessary for us as peoples and churches to re-ascend to our origins.

Lastly, a word to the reader that he may find his way through this book to the best advantage. Two-thirds of it is devoted to general history, but towards the end of the volume will be found a brief recital of the career of every church, obsolete or extant, connected with the Denomination from its beginnings. I have taken the liberty in these local notes, and sometimes less frequently in the body of the book, of leavening the cold facts here and there with a few lighter touches, believing that even Church History is better, and indeed loses nothing of piety, for a little discreet humanising. I have also attempted, so far as church records have allowed me, to bring Dr. Ross's list of ministers up to date. In this part of a most difficult task I have had the assistance of many friends but of four in particular—the Rev. R. F. G. Calder, the Rev. A. S. Marshall, Mr. William Gauld and Mr. W. Stewart Smith, without whose help there would have been far more inaccuracies and hiatuses in this section of the work than there must be at present. I am most indebted to these gentlemen, as I am indeed to all who have helped me to lay my hands on relevant material amidst the demands of crowded days. The Rev. Dr. Price and the Rev. Dr. Simpson read the book in manuscript and made some useful suggestions. A generous grant by the Carnegie Trust for the Universities of Scotland has facilitated the publication of the work. May God bless the book and make it an encouraging and reviving message of the Holy Spirit to the Church and the Nation alike.

GLASGOW,

August 1959

CONTENTS

THE RELATION OF CONGREGATIONALISM TO PRESBYTERIANISM IN SCOTLAND

AFTER some abortive attempts in the sixteenth and seventeenth centuries to introduce English Independency into Scotland, modern Scottish Congregationalism arose. It owed its existence to the confluence of two urgent streams of Christian conviction, the Haldanite revival of the French Revolutionary period, and the mid-nineteenth-century Morisonian movement which culminated in the formation of the Evangelical Union in 1843, that *annus mirabilis* of Scottish ecclesiastical history. This book will be concerned mainly to trace these two streams from their sources to 1896, the year of their union; and thereafter to follow the course of the broadened river to the present day, indicating how and where it has brought refreshment to the religious life of Scotland.

Before beginning this task historical sense as well as historical truth compels us to sketch the English affiliations, and to trace some few other streams with a native Congregational source that in the course of time became dried up and exhausted, never meeting in blest union as did the other two. Such were the Glasites, the Bereans, and the Old Scotch Independents, democratic movements of the Spirit, naïve sometimes to the point of crudity, yet too intense and parochial to flow far afield. Consequently these streamlets are no more, and it is difficult to trace even the channels through which they once flowed with ebullient if narrow life.

All these—streamlets, streams and river alike—are Scottish, as Scottish as the burns and waters that swell the Forth and Clyde and Dee. As surely as those are coloured by the terrain through which they run so these streams of the Spirit, small and great, belong to Scotland's native spiritual culture. They are as much a part of the nation's religious life as the great Inland Sea of Presbyterianism so markedly is. They are indigenous to the soil of Scotland's heart and mind and life. They are all manifestations of a Congregationalism which is unashamedly Scottish.

This does not imply, as some historians have thought, that the first native expression of the Reformed Faith in Scotland was Congregationalist, and that Presbyterianism was a subsequent falling away from the ideal of church life. Doubtless the earliest reformed churches in Scotland had not a few Congregational features. In 1560 appeared *The Scots Confession,* and *The First Book of Discipline* in the year following, both the offspring of John Knox's ardent Christian spirit. These symbols of the Reformation are indeed remarkable for the clarity and force with which they declare the principle of religious Independency. Illustrations of this are found in both documents. For example, the *independence* of the several churches was stressed: the notes of the true kirk of God were declared to be, 'First, the true preaching of the Word of God. . . . Secondly, the right administration of the sacraments. . . . Lastly, ecclesiastical discipline rightly administered, as God's Word prescribed, whereby vice is repressed and virtue nourished. Wheresoever, then, these notes are seen, and of any time continue (be the number never so few, above two or three), there, without all doubt, is the true kirk of Christ, who, according to His promise, is in the midst of them. . . . And such like we, the inhabitants of the realm of Scotland, professors of Christ Jesus, confess us to have in our cities, towns, and places reformed.'[1] There was at first, it is true, no provision made for the government of churches by ecclesiastical courts external to the local congregation, but that arrangement did come into full operation in 1581, when *The Second Book of Discipline* appeared, and was in the mind of Knox from the beginning from his warm admiration for Calvin's Genevan experiment, though at first circumstances delayed its adoption in Scotland.

Congregational features are traceable also in the Call of a minister. Both in *The Scots Confession* of 1560 and *The First Book of Discipline,* the call and appointment of the minister was in the hands of the people—a privilege and duty for which Congregationalists have always strongly contended. But it should be remembered that even in *The First Book of Discipline,* to go no further, it is distinctly laid down that, should any congregation neglect to exercise its duty in this regard, 'the best reformed church, to wit, the church of the superintendent with his council, may present unto them a man whom they judge apt to feed the

---

[1] *The Scots Confession,* Chapter XVIII.

flock of Christ Jesus'.[1] Such a step is not in accordance with traditional Congregational procedure.

Again, according to *The First Book of Discipline*, 'ordinary vocation consisteth in election, examination, and admission'.[2] The congregation had the right to elect its minister, but before the person elected could take up the charge he had to be examined as to doctrine, life and knowledge, and his power to preach by 'the learned ministers and next reformed church'.[3] Should he 'be judged unable of the regiment by the learned' the people's election was null and void. Such churches can hardly be described as 'independent and Congregational'.[4]

The Congregational view is that every church is spiritually independent of other churches, and by virtue of the presence of Christ in it, has the right to choose its own officers, and that no ecclesiastical court or assembly outside of itself is warranted to wield authority over it. The early Reformation churches of Scotland were manifestly not of this kind, even at the very first; and were never intended to be.

If further proof of the non-congregational character of the churches of the Scottish Reformation be required, it is forthcoming in the fact that as early as December 1560 a General Assembly of the Kirk of Scotland met in Edinburgh, constituted of only six ministers and thirty-five laymen, and proceeded to legislate for the internal affairs of the Church at large. Furthermore, as early as the General Assembly of June 1563 the formal style of authority was used: 'The Kirk appoints and decerns.' The subsequent Assembly (December 1562) elected provincial synods to meet regularly twice a year with powers to translate as well as appoint ministers. In the face of such evidence any claim that Knox and his colleagues intended the Scottish Church at the Reformation to be Congregational in polity is unwarranted. The seed of the subsequent Presbyterian way of worship and life is all there in the first symbols of the Scottish Reformed Church, in 1560.

In addition it should be said, that in its definition of the notes that make a true Church, *The Scots Confession* is not in so close rapprochement with the Congregational idea of the Church as

[1] *The First Book of Discipline*, Chapter IV, para. 2.
[2] *Ibid.* para. 1.
[3] *Ibid.* para. 4.
[4] Ross, *A History of Congregational Independency in Scotland*, p. 6.

some have imagined. The functions of the Church: preaching, sacraments, discipline are rightly enumerated, but nothing is said in the Confession about the Christian life and calling of those who compose the Church, upon which Congregationalism, when true to itself, has laid considerable stress. The Kirk to the Scots Reformers was not a gathered fellowship of those who had passed from darkness into light; *every* parishioner had his place in its membership and was subject to its discipline. Church and nation were thus identified. That such were the views of Knox and his co-workers, *The Scots Confession* and *The First Book of Discipline* leave us in no doubt. Only by shutting our eyes to historical fact can it be held that the Reformation movement in Scotland in its intentions and beginnings proceeded along Congregational lines. The Scot has always had a leaning towards the concept of the Church as an all-embracing structure—a mighty institution. Democratic though he be at heart, his desire for orderliness, authority, soldierly array and discipline finds satisfaction in the Presbyterial system. His pragmatic bent of mind responds to the practical witness to itself confirmed daily by Presbyterianism. Robert Rainy has expressed clearly and eloquently the attraction of Presbyterianism for the Scottish mind and spirit. It was due, he said, 'to something else besides the confidence men had in their theoretical conclusions about Church government. . . . It meant organised life, regulated distribution of forces, graduated recognition of gifts, freedom to discuss, authority to control, agency to administer.'[1]

A just appraisement of the Scottishness of the Congregational churches and of their contribution for two and a half centuries to the national life and culture will not, therefore, depend, as some have believed, on proving the chronological priority in Scotland of the Congregational conception of the Church. That cannot be done without violating historical fact. The rôle of Congregationalism in the drama of the spiritual life of Scotland has been, for all that, a considerable and essential one. It has arisen largely through the failure of the National Church and its offshoots to maintain in equilibrium the tension between authority and freedom that characterises that communion at its truest and best. The Congregational churches in all their branches have been the custodians of spiritual freedom which, although an avowed

---

[1] *Three Lectures on the Church of Scotland* (1872), p. 15.

and cherished constituent of Presbyterianism, has tended sometimes to become submerged under the weight of mere ecclesiastical
opinion or convenience. On the other hand, it should be borne in
mind, that the Scottish brand of Congregational churchmanship,
just because of its Presbyterian provenance, reveals some resem-
blances to Presbyterianism, regarding wistfully sometimes the
practical and orderly administrative machinery which the Presbyterian system has at its disposal. This is why, much to the
surprise and chagrin of our Congregational brethren of other
traditions, whose historical provenance is different, the Congregational churches of Scotland appear to imitate their Presbyterian
mother in aspects of dress and deportment.

PART ONE

SOME EARLY ATTEMPTS TO INTRODUCE CONGREGATIONALISM TO SCOTLAND

CHAPTER I

ROBERT BROWNE, JOHN PENRY AND OTHERS IN SCOTLAND

I

IT was an English refugee Robert Browne, generally credited with being the founder of Congregationalism in the south, who introduced the new type of church polity and witness to Scotland, at the end of the sixteenth century.

Driven from his native country by the persecution of Episcopalian churchmen, Browne sought asylum first in Flanders, and then along with four or five companions and their families resolved to visit Scotland, in the hope of finding here a more favourable field for his work as a preacher. He landed at Dundee towards the close of 1583, and very early in the following year we find him settled in Edinburgh.

On landing at Dundee Browne and his friends had been cordially received. At St. Andrews also they had not been without encouragement. From Andrew Melville, Browne had procured a letter of introduction to Mr. James Lowsone one of the Edinburgh ministers. When, however, they reached the capital and took up their residence 'at the head of the Canongate' on Thursday, 9 January 1584, their experience was somewhat different. They soon discovered that the Kirk of Scotland was as intolerant of Congregationalism and as ready to persecute its devotees as the Church of England had been.

Browne seems to have lost no time in beginning to proclaim his principles, of which Calderwood presents us with this summary: 'They held opinioun of separatioun from all Kirks where excommunicatioun was not rigerouslie used against open offenders not repenting. They would not admit witnesses in baptisme; and sundrie other opiniouns they had.' With these principles and their English exponent the Edinburgh ecclesiastics had no sympathy, and action was taken immediately to prevent Browne from spreading his doctrine. Less than a week after his arrival he was on his defence before the Session of the Kirk of Edinburgh. A week later, on Thursday, 21 January, Browne was examined by

the Presbytery. The attitude which he took up before the latter
court, 'that the whole discipline of Scotland was amisse, that he
and his companie were not subject to it', and his appeal on that
ground from the Kirk to the Magistrate did not make his Presbyterian critics more kindly disposed towards him. On the contrary, it seems to have made them more determined to prevent
further opportunity being afforded him for spreading his beliefs.
Browne was not allowed to continue in his lodgings, but was
committed to prison, a treatment which he keenly resented. 'In
Scotland', he writes, 'the preachers having no names of byshops
did imprison me more wrongfully than anie byshop would have
done'.

It has been claimed by some historians that Browne stayed in
Scotland for close upon a year, but this is an exaggeration. A letter
from Lord Burleigh to the Archbishop of Canterbury, dated 17
July 1584, indicates that at that date his kinsman had returned to
England. It would seem rather that Browne remained in Scotland
for some months in which, as he himself had claimed, he travelled
extensively, studying Presbyterianism at first hand in the 'best
places as in Dundee, St. Andrewes, Edinborowe and sundrie other
townes'.[1] One cannot imagine, however, that he was silent as to
his own beliefs, or that he hesitated to attempt to convert to them
the Scots whom he encountered on his journeying, but there is no
record whatever of any success in this connection. The time was
manifestly an evil one for any such missionary purpose. The Scots
were in no mood to welcome the new faith. Indeed Presbyterianism
had by this time become indissolubly bound up with the religious
life of the Scottish people, only the Court and all under its influence
did not like it, and at this moment it was fighting strenuously for
its existence. Browne's own testimony was that when he 'came
away, the whole land was in a manner divided into parts, much
people in armes and redie to joine battel, some with the King and
some against him, and all about the preachers' discipline'.[2] In
circumstances such as these any attempt to establish Congregationalism among the Scots was doomed to failure, and it is not
surprising to learn that there is no record of any churches after the
Congregational pattern having been formed by Robert Browne
during his brief but stormy visit to Scotland.

[1] Browne, *A New Year's Gift*, p. 25.   [2] *Ibid.* p. 26.

II

In 1589, some five years after Browne's tempestuous sojourn here, John Penry, whose devotion to Congregationalism later cost him his life, fled from his persecutors across the Border and for a time found refuge in Edinburgh. James Ross, in the absence of any definite factual proof, thinks that so bold and earnest a champion of Congregationalism could not have been silent and inactive during his residence in Scotland.[1] Are we then justified in regarding the Welsh martyr as the second Congregational missionary to these northern parts? What do the known facts suggest?

Until quite recently it was believed that Penry's stay in Scotland extended from 1589 to 1592, some four years. According to a modern scholar the Welshman's exile lasted only till December 1590, and was a peaceful one. Thereafter we are to think of him as hiding in different parts of England, joining the ranks of the English Separatists, formally at least, only in the autumn of 1592.[2] Penry then was not a Congregationalist during his Scottish sojourn but a Puritan, or more correctly a Presbyterian. His views on the nature of the Church and on questions of Church government, abundantly illustrated in his writings up to the year 1592, reveal him as holding views peculiar to himself, yet mainly in alignment with Presbyterian theologians like Thomas Cartwright, rather than with Congregational churchmen like Robert Browne. We notice, for example, in his *A Brief Discovery* (1590), that he stands forth not as the champion of the Congregational way but of the Church of Scotland. Far from continuing the work Browne had begun in Scotland, Penry describes the English Independent as 'that noted schismatic' whose treatment in Scotland was such as 'a proud ungodly man deserved to have'.[3]

From the foregoing facts it must be abundantly clear that the customary picture of John Penry as the bold protagonist of the 'Congregational Way' during his Scottish exile has no historical foundation. His public espousal of Congregationalism was not a Scottish phenomenon: it came later, and his service to Congregationalism was rendered on English soil.

---

[1] *A History of Congregational Independency in Scotland*, pp. 16-17.
[2] *Transactions of the Congregational Historical Society*, pp. 111, 182; *A Brief Discovery*, p. 44.
[3] *A Brief Discovery*, p. 44.

III

After John Penry's departure from Scottish shores at the close of 1590, there is no trace of any other visits of notable English Congregational churchmen till the first quarter of the seventeenth century. This is not surprising. The London church of Barrowe and Greenwood was dissolved in 1593, and its members were driven to seek refuge in Amsterdam. Indeed, so completely was Congregationalism in England suppressed, that for the next decade or so it was unable to assert itself against the political authorities let alone send missionaries to Scotland, whose king, be it remembered, enamoured of Episcopacy and whose people 'thirled' to Presbyterianism, would most certainly have made common cause against its encroachment.

In 1616, however, there was a change in the situation in England. In that year Henry Jacob reached London from Leyden, formed a church in the metropolis, and so commenced a new Congregationalist movement. This revival had far-reaching effects on the religious life of Scotland. As early as 1624 both king and clergy were convinced that 'Brownism', as they called it, had reappeared in Scotland, and indeed to such an extent that endeavour must be made to suppress it.

Calderwood tells us that on 23 March 1624 certain influential men of Edinburgh had ventured to criticise the doctrine preached by one of the city ministers. The king, greatly incensed by this attitude, 'sent down a direction to a select number of the Secrete Council' to try these individuals, six in number, for their boldness, which trial took place on 'the last of Aprile 1624'.[1] In the course of the trial the Bishop of St. Andrews charged one of the critics, John Meine, a merchant, with keeping private conventicles and giving hospitality to a Brownist minister in his house—a charge which the man denied.

What are we to understand by this accusation? Undoubtedly that one of the Presbyterian ministers who had refused to conform to Episcopacy and some people who shared his views had been holding private meetings after the manner of the Brownists. It would appear, therefore, that Congregationalism of a sort did exist in Edinburgh as early as 1624. Nor is this the only evidence of its existence. A royal proclamation of the same year, prohibiting meetings for hearing deprived Presbyterian ministers, aimed also

---

[1] Calderwood, *The History of the Kirk of Scotland*, Vol. VII, pp. 596-604.

at preventing meetings of Brownist, Anabaptist and other sects. It is bluntly asserted in reference to contemporary happenings that 'such seeds of separation . . . have brought forth damned sects of Anabaptists, Families of Love, Brownists . . . and manie such pests'.[1] It would appear, therefore, that as early as 1624, sixteen years prior to the usually accepted date,[2] Congregational principles were in a measure being tried out in Scotland. Indeed all through the years in which the episcopalian party was dominant, there were those up and down the country who refused to conform and adopted the measure of meeting together in private, engaging in Scripture reading, exhortation and prayers for their mutual edification.

When in 1638 the Glasgow Assembly abolished Episcopacy and re-established Presbyterianism the reason for these 'cells of Congregationalism' no longer existed. They might have ceased completely but for the settlement in the West of Scotland about this time of Congregationalists from England and Ireland. We hear, for instance, of 'one, Thomas Livingston, a taylor, and another, Mr. Cornall, a chirurgeon' (both supposed to favour the Brownistical way) who 'came from England as soon as Episcopacy had been thrust out', and also of the arrival from Ireland of 'a fleece of Scots people who being dissatisfied with the forms of that church had long ago forsaken the public assemblies thereof and betaken themselves to conventicles'.[3] Principal Baillie informs us that his countrymen in Ireland, most of whom now sought shelter in Scotland, had become acquainted with the discipline of the Congregational churches of New England, that some of them, who had thought of trying their fortunes there, inclined towards the discipline of these churches, while others of them had been influenced by Brownists 'towards these conceits'.[4]

However, there was no attempt at this time to set up separate independent churches. While it is true that the settlers from the north of Ireland had started family meetings and that these gatherings were conducted by laymen, there were no innovations in church government and no scruples about the Presbyterian polity. The innovations introduced at this time, apart from the

[1] Calderwood, *The History of the Kirk of Scotland*, Vol. VII, p. 612.

[2] Fletcher, Waddington, Orm and Ross regard 1640 or 1642 as the earliest date in the seventeenth century when anything resembling Congregationalism dared to raise its head north of the Tweed.

[3] Bishop Guthrie's *Memoirs*, p. 77; Gordon, *Scots Affairs*, Vol. III, p. 272.

[4] Baillie, *Letters and Journals*, Vol. I, p. 249.

family meetings, were mainly innovations in worship, a movement towards greater simplicity and spontaneity in worship, and a further opportunity for the fellowship to develop its own spiritual life. But even these innovations did not escape the critical eye of the National Church and the whip of its scorn. In 1641 the Assembly passed, in addition to the 'Act against impiety and Schism', a further 'Act against Novations', which forbade the introduction of any novation in doctrine, worship or government, and ordered Presbyteries and Synods to deal with transgressors.[1] Whilst Congregational ideas of church government can never be said at any time to have commended themselves generally to the people of Scotland, Congregational conceptions of worship, which about this time first appeared in Scotland, did eventually find much acceptance and gave to Scottish services those characteristics of plainness and simplicity, freedom and spontaneity, which have distinguished them for two hundred years. Indeed only in recent times have attempts to depart therefrom achieved any measure of success.

Scottish churchmen in the tempestuous seventeenth century believed in the 'jus divinum' of Presbytery. The Presbyterian way to them was neither an accident of history nor made by man; it was divine in its origin and had the warrant of Scripture. The Presbyterian polity, therefore, was right and all others wrong. In such a situation there was as little room for Congregationalism as there had been as little previously for Episcopacy. Religious Independency, with its insistence on the right of each company of Christians to manage their own affairs under the guidance of the Holy Spirit, must have been, in that age of dogmatisms and strong passions, anathema to the Scottish presbyterian—the very antithesis of the national religious system with its 'Assemblies higher and lower in their strong and beautiful subordinations' directing and controlling the wayward moods of men as well as of churches.

[1] Peterkin, *Records of the Kirk of Scotland*, p. 294.

CHAPTER II

THE INFLUENCE OF CROMWELLIAN CONGREGATIONALISM

IT was not until the Cromwellian period that Congregationalism was introduced into Scotland in an open manner and on a large scale. Early in 1650 the English army—in which Congregationalists and Baptists predominated—invaded Scotland under Cromwell to revenge the injuries done by the Scots during their invasion of England, and to exterminate the powerful party which in the north supported the pretensions of Charles II. Accompanying that army as chaplains were such stalwarts and distinguished Congregationalists as John Owen and Joseph Caryl, who regularly preached not only to the English troops but also to the Scottish people. The troops themselves, however, soldiers and officers alike, were not slow to give a reason for the faith that was in them. Cromwell's 'booted apostles' were indeed 'sui generis'; Scotland had never seen their like before. They carried with them the message of the Gospel as well as the munitions of war; and when occasion presented itself they did not hesitate to take possession of the pulpit, and preach with zeal and fervour, and, sometimes at least, with a certain measure of acceptability. We are told that General Lambert secured for himself the East Kirk of Edinburgh, 'quhairin thair was dyveris and sindrie sermounis preached, alsiweill by Captaines and Lieutenantis and trooperis of his Army, as by ordiner pastouris and Englische ministeris. . . . It was thocht that these men were weill giftit yet wer not ordourlie callit according to the discipline observit within the Kingdom of Scotland.'[1]

It has commonly been maintained that Congregationalism made no headway in Scotland in this period, and that no Congregational churches were formed as a result of the missionary efforts of the Cromwellian soldiers.[2] Baillie, however, in his *Letters* tells us that in the Kirk of Kilbryde, 'the best stipend in the West', one, Thomas Charteris, was settled and gathered round him a small fellowship of Congregationalists, while the great majority of the parishioners who adhered to Presbyterianism had

---

[1] J. Nichol, *Diary*, pp. 68-69; see also Chapter IX in the present book.
[2] J. Ross, *A History of Congregational Independency in Scotland*, p. 20.

to build a meeting place for themselves and find a salary for their minister. Another 'Sectarie', he further informs us, was planted at Lenzie; and in other parts of the country similar settlements took place, or were, at least, attempted.[1]

To evaluate at all correctly the influence Cromwellian Congregationalism must have exerted upon Scottish religion we should bear in mind that the sojourn of the English army in Scotland was not merely a matter of weeks or months, but lasted for eight years. After Cromwell had fully established himself, the army of occupation, never less than seven thousand strong, was quartered in eighteen garrison towns as well as in the Citadels of Leith, Perth, Ayr, and Inverness. Many of these troops, officers and men, were Congregationalists and were imbued with the missionary spirit and eager to win the Scots among whom they dwelt to their way of thinking.

After the crushing defeat of the Scots at Dunbar, in 1650, one Scottish writer laments that there were in the Scottish army 'mony Independents and Sectareis quho had too much relatioun and correspondence with General Cromwell'.[2] A careful reading of contemporary documents would, we think, reveal that the Scots were not so indifferent to the preaching and teaching of Cromwell's 'booted apostles' as conservative historians have led us to believe.

Baillie relates of some in Fenwick in Ayrshire who about this time declared for Congregationalism despite the arguments and entreaties of their ministers, who preached against it with tears.[3] There were also, as is more well known, Aberdeen Congregationalists of whose activities we may learn from various sources.

Among the prisoners taken by the English at the battle of Dunbar was Alexander Jaffray, the Provost of Aberdeen. He relates in his *Diary* how, while a prisoner, he had frequent conversations with Cromwell, General Fleetwood, and Dr. Owen. As a result of these interviews Jaffray was led to serious reflections first of all on the justification of the Scottish quarrel with the English. He had fought for the king and the Covenant, but doubts now began to arise in his mind about both. These questionings inevitably raised others about Church government; for what had prompted his zeal and that of the best men of the nation for the Covenant? A desire to maintain the doctrine, worship, and government of the Kirk of

---

[1] Baillie, *Letters and Journals*, Vol. III, p. 244.
[2] J. Nichol, *Diary*, p. 27.
[3] Baillie, *Letters and Journals*, Vol. III, p. 193.

Scotland had certainly had much to do with the contriving and carrying on of the Covenant. But if they had mistaken the mind and will of God against them at Dunbar—and the subsequent dissensions among themselves convinced Jaffray they had—might they not also have mistaken the mind and will of God about the other? Was Presbyterianism a 'jus divinum', and the only way of Christ, as they had claimed? This was the question that now forced itself upon him. After much thought and prayer he came to the conclusion that Presbyterianism was very far from being the only way of Christ. After the most diligent search Jaffray could see in Presbyterianism 'but a human invention composed with much prudence and policy of man's wit, fitted for those times when it had its rise in Geneva'.[1]

On his return to Aberdeen Alexander Jaffray consulted with some of his friends and was surprised to find that not a few of them had been thinking along the same lines long before his own mind had been exercised by these problems. The outcome of these conversations was the expression of the desire to 'have the ordinances administered in a more pure way, than there was any hope ever to attain to have them in the national way'.[2] They resolved, however, before proceeding further to communicate their intention to some Christian friends and learn how they looked upon such an action.

Accordingly a letter was drawn up and sent to certain leading men. This letter probably furnishes the first manifesto of Congregationalism in Scotland promulgated by Scots, though the Aberdeen venture can hardly be regarded as an expression of a truly native Congregationalism, as it has a largely English provenance and inspiration. The letter opens with an acknowledgement that fear of offending their fellows has made them endure for a long time things grievous to their spirits, but they can be silent no longer and must venture to set forth their thoughts. They are at variance with the Church as at present established in Scotland on two grounds. The first is, on the question of the nature of the Church and the qualifications for church membership. They are of the opinion that 'none should be admitted as constituent members of the visible Church, but such as with a profession of the Truth join such a blameless and gospel-like behaviour as they may be esteemed, in a rational judgment of Charity, believers, and

---

[1] *Diary of Alexander Jaffray*, pp. 59, 61-63.   [2] *Ibid.* p. 65.

their children, for such were the churches founded by the Apostles, which ought to be patterns for us'. They are sure that 'holiness becomes the house of our God', but the churches of Scotland are 'not constituted according to this rule in the full extent of it'. Their consciences convince them that they are under a snare by reason of their sinful mixtures being as they are, and some of the most holy ordinances of Jesus Christ, as the Sacrament of the Supper, they cannot partake of without sin. To them the call has come, 'Come out from among them and be ye separate'.[1]

Their second ground of objection to the Church of Scotland is on the question of polity. They have come to see that 'the Congregational way comes nearer to the pattern of the Word than our classical form and that Christ has furnished a congregation with their elderships, with complete power of jurisdiction and censure within themselves'. These views of church polity they support by many texts from the Scripture and other arguments. The remarkable document is dated 24 May 1652 and bears the signatures of Alexander Jaffray, John Row, William Moore, John Meinzies, and Andrew Birnie.

The letter greatly distressed the leaders of the National Church; and when other methods failed to dissuade Jaffray and his friends from taking what they judged to be such a disastrous step, they at last sent Samuel Rutherford, James Guthrie, Patrick Gillespie, and John Carstairs to Aberdeen to confer with them, which they did for the space of six days, but with no success. Some weeks later in the month of November Jaffray and his companions carried out their original intention and 'did together partake of the ordinance of the Supper of the Lord publicly in the meeting place called Greyfriars'.[2]

There is no ground for the view held by some historians that Jaffray later declared against Congregationalism and departed from the high ground he had first taken. He never returned to the Presbyterian Church but ultimately went by way of religious Independency to Quakerism.[3]

We are not without evidence that there were Congregational churches elsewhere than in Aberdeen at this time. Alexander Jaffray explains in his *Diary* (p. 98) that he is not a member of any

---

[1] Woodrow MSS. fol. 30; Jaffray, *Diary*, pp. 167-169.

[2] Jaffray, *Diary*, p. 66.

[3] *Diary of Alexander Jaffray*, pp. 98-99; Barclay, *Memoirs of People called Quakers*, p. 197.

gathered church, but points out that there are such churches up and down the country. A letter from Edinburgh, dated 20 November 1652, makes mention of 'the gathered churches in Scotland' which, the writer says, 'go on so successfully, that many who derided them, begin to admire them and love them'.[1] Moreover, Robert Pittillok in his *Hammer of Persecution* (1659) furnishes the names of eight ministers who became converts to Congregationalism about this period.[2] He tells us too that there was at least one Congregational church at Leith.

Sufficient has been said in this chapter to convince the reader that Congregationalism was a much stronger religious force in Scotland in Cromwellian times than has hitherto been supposed.[3] At the same time it could not be said by any stretch of the historical imagination that Congregationalism swept the country in that period. Presbyterianism as we have seen was linked too closely with the life and liberty of the Scottish people and revered in some quarters almost with superstitious dread to be deserted for any other type of religious faith and order. Besides the General Assembly of the Church in that time of political stress served as the Parliament of the people. And so when the English army returned to England the great majority of the population were as devoted to Presbyterianism as they had been when the invasion started. It seems to us that as time went on even Cromwell himself saw very clearly that there was little hope of converting Scotland to Congregationalism, and that anything like interference on his part would only arouse the jealousy of the National Kirk, and add to the numerous difficulties which already beset the government of the country.

[1] *Scotland and the Commonwealth*, ed. Firth, p. 370.
[2] Pp. 10, 13.
[3] It should be noted that some of these Independent churches might have been Baptist.

PART TWO
SOME NATIVE MOVEMENTS

CHAPTER III

THE GLASITES

THE departure of the Commonwealth troops from Scotland on New Year's Day 1660 emptied the Congregational churches of their leading members, and the native element remaining in them was so scant that the churches soon entirely disappeared. Some sixty-five years measure the gap between this eclipse of Congregationalism and its re-appearance at the end of the first quarter of the eighteenth century. The differentia of the return is that Congregationalism on this occasion was not transplanted but grown from native seed, and afterwards was carried to England and America.

John Glas,[1] through whose action Congregationalism was revived, was born at Auchtermuchty on 21 September 1695. He was ordained and inducted to the rural parish of Tealing, some five miles from Dundee, in March 1719. There he exercised a memorable ministry, his powerful preaching attracting many in the neighbouring parishes to the services of his church.

At the time of his ordination Glas gave both to Presbytery and Covenant alike a loyal and unquestioning obedience, and 'took up the common report against the Congregational Business, that it is mere confusion, and was the mother of all the Sectaries'.[2] It was the zeal of certain of his parishioners for the Covenants that first set Glas pondering on the nature of Christ's Kingdom and the difference between the Old Testament and the New. He came to the conclusion that National Christianity is not New Testament Christianity; that there is no authority in the New Testament for either the National Covenant or the Solemn League and Covenant; that Magistrates as such have no function in Christ's Church, and have no right to punish for heresy; and that the use of political and secular weapons as a means of reformation instead of Christ's word and spirit is wrong. These conclusions, novel and startling then in Covenanting Presbyterian Scotland, Glas gave to the world in his first and greatest work, *The Testimony of the King of Martyrs* (1729).

[1] Glas is regarded by some as 'the Father of Scottish Congregationalism'.
[2] Preface to *Continuation of Mr. Glas's Narrative*, pp. vii-viii.

Even before the publication of this book the new ideas began to appear in his preaching which provoked opposition from the upholders of the Covenants, who did not hesitate to decry both the new doctrines and their originator. Indeed his own father branded him an Ishmael, and declared 'His hand was against every man's hand, and every man's hand against him'. He was the first who told him he was a Congregationalist; while his father-in-law said, 'He was fighting in vain, for what he aimed at never would nor could take place'.[1]

It should be stated that there was soon to be a development in Glas's thought respecting the *nature* and *constitution* of the Church. From a belief in its spirituality he was to advance to the view that such a Church must needs be composed of true believers, who possessed a real experience of saving grace, and had been moved to separate themselves from the world. Thus unconsciously he had approximated to the principle of the Congregationalists, who maintained the necessity of gathered churches as distinct from parochial congregations.

Some of his parishioners after a time embraced his views. These Glas began to separate from the multitude, and so to form a little Congregational church in his own parish. Their number, according to the first roll of their names, dated, Tealing 13 July 1725, amounted to nearly one hundred. They agreed to observe the ordinance of the Lord's Supper monthly, and recommended that members living near to one another should form themselves into societies, and have weekly meetings for prayer and exhortation.

Glas's principles and divisive practices were very soon known beyond the bounds of his parish, and open battle against them was declared from several pulpits. On 6 August 1726, which was a Fastday before the Sacrament at Strathmartine (now a suburb of Dundee), Glas and John Willison of Dundee were engaged to preach there, and from all parts of the country a great concourse of people had assembled. Glas took for his text John vi. 69—'And we believe and are sure that thou art that Christ, the Son of the living God'—and in the unfolding of his theme was led to speak of Christ's Kingdom and the nature of it. He publicly confessed his faith that it is not an earthly kingdom, like the kingdoms of the world, defended by human policy or eloquence, or worldly power and wisdom. 'I confess', he concluded, 'my adherence to our

---

[1] *An Account of the Life and Character of Mr. John Glas* (Edinburgh, 1813), pp. ix-x.

fathers and martyrs in their testimony for the Kingdom of Christ
in opposition to any earthly head of the Church not appointed by
the Lord Christ . . . but as far as they contended for any national
covenants . . . so far they were not enlightened.'[1]

Such an utterance was too public and too remarkable to be
overlooked by a champion of the Covenants like Willison. At the
next meeting of the Presbytery of Dundee on 7 September 1726
he accordingly charged Glas with opposing the doctrine and
authority of the Church in his Strathmartine sermon, and also
mentioned an act of Assembly enjoining the deposition of ministers
who spoke against the Covenants.[2] So began the lengthy proceeding against Glas which culminated in his deposition by the Synod
of Angus and Mearns on 16 April 1728, which deposition after
Glas's appeal against it was confirmed by the Commission of
Assembly on 12 March 1730, chiefly on the grounds that he
showed contempt of the judicatories of the Church.

For a time after his deposition Glas remained in Tealing
ministering to the church he had formed there in 1725. A little
later, however, he removed to Dundee, where some who had been
in the habit of coming to Tealing on Sundays, formed the nucleus
of a second congregation.

From this time onwards one principle appears to have guided
him and his followers, namely, to make their churches approximate
in detail to the order and discipline of the primitive churches. This
aim led first of all to the abandonment of the monthly Communion
for a weekly observance of the Supper, since on the first day of the
week the first disciples came together for the breaking of bread.

A more careful consideration of the primitive churches disclosed the further fact that in every one of them there was a
plurality of elders.[3] Glas had, therefore, to have a colleague. The
elder chosen was Mr. Archibald, the minister of Guthrie, who had
followed in his own parish the practices Glas had adopted in
Tealing.

The possibility of forming other churches was discussed, but
the question invariably arose, how could elders for these new
causes be found? This led to the study of the qualifications required
for the eldership as laid down by Paul in his epistles to Timothy
and Titus. Glas and his followers found there no mention of a

---

[1] *An Account of the Life and Character of Mr. John Glas* (Edinburgh, 1813),
pp. xi-xiv.   [2] *Ibid.* p. xvi.
[3] Glas, *Works*, Vol. II, p. 213; *An Account of the Life and Character of Mr.
John Glas*, p. xiv.

university education, or of the necessity of understanding the learned languages, but an insistence on character. They saw some of their brethren in possession of the characters laid down by the Apostle, and therefore 'to their conviction, able by sound doctrine, both to exhort and convince the gainsayers'. These after fasting and prayer they accordingly appointed.

About the year 1736 Glas was joined by Robert Sandeman, who had been an elder in the Glasite church formed in Perth three years earlier and had married Glas's daughter. Churches formed by Glas and Sandeman thereafter sprang up in various parts of Scotland. They had to encounter much opposition, for the Scottish people in the first half of the eighteenth century were for the most part inclined to look askance at their sometimes naïve and uncouth experiments in primitive Christianity. Moreover the acrimony and bitterness with which Glas and his followers attacked all other religious parties and professions did not make things easier for them. However, considerable progress was made by the Glasite movement both in Scotland and England.[1] Two ministers of the Church of Scotland, Byers of St. Boswells and Ferrier of Largo, joined the movement, as did several English Congregational ministers.

In 1760 Sandeman went to London and attracted considerable congregations. At St. Martins-le-Grand a Sandemanian Society started, of which the most illustrious member was that scientific genius, Michael Faraday. In some parts of the north of England societies were also formed and for a time prospered.[2]

The fame of Sandeman's writings having reached America, he received an invitation to visit that country. With this request he complied and undertook the voyage in 1764, accompanied by two of his brethren, one of whom was a Scot, James Cargil, a glover by trade, who had attracted much notice as the first unclerical and unlearned man to dare ascend the pulpit and exercise the office of a teaching elder. In America Sandeman laboured till his death in 1770, and not altogether in vain, for he succeeded in establishing several churches, particularly in New England, where his senti-ments gained most ground.

Glasite churches were formed in Paisley, Glasgow, Edinburgh, Leith, Arbroath, Perth, Montrose, Aberdeen, Dunkeld, Leslie, Cupar, and Galashiels.

---

[1] Cf. R. W. Thompson, *Benjamin Ingham and the Inghamites* (1958).
[2] *Ibid.*

After labouring for forty-four years and suffering many hardships John Glas himself died at Dundee in 1773. In that city a monument to his memory bears the somewhat ambiguous inscription: 'John Glas, minister of the Congregational Church in this place, died November 1773, aged 78 years. . . . His character in the churches of Christ is well known, and will outlive all monumental inscriptions.'

It is high testimony to the singular worth and Christian excellence of the man, as well as of the impressive character of his preaching, that on one occasion after preaching at Alyth, the minister of the parish, Mr. Ayton, came to him, and embracing him said, 'Oh, Jock, what would become of me but for *that* New Covenant'.

Indeed it may be doubted if the Church of Scotland would have deposed Glas merely on account of his Congregational views. At that time friendly relations existed between the Scottish Presbyterians and the English Congregationalists. Many influential Scottish churchmen were anxious not to give offence to 'our brethren of these sentiments in England and New England'. Two of Glas's contemporaries in the ministry (as we shall later see in Chapter IV) Gabriel Wilson of Maxton and Henry Davidson of Galashiels had adopted congregational principles and formed a Congregational Church at Maxton, but they were not interfered with on that account. When Davidson offered to resign his parochial charge the Presbytery requested him to remain. This irregularity continued for twenty years and would appear to have been winked at by the Church authorities.

It was more likely because of Glas's contumacy that he suffered deprivation. Nine years later the Assembly restored his ministerial status, and it is significant that the same Assembly 'prepared the way for the deposition of the Erskines', which seems to justify the statement that 'when the Church of Scotland became harsher towards the founders of an opposition Presbytery, it became lenient towards Congregationalism'.[1]

The type of church order taught by Glas and practised in his churches may perhaps be described as Congregational Presbyterianism rather than strict Congregationalism as taught by Robert Browne and other Fathers of English Independency. Glas regarded

---

[1] J. T. Hornsby, 'John Glass : His Later Life and Work' : *Records of the Scottish Church History Society*, Vol. VII, 1940, pp. 94-113, to which I am indebted for practically the whole of this section.

the Eldership, for example, as of the *esse* and not merely of the *bene esse* of a Scripturally constituted Church.[1] Significantly he had no connection with southern Congregationalism which gave him the cold shoulder when he did appeal thither for sympathy and support. Indeed at a later time he accused the English Congregationalists of thinking more of their good relations with the Church of Scotland than of interesting themselves in the small Congregational churches of his own connection. Dr. Hornsby thinks that the English Congregationalists lost a great opportunity of promoting Congregationalism in Scotland by neglecting the Glasite churches. They could have saved the Glasites from many mistakes which crippled them in their testimony, and also have helped to establish a strong Congregational communion north of the Border. Many who later became leaders of the seceding Presbyterians, this authority maintains, would have been favourably disposed towards a similar kind of independency.

Internal dissensions and the adoption of practices repulsive to the good sense and Christian feeling of many who sympathised with the leading principles, as well as the narrowness and exclusiveness of the Glasite movement, contributed to its gradual extinction in Scotland. J. T. Hornsby believes that had Glas been content with the spiritual and evangelical principles with which he began his witness and work, he might have become one of the outstanding figures of his century, but unfortunately he was ensnared by the pitfalls which beset ecclesiastical and doctrinal particularisms, repelling many who otherwise would have followed him in a great venture of faith and service. Moreover, his distorted view of saving faith as 'mere belief' sapped the evangelical zeal of Glas and his churches, while his depreciation of missionary effort made him no more than the founder and leader of a relatively small and narrow religious coterie.

But we may not dismiss Glas's witness as of no account. His views of church order and discipline influenced, and were to a considerable extent adopted by many who repudiated his doctrinal position. The Old Scots Independents, old Scotch Baptists, and the societies in connection with Robert and James· Haldane, after they became Baptists in 1808, were according to the Glasite plan, although in all cases the leaders denied that they were Glasites.

[1] J. T. Hornsby, 'John Glas: His Later Life and Work': *Records of the Scottish Church Society*, Vol. VII, 1940, p. 108.

There is no doubt that Glas's writings on the nature of the Church were familiar to many who formed our modern Scottish Congregational churches and that his teaching influenced them towards Congregationalism.[1] But more important still is it to remember that Voluntaryism, which agitated Scotland for about two hundred years, originated with John Glas.[2]

Finally, it is not commonly known that the Glasite churches have influenced, if only indirectly, the worship of nearly all the Churches in Scotland. They were probably the first to use hymns in public worship. *Christian Songs*, including a number of compositions by Glas himself, first published in Edinburgh in 1749, was adopted by all the Glasite churches as their hymnal. A considerable number of these songs, never of high poetical or liturgical merit, nevertheless passed in more or less altered forms into the hymn books of the Baptists, the old Scots Independents and other Congregational churches in Scotland, from 1781 to 1867.

[1] R. Philip, *The Life of John Campbell*, p. 281.
[2] G. Struthers, *History of the Relief Church*, p. 179; A. J. Campbell, *Two Centuries of the Church of Scotland*, p. 90.

CHAPTER IV

THE OLD SCOTS INDEPENDENTS

I

IN 1768 a new movement arose in Scotland which came to be known by the name of the Old Scots Independents. In doctrine and polity this new body, as we have already suggested, had much in common with John Glas and his followers, but happily it was free from the somewhat harsh and uncharitable spirit of the Glasites.

Any attempt to outline the history and progress of this body of Congregationalists must begin with the careers of Henry Davidson, minister of Galashiels from 1714 till his death in 1756, and Gabriel Wilson, minister of the parish of Maxton (in Roxburghshire) about the same time; for while these did not bring the movement into being, forecasts of it can be found in their action.

Davidson and Wilson who were close friends lived and died ministers of the Church of Scotland. The Assembly of 1732, however, by its restoration of patronage and other high-handed measures so disgusted the two men that they renounced Sacramental communion with the Established Church. They continued to preach, baptise, and catechise in their respective parishes, but from this time onwards they declined to dispense the Sacrament of the Supper to their people. They actually started round about 1736 a Congregational Church at Maxton, and there they had Communion on Sunday evenings, when Davidson could go down from Galashiels. They continued this practice for more than twenty years, no man forbidding them.[1] It was a most extraordinary situation. Though *in* the National Church they were not *of* it; guilty of disobedience they undoubtedly were, yet they were never expelled nor libelled for following divisive practices; and to the end their irregularity was winked at. When both Davidson and Wilson had died, the church founded by them on the Congregational pattern continued to meet, and the remains of it formed a connection with the Old Scots Independents after their appearance.

[1] J. W. Brown, *Gospel Truth Accurately Stated* (1831), pp. 163 ff.

II

The real founders of the Old Scots Independents were James Smith and Robert Ferrier, ministers respectively of Newburn and Largo, neighbouring parishes in Fife. Their 'Case'[1] is interesting because it shows that they adopted Congregational principles after an independent investigation of the whole subject of church order. Both of them, however, had been influenced by the writings of John Glas. As a result of their inquiry they decided to sever their connection with the Church of Scotland, which they did in 1768.

Their doctrinal and ecclesiastical positions are fully set forth by Smith and Ferrier themselves in the document referred to, and were clearly restated in 1814 by James McGavin of Paisley in *A Concise Abstract of the Faith, Hope and Practice of the Old Scots Independents*.

Smith and Ferrier acknowledged that the Westminster Confession 'contains many most precious and impartial truths', and that in their view 'it is mostly founded upon the word of God', but it contains certain doctrines which they cannot accept. The chief of these are: (1) The Eternal Sonship of Christ: They admit that the Saviour is spoken of in Scripture as the only-begotten of the Father, but they add, 'He is never said to be eternally begotten'. (2) The Eternal Procession of the Holy Spirit from the Father and from the Son: On the latter part they take up the position of the Eastern Church and reject the *Filioque* clause. (3) Saving Faith: They hold that faith is not a complex but a simple act, and consists of the acceptance of God's testimony concerning His Son which produces 'a receiving, resting and relying on Him for salvation'. (4) The authority of the civil magistrate in ecclesiastical affairs: To this they objected and sided with Glas. (5) The civil magistrates' powers to call Synods. (6) That the power of Church censure and discipline should be placed in the hands of Church officers only, to the exclusion of the members. To these objections they added 'there are several others expressions in that Confession with which we are not fully satisfied', but these they forebore mentioning.[2]

In church polity and practice the Old Scots Independents from their beginnings under Smith and Ferrier departed from the standards of the Church of Scotland. Like Glas they looked upon civil establishments of religion as opposed to the spiritual nature

---

[1] *The Case of James Smith, late minister at Newburn and Robert Ferrier, late minister at Largo, truly represented and defended* (1768).   [2] *Ibid.*

of the Kingdom of Christ. They found in Scripture no support for the Presbyterian form of church government, but held to the Congregational way, that every single congregation united in the faith, hope, and obedience of the Gospel, is independent of any other congregation, and that having Christ as their head they are complete in themselves.[1] Their services were conducted in almost the same manner as the Glasite churches. Like them they had a plurality of elders or pastors in every church, and were inimical to anything like education for the ministry; and received their members by a public profession of their faith before the whole church, each receiving not only the right hand of fellowship but the kiss of charity. They resembled the Glasites also in other ways. On the first day of the week they gathered to observe the dying command of Jesus to keep up the remembrance of his death and sufferings. It should be added, however, that on the whole the Old Scots Independents were men of a wider and better spirit than the Glasites.

After the secession of Smith and Ferrier from the National Church, the first church of the new movement was started at Balchristie, an ancient village in Fife, where, according to tradition, the first Christian Church in Scotland had been founded. The original congregation was composed of a few members from each of the churches to which the two pastors had ministered. In due course Smith and Ferrier were ordained as 'elders', and before long there were some sixty or eighty members in the new Congregational church.

The second church was formed in Glasgow. About the time when Smith and Ferrier were abandoning Presbyterianism, a small party were in the act of seceding from the Relief Church at Glasgow under the pastoral care of the Rev. William Cruden, whom they did not consider qualified to preside over a congregation. At the head of these dissenters were Archibald Paterson, Matthew Alexander and David Dale, the founder of the New Lanark Mills. Doubts had arisen in Dale's mind, and in the minds of the others as to the Scriptural warrant for the Presbyterian form of church government, and they proceeded to hold meetings of their own in a private house. By the end of 1768, the membership having grown to twenty-five, a chapel was built in Greyfriars Wynd (now Shuttle Street) through the liberality of Paterson, a wealthy

[1] *The Case of James Smith, late minister at Newburn and Robert Ferrier, late minister at Largo, truly represented and defended* (1768).

candlemaker. From this connection the building was commonly known as the ' Candle Kirk'.

It was at this time that the 'Case' of the two Fife ministers came into their hands; and finding themselves in full agreement with the views put forward therein, they sent a deputation to the church at Balchristie, to confer with the elders. After some discussion it was proposed that Ferrier should come to Glasgow, which he did in 1769. Dale and he were ordained as joint-elders over the Glasgow congregation, while James Simpson, a Largo weaver, became Smith's colleague at Balchristie.

The new denomination had its adversaries, and the Glasgow congregation had to endure not a little of the general persecution. Their meeting-house was violently assaulted with stones and other missiles. But the patient endurance of the members, and their unwearied witness to Christian charity and forbearance prevailed over all difficulties. As the years passed they were joined by others, not only residing in the city, but also from Hamilton and Paisley.

The attitude of increasing tolerance towards the new movement, particularly in Glasgow and the West, was due in large measure to the character of David Dale. The recent demolition of Dale's house in South Charlotte Street has brought his name before our eyes; would that the spirit of this great man possessed our hearts! As he is one of the Fathers and Founders of Congregationalism in Scotland, it is fitting that his life and work should be put on record in this book.

David Dale, whom some believe was the original of Sir Walter Scott's Bailie Nicol Jarvie, and who during his lifetime was known throughout the West country of Scotland as the 'Benevolent Magistrate', was born the son of a shopkeeper in the Ayrshire town of Stewarton on 6 January 1739. He commenced his working life as a herd boy in his native district, but early came to Paisley where he was engaged as an apprentice weaver. As a young man he moved to Glasgow, was first an assistant shopkeeper there, and afterwards the proud owner of a business devoted to the importing of French and Dutch linen yarns, which was situated in Hopkirk's Land a few doors north of the Cross in the High Street. He soon realised, however, that manufacturing offered greater opportunities than distribution; and, having purchased the necessary machinery, he began to weave the inkles and other linen cloths. By 1782 his business had so greatly prospered that it was designated 'David Dale and Company'.

Dale had already become interested in cotton manufacture, especially in Richard Arkwright's Spinning Frame. He was in fact one of the manufacturers who invited the inventor to visit Glasgow in 1783. He gave the visitor hospitality at his attractive house in South Charlotte Street. He later conducted him to some land near the Falls of Clyde, which seemed to Dale an excellent situation for the erection of a cotton-spinning mill. The outcome was that he and Arkwright went into partnership, and the historic New Lanark Mills were opened in 1786.

By 1793 the mills had grown to be the largest of their kind in Britain, with 1,300 employees, including many formerly destitute men and women from various parts of Scotland, whom Dale fed, clothed, housed, and trained. He was probably the pioneer of Industrial Welfare in Scotland, and inaugurated many of the schemes usually associated with the name of his noted son-in-law, Robert Owen. Greville Ewing, minister of the first Haldanite Congregational church in Glasgow, who often itinerated as a preacher throughout Lanarkshire, wrote in 1799 of Dale's experiments in Christian philanthrophy: 'About five-hundred children, between the ages of seven and fourteen taken from poor-houses, cottages, and even from the streets, are employed; they are taught reading and writing, and the principles of religion by teachers appointed for the purpose; their morals are carefnlly inspected; all of them who are able attend regularly the Church, or the Seceding meeting-house, where seats are provided for them. Mr. Dale likewise encourages Gospel ministers to preach to the children on Sabbath or week-day evenings; several have already done so, and the prospect of utility is considerable'.[1] Ewing delighted to dwell on the excellence of Dale's character, and often remarked that whatever was truly valuable in the 'social system' at New Lanark was originated by Dale himself and based upon Christian principles.

Dale was associated too in the building of several other factories. In every case he was anxious that the workers should be properly housed. When the mills at Catrine in Ayrshire were planned and erected he laid down that the houses should be sixty-six feet apart, two storeys high, slated, and equipped with what were then all modern conveniences. That was in 1786! He was

---

[1] *A Memoir of Greville Ewing*, p. 202. See also T. Johnston, *A History of the Working Classes in Scotland*, pp. 302, 304, for an opposite view of Dale's philanthropy.

also connected with the building of the mills at Blantyre that are linked with the immortal memory of another renowned Scottish Congregationalist, David Livingstone.

The real business of Dale's life was Christian philanthropy. It has been said that to make men happier and better he gave his money ' by sho'ls fu' '. He is computed to have given away during his lifetime more than £52,000 to charity. In the terrible years between 1782 and 1799, when the cost of meal rose to 21s. 4d. a boll, he chartered ships and imported great quantities of grain to be sold cheaply to the poor. He visited Bridewell to preach to the prisoners. He helped to found in Glasgow the earliest Auxiliary of the Bible Society and to the day of his death acted as the Society's treasurer for Glasgow and the West of Scotland. He was also an enthusiastic supporter of missions.

Recounting all these good works of David Dale, and remembering his warm humanity (for his contemporaries have put it on record that he could sing a guid Scots sang with such feeling as to bring tears to the eyes), we are not surprised that the little kirk in Greyfriars Wynd won in the end the affection and sympathy of many of the citizens of Glasgow. For thirty-seven years Dale was its faithful pastor, preaching regularly every Sunday. We are told that he taught himself to read the Bible in its original Hebrew and Greek that he might be better equipped for his pulpit ministry.

In 1800, his business labours and ventures over, Dale purchased 'Rosebank' near Cambuslang, and it was there that he died on 7 March 1806. His mortal remains lie in the Ramshorn churchyard, near Candleriggs. Except for a stone let into the east wall bearing these words: 'This burying ground is the property of David Dale, merchant in Glasgow, 1780'—he has no monument. But who will say that he has left no memorial? Wherever men rejoice in the freedom of the Congregational way and the benefits of Christian charity, the spirit of David Dale lives on.

After this long but not irrelevant interlude, we return to consider the fortunes of the congregation at Greyfriars Wynd. Unfortunately within two years of its existence a spirit of division arose among its members. It was occasioned by differences of opinion on such points as to whether the Lord's Prayer should form part of public worship; whether 'Amen' should be audibly pronounced by the congregation at the close of prayers offered in public; and whether the people should stand while singing, as well

as while praying. Dale, with characteristic tolerance, urged forbearance until they should see whether they could not ultimately
come to be of one mind in such matters. But Ferrier strongly
advocated 'unity of judgment'. The result was that the latter, and
a few who adhered to him, left the congregation and joined the
Glasite church in Glasgow. From that time onwards until his
death in 1806 Dale appears to have been sole pastor of the fellowship in Greyfriars Wynd, and to have piloted it to safety through
stormy seas. Only in recent times did this historic church, which
twenty years or so ago was meeting monthly in the Christian
Institute of Glasgow, cease altogether.

III

It has been said elsewhere in this volume that history worthy
the name should be a resurrection of the past, and not a mere
excavation of facts and figures. Perhaps the chief misfortune of the
ecclesiastical historian is that the warm human side of religious
annals is either no longer accessible or else escapes his notice.
What would he not give, for instance, for an opportunity to visit
David Dale's congregation in the old Greyfriars Wynd? Although
that is denied him, the chronicler of an almost contemporary
congregation of Paisley Independents has left for his instruction
and delight a living picture of their manner of life and worship.
They were known as 'The Pen Folk' of Paisley, a small but
vigorous body of Old Scots Independents which flourished at the
end of the eighteenth century, contemporaneously with the Abbey
Close Independents, established in that town by David Dale. They
took their name from worshipping in a hall entered by a 'pend'
close.[1] The congregation was formed in 1796. The following year
some of its members adopted the doctrine of believer's baptism
and the church divided. Again, in 1798, there was a split over a
theological difference. The members adopted Calvinism in its
strictest form. An old 'Penite' said, in criticism of the Paisley
Baptists of that time, 'Frae the verra beginnin' the Storie Street
Baptists were tainted wi' the heresy o' free will, contrair tae the
hale tenour o' Scripture, seestu'. As a consequence of their
theological rigidity, their historian says, using the common idiom
of the day, 'they would neither "pick nor dab" with others'.

---

[1] D. Gilmour, *Reminiscences of the Pen Folk.*

Admission to membership was by vote of the congregation. The conviction and opinions of the applicant were discussed, and if considered suitable he was admitted by a majority of votes. 'Callings off' took place in the same manner, after prayers and admonition, and opportunity given to recant.

Notwithstanding this stringent code of behaviour there were occasions in which human nature unregenerated was much in evidence. One member in discussion with another admitted that when he was tempted to do what his better judgment told him was wrong, he always took the easiest course and yielded to the temptation. Thereupon he was eagerly asked, 'At sic time does thy conscience no gie thee a twitching?' 'Oo', replied Johnny, 'Weel, I get whiles a glouf o' conscience, but I aye get twa gaups o' gratification afore hand'.

The members were extremely kind and helpful to one another in sickness and distress, even leaving their work to nurse and tend the sick. Indeed the property which they built had to be sold to meet the mortgage incurred in supplying the wants of their poor.

The church continued in vigour for twenty-one years. During that time the total membership was 164. Of these, however, 79 withdrew, 30 were 'cut off' chiefly for heresy, 11 emigrated, and 18 died. The remaining 26 left 'the pend' for less pretentious premises at 8 Barr Street, Paisley, where they continued to decrease for nearly thirty years, and finally the church became extinct.

David Gilmour's interesting and sympathetic account of this church and its members helps us to form an imaginative reconstruction of the type of congregation found amongst the Old Scots Independents; and to understand in some measure their inner life. Recalling the look and feel of the chapel at Paisley, he writes: 'How I well remember the original interior appearance. Against the west gable, below and between the gable windows stood the pulpit; in front of which, and facing the passage running to the east gable, where stood the stove with a long red-hot pipe, was the precentor's desk. At either side of the pulpit were the elders' seats, on a level with the others, which were so placed that all the occupants looked towards the presiding elder. The large space round the stove was fitted with forms, and was set apart for social intercourse between services, and there love-feasts were eaten.' He goes on to tell us about the subjects discussed in the sermons of the meeting-house. One brother delighted in showing the ugliness of sin; another in denouncing the heresy of Arminianism, which he described as an attempt 'tae big hauf-gable wi' the Lord'; a third preferred to portray the loveliness and harmony of revealed truth; whilst others, and they were a large majority, inculcated purity of mind and life.

Of all the Scottish towns Paisley had been influenced most deeply by the French Revolution, and at this time was a hot-bed of revolutionary tendencies.[1] Some of the town's political radicals were attracted to the Independent churches with their democratic polity, which realised more manifestly the declarations of the Gospel —'All ye are brethren' and 'One is your Master, even Christ'.[2] Gilmour spot-lights one of these democrats. 'Young as I was', he says, 'there was to my mind something outrageously grotesque in the appearance of Daniel (pronounced *Dawniel*) Cameron, as he rose in his pew, Bible in hand, spectacles astride his nose, the end of his cutty-pipe cropping from under the pocket-flap of his waistcoat, craving attention to a few stray remarks on a passage in *Hebrews. Hebrews* was Dawniel's decalogue and lawgiver, profound and inexhaustible. Once a month, at least, he returned to his exposition; complex, diffuse, and sadly in want of arrangement.' Cameron, we learn, was a '93 'black-neb' Democrat and had a great fund of solid information on almost every subject then known.

Besides the regular members and their families, there were the occasional hearers—'wanderers'; and the constant attenders, 'waverers', 'doubters', 'outsiders', as they were variously designated. Of these Gilmour sketches one or two memorable portraits. There is James Andrew, or, as he was familiarly called 'big Jamie An'rew', a slovenly, loosely-clad mortal, whose clothes appeared as if made for somebody much larger than he. Everything he wore, from hat to shoes, was too large for him; the former was partly without brim, the latter frequently without laces; stockings without garters; kneebreeches unbuttoned; coat and vest flying in the wind. However, his face beamed with good nature; and he had the softest hands and voice, and mild liquid soft eyes. To men, women and children alike he was uniformly the same genial, earnest, humble man—full of warmth and downright honesty— too honest to profess a truth of which he had the faintest doubt, and esteeming himself too unworthy to be called a Christian.

---

[1] *The Life and Opinions of Arthur Sneddon* (of Paisley), 1860.
[2] Gilmour, *Reminiscences of the Pen Folk*, p. 13.

John Killock, another of these 'hearers' on the circumference of the membership, was 'a bean of a different kidney from James Andrew'. John was a little spare man with large, rheumy bloodshot unsteady eyes, heavy under-jaw, and open, flabby purposeless mouth. He wore buckle-shoes, grey worsted stockings, cord knee-breeches; wine coloured jockey coat, buttoned to the chin; a discoloured hat, turned up behind, as if disgusted with the drab-coloured wig on which it rested. He was a fussy little man and could often be seen hurrying along the streets of Paisley, stooping over the books of Friendly Societies, for which he was officer; his watch chain heavy with sundry rings and coins attached, rattling like snakes as they bobbed from side to side. John Killock was a man 'wi' an extraordinar' grip o' gospel truth, but without ony evidence i' Christian goodness'.

IV

We must now say something in a less detailed manner about the progress of the other Old Scots Independent congregations which sprang up in different parts of the country.

From the first church at Balchristie stemmed churches in Kirkcaldy, Perth, and Methven, while from the Glasgow church came the churches at Hamilton, New Lanark, and Paisley. In Montrose, Marykirk, Galashiels, and Edinburgh churches were also formed. At Airdrie in 1807 a church was started but its existence was short owing to a bitter division on the question of baptism. The Congregational church at Earlsferry, which owed its inception to the Haldanes, went over to the Old Scots Independents in 1813.

In Dundee a church was formed in 1769 by Andrew Scott the minister of Bell Street Anti-burgher congregation in that town. Scott had protested against his denomination's views of 'swearing covenants'. In consequence he was suspended by his presbytery in 1768. He continued to preach in defiance of their sentence, with the result that he was deposed for contumacy in November of that year. He then formed a meeting-house in Barrack Street, and formed a congregation there over which he presided for fully twenty years.

There was for some time a small congregation at Newburgh, Fife, under the care of Alexander Pirie, who had a varied ecclesiastical career and caused much disturbance in three rival denominations—Anti-burgher, Burgher, and Relief. When in 1778, the

C

Relief Synod for the fourth time refused to receive him, he returned to Newburgh, in the neighbourhood of which town he had started his career as a minister of the Burgher Secession Church. There he set up a congregation on Independent principles and a few of his former members joined him.

Between the Independent churches at Dundee and Newburgh and the Berean congregation at Sauchieburn a correspondence was kept up for many years, their ministers freely exchanging pulpits with each other and bearing greetings and exhortations on behalf of their people to their fellow Independents.[1] These three congregations, it would appear, did not follow the practices of the Old Scots Independents in all respects. Plurality of elders, for example, never prevailed in the Newburgh church or in the Berean society at Sauchieburn, while in the Dundee church during the first twenty years of its history Scott was without a colleague. It was not until 1789 that this congregation adopted the principle of plurality of elders, and Alexander Kirkcaldy was associated with Scott as elder.

The churches of the Old Scots Independents were never very numerous or large, and almost from the first were weakened by internal dissensions and by members drifting away to other denominations, more especially to the Old Scots Baptists. As early as 1776 the subject of believer's baptism much disturbed the members of the Glasgow congregation. They had been accustomed to regard infant baptism as defended by the authority of Scripture, but other views were then adopted by many, including one of the elders of the church, Robert Moncrieff, brother of Sir Henry Moncrieff, and Mrs. Dale. Nothing daunted David Dale stuck to his colours, but the church was reduced to a mere skeleton and years were to elapse before it recovered its former vigour and members. More particularly, however, in the early years of the nineteenth century, when the question of baptism was very much to the front, were the Old Scots Independent churches all over the country depleted by the departure of members who adopted Baptist views.

In 1814 a union was formed between the Old Scots Independent churches with some small churches in the north and west of England, which promised for a time to infuse new life into the denomination. The English churches concerned had been gathered some years before by Benjamin Ingham, a colleague of John

[1] See Chapter V below.

Wesley, and son-in-law of the Countess of Huntingdon. Ingham had been with Wesley in America, and, on his return to England, he had succeeded in founding certain religious societies or congregations.

Wesley sought to persuade him to join the Methodists, but this, owing to disagreements with some of Wesley's views, he refused to do. In 1761 the Inghamites disagreed and divided on the question of church polity. Those who remained adopted sentiments and practices very similar to those of the Old Scots Independents, which made the 1814 union possible.

At the time of the union there were thirteen Inghamite churches; in Kendal, Nottingham, Bulwell, Tadcaster, Howden, Leeds, Bradford and Wibsey, Todmorden, Salterforth, Ruthwell and Tosside, Winewall near Colne, Wheateley and Haslingden. The number of members in all these churches was 252. The Scots Independent churches were twelve in number, namely, Perth, Dundee, Kirkcaldy, Balchristie, Earlsferry, New Lanark, Hamilton, Edinburgh, Glasgow, Marykirk, Methven, and Paisley. There was also a church in London which was in fellowship with the Scots churches. The total membership of these thirteen churches was 501.

Although much appears to have been expected from this union, the only practical result was the occasional exchange of a circular letter by the churches in England and Scotland. From a pamphlet which appeared in 1835 we learn that several of the churches were in a declining state, and gave the members great concern.[1] While churches had been formed between 1814 and 1837 in Falkirk, Glassford, and Lesmahagow, the churches in Earlsferry, Marykirk, and Montrose had become extinct, and the majority of the others were not in a prosperous state. Among the causes for this decline the following predominate:

1. The Congregational and Baptist churches which sprang up under the preaching and leadership of the Haldanes seem to have attracted the class of people who formerly were disposed to join the Old Scots Independents.[2]

2. These Haldanite churches also afforded an open door to those Old Scots Independents who were dissatisfied with conditions in their own congregations.

[1] *The Substance of a Correspondence between the Old Scots Independent Church in Dundee and the churches of the same denomination in the West of Scotland.*　　　　　[2] See Chapter V below.

3. The chief cause of the decay among the Old Scots Independents was their non-aggressive and non-evangelistic character. They appear to have done little or nothing in the way of preaching the Gospel to the multitude, but to have been satisfied with the enjoyment of church privileges for themselves.[1]

[1] McGavin, *A Short Account of the Rise and Establishment of the churches in Scotland commonly denominated the Old Scots Independents.*

CHAPTER V

THE BEREANS

I

THE last of these tentative native Congregational movements has received no detailed consideration, so far as we can trace, in any published or unpublished account of the beginnings of Congregationalism. We refer to the Bereans, to whom on one or two occasions we have had cause to allude in the above narrative.

The movement bearing this name began at Fettercairn, Kincardineshire, in 1773, and continued for about seventy years. Its founder was John Barclay, a licentiate of the Church of Scotland, and a minister therein for fourteen years or so. He was the son of a Perthshire farmer and was born at Muthill in that county, in 1734.

He received his education at the parish school there and afterwards at St. Andrews University, where he graduated about 1755. In September 1759 he was licensed by the Presbytery of Auchterarder and became assistant to James Jobson, minister of Errol, with whom he remained for four years. He was dismissed at the end of that period for teaching what Jobson considered dangerous doctrines.

On leaving Errol he became in 1763 assistant to Anthony Dow, minister of Fettercairn, whom failing health precluded from performing the full duties of the pastorate. Here he remained for the next nine years, until the death of Dow in 1772. We learn from contemporary sources that the popularity of Barclay's preaching was unprecedented in that part of the country. Multitudes from distant places came to hear him. Indeed the crowds were so great that the church, which was an old fashioned building, could not contain them. Wherever a seat could be found it was occupied—in the windows, on the rafters of the church, and on forms placed outside for those who were not able to endure the heat within.[1]

In other respects Barclay found Fettercairn a congenial field of service, as Dow's son who had been with him at College was

[1] J. Campbell, 'The Berean Church—especially in Edinburgh', *Records of the Scottish Church History Society*, Vol. VI, pp. 138 ff.

minister of the neighbouring parish of Dron, and a sympathetic supporter of his opinions.

Furthermore, Barclay was most assiduous in the performance of his pastoral duties and exercised a strong moral influence over the people. He was, moreover, the possessor of a considerable gift of verse, though his productions scarcely rise into the region of poetry. Many of his verses, however, were afterwards collected in a hymnary which was used in his own church at Edinburgh.[1]

In 1766 he published a paraphrase of the Book of Psalms, and because of some questionable statements made in it he was summoned before the Presbytery of Fordoun; but he escaped without censure. The publication of another book, *Rejoice Evermore; or Christ all in all*, in 1767, caused a revival of suspicion regarding his teaching. A list of Barclay's heresies was drawn up by the Presbytery and proclaimed in the church of Fettercairn.

This treatment apparently only increased his popularity, for when Dow died the parishioners were almost unanimous in their desire to have Barclay as their minister. The Presbytery, however, remained antagonistic to him. Indeed when his connection with the parish ceased, and he asked for the customary presbyterial certificate of character, it was refused, on the ground that he was obstructing the peaceable settlement of the presentee. Thereupon he appealed to Synod and Assembly, but the appeal was dismissed on 24 May 1773. The result was he separated himself from the Church of Scotland, and the majority of the members of the church at Fettercairn retired from communion with the National Church. They formed a congregation under Barclay's ministry, erecting a chapel at Sauchieburn in the parish of Marykirk.

About the same time a congregation of Barclay's sympathisers was formed in Edinburgh, which invited him to become their minister.

His pastoral oversight of the Sauchieburn congregation must have been very brief, for towards the close of 1773 we find him as minister of the Edinburgh church. James MacRae, grandfather of the famous David MacRae of Dundee, was called by the Sauchieburn fellowship, and set aside as their pastor in 1774. It should be added that during Barclay's ministry at Sauchieburn another congregation had been formed at Crieff, which, by its proximity to Muthill had probably come under the influence of Barclay's teaching.

[1] *Encyclopaedia of Religion and Ethics*, Vol. II, p. 520; Julian, *Dictionary of Hymnology* (1892), p. 1031, and below.

After spending three years with the congregation in Edinburgh, which appears to have worshipped in the Cowgate, Barclay was invited by friends and readers of his writings in London to visit that city. This he did for two years, and while there planted several churches, and one in Bristol. William Nelson, a Londoner, who had been 'judged by him and the brethren there well qualified to preach the Gospel' took charge of the Edinburgh congregation till Barclay's return in 1778.

Barclay often visited the Berean fellowships in Scotland, travelling on foot to such places as Glasgow, Stirling, Crieff, Kirkcaldy, Dundee, Arbroath, Montrose, Brechin, and Fettercairn where congregations had been formed. He died on 29 July 1798, and was buried in the Old Calton churchyard, where a monument was afterwards erected to his memory.

The ruling principle of Barclay's teaching was the perfection and supreme authority of the Scriptures as the sole test of divine truth; and it is highly probable that it was he himself who gave the name 'Bereans' to the new movement, because of his fellow feeling with the disciples at Berea who searched the Scriptures daily to see whether the apostle was preaching the truth (Acts xvii. 11). Barclay and his followers applied most of the Old Testament prophecies, and in particular the Psalms, to Christ, discerning in them types or predictions of Christ's atoning death, mediation and Kingdom. They strongly objected to the application of the Psalms to the experience of Christian believers, as they maintained that no prophecy of Scripture is of any private interpretation. They held also that assurance was of the essence of faith.

With regard to the Sacraments, they believed that infant baptism was a divine ordinance and was the substitute in the Christian church for the rite of circumcision in the Jewish; but they strongly disapproved of the practice of consecrating the water, or setting it apart from common to sacred use. Likewise they would not consecrate the bread and wine of the Communion, holding that whatever form of words might be used, no change could be produced in the substance of the elements. Nor did they refer to either Baptism or the Lord's Supper as a 'Sacrament', believing that the word meant the taking of an oath, which they held was in no way connected with either of these ordinances.

Their conception and practice of the other parts of public worship were not dissimilar to those of the Church of Scotland at that time, except that in singing they used hymns composed by Barclay himself.

Barclay, like Glas, was a pioneer in the introduction of the hymn to public worship in Scotland. In 1767 in his book *Rejoice Evermore* he published 196 spiritual songs 'collected from the Holy Scriptures' and versified by himself. He is said to have written thousands of verses on religious themes. None of them, however, would appear to have any literary or liturgical merit, not a few indeed are marred by bad taste and grotesqueness. But nevertheless Barclay's aim was laudable. Noticing how eagerly the common people took to singing, he wedded words on moral and evangelistic themes to common tunes, tunes which unfortunately had been consecrated too long to opposite and sometimes demoralising sentiments. These songs he distributed in his visitation. His *Spiritual Songs* were used in all the Berean congregations.

Little else can be said with certainty about the subsequent history of the Berean movement in Scotland. Few records of it are extant. However, we do know that in 1823 the Glasgow congregation had 96 adherents, the one in Stirling about 33, and the congregation at Crieff 8. The Editor of *The Scottish Ecclesiastical Register and National Almanac* for 1843 has raised from oblivion a few more interesting facts. He informs us that 'for many years the denomination has been in a state of decline. It has now no connections in England, but small congregations still exist in some places in Scotland. They have only four ordained ministers, at Edinburgh, Glasgow, Laurencekirk, and Dundee; but meetings conducted by deacons are still kept up in a few other places. Their form of church worship is Independency. They choose their ministers from among themselves and make no account of human learning . . ., on receiving a call from the congregation, they are set apart by one or more ministers who have themselves been ordained. The number of regular meetings is reported to be seven, with some stations without speakers.' That was the situation in 1843, and it would seem that not long afterwards the Berean churches died out altogether.

The Berean Assembly at Sauchieburn became a Congregational church in 1809. From 1777 to that date James MacRae had ministered there as a Berean pastor. He was a popular preacher and an earnest Christian, and one of the first in Scotland to hold and conduct a Sunday school. From 1809 to 1811 he served the church at Sauchieburn as a Congregational minister, Thomas MacKinnon succeeding him in that capacity from 1812 to 1854.

The church ceased only some ten years ago. In the later years of its existence, an annual service was held within the ancient building, organised from Montrose.

II

A. C. Cameron in his *History of Fettercairn* has left us a few verbal thumb-nail sketches of Berean Christians in that neighbourhood. He tells us that when the Berean party dwindled and many returned to the parish church, a few lay preachers kept up weekly meetings in their own houses.

Among these was Anthony Glen who used to say that if not allowed to preach he would *rive*. His discourses were homely. When preaching on the love of money, he would say 'Fowk wud do a' things for the love o' money. They wud gang ower seas, an' into pairts whar naebody kenn'd them, an' a' for a greed o' gain. Their grace afore meat an' after meat, an' their prayers at a' time, was, bawbees—Amen.'

Another worthy sketched by Cameron's pen was William Taylor, carrier, the last of the Berean preachers. After walking five miles he officiated regularly, along with others, at the Sunday meetings in Laurencekirk. He survived all his colleagues; and with the last of them, John Todd, farmer at Butterybraes, divided the duties of the Sunday, with a remark such as 'Noo John, ye'll come up and lat's see daylight through the Romans'. The chapel a small building stood in what was known at the end of last century as 'Berean Lane'. About 1844 the services there ceased and Taylor conducted Sunday meetings in his own barn at Balmain, to which not a few repaired to take stock of his sayings and to benefit by his naïve wisdom.

The last of the sect in Laurencekirk were two old women, and when one of them died the other feelingly remarked, 'Wae's me! when I gang too the Bereans'll be clean licket aff!'

III

The extravagances and crudities of the Berean movement, particularly in their later manifestations, came in for much criticism. The sect was attacked because its pastors were mostly tradesmen and its members 'the very dregs of the people, who,

having lived loosely, took at last a serious turn'.[1] Doubtless there
were undesirable features in the movement. But it should be said
that Barclay himself was a respectable man, his enthusiasm
considerable and his teaching, if sometimes fantastic, was serious
and helpful, and did draw attention to points which had been
forgotten. Wherever Berean congregations were planted 'a taste
for religious knowledge, the reading and study of the Bible began
to prevail to a great extent; the morals of the people were improved,
and vice and profaneness, as ashamed, were made to hide their
heads. Temperance, sobriety and regularity of behaviour sensibly
discovered themselves throughout all ranks.'[2] It must be admitted
that the Bereans did dress religion in the homespun of the people
and related it to their daily lives and habits.[3]

In concluding this section on native Congregational movements
prior to the Haldane revival, one must admit that the churches of
Glas, Dale, and Barclay, for all their shortcomings, did arise in an
eager desire to attain a purer and more ardent life than seemed
possible in the Church of Scotland of that day. And it is to their
credit that they earnestly searched the New Testament for the
primitive church type of order, believing that this was nearest to
the mind of Christ and so was alone legitimate. But unfortunately
they came to exalt the letter above the spirit of Scripture. For
example, the churches of Glas and Ferrier were careful to obtain
a plurality of elders in each church, and to practise weekly Communion; and they even descended, in the case of the Glasites, to the
bathos of the kiss of charity, because all these things seemed to
have obtained in the Apostolic churches. The order and constitution of the Church thus came to be considered as of supreme
importance, to be regarded as the end of Christian fellowship and
not as the means of Christian edification and Christian effort.
Negatively these movements, for all their eccentricities and weak-
nesses, did teach the Scottish churches that it is not by repro-
ducing to the minutest detail every feature of the Church of the
Apostles that churches live, but by their possession of the Spirit
of Him who came to seek and to save. It was, however, the non-
aggressive and unevangelical character of these three native
religious movements and their lack of missionary zeal that caused
their decline and extinction.

[1] *The Manuscript of John Ramsay of Ochertyre*, edited by Allardyce in
Scotland and Scotsmen.
[2] A. Philip, *The Evangel in Gowrie*, p. 240.
[3] Archibald C. Cameron, *The History of Fettercairn*, p. 206.

PART THREE

THE HALDANE REVIVAL

CHAPTER VI

THE SPIRIT OF REVIVAL

I

HAVING dealt with the early attempts to introduce English Congregationalism into Scotland in the sixteenth and seventeenth centuries, and having outlined the very minute older native Congregational Independency of John Glas, David Dale and John Barclay, we proceed now to consider the beginnings of the present Scottish Congregational Communion at the end of the eighteenth and the opening of the nineteenth centuries.

The first thing that strikes the historian, when he reviews this period, is that most of the modern Congregational churches which then arose were the fruit of spiritual revival. It may sound paradoxical, but nevertheless it is true, that Congregationalism as a church polity had not, in the first instance, much of a place in the formation of the great majority of the oldest Congregational churches at present existing in Scotland. Not to any sectarian motive, not to any ecclesiastical or theological controversy, but to a deepening sense of God and His claims upon men in Jesus Christ does modern Scottish Congregationalism owe its existence.[1]

It was the outcome of a revival of religion associated notably with the names of Robert and James Haldane, who have not had justice done to them by Scottish ecclesiastical historians, but of whom it may be justly claimed that they did for Scotland what Wesley and Whitefield had done for England. If we are to understand this revival movement in which modern Scottish Congregationalism originated we must look at religion and life in Scotland at the time when the Haldanes began their labours.

One outstanding characteristic which clearly distinguished the eighteenth century in Scotland from the century that preceded it was the predominance of secular over religious interests. Many influences were at work towards that end. There was, for example, the Industrial Revolution, which was not so much an event as

---

[1] See J. Haldane, *Journal of a Tour*, p. 25: 'The true Church is not to be found in one sect or denomination, but scattered among all who had heard the gospel.'

an atmospheric change. Perhaps the opening of the Carron Iron works in 1760 may be said to mark its commencement in Scotland. The Industrial Revolution altered the habits and thoughts of people as they had never been altered before. The changes were greatest, of course, in the Scottish Midlands where lay the mineral wealth of the country, but Dundee and Aberdeen, and even far away Wick, shared in the progress of the period.

In the towns and villages we see a new population gathering, different from the peasantry from which they had descended, sharing no longer the theological interests of their fathers and mothers, caring little about the next world if only their feet were firmly planted on this one. David Wilkie the painter embodies the spirit of the new age in his picture *Village Politicians*, and in Scottish prose literature none illustrates it so well as Galt in *Annals of the Parish* where the main character is represented as saying: 'The minds of men were excited to new enterprises; a new genius, as it were, had descended upon the earth, and there was an erect and outlooking spirit abroad that was not to be satisfied with the taciturn regularity of ancient affairs. . . . In the midst of all his commercing and manufacturing, I began to discover signs of decay in the wonted simplicity of our country ways. Among the cotton-spinners and muslin-weavers . . . were several unsatisfied and ambitious spirits, who clubbed together, and got a London news-paper to the Cross Keys, where they were nightly in the habit of meeting and debating about the affairs of the French, which were then gathering towards a head.'

Equally important was the spirit of scepticism widely prevalent among the educated classes. Rationalism affected everything in Scottish life, literature, politics, philosophy, and religion. Scotland was feeling the baneful influences of a general European move-ment: the Latitudinarianism of England, made more accessible since the Union; the *Aufklärung* of Germany; the Newtonianism of France; were sending waves to Scotland whose impact threatened to sweep away the old landmarks of the faith.

It is only against this rationalistic background that we can understand the growth of Moderatism within the Scottish Church, which was increased in extent as the century progressed. The real aim of the Moderates was to meet and win the educated opinion of their day, which had been carried away from dogmatic theology and Puritanism of life. They were out to effect an under-standing with the world as it seemed to be going.

Their creed was deeply tinged with Deism and their grasp on the Evangel was cold and loose. They preferred Francis Hutcheson to John Calvin. They set the new deistic doctrine of man and his natural goodness in place of the ancient theological doctrine of man and his depravity; and as a consequence a system of naturalistic ethics supplanted the old supernaturalism. They put the emphasis on the ethical teaching of the Bible, not on its mysteries. A contemporary complains of them, that to deliver a Gospel sermon or preach to the hearts and consciences of their hearers was as completely beyond the Moderates' abilities as to speak the language of angels.[1] 'The great realities which sent a shudder of awe through the soul of the Covenanter, the vivid apprehension of the Unseen which fortified the Cameronian in his heroic battle for the truth—these by the Moderates were treated as products of morbid spirituality, excrescences of fanaticism.'[2] The ideal virtue of the Moderates was a sanctified commonsense nurtured by general culture, and they were the sedatives to all enthusiasm.

But not only in their teaching and preaching did the Moderates aim at an adjustment to the spirit of the age; their standard of conduct also was an accommodation to it. Alexander Carlyle of Inveresk, nicknamed *Jupiter* from his personal appearance—'the grandest demigod I ever saw' said Scott—may be regarded as the apotheosis of Moderatism, and his *Autobiography* as its vivid personal manifesto. Carlyle was the social as Principal Robertson was the official head of the Moderates, and regretted that religion was too often prescribed in such an austere and ungainly form that a gentleman could not bring himself to like it. It was exactly that reproach and stumbling block that he and his party set about to remove. And they did not demand too much of human nature, as Carlyle's *Autobiography* abundantly attests. In its pages we read much of 'fine dinners', 'fine scenery', and 'fine women', but religion, except in the convivial form of Assembly politics, is hardly mentioned. Indeed of Carlyle it has been said that he scarcely acknowledged God out of the pulpit and spent the whole Sunday, except when at church, in calling at country houses and 'gallanting' the ladies. He played cards for money, danced and drank to excess, and delighted in profane songs such as 'De'il stick the Minister'.[3]

[1] A. Haldane, *Memoirs of the Lives of Robert Haldane . . . and James Alexander Haldane*, p. 129.

[2] H. Macpherson, *Scotland's Battles for Spiritual Independence*, p. 138.

[3] W. L. Mathieson, *The Awakening of Scotland*, pp. 209-210.

The biographer of the Haldanes mentions, as an example of the degraded state of the dominant party in the Church at this time, a Presbytery dinner to which James Haldane was invited in Edinburgh. The company were treated to Bacchanalian songs, the folly of which was aggravated into something approaching to wickedness by an admixture of ridiculous, if not profane, allusions to their own sacred calling and functions. The burden of one song was the prescription of a bumper of Nottingham ale in the pulpit at different stages of the Presbyterian discourse.[1]

It is no surprise that the morals and habits of the people deteriorated under the guidance of such shepherds as these. In 1783 church attendances, which twenty years earlier had been widely observed by all ranks of the people, had greatly fallen off; family worship which had been frequent was now almost totally disused. Moreover, the riotousness and licentiousness of the lower ranks compared unfavourably with their sobriety in the earlier period. During these twenty years, when the system of Moderatism was in full force, there had been such an increase in immorality that the annual amount of fines had risen from £154 to £600.

The anti-democratic policy of the Moderates caused the name of Moderatism to stink in the nostrils of later generations, and indeed prepared the people for the Haldane movement which was essentially democratic. That policy stood unmistakably for clerical privilege and its aim was to fill the Church with ministers who, by their sermons and social graces, would commend religion to the classes whose adhesion it was deemed the interest of the National Church to secure. As a means to that end the law of patronage was firmly upheld and rigidly enforced.

On the eve of the Haldanite revival it would seem the unchallenged supremacy of Moderatism was drawing to a close. The rationalistic philosophy which had fostered it had received a staggering blow from Kant's *Critique of Pure Reason* (1781) which was soon followed by another more widely felt blow and indeed a mortal one in the French Revolution, that volcanic disturbance which rocked or destroyed the whole human structure of thought and action in the West.

In Scotland, as elsewhere, the effect of the French Revolution was immediate. The wealthy and the privileged dreaded what it might portend in regard to their own fortunes, and, for the most part, the Church shared their attitude. But from the first the

---

[1] *Memoirs of the Haldanes*, p. 126.

common folk received the news of it with delight. Even some whose disposition was anything but revolutionary hailed the downfall of feudal France, as the breaking of a new dawn for humanity. Thomas Paine's *The Rights of Man* became a familiar book, especially among the industrial class. It was even translated into Gaelic. In some homes it began to displace theological literature in popularity and favour. Passions and hopes which had long lain dormant were roused into activity. To many was suggested the need for the immediate reform of Parliament and of the burghs; in many others larger hopes were awakened too vague perhaps to be expressed plainly but bearing issue in excited gatherings, in banquets, even in local riots.[1]

The new Society of the Friends of the People gained hundreds of recruits and organised branches throughout the length and breadth of Scotland.[2] The result among the conservative element of the population was that everything was suspect which brought men together after any unfamiliar fashion or for any new object. Innocent ventures, such as the new Sunday schools or Missionary societies, were regarded by them as cloaking secret plans of sedition.

At a time like this when men were either unduly excited or unnerved the Church of Scotland, largely Moderate in persuasion, was helpless. It had no message of hope for the alarmed: it had no spiritual balm for minds inflamed. When the heavens and the earth were shaken and men's hearts were failing them for fear, they needed and desired a refuge more positive than the vague tenets of Moderatism. Nor indeed were the Seceders more capable of providing the required refuge. For all their orthodoxy they were too concerned with the minutiae of their peculiar doctrines than with the great movements of the human spirit that were agitating the world.[3]

But in the darkening firmament of Scotland's life and religion there were streaks of the approaching dawn. For at this time of bewilderment and fear God raised up two intelligent, God-fearing Scotsmen, loyal sons of the Church, the brothers Robert and James Alexander Haldane—laymen with no clerical axe to grind, who

---

[1] See *The Life and Opinions of Arthur Sneddon* (Paisley, 1860) for a description of happenings in Paisley in the Revolutionary era.

[2] See *A History of the Working Classes in Scotland* (T. Johnston), pp. 217 ff. and *Scotland and the French Revolution* (H. W. Meikle), *passim*.

[3] The Relief Church *was* concerned about the people. See Chapter VII below.

D

were not engrossed in questions of church government and discipline, but alive to the spiritual situation and need of Scotland in this momentous and decisive hour. These men having found, after much adventuring upon the sea (for they were sailors) and more perilous adventuring upon the sea of life, the treasure of the Gospel were moved to share their fortune with all whom they could reach. Through them God wrought a great work in Scotland. And through that mighty work of the Lord many Scottish Congregational churches were born.[1]

II

Robert and James Alexander Haldane, born respectively in 1764 and 1768, were scions of an ancient Scottish family, the Haldanes of Gleneagles, in Perthshire. Their father, James Haldane, a captain under the East India Company distinguished himself in that service. He inherited the estate of Airthrey near Stirling from a kinsman, married a sister of Admiral Duncan of 'Camperdown' fame, and was on the eve of being elected an East India director when he died on 30 June 1768. Robert was then but four years old, James was not yet born. Their first religious instruction was received from their mother a devout Christian of whom Robert once said, 'She lived very near God and much grace was given to her'. When she died, the two boys were placed under the guardianship, first of their maternal grandmother, and afterwards of their uncle; and by the latter were sent to the High School of Edinburgh in 1777. They boarded with Dr. Adam, the renowned Rector of the School; and in the house opposite to them in Charles Street dwelt Henry Dundas, afterwards Lord Melville, to whose candle, early lit in the mornings, Dr. Adam would point in order to stir them to emulation.

For a short time Robert was a student at the University of Edinburgh, but the exploits of his famous uncle kindled in him a desire to follow him into the navy. Accordingly, in 1780, he abruptly left his academic studies and joined the *Monarch* at Portsmouth.

In 1781 James too went to the University and spent three sessions attending classes in Greek, Latin, Mathematics, Logic, Metaphysics, and Natural Philosophy. At the age of seventeen he entered the service of the East India Company.

[1] See *A Chronicle of the Churches*, below.

In the Royal Navy Robert had a distinguished career but to the great regret of his uncle, Admiral Duncan, he withdrew from the naval service in 1783; and thereafter pursued a further period of study at Edinburgh University followed by foreign travel. Then he retired to Airthrey, where he lived for the next ten years or so the life of a country gentleman.

James quickly made good in his chosen career. He made four adventurous voyages, plunged into the gaieties of Anglo-Indian life in Calcutta, and even fought a duel, in which happily, his pistol burst and his opponent's missed fire. By 1794 he had passed his Master's examination, and had been nominated Captain of the East Indiaman *Melville Castle*. Suddenly he too gave up his post, sold out, and retired into private life.

Both brothers about this period were passing through an intense and momentous spiritual experience. James speaking about it says, 'I lived on board my ship nearly four months at Portsmouth, and having much spare time and being always fond of reading, I was employed in this way, and began more from conviction of its propriety than any real concern about eternity, to read the Bible and religious books, not only on the Sabbath, but a portion of Scripture every day. I also began to pray to God, although almost entirely about the concerns of the present world.' So God—as Haldane himself tells us—had begun a work of grace in his soul while he was on board the *Melville Castle*. On his return to Scotland in 1794 he had serious conversations with several friends, clerical and lay, and was greatly influenced thereby. He became convinced that Jesus was indeed the Son of the Living God, and he was anxious to know more about the way of salvation through Him. Slowly but surely, after much heart-searching and meditation in religious books, there came to him clearer views of the truth, of the freeness of the grace of the Gospel and the necessity of being born again.

Robert had a like experience. For some ten years he had lived the quiet life of a country squire taking little interest in politics, contenting himself with the improvement of his estate. The tremendous happenings of the French Revolution—he himself has left it on record—shook him out of his lethargy and stirred him to the deeps of his being. Like many others he hailed the downfall of feudal France as the dawning of a new and better age for humanity. 'A scene of melioration and improvement in the affairs of mankind, seemed to open itself to my mind, which, I trusted, would speedily take place in the world; such as the universal abolition of slavery, of war, and of many other miseries, that mankind were exposed to, and which appeared to me wholly to result from the false principles upon which the ancient governments had been constructed. I exulted in this prospect, from motives of benevolence, and, as far as I know, without any allowed mixture of selfishness. I rejoiced in the experiment that was making in France, of the construction of a government, at once from its foundation upon a regular plan, which Hume, in his essays, speaks of as an event so much to be desired.'[1]

These views Robert Haldane did not hesitate to make known, and they were the subject of many discussions he had from time to time with ministers in the neighbourhood of his home. These to a man disagreed with Haldane's humanist philosophy and assured him that he was only cherishing a vain dream, as the Utopia of his vision could never issue from human nature which was totally corrupt. At long last he was led to consider religion and to discern 'the glory of the doctrines held out in Scripture, and the consistency of the truth as it is in Jesus'. As an anxious enquirer, he read much and deeply on the evidences of Christianity, asking the Lord to lead him from the darkness of error into the light of truth. 'When politics began to be talked of, I was led to consider everything anew. I eagerly catched at them as a pleasing speculation. As a fleeting phantom, they eluded my grasp; but, missing the shadow, I caught the substance; and while obliged to abandon these confessedly empty and unsatisfactory pursuits, I obtained, in some measure, the solid consolation of the gospel; as that I may say, as Paul, concerning the Gentiles of old, He was found of *me* who sought him not.'[2]

Thus it came to pass within a short time of each other the two brothers had experienced the change in feeling, thought and motive, and in the principles and aims of action which we call conversion. Each by the rich mercies of the Lord had passed 'from death to life'. Each was in Jesus Christ 'a new creature'.

Spurgeon used to say that grace is not given for ornament but for service. The genuineness of this dual conversion was soon attested by Christian action. To the elder brother, Robert, it would seem, belongs the honour of attempting the initial effort of

---

[1] R. Haldane, *Address to the Public Concerning Political Opinions, etc.* (1800), p. 4.
[2] *Ibid.* pp. 11, 13, 14.

inaugurating, unsuccessfully alas, their missionary endeavours. His friend William Innes of Stirling had given him an account of Carey's missionary labours at Serampore. The Baptist missionary's plunge into the Indian abyss made such a deep and indelible impression on Robert Haldane's mind that he was impelled to think how he himself might serve the interests of Christ's wider Kingdom.

As a result he resolved to sell his estate of Airthrey, and with the proceeds to finance a mission—on the lines of Carey's—to the Hindoos living under British rule. He proposed to take with him to this work William Innes, David Bogue of Gosport, Greville Ewing, assistant minister of Lady Glenorchy's chapel, Edinburgh, and John Ritchie 'a respectable pious Edinburgh printer' who was to superintend a printing establishment which was to be an important part of the mission. In addition to these four intimate friends, some others were to have gone out as catechists, city missionaries or teachers.

The scheme was a worthy and magnificent one and manifested the measure of Robert Haldane's dedication to his Lord, but it met with such opposition that it was never put into operation, and the funds intended to launch and maintain it were directed into other channels. The directors of that powerful commercial body that had long ruled India, the East India Company, refused their consent. Robert Haldane, always indomitable, tried to bring pressure to bear both upon the Directors of the Company and the British Government. In September 1796 we find him threatening in a letter to bring the India project before the general public, for, he writes: 'We have not a doubt but we shall interest in our favour all the numerous friends of religion and of human happiness of every denomination in every part of the country. The lively concern that they will feel for our success, the numerous petitions with thousands of signatures they will present, will so fully express the sentiments and the wishes of the most virtuous and respectable part of the community that we are confident the Government would feel it a duty to comply with their request.'[1]

From letters by Dr. Porteous and Dr. Hill of St. Andrews it is plain that this threat Haldane tried to carry out. A circular letter was 'sent over all the three kingdoms inviting people to petition in the same manner as was done about the slave trade'.[2] This

[1] *Edinburgh University Laing MSS.*, No. 501, dated 28 September 1796.
[2] *Ibid.* 20 February 1797; 21 March 1797.

letter is headed 'Edinburgh, Feb. 16, 1797' and bears the signatures
of Robert Haldane, David Bogue, William Innes, and Greville
Ewing. Bengal they consider is the field of labour in which they
can best use their substance and talents committed unto them by
God. Their plan is 'to proceed to India as soon as possible to make
themselves acquainted with the language of the country, to preach
the Word to the natives, to translate the Scriptures and circulate
them extensively, and to erect schools in the populous cities, for
the education of their youth; and they have sufficient funds among
themselves for the execution of their designs. By the charter,
however, given to the India Company they find it impossible to
get out without their leave.'

Even the Missionary Societies, from which they were entitled
to expect sympathy and support, do not appear either to have
given them the assistance they desired; though importuned by
Haldane and his associates they would not move in their favour.
Reaction and panic were then in the ascendant. Robert Haldane's
politics were suspect, and had they countenanced his missionary
scheme they might have been thought to countenance his sup-
posedly revolutionary sentiments too. That risk they would not
run, and therefore declined to memorialise the East India Company on his behalf.

So terminated Robert Haldane's first missionary scheme. A
like disappointment would have deterred most men from further
effort in the interests of the Kingdom but happily it was not so
in his case. His frustrated energies found an outlet in other
channels of Christian service nearer home to the blessing of
countless multitudes of his countrymen and Christian brethren
overseas.

One of the results of the French Revolution was that by
changing the temper of the times it helped to hasten in an era of
religious interest. This displayed itself, as we have already suggested, in a manifestation of missionary activity first abroad and
then at home. The Baptist Missionary Society was founded in
England in 1792 and the London Missionary Society three years
later. The enthusiasm evoked speedily spread to Scotland, so that
in 1796 missionary associations were established in Edinburgh,
Glasgow, and other towns. In July of the same year Greville
Ewing and Charles Stuart, an Edinburgh physician, founded the
Missionary Magazine, a monthly publication intended 'as a repository of discussion, and intelligence respecting the progress of the

Gospel throughout the world'.[1] The very idea of producing an unsectarian religious periodical in Scotland was altogether new: it was another one of the signs of the times. The magazine rapidly reached a circulation of five to six thousand copies. From the perusal of its pages one can gather something of the spirit that was abroad. It was a time of awakening. Men were astonished at their former apathy and alarmed at the condition of every religious denomination. Scarcely one number of the magazine appeared without the suggestion of some 'plan for spreading the Gospel at home' or 'Hints towards the promoting of the Gospel in Scotland'.[2] Meetings for united prayer gathered all over the country. Religious tracts were numerously and widely distributed—Sunday schools were extensively organised and taught. There was aroused up and down the land an aggressive spirit of Christian zeal.

In the many and varied activities of the time many friends of the Haldanes—John Erskine, Walter Buchanan, David Black of Lady Yester's Church, and others—were taking a prominent part, and it was inevitable, when one remembers their temperament and spiritual experience, that to such labours they should give their hearty support. But neither Robert nor James Haldane knew whither he was being led: neither realised that in this way he would find his life's work—the opportunity of advancing the Kingdom of God he so ardently desired.

To John Campbell, at this time an ironmonger in the Grassmarket, Edinburgh, and the zealous indefatigable promoter of all good works belongs the honour of inducing James Haldane to make a beginning in Christian service of a public nature. Campbell resolved to start a Sunday school in a colliery village about five miles south of Edinburgh. Sunday schools, of course, there were before this time, but Campbell's was on a new plan: it was independent of clerical superintendence, and older folk, who were welcome as well as the children, were included in the address with which the school concluded. Such sympathy had James Haldane with the new effort that he rode out with Campbell to witness its commencement. He had not, however, the confidence to address a few words to the assembled people although the day was soon to come when he could address three thousand with ease. By the success of Campbell's school and the others which sprang up about this time in and around Edinburgh, resulting in 1797 in the

[1] A Memoir of Greville Ewing, pp. 83-85.   [2] Ibid. pp. 124-126.

formation of the Edinburgh Gratis Sabbath-School Society, James Haldane was led to think of the possibility of holding similar meetings in other parts of Scotland. Accordingly in the spring of 1797 John Campbell and he began a week's tour with this end in view. 'We set off on Monday morning', Campbell relates, 'taking some thousands of tracts with us in a one horse chaise, distributing tracts to rich and poor as we proceeded. We obtained a meeting in Glasgow from a few friends of the cause of God. We laid before them the general neglect of giving religious instruction to the youth of our country except in pious families—described the plan pursued in Edinburgh for educating the youth in the principles of the Gospel by the formation of schools on the Sabbath evenings, and the countenance that was given to the plan, and the ease with which children were collected, with the trifling expense that attended its execution. After some conversation those present were formed into a Society for establishing and conducting Sabbath evening schools in Glasgow and the surrounding towns and villages. We acted in the same way and with the same success in Paisley and Greenock.' The result of that week's tour was the formation of sixty Sunday schools, truly a magnificent beginning to James Haldane's long career of usefulness.[1]

Neither of the Haldanes as yet attempted to preach. James was diffident, but, when it was remarked by some of his friends that he would by and by become a preacher, he was much pleased and in his heart began to cherish a desire for that work, which he considered 'the most important as well as the most honourable' of all labour. The journey with Campbell to the West country doubtless strengthened and whetted his appetite for the work of preaching; and so when the opportunity afforded itself 'of being allowed to speak a word for Jesus' James Haldane hesitated no longer to avail himself of it.

That opportunity eventually came, and in this way. John Campbell, who was always on the lookout for new fields of Christian usefulness, was much concerned about the religious destitution of the people (chiefly miners and their families) in the village of Gilmerton near Edinburgh, and secured a student from England, Joseph Rate from David Bogue's academy at Gosport, to conduct services there for a few weeks. These met with consider-

---

[1] R. Philip, *John Campbell*, pp. 125-126, 129-130.

able success, folks coming from a wide area. After two meetings, however, Rate was unexpectedly called south, and the difficulty arose of finding a preacher for the approaching Sunday. Campbell consulted James Haldane on the matter, and he suggested John Aikman, then a divinity student at the university and subsequently founder-minister of North College Street Chapel (now Augustine Church) Edinburgh; but Aikman would not consent. He, however, afterwards agreed to preach on James Haldane promising that if he did take the service the next Sunday and Mr. Rate did not return during the week, he (Haldane) would officiate the following Sunday. John Aikman preached as he had promised. Mr. Rate still being in the south when the succeeding Sunday came, Mr. Haldane was obliged to take his place. Thus it happened that James Haldane preached his first sermon on 6 May 1797. One of his friends who was in the congregation that day pronounced him to be a *Boanerges*; the earnestness, the energy, and the power of the preacher created a profound impression and in the estimation of competent judges, James Haldane had found his proper work.

The soundness of this judgment was soon to be made manifest in a conspicuous manner. A few weeks later he launched out on his career as an evangelist among his fellow countrymen. Having heard much of the low state of religion in the north of Scotland he and Aikman, encouraged by the success of their efforts at Gilmerton, resolved to make an evangelistic tour through these parts. On Wednesday, 12 July 1797, accompanied by Joseph Rate, they left Edinburgh, after being commended to God in prayer in the house of their friend David Black, minister of Lady Yester's church.

Prior to setting out they had addressed to the public through the medium of the *Missionary Magazine* a manifesto of their designs. They were undertaking this journey, they declared, 'not to disseminate matters of doubtful disputation or to make converts to this or the other sect, but to endeavour to stir up their brethren to flee from the wrath to come, and not to rest in an empty profession of religion'. They proposed to preach the word of life, distribute pamphlets, and 'endeavour to excite their Christian brethren to employ the talents committed to their charge, especially by erecting schools for the instruction of youth'. They were well aware that their object would be misrepresented but they avowed their determination nevertheless to know nothing but

Jesus Christ and Him crucified. They appealed for the prayer of their fellow-Christians that their endeavours might be owned and blessed of God.

The three evangelists travelled at their own expense in a roomy chaise capable of accommodating them and a large portion of their tracts. Those they could not take were sent on before them to different towns. The distribution of Christian literature was an important feature of the tour, more than 20,000 pamphlets being given away. They preached in every town and large village to the extreme north of Scotland, and crossing over to the Orkney Islands they visited and proclaimed the Gospel over them all. Indeed, wherever the itinerants came they preached, taking their stand at the market cross or in the public street. Sometimes the Town Bellman or the Town Drummer announced to the inhabitants where the evangelists were to hold forth and almost invariably large audiences gathered. We read in the *Journal of a Tour* of attendances of 2,000, 3,000, and 4,000. Even at six or seven o'clock in the morning they could sometimes attract a crowd of several hundreds.

Doubtless the novelty of this undertaking helped to create interest and command attention. Not that Missionary Tours were unknown in Scotland prior to 1797. Both Wesley and Whitefield had paid visits to Scotland; and the Relief Church had sent its missioner, Neil Douglas, to Kintyre a few days before James Haldane set out on this tour.[1] Only the previous year (1796) Haldane had accompanied Charles Simeon of Cambridge on a preaching journey through the Highlands. But the evangelists on the earlier occasions had been ministers—on this occasion they were laymen. Lay preaching was not unknown in Scotland but it had hitherto been confined almost exclusively to Wesleyan itinerants, whose labours were usually inoffensive, and always obscure. But this was of a different type. James Haldane was young and handsome, of commanding presence and powerful voice. The fact that he had the education and the bearing of a gentleman, and had mounted the pulpit from the quarterdeck gave a certain piquancy to his utterance.

Equally calculated to create interest was the fearless way in which the itinerants denounced the false doctrine they heard from certain ministers of the Established Church. 'They attended the

[1] N. Douglas, *Journal of a Mission*; G. Struthers, *The History . . . of the Relief Church*, p. 397.

local church', says a recent historian, 'only to find as a rule that the minister did not preach the Gospel. Later they convoked the people by a summons from the town crier, and preached to them in the open air. . . . In their discourses they attacked those clergy, who failed to win their approval, in the virulent language which evangelicalism had always been prone to use.'[1] The statement does James Haldane and his colleagues less than justice. They did not attend public worship in the place in which they happened to be of a Sunday morning simply to find fault with the preacher. They went to join their fellow-Christians in the worship of God. Actually they had advanced as far as Kirriemuir before they ventured to offer a word of criticism of the preaching to which they had listened. But there and on subsequent occasions, they did not hesitate in their concern for the souls of men, fearlessly and faithfully to warn their hearers against doctrine which to them was in flat contradiction of the plain teaching of the Bible. That they were somewhat unwise in making these attacks on individuals they seem to have realised, for in the intimation of the Missionary Tour of the following year they announced their intention 'of adopting a different line of conduct from that which they formerly pursued, in animadverting upon the conduct of particular ministers'.[2]

Certainly laymen venturing to cross swords with ministers on matters theological in those days must have aroused interest and provoked discussion. But the success of James Haldane and his fellow evangelists in their first itinerary is not to be explained on these grounds alone. The power and passion of the preachers, their tremendous earnestness and concern for the souls of men counted for far more. Above all, it has to be remembered that many amid the distresses and upheavals of the time were eager to hear just such a message as they so eloquently proclaimed, and when it came it thrilled their hearts and was welcome as cool water to a thirsty soul. It was truly a time of refreshing from the Lord. 'Multitudes dated their turning to God from the period of this awakening. Several years later, the Rev. John Cleghorn names, as within his knowledge, in the small town of Wick alone, forty cases in which there had been a solid work of conversion.'[3]

But not merely from such instances must the good that was

---

[1] A. J. Campbell, *Two Centuries of the Church of Scotland, 1707-1920,* p. 158.
[2] *The Missionary Magazine* (1798), p. 337.
[3] *Memoirs of the Haldanes,* p. 188.

done be estimated. It was far more visible in the impulse given to the Church of Scotland and to the other denominations of the land. The words of James Haldane and his friends were life from the dead not only to numerous individuals but to all the Scottish Churches.

CHAPTER VII

THE NEW CONGREGATIONALISM

I

THE remarkable success of the evangelistic tour of the north convinced James Haldane and his supporters of the necessity of having the same sort of work continued on a large scale. Very soon after the completion of the tour, therefore, and before the account of it was published, Haldane and Aikman communicated to several interested friends something of the religious situation as they had witnessed it. The result was that on 20 December 1797 a meeting of some of their friends was held in Edinburgh to consult as to how they might effectively help to bring about a better state of things. A plan having been submitted for spreading the Gospel in the more destitute parts of Scotland, those present agreed to form themselves into a society for the purpose, under a designation exactly expressing their object, namely, 'The Society for Propagating the Gospel at Home' (S.P.G.H.).[1]

The first General Meeting of the Society was held on 11 January 1798, when a committee of directors was appointed, all of whom were laymen, and a statement of its origin and progress was ordered to be published. From this statement we learn that the Society was instituted from a conviction in the minds of the members, that sufficient means of religious instruction were not enjoyed in many parts of the country; and its avowed object was, therefore, to disseminate religious knowledge in Scotland.

The Society was non-sectarian and interdenominational. Christians of all communions were invited to unite in its truly ecumenical purpose 'to promote pure and undefiled religion'. Its promoters definitely declared that it was not their design 'to form or to extend the influence of any sect'. Their sole intention, they are at great pains to remind the people of Scotland, 'is to make known the everlasting Gospel of our Lord Jesus Christ'. To this

---

[1] Robert Haldane was most probably the mainspring of this movement; for he considered 'the old staid formalities of Presbyterian order as the consummation of dust and idleness'. He wanted a new spiritual agency untrammelled in its evangelistic labours by courts and clerical rules.

end they proposed to employ approved men as itinerant evangelists, to whom a certain district should be assigned, and who should work under the direction of the Society. The main work of the Society was to encourage Sunday schools, to promote the reading of the Scriptures, circulate tracts, establish libraries of devotional books, and defray the expenses of such ministers as were willing to preach in towns and villages in their neighbourhood on Sundays or week-days. In the winter of 1798 we find Greville Ewing itinerating on behalf of the Society in the north, his Journal being published in its *Proceedings*. In April of the same year the Society had been strengthened by the accession of two evangelists originally connected with the Secession Church, William Ballantine and John Cleghorn, who were soon to play an important rôle in the young Denomination.

Two classes of agents were employed—first, catechists, pious young men, whose duty it was to organise and superintend evening schools for children and who, even if they had the opportunity of addressing adults, were not to attempt to preach but to confine themselves to catechetical exercises; the second class of agents were ministers of religion of different denominations, who itinerated under the auspices of the Society. Highly popular ministers like Ewing, Burder, and Parsons were so employed and drew immense crowds.

It was one of the principles of the S.P.G.H. that its agents should neither make public collections, nor take money privately from those amongst whom they preached. Very definite instructions were also given to both itinerants and catechists that they were to avoid entirely speaking on politics, to show no partiality for any denomination of Christians, either established or dissenting, and to exhort the people to attend wherever the Gospel was preached in purity. A letter of instructions given to each of them admonished the Missionary to 'study scriptural simplicity in your discourses. Those sermons are always most useful which are most simple.' It added, 'Let not your sermons and prayer be too long. Much better your hearers should wish you had been longer than be wearied till you close. We are disposed to speak longest, when we have least to say.'

Early in 1798 John Cleghorn and William Ballantine, to whom we have already referred, went forth as the Society's itinerants in Caithness. The success of these, their first agents, encouraged the S.P.G.H. to send out others as opportunity offered. By the end of

1799 many ministers of different denominations—Presbyterians, Episcopalians, Congregationalists, and Baptists[1]—had been employed in preaching tours, and forty catechists were travelling throughout the length and breadth of the land, while thirty or forty thousand tracts had been distributed. 'The whole of the North of Scotland', says Gavin Struthers in his *History of the Relief Church*, 'was thrown into a blaze. The Established clergy complained that the world was going out of its place, and the old landmarks of things, both secular and sacred, were fast disappearing.'

One of the most important contributions of the Society towards the reviving of the spiritual life of Scotland was the sending of Gaelic catechists and preachers to the Highlands. In that region for a great many years the work of the Church had proceeded with great difficulty, owing to geographical and linguistic barriers, besides a considerable part of it was Roman Catholic or Episcopalian in religious persuasion. In 1725 George I had instituted the Royal Bounty—an annual gift of £1,000, afterwards increased to £2,000, to maintain preachers and catechists in the Highlands and Islands. The Society for the Propagation of Christian Knowledge (S.P.C.K.), founded in 1707, undertook the work of planting schools. But it was only after the suppression of the Jacobite rising of 1745 that some of the obstacles in the way of evangelising the Gaelic area were at last surmounted. The Relief Church appears to have been foremost in this field. In 1797 the Relief Synod sent Neil Douglas and Macnaught, a minister in Dumbarton, on an evangelistic tour of Kintyre. They were instructed to preach the Gospel, distribute Gaelic literature, avoid politics, establish fellowship meetings, refrain from declaiming against other denominations, and take note of the most destitute places with a view to further missionary work. Unhappily the venture failed owing to Douglas's espousal of radical views and involvement in the political troubles of the time. In 1798 the Relief Synod sent three more missionaries into Kintyre, but seemingly their predecessor's political record prejudiced their success.[2] Early in 1798 the S.P.G.H. sent a Gaelic catechist, Hugh Ross, into the same

[1] *History of the Baptists in Scotland*, p. 53.

[2] The Relief Church doubtless owed its more liberal attitude in this respect, as in others, to its affiliations with Congregationalism. Following in the footsteps of Doddridge and Whitefield, Gillespie, its founder, maintained that ecclesiastical distinctions were not essential elements of the Christian faith. 'I hold communion', he once said, 'with all that visibly hold the Head'.

region. Others acquainted with the Gaelic language followed, and laboured with considerable success.

Although James Haldane and John Aikman had private means and did not need to draw upon the financial resources of the Society, they supported and supplemented its efforts by their own preaching labours.[1] In the summer of 1798 we find them engaged in a second preaching tour, this time through the south and west country. They set out on Tuesday, 14 June and travelled by Peebles, Biggar, Hamilton, Greenock into Ayrshire and Galloway, preaching in all these parts, and returning home via Berwick. Again a profound impression was made. Men and women were not proof against the power of such applied Christianity as they exhibited. Their manifest desire to serve the best interests of their fellows without fee or reward, and the singleness of purpose with which they laboured to bring other lives under the rule of Christ, appealed with irresistible force to many around them.

Thus from the Solway to the Orkneys Scotland experienced a great spiritual awakening. Great things had been done for Christ, but greater things were yet to be achieved.

II

In the summer of 1798, Robert Haldane, the mainspring of the S.P.G.H., put at its disposal the proceeds of the sale of his estate of Airthrey. From now on the greater part of its funds was supplied by this devoted steward of the Lord's work. In that same year a further development in evangelistic activity was made by the Society, which called for a more self-sacrificing liberality on the part of this generous giver. The first step in this new venture was the opening of the 'Circus', in Little King Street, Edinburgh, as a place of worship. During the time the Relief church was rebuilding, the congregation used the Circus, originally a variety theatre, for their Sunday services. Large congregations had gathered there, many came doubtless out of curiosity, for a minister preaching from a stage was in those days a novelty indeed. When the Relief church vacated the building, Robert Haldane and some associated with him in the work of the S.P.G.H. conceived the idea of utilising it as a Tabernacle, after the plan of those of Whitefield, where preaching would be kept up by a succession of

[1] Aikman had been a wealthy West Indian merchant.

ministers, and where the accommodation would be free to all. The Tabernacle idea was most probably first suggested to Haldane by John Campbell, that man ever foremost in all good ventures in the cause of Christ's kingdom.

The Circus was engaged for a few months as an experiment and Rowland Hill, who was the first preacher there, spent a month in Scotland preaching on Sundays in Edinburgh and itinerating during the week from the Clyde to the Tay. The opening services were held on Sunday, 19 July 1798.[1] Describing them Hill wrote in his Journal: 'Preached for the first time in the Circus. The building is large, and supposed to contain about two thousand five hundred people. This morning the congregation was decently attended. . . . My morning subject was the prayer of Moses, "If Thy presence go not up with me, carry us not up hence", Exodus xxxiii. 14, 15. I preached to the people the feelings of my heart. I felt the call to this city to be solemn and important . . . without our God we can do nothing. A much larger congregation attended the evening service, and I took another subject, just suited to the frame of my own mind, 1 Corinthians i. 22-24—and employed some time in showing Paul's method of treating his proud Corinthian hearers. How very different is the immediate and direct simplicity of the Apostle, compared to too many of the cold and formal productions of the present day!'

On subsequent Sundays, as Hill's Journal indicates, the attendance so increased that the place was crowded even at 7 o'clock in the morning, and it was quite out of the question to hold the evening service within doors. On the Calton Hill, therefore, the Evangelist took his stand and addressed, like Wesley before him, a congregation of 'fifteen thousand, on the most moderate computation', whom he describes as being composed of the most solemn people he had addressed for many years.[2]

During Rowland Hill's stay in Edinburgh many were converted, some of whom had been grossly immoral characters. When he left the city the work was continued by a succession of ministers from England. Large and attentive congregations, particularly in the evening when usually there were no services held in the churches, were the rule; and so Robert Haldane was led to go on with the

[1] See *A Chronicle of the Churches* at the end of this book for historical details of this and all the other churches.
[2] R. Hill, *Journal Through the North of England and Parts of Scotland* (1799), p. 38.

E

Tabernacle plan. It should be added, however, that he had, at this time, no intention whatever of forming a new denomination. His sole aim was to aid the S.P.G.H. in the conversion of souls and the revival of religion.

As time went on, and encouraged by the success of the Edinburgh venture, Robert Haldane turned his thoughts to the possibility of extending the Tabernacle scheme to other centres of population in Scotland. With this end in view he purchased, in 1799, the Circus in Jamaica Street, Glasgow, at a cost of £3,000, and converted it into a Tabernacle and opened it for public worship in July of that year. Similar places he proceeded to erect in Dundee, Perth, Elgin, and Caithness.[1] All these tabernacles Robert Haldane secured or built mainly as centres for evangelistic enterprise. Indeed his brother was careful to state that 'the opening of the Edinburgh Tabernacle was no separation from the Establishment. It was merely the opening of another place of worship for preaching the Gospel where all regard to forms of external arrangement of church order was represented as bigotry.' There was no shadow of an intention of founding Congregational churches, let alone of setting up a new denominational structure alongside of the Presbyterian churches.

The Tabernacle plan did achieve its avowed purpose of attracting the masses to listen to the message of the Gospel unto the saving of their souls. Great crowds on the fringes of the Churches and impervious to their spiritual influence, were drawn to the Tabernacles, where the word was preached 'more plainly, and in a more striking manner than heretofore'.[2] Alehouses that formerly had been crowded on the Lord's Day were emptied and shut up, the frequenters of them having gone to the Edinburgh Circus. The same results happened everywhere. Many 'who came to scoff, remained to pray', and those who entered the Tabernacle out of idle curiosity or because they got a free seat were soundly converted. Incalculable good was undoubtedly done both to individual men and women as well as to the Churches of Scotland.

III

The Circus in Edinburgh was opened, as we have seen, as an effort in undenominational evangelism, the promoters of which still retained their membership of the Church of Scotland. From

[1] See *A Chronicle of the Churches*, below.
[2] *Edinburgh Quarterly Review*, Vol. I, p. 315.

that Church they had no thought of departing. It was not, however, very long before they began to consider the desirability of constituting a church. Indeed early in December 1798, a few days after Greville Ewing withdrew from the National Church,[1] fourteen of Robert Haldane's helpers both at the Circus and in the work of the S.P.G.H. met at his house in George Street to consult as to the wisdom of such a step. As a result they resolved to form themselves into a Congregational church, and to Ewing was entrusted the task of drawing up a plan for its government. After further conference they invited James Haldane to be their pastor, to which urgent request he at length yielded. The formal constitution of the church, however, did not take place till January 1799, when 272 became members, besides thirty-eight others who were received as occasional communicants. On Sunday, 3 February 1799, James Haldane was ordained to the Ministry and inducted to the pastoral charge of the Circus Church.[2]

This church, which soon afterwards entered new premises in Leith Walk and was known henceforth as The Tabernacle, was not the first of the Scottish Congregational churches to come into existence at the end of the eighteenth century,[3] but it certainly was the first of the many churches that were to owe their inception to the preaching of James Haldane and the generosity of his brother. Others soon followed in rapid succession in Glasgow, Wick, Dundee, and elsewhere—but the Edinburgh Church was referred to, and very rightly too, as the mother church, and according to the plan of the Edinburgh Tabernacle the other Haldanite churches were manifestly fashioned.[4]

The plan of the Circus Church was drawn up by Greville Ewing who, as we shall see in a later chapter, was a Congregationalist by conviction and not, as in the case of the Haldanes, by necessity, and the architect of the new Denomination.

Robert Haldane thus describes the plan proposed by Greville Ewing and adopted by the Circus Church: 'The form of church government is what has been called Congregational. It is exercised in the presence of the church itself, by its pastor and church officers, and with the consent of its members, independent of any other jurisdiction; . . . A strict discipline also is maintained. The characters of all persons admitted as church members are particularly examined, and great numbers have been rejected, either

[1] See Chapter ix, below.
[2] See *A Chronicle of the Churches*, below.   [3] *Ibid.*   [4] *Ibid.*

from ignorance of the Gospel, or from not appearing to maintain a becoming walk and conversation. . . . The church members are exhorted to watch over each other in love; if anyone be overtaken in a fault, he is reproved, but if convicted of departing from the faith of the Gospel, or deliberate immorality, or allowed and continued indulgence in sin, he is put away; and restored only upon credible proofs of repentance. Such regulations, we believe, to be according to Scripture, and calculated to promote edification.'[1] That was also the general plan of all the churches that sprang up in Scotland, as a result of the evangelistic labours of the Haldanes.

How did the form of church government known as Congregationalism come to be adopted by the party brought together by the Haldanes in their attempt to evangelise Scotland? Three combined influences, we think, led to the adoption of Congregationalism: the influence of English ministers of that persuasion; the writings of John Glas and others; and the lack of hospitality for the new life within the Established Church. These three, along with the creative congregational thinking of Greville Ewing, determined the choice of Congregationalism as the polity of the new denomination.

IV

Of the three reasons given for the adoption of the Congregational way, perhaps the opposition and subsequent persecution of the National Church was the most decisive. From the first, that Church refused the requests of the evangelists, scorned their longings, and repressed their efforts. Many examples of its unsympathetic attitude to the labours of the Haldanes and their colleagues will be found in *A Chronicle of the Churches* in the present book.[2] But as the new movement gathered strength and momentum opposition developed into persecution.

The Moderate party which, as we have seen, held sway in the courts of the Church was soon up in arms against the Haldanes. They resented their unconservative methods, and still more their open and daring criticism of clerical prerogative. That resentment was brought to a head in 1799, when Rowland Hill published the Journal of his Scottish visit. In it he called for a union of all

---

[1] *Address to the Public*, pp. 72 and 73.
[2] See, in particular, Aberfeldy, Kintyre, and Oban.

Christians, who were requested to throw aside their prejudices and unite on the broad principle of Christian love. Seemingly he forgot that gracious principle himself by his caustic remarks on Scottish religious life. However, the outcome was that the Established Church, and the other Presbyterian churches as well, had little love left for the English Evangelist. Instead of smoothing the way for the Haldanes and their friends, Hill apparently only put great obstacles in their path.

The times, moreover, as we have said, were not conducive to the adoption of new ideas. Everything was suspected which brought men together after any unfamiliar fashion, or for any novel purpose. To Rowland Hill's charge of heresy and intolerance the Scottish clergy therefore retaliated with an accusation of sedition and disloyalty. They professed to see in the planting of Sunday schools without clerical authority, the distribution of Christian literature, the preaching excursions of laymen, and in the Tabernacle plan, and other schemes of the Haldanes dark and sinister designs. Their aims, they maintained, were not religious but revolutionary. Their good works were really only a cloak for political propaganda.

The correspondence of William Porteous of Glasgow with the Lord Advocate made articulate what a great many must have felt in those days about the Haldanes and their religious ventures. 'Many of us have reason to believe', he wrote on 24 January 1797, 'that the whole of this missionary business grows from a democratical root, and that the intention of those who planned it was to get hold of the Publick mind, and hereafter these societies may employ its energy as circumstances may direct,'.[1] Again on 21 February 1798, Porteous professed to be further alarmed. This time the Sunday School Movement gave cause for concern. He had no criticism to make of schools property manned and organised such as had been founded in Scotland ten years earlier, on the model of those of Raikes, and were countenanced by the authorities.[2] It was the schools promoted by the laymen John Campbell and James Haldane on a new plan that earned the disapproval of Porteous. In Glasgow old and young attended these schools 'in multitudes', and in one of them 'a loquacious manufacturer preached and prayed with vehemence till a late hour'. No charge of meddling with politics could be made against them, but, our correspondent

[1] H. W. Meikle, *Scotland and the French Revolution*, p. 208.
[2] *Ibid.* p. 209, footnote.

says, 'obliquely or directly' they had attacked religious establishments. 'Within a few miles of Glasgow we have at present no
fewer than twenty of these schools.' Lay preaching was also a cause
of concern and anxiety. 'The ministers of the Church of Scotland',
Porteous naïvely admitted, 'have enjoyed ease and quiet so long
that few of them have directed their studies to subjects of this
kind; and as they are not prepared for the attack, so I am afraid
they are in danger of giving a handle against themselves by an
ill-tempered zeal. If any method could be fallen upon to direct
attention to the subject of Lay Preaching in a way that would not
irritate, it would be a very seasonable service, but I am afraid the
difficulties and perils of meeting a set of enthusiasts will prevent
it.'[1]

This 'seasonable service' the General Assembly of May 1799
proceeded to perform. Two restrictive measures were passed. One
of these closed the livings of the Church to all but its own licen-
tiates. This part of the Act was prompted by the case of a
dissenter, James Garie, who had received a presentation to the
Parish of Brechin, and who on his presentation being rejected,
became the first minister of the Congregational Church at Perth.[2]
The concluding part of the Act went further: it prohibited
ministers of the Church 'from employing to preach, upon any
occasion, or to dispense any of the ordinances of the Gospel
persons not qualified to accept such a presentation', and also 'from
holding ministerial communion in any other manner with such
persons'. By this Act such men as Rowland Hill and Charles
Simeon of Cambridge were expressly aimed at and excluded from
every pulpit in the Established Church. The other measure was
based on a *Report concerning Vagrant Teachers and Sunday Schools*.
It recited various Acts of the Scottish Parliament which had
established clerical censorship of education, enjoined the presbyteries to examine all teachers, and invited the concurrence of
the Lord Advocate and the Solicitor General in vindicating and
enforcing the jurisdiction of the Church.[3]

The wrath of the Assembly was not to be appeased by these
measures alone. A *Pastoral Admonition*, which the clergy were
ordered to read from their pulpits, was drawn up. This strange
document reveals how strong was the feeling against the movement

[1] *Edinburgh University Laing MSS.*, No. 501, 21 February, 1798.
[2] See *A Chronicle of the Churches*, below.
[3] *Acts of Assembly*, Year 1799, pp. 870-875.

launched by the labours of the Haldanes. At a time when 'the unhappy nation of the French' (states the *Admonition*) was diffusing 'like a pestilential vapour' its revolutionary and atheistical ideas, 'a set of men' had appeared 'whose proceedings threaten no small disorder' throughout the country. The individuals referred to are 'those who, assuming the name of missionaries from what they call the *Society for the Propagation of the Gospel at Home*', are perambulating Scotland as 'universal itinerant teachers', setting up Sunday Schools in which ignorant or notoriously disaffected persons 'presume not only to catechise but also to expound the Scriptures', and 'bringing together assemblies of men in the fields or in places not intended for public worship, where pouring forth their loose harangues, they frequently take the liberty of censuring the doctrines or character of the minister of the parish, studying to alienate the affections of the people from their own pastors, and engaging them to join this new sect, as if they alone were possessed of some secret or novel method of bringing men to Heaven'. These persons had the temerity to maintain that every man had a right to preach the Gospel, and there was much reason to fear that 'the name of liberty is abused by them, as it has been by others, to cover a secret democracy and anarchy'.[1]

This indictment was not allowed to pass unchallenged. Answers were published by the S.P.G.H., Greville Ewing, and others.[2] Rowland Hill, who arrived in Edinburgh shortly after the Admonition was published, attacked the Assembly in pamphlet and sermon, lashing the Moderates for their bigotry and the Evangelists for 'their criminal silence', which had betrayed the Haldanes and handed them over to their 'most malignant and avowed opposers'.

But it was not only the Church of Scotland that was antagonistic to the new movement. Other religious bodies also gave public expression of their disapproval. The General Associate or Antiburgher Synod as early as 1796 passed a resolution against the constitution of Missionary Societies, and testified against co-operating in religious matters with persons to whose religious opinions they were opposed as a Church. In 1798 a further resolution was passed in the same illiberal spirit declaring unanimously that lay-preaching had no warrant from the Word of God, and that, while they did not wholly condemn Sunday schools, they

---

[1] *Pastoral Admonition, passim.*   [2] See below.

judged that 'no person under their inspection could, consistently with their principles, send their children to such schools, or otherwise give them any countenance if discourses were delivered in them tending to encroach on the work of the ministry', or if other persons were permitted to be present besides the children.[1] The Cameronians at Glasgow in 1796 excommunicated some of their members for attending a sermon which a minister of the Church of Scotland had preached on behalf of the Glasgow Missionary Society.[2] The Relief Church, surprisingly despite its liberal attitude in other directions, unanimously decreed in 1798: 'No minister belonging to their body shall give, or allow his pulpit to be given, to any person who has not attended a regular course of philosophy and divinity in some of the Universities of the Nation; and who has not been regularly licensed to preach the Gospel'.[3] In explanation of this illiberal decree, so out of harmony with the customary witness of that communion, it should be remembered that one of its itinerants, who had belonged to the Friends of the People, had been guilty of a political indiscretion which had been used against their Church. They sought to save their reputation by this measure so contrary to their tradition.[4]

The National Church, as we have seen, sought the support of the civil power in its antipathy towards the innovators. A copy of the *Pastoral Admonition* was sent to the Sheriffs-depute of counties and the chief magistrates of all burghs. The Duke of Atholl at the same time appealed to the Home Secretary for more severe measures. He hoped that 'energetic measures will be taken under the authority of Parliament, to annihilate the further progress of unlicensed missionaries and free schools, whether under the auspices of Mr. Haldane, or any other enthusiastic and designing man whatever'. In another letter, this time to the Lord Advocate, the Duke expressed the conviction that an Act of Parliament would prove the only remedy to check the practices which otherwise would lay a sure foundation in the rising generation for the overthrow of every constitutional and loyal principle.[5] That such a Bill was not only contemplated but actually being prepared by the Government we learn from various sources. It was designed primarily to restrain the activities of the Methodists and other

[1] J. McKerrow, *History of the Secession Church*, pp. 384, 393-394.
[2] G. Struthers, *History of the Relief Church*.   [3] *Ibid.* p. 455.
[4] See reference to Neil Douglas earlier in this chapter; also H. W. Meikle, *Scotland and the French Revolution*, pp. 210-211.
[5] *Edinburgh University Laing MSS.*, No. 500, 20 May 1799; 24 May 1799.

Dissenters in England, but it would have been equally disastrous to the Haldanes and their supporters in Scotland. Happily the appeals which Wilberforce addressed to Pitt were successful in averting the threatened blow. Robert Haldane, who was not easily susceptible to fear, was thoroughly alarmed by the turn things were taking, and published in May 1800 his *Address to the Public*. This candid explanation proved exceedingly timely and useful, for it convinced the public that the authors of all this commotion were neither turbulent nor seditious, and that their aims were not political but evangelistic.[1] Henceforth they were left to carry on their work free from official censure.

We must not, however, conclude that the Haldanes and their agents were to encounter no more opposition in their endeavours to spread the Gospel. Efforts were still made all over the land by individuals and Church courts to put an end to their labours. Their disciples, moreover, were frequently subjected to persecutions.[2] For example, in May 1800 George Cowie, minister of the Antiburgher Church at Huntly, who became the morning star of Congregationalism in the north, was deposed from the office of the ministry by the Secession Church, because he allowed James Haldane and his colleagues the use of his pulpit, supported missionary societies, and founded Sunday schools.[3] Sunday school work, however, found little favour with many of the clergy, and those engaged in it sometimes had to face opposition and endure hardship. In a Morayshire parish, for example, a Sabbath evening school was opened. The indignant clergy summoned, cajoled, and threatened the teachers, but no impression being made, the strong arm of the law was invoked against them. This, of course, was in accordance with the decision of the general Assembly of 1799. An interdict was laid upon them, but this too failed, for teachers from Elgin—a distance of fifteen miles—went and taught the school until the original teachers were honourably acquitted. Recourse to such methods was really unnecessary, for at the request of the S.P.G.H., three of the ablest advocates in Edinburgh after diligent search of the law of Scotland expressed the opinion, 'that Sabbath schools are of the nature of religious exercises and come under the Toleration Act which in Scotland is very ample and full. . . .

[1] *Memoirs of the Haldanes*, p. 278; *Address to the Public*, p. 111.

[2] See *A Chronicle of the Churches*, Oban, where their followers were harried 'at the point of the bayonet'.

[3] H. Escott, *Beacons of Independency*, pp. 21 ff. See *A Chronicle of the Churches*, below.

The Act which the Church of Scotland builds upon was made upon the back of the Rebellion of 1745, against Papists to keep them from teaching schools, and it refers only to schools for reading, arithmetic, language, etc.'

Opponents of the new movement were not always careful to have the law on their side in their treatment of its teachers and preachers. Numerous were the instances in which the missionaries were arrested. Some of them were sent to jail more than once. In two instances they were put on board ship as impressed sailors, in the hope of ridding the country of them. James Haldane himself was threatened with imprisonment for preaching at the Cross of Ayr, and from the village of Whitehouse in Kintyre he and John Campbell were sent to the Sheriff of Argyll, thirty miles distant, under an escort of volunteers, as vagrant preachers, but the Sheriff finding no legal fault in them set them at liberty. They returned to the village whence they had been removed, and to the mortification of the minister, who had been instrumental in having them arrested, preached from Philippians, i. 12, 'The things which happened unto me have fallen out rather unto the furtherance of the gospel'.

In some parts of the country those, too, who sympathised with the preachers were often-times made to suffer. False reports were raised and circulated for bringing them into disrepute. Violent measures were designed and employed to deprive them of their houses and farms, and in not a few instances were their lives in jeopardy.[1]

Only a man of James Haldane's mental and spiritual stature could have withstood such opposition, and inspired endurance in others. 'Dignified in manner, commanding in speech, fearless in courage, unhesitating in action, he everywhere met the rising storm with the boldness of a British sailor and the courtesy of a British gentleman, as well as with the uprightness and unoffensiveness of a true Christian.'[2]

V

At the very time when the General Assembly of the Church of Scotland was making such determined efforts to overthrow their schemes, James Haldane, John Aikman, and William Innes were

---

[1] *Scottish Congregational Jubilee Services*, p. 76; *Missionary Magazine* (1803), p. 364; *A Chronicle of the Churches*, below.
[2] *Memoirs of the Haldanes*, p. 290.

engaged in a preaching tour in the north which took them as far as Shetland. Everywhere, despite the Assembly's fulminations, crowds flocked to hear them, and the nuclei of churches were formed. So it proved, north and south, east and west, it was for the new movement a time of amazing progress and advance.

During the building of the Tabernacle in Leith Walk, Edinburgh, which was opened in May 1801, and thereafter was full to overflowing every Sunday evening, Greville Ewing took charge of the services in the Glasgow Circus. There also large congregations were attracted, and a Congregational church was formed on 15 August 1800.[1] In October of the same year the Tabernacle at Dundee was opened, with William Innes as pastor. Here, as in Edinburgh and Glasgow, large crowds assembled to hear the Gospel preached.[2] Not in these busy centres alone, but even in far away Thurso and Wick meeting-houses were opened, large congregations drawn, and Congregational churches formed.[3]

Besides these churches, which may be regarded as the direct outcome of Robert Haldane's liberality and the preaching of James Haldane and his colleagues, others of the Scottish Congregational churches originated about this time. Belmont Street Church, Aberdeen (originally George Street Church) was formally constituted on 16 September 1798, and originated in the conviction of its founders that the Congregational way approximated most nearly to the pattern of the primitive churches.[4] About the same time, or perhaps even earlier, a Congregational church was formed in Paisley.[5] In Perth as early as 1794 there were men who desired to form a Congregational church in that city, which purpose was achieved four years later.[6]

A Congregational church was formed at Huntly in 1800 by the members of the Antiburgher Church adhering to their minister, George Cowie, who, as we have seen, was deposed by the Synod for countenancing James Haldane and his preachers.[7] None of these churches directly owed its existence to the labours of the Haldanes; but the success that attended them in their early years was in part due to the stir that the Haldanes had created, and very soon they were swept into the Haldane movement. By the close of

---

[1] See *A Chronicle of the Churches*, below.   [2] *Ibid.*
[3] *Ibid.*   [4] *Ibid.*   [5] *Ibid.*   [6] *Ibid.*
[7] H. Escott, *Beacons of Independency*, pp. 20 ff. and *A Chronicle of the Churches*, below.

the eighteenth century fourteen Congregational churches had been formed throughout Scotland; seven years later that number had increased to eighty-five.

VI

How are we to explain this phenomenal development in the religious life of Scotland? The spiritual fervour and aggressive energy of the missionaries and their converts, and the munificent liberality of Robert Haldane had much to do with it. But we should not forget that the climate of the public mind, influenced by the French Revolution, made the movement a desirable and emancipating one in many quarters. The troubles in France had roused many out of an intellectual and spiritual torpor, and awakened needs which craved immediate relief. None of the churches existing in Scotland could supply the spiritual enlightenment and nutriment which that time of turmoil and tension made so necessary. The people, therefore, went elsewhere for the help they were refused and denied at home. Hence the crowds that followed James Haldane and John Aikman on their early missionary journeys, and later assembled in the Tabernacles at Edinburgh, Glasgow, Dundee and in the distant north.

Two other factors contributed greatly to the success of the new Denomination in its early stages: one, Robert Haldane's interest in the training of preachers, and, two, the firm grasp both brothers had of evangelical theology.

The Tabernacle scheme soon presented Robert Haldane with the necessity of securing a regular supply of ministers, who by grace and training should be fitted to carry forward the work he had inaugurated. The same problem arose in the evangelistic ventures of the S.P.G.H. The work in that field was held up by the lack of suitable agents. It was under these circumstances that in 1798, he conceived the idea of educating 'a number of pious young men for the ministry, who might be taken, as in primitive times from the various occupations of life, and chosen for the ministry on account of their piety, and promising talents'.[1] Haldane divulged the idea to John Campbell in a letter, written under date of 6 October 1798, 'I intend to give one year's education to ten or twelve persons, of any age that may be fit for it, under Mr. Bogue, with a view to the ministry. Will you and my brother be looking

---

[1] R. Haldane, *Address to the Public*, p. 83.

out for suitable persons to be ready by the time I return.'[1] This marks the origin of those theological seminaries, which were afterwards carried out by Robert Haldane on so great a scale.

It was not, however, to David Bogue, Congregational minister at Gosport, that the instruction of the first class of students was committed. Representations were made to Haldane that if the students were sent south it would only react unfavourably on his projects for evangelising Scotland, as Bogue's politics were suspect. Thus to Greville Ewing was entrusted the charge of the first class in the new seminary. This was formed in January 1799 in Edinburgh but removed to Glasgow, when their tutor took charge of the Tabernacle there. It commenced with twenty-four students, all of them being Presbyterian and not Congregationalist in sentiment; but before the end of their course they were, as one of them avowed, 'decided and intelligent Congregationalists'. Their course of study over in November 1800, there were applications for their services from various towns of Scotland.[2]

The second class commenced in January 1800 at Dundee under William Innes's direction.[3] It numbered between fifty and sixty and included some who had been catechists in the service of the S.P.G.H. After a year with Innes they removed to Glasgow and continued under Greville Ewing's instruction for fifteen months. On this class terminating their studies, and being sent to various parts of Scotland, Ewing relinquished his connection with the seminary, which was later transferred to Edinburgh and brought more directly under the control of Robert Haldane and his brother.[4]

In July 1801 a third class of twenty-two students was gathered at Dundee, and removed to Edinburgh twelve months later. The students' course of study was interrupted by their being sent out to officiate as preachers at the end of their first year, and therefore they did not finish until 1804. In 1802 the fourth class, with which the third was united, began in Edinburgh. The combined class numbered about fifty, some of whom were married men with families. Aikman and Campbell acted as theological tutors and Thomas Wemyss as classical tutor.[5]

---

[1] *Memoirs of the Haldanes*, p. 231.

[2] *Memoir of Greville Ewing*, p. 196.

[3] Innes was a brother-in-law of the Haldanes; he had been minister of the Established Church in Stirling and chaplain of the Garrison.

[4] *Memoirs of the Haldanes*, p. 329.

[5] Wemyss was well-known in theological circles as the author of *Job and his Times* (1839) and *Clavis Symbolica* (1840).

A fifth class was started in 1803 under the instruction of Aikman, Wemyss, and William Stephens.[1] Among the students were two young men who were later to take a prominent place in the denomination: David Russell and John Watson, the first Secretary of the Congregational Union of Scotland. This class, Lindsay Alexander declares, was divided into two parties, the liberals and the conservatives, or more accurately, the Sandemanians and the Anti-Sandemanians. He further contends that the former had the sanction of ' one of the tutors if not also the patron of the institution'. As regards the latter's leanings to Sandemanianism, or at least to the Sandemanian idea of church order and discipline there can be little doubt. Later events at the Tabernacle were to prove it. The writings of Glas and Sandeman undoubtedly influence for a time many of this class, so that there were frequent heated discussions.

The sixth class was formed in 1804 under Wemyss, Stephens, and George Cowie[2] for the first year, but under Cowie alone for the second.

In 1805 the seventh class was started under Cowie and William Walker, student of the fifth class. The eighth under the same tutors, commenced in September 1806, but Cowie resigned in the spring of 1808, when most of the men were sent by Robert Haldane to England, as the S.P.G.H. had been broken up some time before. A ninth class was, however, organised under William Walker at the end of 1807, and met till December of the following year, when the seminary ceased, after having sent out nearly 300 students into the world.[3]

The cause of the cessation was the withdrawal of the financial support which made the classes possible. For some time Robert Haldane had been inclined, with not a few others, to alter his views about the fundamentals of the body he had done so much to form, notably about 'mutual exhortation', the 'plurality of elders', and baptism. In 1808 the two Haldanes, Innes, and others became Baptists, and the source of liberal financial aid on which

[1] Stephens had been minister for three years of George Street Church Aberdeen, and was now assisting James Haldane at the Tabernacle in Edinburgh.

[2] Cowie resigned from the Church of Scotland to join the new body, becoming minister of the Montrose Church, 1801-4.

[3] *Scottish Congregational Jubilee Services*, pp. 69-70; R. F. G. Calder, ' Robert Haldane's Theological Seminary ', *Transactions of the Congregational Historical Society*, Vol. XIII, No. 1 (September 1937), pp. 59 ff.

the Seminary, and indeed many of the churches depended, dried up. The Seminary had to be closed at once.

In addition to the classes conducted under Robert Haldane's direction during the decade of the academy's existence, there were others up and down the land. There was one at Armagh under the instruction of a Mr. Hamilton; and at least another in Scotland, at Elgin, under William Ballantine.[1] Quite a number of students appear to have been sent up to the academy from these classes, which were of a preparatory character.

The students in the academy were entirely maintained by Robert Haldane, who paid for their lodgings, medical attendance, education and books, and gave to each student £24 for the first year and £30 for the second. He provided a well-stocked library for their use. It is computed that the seminary must have cost him upwards of £20,000. His total expenditure in ten years on the spreading of the Gospel is said to have been fully £80,000.[2]

The students came from all parts of Scotland and Ireland, and were divided into three bodies: Highlanders, Lowlanders, and Irishmen. A student was appointed as censor over each body to watch over the sayings, doings, and opinions of all, and report anything unusual to Haldane. There is no indication of any resentment being shown at this petty tyranny.[3]

The course of study prescribed lasted two years, with an annual vacation in the summer of each year. The curriculum covered English Grammar and Rhetoric, the elements of Greek and Hebrew, and Systematic Theology. A teacher of French was provided for those who wished to acquire the language, and, that they might lack nothing when sent out as preachers, they received instruction in Church Music. Latin was also taught on request.

During vacations those students who were deemed suitable for the work were sent out, frequently in twos, to itinerate in different parts of the country, preaching as they had opportunity. Thus in the vacation of 1804, we find John Watson and William Walker touring Clackmannanshire, Fife, Kinross, Angus, Forfar, and Aberdeen, preaching as they journeyed. On Sundays in term time the senior students were often sent to assist ministers and vacant churches.

---

[1] Ballantine had been minister of the Free Presbyterian Church in Elgin for three years before becoming minister of the Tabernacle built there in 1804.

[2] *The Evangelical Magazine*, 1843; W. L. Alexander, *Memoirs of Revd. John Watson*, pp. 29-30.

[3] 'Robert Haldane's Theological Seminary' (Calder).

Several preaching stations in Edinburgh and district were regularly maintained by them. Juniors 'were but sparingly engaged; but by way of compensation they were required to go through a certain amount of historical reading in the works of Mosheim, Milner, Rollin, and Robertson'.[1]

In the light of what has been written above it will be seen that the success of Congregationalism in the opening years of the nineteenth century depended largely on Robert Haldane's zeal and liberality in the training of its evangelists and ministers. His generous enthusiasm in this work, along with the influence of the Christian character and faithful labours of the men he trained, built up the churches, quickening their spiritual life and widening their witness.

Their sure grasp of evangelical truth was the other thing that furthered the success of the revival movement under the Haldanes. The two brothers used their pens and purses in producing books and pamphlets in defence of the Gospel. If James was the better preacher, Robert was the abler writer, who will also be remembered gratefully for the work he did as a Christian teacher at Geneva. Early in the century he spent a few years at Geneva and Mont-auban, the headquarters of French protestantism, then under the dark cloud of rationalism. His Biblical expositions at Geneva were attended by the whole body of Theological students. And when among those to whom his labours were blessed one must mention such names as Merle D'Aubigné, Malan, and Monod it will be recognised what a far-reaching influence his work exerted in ecumenical religion. One of his student converts said of him: 'He knew the Scriptures like a Christian who has had for his Master the same Holy Spirit by whom they were dictated.' D'Aubigné, the historian of the Reformation, who owed his soul to Haldane's teaching has written: 'If Geneva gave something to Scotland at the time of the Reformation—if she communicated light to John Knox—Geneva has received something in return in the blessed exertions of Robert Haldane.'

At home and abroad the original teaching of the Haldanes was never narrowly denominational. The mainspring of the movement they initiated was not the advocacy of Congregationalism or any other church polity, but ecumenical Christianity, the proclamation of the simple Gospel—salvation by grace; justification by faith,

---

[1] W. L. Alexander, *Memoir of the Revd. John Watson*, pp. 31-33.

irrespective of frames of feeling; free forgiveness through the Cross of Christ; implicit trust in Him as the only and all-sufficient Saviour: doctrines indeed which in substance have been the spring of every great religious revival throughout the world.[1]

[1] See J. Macleod, *Scottish Theology*, pp. 225-228, for an appraisement of the Haldanes as theologians.

F

CHAPTER VIII

DIVISION AND SEPARATION

WE have seen that by the end of 1807 eighty-five churches had been formed on the Congregational plan, and we have given some reasons for this phenomenal growth of Congregationalism in a Presbyterian land. The wonderful progress and achievements of the first decade of the history of these churches augured well for future successes and triumphs. But a time of testing was at hand. Questions were soon to be raised which seriously affected the movement—questions relating to church order and to the ordinances of Christ, which unfortunately were discussed with an acerbity which rent the denomination, and even for a while threatened its very existence.

'The first public manifestation of a difference of opinion likely to issue in a change of practice', says William Orme, 'was given in Mr. Haldane's *Social Worship*, in which he contends for public exhortation in the churches on the Lord's Day, by the brethren; and for a plurality of pastors in every church, though the most of them should be employed in secular business '.[1] Mutual exhortation was not unknown among the churches. Provision had been made for it in the rules which Greville Ewing had drawn up for the Tabernacle at Glasgow, but as a part, and an essential part of the Sunday services (and for this James Haldane argued) it was a novelty, for hitherto it had been confined to a week-night meeting of the congregation. In *An Address to the Church of Christ, Leith Walk, Edinburgh*, James Haldane maintained that not only exhortation but also the exercise of discipline should take place publicly at the Sunday services. Here, too, was an innovation, for discipline until then had been exercised in the presence of the members alone. It was otherwise in the Apostolic churches argued Haldane. These had public exhortations by the brethren and public exercise of discipline on the Lord's Day. Therefore it must be so in *all* true Churches of Christ, for God had established an order and to that order we must adhere. 'No dispensing power has He given us respecting any of His ordinances.'[2]

[1] W. Orme, *London Christian Instructor* (1819), p. 782.
[2] J. Haldane, *An Address to the Church . . .*, p. 4.

According to Greville Ewing, even before this time, Robert Haldane having been persuaded to study the writings of Glas and Sandeman had become enamoured of their teaching, as previously he had been prejudiced against it, and their view of church government had become his.[1] His brother, it would appear, had become similarly convinced, for it was the Glasite ideal of churches which would be replicas to the minutest detail of the primitive apostolic churches, that he had in view, and it was some of the distinctive practices of the Glasites that he desired to introduce.

James Haldane's *Social Worship* and *Address* were followed by a treatise on the Elder's office by William Ballantyne. This pamphlet advocated a plurality of elders and indeed struck at the entire order of the public worship of the churches, and was widely circulated by Robert Haldane as representing his own views.[2] It provoked much discussion as to the pastor's or elder's office in the church, but, unfortunately, the discussion developed into dispute; and a restless passion for novelty raged in the bosom of many influential members of the Congregational churches, and infected even some of the pastors. 'Matters came to such a pitch that to train pious men for the ministry—to have public collections for the support of Gospel ordinances—for ministers to wear black clothes—was pronounced anti-Christian. Various other novelties were zealously enforced; while those who would not embrace these things, were accused of opposing the cause of God.'[3]

All likelihood of reconciling the two parties in the churches vanished when another and greater question was raised between them—that of Baptism. This further crisis was brought about by James Haldane and his brother adopting and advocating Baptist views. The former is said, erroneously we believe, to have made this sudden change immediately after Archibald McLean's *Review of Wardlaw's Lectures on Infant Baptism* appeared; for whereas the review was published in 1807, James Haldane was not baptised till the following year. From a letter to John Campbell dated 19 February 1808, it is plain that on the question of baptism he had been thinking for a considerable time. He writes that, at various times he had entertained doubts as to the Scriptural authority for Infant Baptism. The persistence of these doubts

---

[1] Greville Ewing, *Facts and Documents Respecting the Communications . . . between Robert Haldane, Esq., and Greville Ewing*, p. 82; see also Chapter VII, VI, above.
[2] W. Ballantyne, *A Treatise on the Elder's Office*.
[3] *Memoir of Greville Ewing*, pp. 327-328.

made him determine, at the end of 1804, fully to examine the Scriptures at his leisure, 'with prayer for direction and a desire to be led to a right conclusion'. The result was that, after much reading and thought on the subject, his doubts so much increased that a request being made to him to baptise a child, he was obliged to inform the church that, although his mind was not made up to become himself a Baptist, yet he could not conscientiously baptise children.[1] In that undecided condition, however, he did not long remain, for it would seem that early in March 1808 he definitely adopted Baptist views and submitted to the ordinance. Robert, his brother, about this time also changed his sentiments on infant baptism, and later in the year was immersed.[2]

It was not James Haldane's intention that his adoption of Baptist views should affect his relations with the Tabernacle congregation. In the letter to John Campbell already referred to, this is made clear, for he concludes: 'I informed the Church that, although I were baptised, I should be of the same mind as formerly, that the Baptists and Paedo-Baptists, might have fellowhip together.' In a subsequent letter of 21 April he is still of the opinion that, although he himself has adopted Baptist views and been baptised, with regard to the Church this will be a matter of forbearance. 'If we are all acting on conviction', he writes, and both desiring to know the will of Jesus in this, and in all other respects, I have no apprehension of disunion. Of one thing I am sure, that all who love the Lord Jesus should, so far as they are agreed, walk by the same rule, and mind the same things; and if it be improper for Baptists to be in fellowship in the same church it must be equally improper to have occasional fellowship in private.'[3] But these expectations were not realised. His views of mutual forbearance were not reciprocated, and a rupture took place in the Tabernacle congregation. Two hundred of the members adhered to their pastor, but a considerable number withdrew. Some of these joined Presbyterian churches; some went to John Aikman's Church in North College Street; while about a hundred formed themselves into a Congregational church in Bernard's Rooms, West Thistle Street on Sunday, 26 March 1808, and in the summer of that year called William Innes of Dundee to be their minister.[4]

[1] *Memoirs of the Haldanes*, p. 357.
[2] *History of the Baptists in Scotland*, p. 58.
[3] *Memoirs of the Haldanes*, p. 358.
[4] See *A Chronicle of the Churches*, below.

Mr. Haldane's renouncing of Infant Baptism apparently precipitated this division, but it should be remembered that this was not the *sole* cause of the separation of so many members. Their pastor's changed views regarding various parts of the mode of worship followed hitherto by the church, and his insistence 'on introducing exhortation by many of the brethren who felt inclined to exhort on the Lord's Day—discipline in public and the kiss of charity' was another and important ground of difference, and had something, perhaps much, to do with the decision to separate and form a church that was neither Baptist nor Glasite but Congregational, as the Tabernacle had been at its inception.

This disastrous rupture was repeated elsewhere. The new notions spread throughout most of the churches and contention, strife of words, jealousies and separations followed. In Glasgow, Perth, Wick, Arbroath, Falkirk, and many other towns and villages, considerable numbers holding Haldane's views on baptism, church order and worship withdrew and allied themselves with the Old Scotch Baptists.[1] The denomination was rent in twain and one of the noblest schemes which that age had witnessed for diffusing religion and evangelising the population of the country was in a great measure laid in ruins.

This tragedy, regrettable as it is, could hardly have been avoided; for these first churches were composed of two distinct parties, those who were Congregationalists by conviction and those who were so only by accident. The Haldanes belonged to the latter. It was only a temporary ecclesiastical refuge they found in Congregationalism. The proposals they put forward for the conduct of worship showed, even before they became Baptists, that they had moved away from the Congregational polity. In ecclesiastical outlook, though not in doctrine, they were Sandemanians, and were they living today they would find their spiritual home with the Plymouth Brethren.

To a convinced Congregationalist like Greville Ewing, these views of the Haldanes were 'destructive, both of the pastoral office, and of all order in the House of God'; and the task of rebuilding upon the waste places a goodly edifice fell into his capable hands, as we shall now see.[2]

[1] *History of the Baptists in Scotland*, p. 59.
[2] *Memoirs of the Haldanes*, p. 359.

CHAPTER IX

REBUILDING THE WASTE PLACES

I

THE architect and builder of modern Scottish Congregationalism was Greville Ewing; and the time has arrived in this narrative for a more minute account of his life and work than we have been able so far to give.

He was born in the Parish of Old Greyfriars, Edinburgh, in 1767, and died in Glasgow in 1841, the revered founder-pastor of the first Haldanite Congregational Church to be established there. From his early years he was associated with the Evangelical party in the Church of Scotland. His boyhood was passed under the ministry of John Erskine. Through the influence of his stepmother, a pious woman who had been converted by the preaching of Whitefield in the Orphan Park in Edinburgh, he became a communicant of Lady Glenorchy's Chapel in that city in 1782. Lady Glenorchy was the counterpart in Scotland, albeit a less masterful one, of Selina Countess of Huntingdon, in England. She was the founder of a number of churches that had a more democratic type of churchmanship than was usual, serving as small oases of evangelical interests and life amid the arid wastes of Moderatism. Indeed, Lady Glenorchy's Chapel in Edinburgh had not a little in common with the Congregational churches soon to be established by the Haldanes. It was extra-parochial; it was not endowed or founded by the State, having been built by Christian liberality for the purpose of extending the knowledge of Christ and His salvation; its ministers had no voice in church courts, and could therefore exert little influence ecclesiastically beyond their own congregations; but they had the satisfaction of being elected by the choice of the people. It was a Christian society more truly than the bulk of churches in Edinburgh, and indeed in Scotland, at that time.

In January 1793 Ewing became assistant to Thomas Jones the minister of Lady Glenorchy's Chapel, and in October of that year he was ordained to the ministry as Jones's colleague. In his sermon on that occasion Jones stressed the unsectarian character of the church to which the ordinand had been called, in words which remind us of the spirit of traditional Congregationalism: 'Our great object is to make sound believers and real saints, and our united efforts in this city must be exerted to win souls to Christ, not to make a faction for ourselves.' Connected with this church, moreover, was a Sunday school under the supervision of Lady Maxwell, which met on Sunday evenings, before any society for the support of Sabbath schools was formed in Edinburgh. Here Ewing sometimes assisted. It is interesting also to notice that purity of communion (a favourite topic of the early Congregationalists) was a subject which deeply engaged Ewing's attention. 'Under the notion of being charitable', he said in a sermon preached in 1794, 'we are rash in giving the right hand of fellowship to every one who will give himself the trouble to ask it. Hence, it is, in a great measure, that our societies consist of a motley mixture of ignorant and enlightened; carnal and spiritual; persons who fear God, and persons who fear Him not; lovers of Jesus, and workers of iniquity.'

Like the early Congregationalists too, Greville Ewing was a pioneer in missionary enterprise. Before he became a Congregationalist he supported with voice and pen the work of missions at home and abroad. He once said, 'I will yield to no man living in concern for the cause of Missions, or in joy at the success of Missionary Societies. I am sensible, however, that the Church of Christ is, strictly speaking, the proper, the legitimate Missionary Society.' The beginning of the London Missionary Society kindled his mind and heart. The following statement made by him, dated November 1795 is significant: 'Excited by a desire for the spreading of the Gospel, a number of serious persons in Edinburgh, some time ago, agreed to join together in prayer for that purpose. These meetings are now increased, and are conducted on such a plan, as not to interfere with the duties of the family or closet. They meet at 7 o'clock on Sabbath mornings, and continue about an hour and a half; during which time three or four members usually pray, after having sung part of a psalm and read a portion of Scripture.' As a result of these meetings, apparently, the Edinburgh Missionary Society (later, the Scottish Missionary Society) was formed in March 1796, and Ewing became its first secretary.

In 1794 we find him writing to the *Evangelical Magazine*, then only in the second year of its existence, under the pseudonym of

'Onesimus', in appraisal of the magazine's missionary interests, its determined adherence to evangelical truth and its true catholicity. The last phrase recalls yet another characteristic of the man, which also became the mark of the denomination he may be said to have founded, namely, his ecumenicity. He once wrote: 'It is true, indeed, that the existence of sects in the Church of Christ which is one, although often overruled by Him for good, is a striking proof of our ignorance and depravity; it calls for general humility and mutual forbearance; and should quicken our desire for that blessed world where we shall be made perfect in love.'

Ewing was a pioneer in Christian journalism. In July 1796 he and Charles Stuart, an Edinburgh physician, who had been minister of the Established Church at Cramond, but was now a Baptist, began the *Missionary Magazine* (now *The Scottish Congregationalist*).[1] Ewing ceased to be Editor in 1799. It was a monthly publication intended 'as a Depository of Discussion and Intelligence respecting the Progress of the Gospel throughout the World'. The idea of producing such an unsectarian religious periodical in Scotland was altogether new. It was another child of Ewing's ecumenical mind, though it should be added that the times were ripe for the publication of a journal of Christian world enterprise. Stuart, like his colleague on the editorial bench, was 'the friend and advocate of every undertaking calculated to diffuse the knowledge of Christ, or ameliorate the condition of men'. His own contributions to the magazine bore the signature *Philalethus*. He was, moreover, an intimate friend of Andrew Fuller, through whom he received news for its pages from the Baptist missionaries in India. Amongst frequent contributors who subsequently played leading rôles in the drama of the denomination were John Campbell, George Cowie, and John Cleghorn.

Doubtless Ewing's editorship of the *Missionary Magazine* did much to prepare the ground for the evangelical ventures of James and Robert Haldane, which resulted in the formation of Congregational churches. Ewing was more truly a Congregationalist than either of the Haldane brothers. Even before he met them he was not far out of the Congregational way. His idea of Congregational church polity stemmed from his experience of the

---

[1] The designation was changed first to the *Christian Herald*, and then to *The Scottish Congregational Magazine*, and finally to the present title. See Chapter XIII, III, below.

less rigid Presbyterianism of Lady Glenorchy's Chapel, and from his study of New Testament church order, inspired apparently by Campbell's *Lectures on Ecclesiastical History*, which he had evidently read round about 1799. The essential Ewing was in nowise changed by his association with the Haldanes, except, of course, in that he then espoused Congregationalism in a public manner. 'I am a Dissenter', he wrote in 1800, 'because I think Christianity suffers when civil privileges are claimed by any denomination of Christians in their church capacity: I am, moreover, a dissenter from the Church of Scotland, because I am not convinced of the divine right of Presbytery.'

We shall not weary the reader with an account of Ewing's retiral from the National Church and of the steps by which he became founder-minister of the mother church of the denomination in Glasgow (now *Hillhead*). The whole story is told in *A Chronicle of the Churches* at the close of the present book.[1] The denomination was indeed fortunate to have had such a man in such a place in its formative years; and particularly when the controversies about church order, worship, and baptism arose with such devastating results, as we have noticed in the previous chapter. Ewing was precluded from falling a victim to the fanaticisms which overpowered the Haldanes and many others and tragically disrupted the youthful movement, because his Congregationalism had strong scriptural, ecclesiastical and experiential sources. It was this fact that equipped him to be the deliverer of the denomination in its decisive hour. Fortunately, too, Ewing carried over with him into Congregationalism, in addition to a decided evangelical piety, not a little Presbyterian soberness; and these qualities, combined with a reticence and love of order that were perhaps temperamental, fitted their possessor to build up the depleted churches into a strong and unified organisation.

His critical attitude towards the ideas adopted by the Haldanes, which were largely resuscitations of the doctrines of Glas and Sandeman, was in no sense motivated by personal animosity. Ewing shared the distaste of the eighteenth century for 'enthusiasm'. A classicist by training, he had also the classicist's love of harmony and peace. Lawlessness he detested wherever it was found, in social affairs as well as in religion. This is clearly illustrated in a sermon he preached in 1799 in support of lay preaching, when, as we have seen, that strange phenomenon had roused the

[1] See also Chapter VII, v, above.

ire of the religious and civil authorities alike.[1] Ewing's discourse provoked the criticism of many ministers and the published *Animadversions* of at least one of them, John Robertson, assistant minister at Cambuslang. Apparently this critic had referred to the outrages of the Cromwellian lay-preachers against ecclesiastical dignity and their disruption of the unity and peace of the National church. Ewing, ever the bold champion of the layman, nevertheless agreed with his literary adversary about the aberrations of Cromwell's booted apostles. 'The lay-preachers in the Cromwellian army', he is prepared to admit, 'depended not upon the warrant and direction of Scripture, but upon a kind of miraculous assistance of the Divine Spirit, without any study or preparation. They violated every church order, for they took possession of the country pulpits where they were quartered. In short, they were *bold enthusiasts*, and they introduced all these disorders which enthusiasm will always tend to introduce, both among lay, and clerical preachers.'[2]

In a wide sense one supposes Ewing could be regarded as a child of Whitefield's revival work in Scotland, and yet no one could have been more critical of the enthusiastic concomitants of the 'Cambuslang Wark', with which the English evangelist had been so closely connected, than he. His disapproval of the wild and undisciplined features revealed at Cambuslang, which he had apparently expressed in a letter written in March 1800, to Robert Haldane, earned for him the latter's sharp rebuke: 'I do not much like your remark upon the work at Cambuslang; it was that way the Spirit of God chose to work in many who were really converted.' Robert Haldane and Greville Ewing were equally men of deep dedication, outstanding intellect and piety, but their dispositions and ecclesiastical convictions were so dissimilar that a rift in their association was bound to come sooner or later.

II

The division of 1808 left the churches which had declined to accept the new notions in a weak and shattered condition. Many

---

[1] *A Defence of Itinerant and Field-preaching. A Sermon preached before the Society for Gratis Sabbath Schools, Edinburgh*, 2nd edn., Glasgow, 1832.

[2] *Animadversions on some passages of a pamphlet entitled Lay-preaching Indefensible on Scripture Principles by Mr. John Robertson, assistant minister, Cambuslang*, by Greville Ewing, Glasgow, 1800; see also Chapter II in present book.

of them had lost a large proportion of their members: only in the large towns was the membership now numerous. Most of their congregations were poor, and if previously they had found it difficult to support their pastors, much more difficult was it for them now when they were divided in sentiment, fewer in numbers, and all outside aid was withdrawn from them. A number of the buildings were the property of Robert Haldane and the occupants of others were deeply indebted to him; he claimed the restoration of the former and the immediate payment of the debts due on the latter. A heavy load of debt therefore impeded the efforts of very many congregations. In consequence of these things some promising spheres of usefulness had to be relinquished, and others were carried on only at the cost of much self-denial on the part of the pastors. Some of the latter betook themselves to teaching and other occupations to augment their scanty incomes, while others continued to labour, managing as best they could upon the slender pittances which their people could afford.[1]

The separation from the Haldanes meant also the loss of the Seminary for the training of future ministers, since from the first, as we have seen, this institution had been supported at the sole expense of Robert Haldane. Any further supply therefore of pastors was not to be expected from that quarter.

To these live problems of church aid and theological training it was imperative that the churches should immediately address themselves if the denomination was not to die out in Scotland. With the latter a beginning was made early in 1811.

The leader in this important matter was Greville Ewing. In 1804 he had drawn up a *Memorial Concerning a Theological Academy*, in which he suggested that the training of men for the ministry was the responsibility of the churches and not of one individual. He further emphasised the need for an educated ministry. But the proposals did not find favour with the Haldanes, and the publication of the Memorial was deferred.[2] However, in 1808 in the light of the new situation Ewing returned to the subject and published *A Memorial on Education for the Ministry of the Gospel*, and the matter was brought before the churches. Nothing, however, seems to have been done until 1810 when meetings of representatives from various churches were held in

---

[1] *Memoir of Greville Ewing*, p. 393.
[2] *Facts and Documents respecting the Connexions . . . between Robert Haldane, Esq. and Greville Ewing* (1809).

Perth and Dundee. An address from these meetings was sent to all the churches urging the need of some plan for the education of men for the ministry. The response was of such a nature as to encourage definite action being taken. Accordingly, on 22 January 1811, a meeting of ministers was convened in Glasgow to consider 'what should be done for affording a supply of preachers to meet the wants of the churches'.[1] It was resolved, at Ewing's suggestion, to send a circular invitation to the pastors to meet at Glasgow to consider the matter of supplying preachers for the churches. The result was 'a numerous and very interesting meeting of pastors, and also of brethren belonging to various churches' assembled on 13 March 1811. After a sermon by Ralph Wardlaw it was agreed to form the Glasgow Theological Academy. Ewing and Wardlaw were appointed tutors, and the plan of education was presented 'embracing Latin, Greek, and Hebrew; Logic, Natural Philosophy, Mathematics, General History, and Theology, connected with a comparative view of philosophical and Christian morality. The course to be four years, or five if necessary. The more advanced branches of classical learning to be obtained by attendance at the university; the expense of which, as well as the support of the students, in cases requiring aid, to be borne by the funds of the institution. This support was to be continued, for one year at least, after the commencement of their ministerial labours, if, within that time, they did not obtain a stated charge. All persons received as students, were to be recommended by their respective pastors with the consent of the churches to which they belonged; decided piety being a qualification indispensable.'[2] A committee was appointed to manage the Academy's affairs and an appeal was drawn up and sent to the churches on its behalf. The Academy as soon as possible thereafter came into operation and the first class of students numbered eight. The number of this and subsequent classes would have been much larger but the committee were hampered by the small amount of funds at their disposal.

The new academy was also a centre of evangelistic effort. During vacations the senior students were frequently stationed in one or other of the churches, to enable the pastors to itinerate more exclusively. The younger students were generally engaged in itinerant preaching or in association with some experienced

---

[1] The ministers chiefly concerned were George Robertson (of Paisley) Ralph Wardlaw, and Ewing himself.
[2] *Memoir of Greville Ewing*, pp. 378 ff.

minister. In this regard all the students had the example of their tutors to follow: both Ewing and Wardlaw to the end of their days were busy evangelists.[1] Every encouragement was given to candidates for training who were natives of districts in Scotland where the Gaelic language prevailed, because there the lack of preachers was most pronounced.

It cannot be gainsaid that the efforts put forward by Greville Ewing, that resulted in the formation of the Glasgow Theological Academy in 1811, inaugurated a new era in the history of Scottish Congregationalism; and determined that traditional pattern of academic plus evangelistic training which has always characterised the curricula of its Halls and Colleges.

III

Systematic ministerial training went a long way towards the rebuilding of the denomination after its tragic disruption in 1808. But now something else needed to be done to consolidate the advantage gained. The local churches needed to know one another better, and to share one another's burdens for the good of all. From the sporadic and unexpected manner in which the churches originated, one natural result was the absence of any systematic co-operation. Though regarding each other with the interest of sister churches, they yet lacked some visible bond of union—some regular plan of correspondence and communication. 'They were in the situation of a flock dispersed in a tempest, the losses of which can only be ascertained by bringing together the scattered remnants within one common fold.'[2]

Moreover, the economic difficulties of the local churches made some kind of federation for mutual aid necessary. None was more conscious than Ewing of the gravity of the situation, as may be inferred from a letter, in which he wrote: 'It would require a long letter indeed, to describe the distresses of almost all the smaller churches. Their pastors are either compelled to betake themselves to business, or the people are deprived of all the ordinary means of grace.'[2] On another occasion, he told of an able and much-loved pastor who, except when snow lay thick, assembled his flock on the mountain side. It would require many pages of the present

---

[1] Cf. *Memoir of Greville Ewing, passim,* and W. L. Alexander, *Memoirs of The Life and Writings of Ralph Wardlaw, passim.*

[2] *Memoir of Greville Ewing.*　　　　　　　　[2] *Ibid.*

book to tell of the privations of travelling preachers lodging under roofs open to every blast. But even when at home, there were honoured servants of Christ who brought up a young family, amidst the inconveniences of an earthen floor, affected by every change of weather; or saw their last morsel of food consumed, before they were able to satisfy the inquiries of their children whence the next supply was to come.

With the view of relieving the churches in this crippling and heart-breaking situation the Congregational Union was formed in November 1812.[1] The suggestion that something of this nature might be attempted was first made in the course of conversation among some ministers and office-bearers in the neighbourhood of Musselburgh in September of that year. The company—consisting of Alexander Arthur, pastor of Dalkeith Congregational Church; Messrs. Rae and Leyden, two of its members; John Watson, pastor of the Congregational Church, Musselburgh; and Mr. Tait, one of Watson's deacons—eagerly discussed the suggestion. The matter was further discussed at a district meeting at Dalkeith a week later, and eventually laid before a meeting of delegates from the churches in Edinburgh on the first Wednesday of the ensuing November. This meeting which was held in Thistle Street Chapel[2] was attended by representatives from all over the country. 'After prayer and careful deliberation, the plan of the Society was agreed upon, a committee was appointed for the first year, and an address to the churches drawn up. In the Society thus founded John Watson and George Payne were continued as joint Secretaries. The first Annual Meeting was appointed to be held in Edinburgh on 6 May 1813.' The avowed object of the Union at its inception was 'The relief of Congregational churches in Scotland, united in the faith and hope of the Gospel; who, from debt upon their places of worship, are unable to provide for the ministration of the word of God, in that way which would tend most to their own edification, and the eternal happiness of those around them.'[3] These last words are worthy of special notice, for they reveal the original aims of the Union to have been twofold—Church aid and home missions. The Union originated in the felt necessity of doing

---

[1] It is interesting to notice that before the end of the previous century Robert Haldane had considered the possibility of a union of the Tabernacle churches of Edinburgh, Glasgow, Dundee, and Caithness. He thought that 'if they conformed to the same strict and scriptural discipline they might be united, as far as Congregational principles admit' (*Address to the Public*, p. 82).

[2] Bernard's Rooms.   [3] *Memoir of Greville Ewing*, p. 392.

something for the assistance and support of the poorer churches, but along with that primary object the other went with it, viz. the spreading of the Gospel in the communities in which these churches were set. The Institution thus formed was essentially a Home Missionary Society. This will not appear strange if we remember that the Congregational Union of Scotland, like its College for the training of ministers, sprang in large measure from the influence, counsel and prayers of that great lover and servant of missions—Greville Ewing.

Several churches declined to join the Union on its formation. Some objected to it on the ground that it was incompatible with the independency of the churches, others objected to it because it had not based itself on a declaration of religious opinions, so that people might know what were the sentiments of those on whose behalf it was instituted. Fifty-five churches, however, originally constituted the Union in 1812, and the number was afterwards increased by the addition of others who had stood aloof for a time.

It is interesting to notice that on several occasions Ewing journeyed into England to seek support from the Congregationalists there for the home missionary work of the Union. In 1819 the associated Congregational ministers of the county of Essex sent a donation of £60. The churches of Suffolk and Norfolk similarly assisted the Congregational Union of Scotland, sending in 1820-21 a gift of £300 to its funds. In September 1824 Ewing was deputed by the Committee of the Union to solicit in London and its vicinity financial aid for the funds of that institution as well as for the Theological Academy. On his arrival at the capital he put into circulation a printed statement, in which the number of churches in the Union is now given as seventy-two. Of that number twelve pastors were able to speak the Gaelic language. In referring to extensive itinerancies, the Shetland Islands are named; in some parts of which there 'were persons who never heard a sermon, except on the annual visit of the minister sustained by the Union'.[1] In 1821 the College of Princeton, New Jersey, U.S.A. conferred on Greville Ewing the honorary degree of Doctor of Divinity, but he never used the title. He strongly disapproved of all 'religious titles' and the disapprobation was sacredly regarded by his family and friends. The effects of the institution of the Union speedily became manifest. Many pastors who had been compelled to resort

[1] *Memoir of Greville Ewing, passim.*

to secular work for support were enabled through the help furnished by the Union to give their undivided attention to pastoral and evangelical work, and not a few churches were saved from the extinction that threatened them. Indeed, it is not too much to say that the creation of the Congregational Union of Scotland in 1812 preserved the denomination from that decay which had been the fate of the early experiments in Congregationalism made by the Glasites, the Bereans, and the Old Scots Independents. In the course of a few years the number of churches connected with the Union reached about one hundred, and at a later period exceeded that number; but the number never much exceeded or fell below that figure in any one year of the history of the Union until 1896. The Union was and still is 'one of the chief ornaments and greatest bulwark of our churches'.[1]

IV

For many years the supporters of the Union closely adhered to the distinctive objects for which it was formed; to afford aid to churches and pastors in maintaining the ordinances of the Gospel and in carrying on evangelistic work in various parts of the country. The meetings of brethren from all parts of the country once a year to hear the reports became an occasion of pleasant brotherly intercourse and Christian fellowship. 'If no other benefit had accrued to the churches than the realisation of their fellowship promoted on these occasions, the spirit of sympathy and prayer excited and diffused through the multitudes of hearts and households for self-denying brethren and perishing souls, the formation of the Union would not have been in vain.'[2] To the brethren in remote parts of the kingdom the annual meetings of the Union became the outstanding event of the year, while it became an occasion of happy social intercourse between them and ministers and members of churches in the towns in which the meetings were held, and where they were heartily welcomed and hospitably entertained. No annual gathering was allowed to pass without one or more of the ministers from the country districts being invited to address the meetings, and to tell the story of his work in the district in which he laboured, and these addresses served to keep alive a feeling of personal interest in each of the good men and his

[1] W. L. Alexander, *Memoir of the Rev. John Watson*, p. 106.
[2] *Memoir of Greville Ewing*, p. 395.

work. Nor was a response wanting on the part of the pastors of town and city churches, for many of them—such as Greville Ewing and Ralph Wardlaw, and others—visited the various churches in the north and other parts of the kingdom, moved not only by their desire to renew the fellowship with men whom they had learned to respect and love for their work's sake, but to encourage them in it. Such an interchange of visits and intercourse had the happiest effect on the churches of the Union, and tended to knit them together in the best of Christian bonds—that of brotherly fellowship with each other and common service for Christ.

Notwithstanding the practical unanimity in regard to all the essential doctrines of the Christian faith which prevailed among the churches, and consequently the needlessness of any formal declaration of their faith and order, Presbyterians found it difficult to understand how a body of churches could be united except by their subscription to some doctrinal confession, by which the orthodoxy of those in the Union could be assured and heretics kept out or cast out.[1] They found it equally difficult to understand how a religious body could have its affairs managed without some such authority as resided in church-courts. Hence two charges were made against the churches of the Union, the one that their doctrine was of doubtful orthodoxy, and the other that the Union was virtually a church-court under another name. To the one charge the members of the Union were able to reply by appealing to the known teaching and religious faith common in all their pastors and churches, and which had never been seriously called in question. It might have been well had they dealt in the same way with the other charge—that of being Presbyterians in disguise. They could have appealed to the reports given of the functions and work of the Union at the annual meetings, and challenged anyone to show that in managing the affairs of the Union any attempt had ever been made to interfere with the absolute independence of the churches. But some brethren were rather sensitive to the insinuations of those Presbyterians who alleged that the Union was, after all, a church-court, and exercised authority over it members and the churches. Accordingly, in 1848 it was agreed, though not without strong opposition, that there should be inserted in the rules of the Union a statement to the effect that 'the Union shall

---

[1] This has not precluded the issue of 'Statements of Belief', such as the one published by the Union in 1949.

G

not be regarded as, in any sense, an ecclesiastical court or corporation, possessing or pretending to possess, authority over the
churches, all such authority being contrary to the first principles
of Congregational polity, but simply in the light of a Church Aid
and Home Mission Society'.

Another change in the constitution of the Union was made in
1857 by the insertion in it of the qualifying condition that the
Union consisted of 'churches of the Congregational order, *in
fellowship with each other*'. What led to this change appears to have
been the circumstance that two churches connected with the
Union had had a dispute, and had made it known that they were
no longer in fellowship with each other, though in what particular
ways this absence of fellowship was shown does not appear. The
question then arose as to whether one or both of them could still
be regarded as in connection with the Congregational Union. The
qualifying clause requiring churches to be in fellowship with each
other in order to have connection with the Union was explained
in a footnote to the effect that by this it was not meant that 'every
individual church must be in fellowship with every other individual
church, but only that, in order to have connection with the Union,
every church must be in fellowship with the other churches
generally in the district to which it belongs'. While this change in
the constitution really gave formal expression to the relations of
the churches of the Union to each other which had for a long time
been recognised, it indicated the large departure which had taken
place from the original constitution of the Union. In that nothing
more had been contemplated than the free co-operation of churches
in aiding each other, and in supporting home mission agencies.
Any fellowship or fraternity realised in this common work grew
out of their co-operation, and was regarded rather as a valuable
privilege associated with it than as a distinct aim in itself. Further,
the fact that most of the Congregational churches belonged to the
Congregational Union was regarded as a kind of denominational
distinction, marking them off from any churches of the Congregational order that had no connection with the Union, of which there
have always been some. These two facts—that the association of
the churches of the Union had come to be known and valued as
'a fellowship of the churches', and that connection with the Union
had come to be recognised as a kind of denominational distinction
—were formally recognised in the change made in the constitution
in 1857, by which it was announced that the Union was no longer

exclusively a church-aid and home mission society, but, as such, was also a fraternity of the churches, banded together for the purpose of mutual fellowship. One effect of the change was that, in addition to subscribing to the funds of the Union, which was the only condition of connection with it originally, churches joining the Union had to show that they were in fellowship with churches in their districts already belonging to the Union. Whether this change was a wise one has been doubted by many. It has been contended by those who have never viewed with favour this departure from the original character and aims of the Union, that it has had the effect of affording an inducement to Congregational churches to join the Union which have neither had much sympathy with the practical objects of the Union, nor have valued the fellowship of the churches enjoyed in carrying them out, but whose chief desire has been through connection with it to obtain a standing before the public which they might not otherwise have obtained.

In 1873 the idea of the Union being a fraternity of the churches was further given effect to by an addition to its objects, stating that it existed to 'cultivate fraternal Christian affection, fraternal intercourse, and cordial co-operation in all that relates to the interests of the associated churches'.

A still further change was made in 1878. Prior to that year there had been no formal constituency of the Union. The annual meetings at which all business was transacted were composed of pastors and members of the churches, and any resolutions proposed were carried by acclamation, as at the meetings of missionary or other benevolent societies. As there had seldom or never been any pronounced division of opinion shown at such meetings the need for defining the qualifications of those entitled to vote had not been felt until 1867. At the annual meeting of that year, however, a serious division of opinion was shown in connection with what was known as the 'Cranbrook Case'. The pastor of Albany Street Church, Edinburgh, had been invited to give an address at one of the forthcoming meetings of the Union in Edinburgh. In the interval between the invitation to him and the holding of the meetings, however, that gentleman had startled the community, and the Congregational churches in particular, by his public advocacy of views on prayer and other subjects that were denounced by many Congregationalists and others. In view of this feeling the committee of the Union felt bound to withdraw the invitation to Mr. Cranbrook to address any of the Union meetings, a step which was resented by him and by his congregation. At the annual meeting a motion was proposed expressing regret at the action of the committee, which was carried by a large majority of those present, most of whom were persons in connection with Albany Street Church. In the belief that the vote of this meeting did not express the minds of the members of the churches connected with the Union an adjourned meeting held next day virtually reversed the vote of the previous day by passing a vote of renewed confidence in the committee. Apart altogether from the case in connection with which this regrettable division of opinion was shown, there was a general conviction that the proceeding disclosed a defect in the constitution of the Union by the absence of any definition of the qualifications of those entitled to vote at the annual meetings. Membership of the Union had been loosely described as that of churches or members of churches in fellowship with each other agreeing to promote its objects and contributing to its funds; but inasmuch as the business was transacted by individuals present, there was no provision for ascertaining whether they attended and voted as representing themselves or the churches to which they belonged, and as in either case it was not possible at the time to ascertain whether they had been contributors or not, any vote taken at the annual meeting had but little value or significance as expressing the minds of the supporters of the Union generally. It was not until 1887, however, that any attempt was made to secure a voting constituency of the Union. In that year, after strong opposition by brethren who wished no change to be made, an addition was made to the constitution providing that the annual meeting should consist of (1) the pastor of each contributing church, (2) of one other representative where the membership of the church was under 200, (3) of a third where the membership was over 200, and (4) of an additional representative, irrespective of the number of its members, of a church sending not less than £40 a year to the funds of the Union.

The last change of any importance was made in 1883, when a further defect in the constitution was supplied by directions being given as to the procedure to be followed in order to obtain the admission of churches to the Union, and their separation from it.

Many other minor changes were made in the constitution from time to time, chiefly in connection with the improved arrangements regarded as desirable for the greater facility in transacting the business of the Union; but the changes of radical importance have been those already noted.

It may be well to note that all the changes in the constitution and modes of procedure in connection with the Union were made to meet the unforeseen difficulties of earlier years, and to remove some hindrances to the greater efficiency of the Union in the management of its affairs that had been found in actual experience.[1]

[1] See Chapter XVI, for changes made in the twentieth century.

PART FOUR

THE REVOLT FROM CALVINISM

CHAPTER X

THE REVOLT FROM CALVINISM WITHIN CONGREGATIONALISM

I

A WIDESPREAD intellectual and spiritual awakening took place about 1830. The tidal wave had appeared, as we have noticed elsewhere in this book, first in France, where it produced the Revolution. It rolled on to England and manifested itself mainly there in notable social and political changes—the Reform Bill, for example, which was carried in 1832. Chartist agitation was another result which appeared in all the large centres of population in Britain, and did not leave the churches unaffected.[1] This wave of the Spirit also affected the most conservative of the English universities: the year 1832 marked the rise of the Tractarian Movement which carried many Anglican churchmen in the direction of Rome. This spiritual springtide also influenced our national literature so that, among other things, a new school of poetry appeared.[2]

This strong and lofty wave broke upon the shores of Scottish life too, but with different effects. Although Scotland felt the swell of the tide, like the other nations of Europe, as a quickening of democratic conscience, an urge towards social and political reform, it found its most characteristic and most enduring expression in connection with the life of the Church. The Voluntary Controversy broke out about this time and raged with a violence which of itself was an indication of the electrically charged atmosphere of the age.

The demand put forward on behalf of the people for the removal of their civil disabilities had a very real connection with the rise of the Non-intrusion movement within the National Church. It began to be seen and felt that when the political enfranchisement of heads of households had been conceded, it would not do to keep the same parties in a state of servility in the Church. In 1834 the

---

[1] L. C. Wright, *Scottish Chartism, passim* ; P. Brewster, *The Seven Chartist and Military Discourses*, Paisley, 1843.

[2] J. R. Fleming, *The Church in Scotland, 1843-1874*, to which book I am indebted for the substance of this chapter.

General Assembly passed the Veto Act beginning the Ten Years' Conflict, which ended on 18 May 1843 in that blessed tragedy of the Disruption.

James Ross has gone to great pains to demonstrate how this crisis in Scottish religion is linked with the spiritual witness of the Congregational churches. Speaking at a meeting in Aberdeen a few weeks before the Disruption, Principal Dewar of Aberdeen University, said that 'the future historians of the Church will have to say that the Congregationalists have done much to bring about the present crisis in the Church of Scotland'.[1] As a result the Congregational churches were numerically impoverished. For many years prior to the Disruption their places of worship had been attended by members of the Established Church, who desired a more evangelical kind of preaching than they found in that body. Now their needs were satisfied in the Free Church.[2] The consequent exodus of hearers from the Congregational churches increased the economic difficulties of some of them. Besides they became more isolated from people of other denominations than they had been previously.

The decade immediately prior to the Disruption was the period of the great evangelists Burns and McCheyne; of the Kilsyth revival, of a movement of God's Spirit throughout the length of Scotland which compelled the courts of the Church to investigate (without resulting esteem) the whole matter of religious revivalism. There were a larger number of apparent conversions, we are told, in this period than during the previous half century. It is significant that the newly-formed Free Church had amongst its original ministers such evangelical names as Burns, the two Bonars, Milne, MacDonald, and Mackintosh, the Apostle of the north.

In 1839 there was a remarkable revival of religion among many of the Congregational churches in Scotland, the spirit of which continued for some years. 'Protracted meetings' as they were then called, were held in churches in Edinburgh, Glasgow, Dundee, Paisley, Dumfries, Kilsyth, Hawick, Alexandria, Anstruther, and other places. Many conversions were reported, new churches were planted in places where none had existed before, and the membership of all the churches in places where the meetings had been held was largely increased. There had been no such extensive

---

[1] *A History of Congregational Independency in Scotland*, pp. 121 ff.
[2] Some of these were actually built on the sites of Congregational Sunday schools. See H. Escott, *Beacons of Independency*.

spiritual movement since the beginning of the century, and the gratifying results of the earnest preaching of the Gospel which was carried on recalled the best days of the Haldanes and those who had been their fellow-labourers over forty years before.

II

In this same period there were feelings after a sunnier and less austere type of theology. Perhaps its most popular, because less doctrinaire exponent, was the Congregationalist George Macdonald who in song, story, and 'unspoken sermon' became the 'spokesman of the slow, dumb soul of Scotland, seeking for Infinite Love'. Long before his day, however, Robert Burns had pilloried the inhumanity and hypocrisy of the Calvinist churchmanship of his time. In the realm of pure theology the period under review saw the work of Campbell of Row and Erskine of Linlathen, each in his own way concerned to lead a revolt from rigid Calvinism.

It would indeed have been strange too if the growing democratic spirit in secular life had not influenced in some sort the austere tyrannical features of Scottish theology. Man's increasing concern for the welfare of his brother man would appear in Scotland to have contributed something to the humanising of religion. God's face when visioned was no longer a forbidding shadow, but compassionate and humane, like the face of the Man Jesus.

But this humanising of Scottish theology when it eventually came about did not arise directly from any of the tendencies we have mentioned, though it must have owed something to them all. It arose rather in the awakened minds and hearts of two ministers of dissenting religious bodies: John Kirk, pastor of the Congregational Church at Hamilton, and James Morison, minister of the United Secession congregation in Kilmarnock. Contemporaneously these two men were faced with a similar theological problem.

In 1842 Kirk published a series of addresses entitled *The Way of Life made Plain,* in which he set forth views regarding the work of the Holy Spirit in connection with the conversion of the sinner, which he had been preaching for some time prior to this. He held that 'not only did Jesus die for every man, but that God's Spirit strives with every man, and that they who yield are the saved, and that they who resist are the unsaved'. He thus held that the influence of the Spirit was as universal as the atonement of Christ. This was a view that had been strenuously opposed by Wardlaw and those who with him had been led to accept the position of moderate Calvinists. In his *Extent of the Atonement*, Wardlaw taught that the atonement had universal sufficiency but was limited in its efficacy by the purpose of God in election—a purpose carried out in the bestowment on the elect of the special influence of the Holy Spirit, in virtue of which they are led to accept the Divine offer of salvation. So strongly was this view held by the Congregationalists in general that it was adduced in proof of their continued adherence to the main doctrines of the *Westminster Confession* concerning Divine sovereignty, election, etc., in regard to which they were at one with the Presbyterians. And so the promulgation of Kirk's views concerning the universality of the Spirit's work called forth much opposition on the part of Congregationalists, and many pamphlets and tracts were written at the time in condemnation of the doctrines taught by him and others. The situation was one which was very perplexing to Congregationalists. Not bound by subscription to any doctrinal creed, and not having any ecclesiastical organisation or machinery enabling them to prosecute for what many of them might regard as heresy, each church was free and independent of the others in regard to the religious doctrine it might hold or teach. There was only one course of action open to them in dealing with serious differences of belief on important doctrines, and this became possible owing to the fraternal relations in which they stood to one another. Although not connected with each other by their professed or formal adherence to any doctrinal creed, there had been a general consensus of belief in regard to the leading doctrines of the Christian faith, and this general agreement made it possible for them to co-operate in promoting and supporting the work of the Congregational Union and the Theological Academy. Out of this common co-operation there grew a feeling of Christian 'fellowship' between the churches which led them to regard themselves, if not a denomination in the Presbyterian sense, at least what they called a 'connection', or a congeries of churches holding certain beliefs and promoting certain practical objects in common. Had Kirk's teachings been regarded as involving differences of opinion only on matters of minor importance, or had the churches been prepared to regard them as a matter for Christian forbearance, their fellowship and co-operation would not have been seriously affected. But, as the discussion on both sides proceeded, it became evident that there was a divergence of belief which was regarded by both parties as so seriously affecting the work, conceived as of primary importance by all of them—that of the preaching of the Gospel—that active fellowship and co-operation had become impracticable; at least, this was the view of some at the time, especially of those who opposed the new teaching.

The first step taken which had the effect of disclosing the rupture that had taken place between the two parties was the action of the committee of the Glasgow Theological Academy. Having learned that some of the students attending the Academy were suspected of adopting, or at least of being inclined to adopt, the views of Kirk on the work of the Holy Spirit, the tutors of the Academy prescribed sermon-exercises to the students bearing on the doctrines in dispute. Several of them having given discourses showing that they were favourable to the new doctrine the committee felt bound to deal further with them by requesting each of them to give answers to three questions which were prescribed. The first was put with the view to ascertaining whether any change had taken place in their views on the subject of 'divine influence' since they entered the Academy. The second was as follows: 'Do you hold, or do you not, the necessity of a special influence of the Holy Spirit, in order to the regeneration of the sinner, or his conversion to God, distinct from the influence of the Word or of Providential circumstances, but accompanying these means, and rendering them efficacious?' The third question was put with the view of ascertaining whether the views of the students on the subject of the second query were 'settled', or whether they were in a state of indecision and desirous of time for further consideration of the subject. The answers were varied in their tone and expression, but the result of consideration of them by the committee was that they adopted several resolutions, one of which was that the names of nine of the students should be erased from the roll of the Academy, but that some of them having expressed a desire for more time to consider the doctrines in question, a sub-committee was appointed 'to converse with such of them as desired it for maturing and settling their views', it being understood that they would be re-eligible when they came to 'the profession of sentiments in accordance with the understood principles of the Congregational body'. In vindication of their action one of the resolutions adopted by the committee, and read to the students, was to the effect that the doctrines of personal election to eternal life, and of the necessity of a special influence of the Holy Spirit in the conversion of sinners, as following up and effecting the sovereign purpose of electing grace, having been among the 'things most surely believed' by the members of the Congregational body, it would have been an evident dereliction of their trust for the committee to have received into the Academy or to have retained in it as students any brethren holding views at variance with those mentioned.

About a month after the above action by the committee of the Theological Academy—in May 1844—seven of the nine students whose connection with the Academy had been severed applied to the committee of the Congregational Union to be employed as preachers in connection with the Union, but that committee declined to entertain the application 'until they had satisfied the Academy committee'. In vindication of this action it was subsequently stated that 'the Congregational Union committee, accustomed to act in harmony and co-operation with the committee of the Academy, discern in this decision no violation of their commission; but, having the same conviction with that committee of the views which have been, until now, held by the Congregational churches see no reason why they should run in the face of their determination, and wantonly thwart their brethren in the discharge of a painful and difficult duty'. The action of the Union Committee is worthy of note, because, with the exception of a resolution proposed by Lindsay Alexander a year later at one of the meetings of the Union, it was the only part taken by the Union or its committee in connection with the controversy which took place on the 'new views'. Dr. Alexander's proposed resolution, which was adopted by the Annual Meeting of the Union in 1845, while no doubt intended to reaffirm the adherence of the churches of the Union to the views of the Spirit's work usually held by moderate Calvinists, was so expressed that many, if not all, of those holding the new teaching could have supported it, for there was a careful avoidance of any expression of the distinctive difference between the old and the new doctrines.

The supporters of the Union evidently thought it well not to interfere in connection with differences of doctrinal opinion among them, but that the churches feeling themselves affected by such differences should take such action as they thought proper. In only two instances was this done—in the case of the four Congregational churches then existing in Glasgow and the Congregational churches in Aberdeen. The former sent a letter to each of the churches in Hamilton, Bellshill, Bridgeton (Glasgow), Cambuslang, and Ardrossan, in which they asked for a statement of their views on the work of the Holy Spirit in conversion and on the doctrine of election, with the view of enabling them to decide whether or not they could continue to hold fellowship with them as sister Congregational churches. In this letter two questions were put, viz. 'Do you hold that the influence which the Holy Spirit exerts in the conversion of sinners is a *general*, and in no case a *special*, influence?—meaning by general that the Spirit's influence is put forth upon all alike who hear the Gospel, and that no more or other divine influence is exerted on those who believe the Gospel than on those who reject it. Have you ceased to hold the doctrine of personal and unconditional election?—meaning by that the sovereign and gracious choice of individuals to eternal life by God.' Replies to these queries, with rejoinders from the four churches, were given at great length. The unhappy result of the controversy was that the 'Four Churches in Glasgow' felt compelled to withdraw from fellowship with the churches with which they had corresponded. A pamphlet was subsequently published, extending to 190 pages, giving 'The Entire Correspondence between the Four Congregational Churches in Glasgow and the Congregational Churches in Hamilton, Bellshill, Bridgeton, Cambuslang, and Ardrossan on the Doctrines of Election and the Influence of the Holy Spirit in Conversion'.

A similar correspondence took place between the Congregational churches in Aberdeen and the Congregational churches in Blackhills (now Westhill) and Printfield (now Woodside) with the same result—that the former churches declared themselves out of fellowship with the latter.

The reasons given for the publication of the correspondence were (1) that the Congregational churches throughout Scotland might know the whole grounds on which the four churches in Glasgow declined to hold further fellowship with the churches in their neighbourhood, and that thereby the other churches might have a full supply of evidence on which to judge and to act with regard to the five churches; (2) that the correspondence might show to churches of other denominations that the Congregational churches held 'correct sentiments relative to fundamental truths', and that their principles of church-polity were quite competent to maintain in their communion purity of doctrine; and (3) that by publishing the letters the 'errors' which had been extensively spread by the pastors and churches holding them might be more efficiently met and exposed than perhaps by any other means.

Apart from the doctrinal points and the differences exhibited in this controversy, the discussion of which would be beside the purposes of this history, there are some considerations of a practical nature that may here be noted.

1. The controversial correspondence was throughout conducted in a fine Christian spirit and with great courtesy on both sides, which left no cause for embittered feeling, but enabled brethren to part company with mutual respect, while each party firmly adhered to its own position.

2. The moving causes of the difference of views between the two parties were such as were directly connected with the earnest *practical* work in which preachers on both sides were engaged. The discussion that took place was by no means of an exclusively theoretical or academic nature, but involved issues bearing on the question of the proper presentation of the Gospel of Christ to men. On the one hand, the supporters of the 'new views' felt bound to give special prominence in their teaching to the doctrine that, through the provisions made by the death of Christ for all men and the equally universal influence of the Spirit on the minds and hearts of those who heard the Gospel, every obstacle to the conversion and salvation of the sinner had been removed save his own unbelief. On the other hand, the supporters of the Calvinistic view gave prominence to the doctrine of the absolute sovereignty of God in His purpose to bestow upon individual men the Holy Spirit, whose inner operations on their minds and hearts effectually led them to believe in Christ, and thus to be saved. The one party appeared to be anxious to insist on the responsibility of men for their belief or unbelief, while the other sought to exalt the sovereign power of God at every step in the conversion and salvation of men. Neither view was so presented by the more intelligent and able of the disputants as to exclude the other, though at times words were used that gave occasion for the impression that the one party virtually denied the work of the Holy Spirit and that the other virtually set aside the freeness of the Gospel offer of salvation and the responsibility of those who failed to accept it. In both instances this arose from a misunderstanding, for both parties affirmed the necessity of the Divine influence of the Holy Spirit in order to conversion, the sovereign grace of God in bestowing the gift of

the Spirit, and the responsibility of men for rejection of the offer of salvation. Whatever judgment may be passed on the whole controversy, it is but fair to the memory of the brethren who engaged in it to keep in mind that they did so in the sincere belief that they were bound to defend what they believed to be aspects of Divine truth which had a vital bearing on their work as preachers of the Gospel.

3. The question arises, was the difference of view between the one party and the other such as necessarily led to the rupture of fellowship between them? This question may be said to have divided the churches and ministers of the time in their opinions even more than the points in dispute. Evidently the four churches in Glasgow took their action, both in withdrawing from fellowship with neighbouring churches and in publishing their 'Correspondence' in the expectation that other Congregational churches would take a similar course. Only in the case of the Aberdeen churches was this done. The protest made by several of the respondent churches against the view that any difference of opinion on the questions in dispute should be made a ground of separation from fellowship, seeing that hitherto the chief thing sought in the case of applicants for membership was that 'they had peace with God through our Lord Jesus Christ', was one the force of which was felt by many who did not sympathise with the 'new views' party. This was notably the case with Dr. Alexander, whose 'Counsels' to his church (afterwards published) on the proper attitude of the churches in regard to the whole dispute had much influence in determining the decision of other churches to take no action in the matter. His view may be stated in his own words: 'Whether I am right or wrong in thinking that the views of the churches which have been separated from their sister churches in the west tend to Arminianism, is to me a small matter. What I conceive of moment is the fact that these churches avow their belief in the sovereign agency of the Spirit in conversion and sanctification; and where this avowal is made I, for one, must deprecate the principle that the holding along with this of views which by a clear-thinking and keen logician may be shown to be not perfectly harmonious with it is to be made an occasion for one church's dissolving fellowship with another. Oh, when will controversialists learn that a man is responsible morally only for the opinions he *knowingly* holds, not for every conclusion which a more acute man than he may *deduce* or *extort* from his opinions? When will

H

churches remember that excommunication for *opinions* merely was unknown in Christ's church until introduced by the "man of sin"?' That this view of the situation was adopted by the churches, with one or two exceptions, was an indication that in separating themselves from neighbouring churches on the ground of difference of opinion on the doctrinal questions in dispute the churches in Glasgow and Aberdeen stood alone. The other churches of the connection tacitly agreed to let any difference on the points in dispute be a matter of Christian forbearance.

4. Two of the reasons given for the publication of the *Entire Correspondence*, were evidently also reasons for the action taken by the four Glasgow churches in severing their connection with neighbouring churches. One was that 'other Christian denominations' might be reassured of the 'orthodoxy' of Congregationalists, and the other was that Congregational principles of church-polity were 'quite competent to maintain purity of doctrine'. It is perhaps not too much to say that both these expectations failed to be realised, so far as the action of the Glasgow churches was concerned. Instead of securing a doctrinal declaration on the points in dispute by the Congregational churches in Scotland the Glasgow and Aberdeen churches found themselves alone, and the very smallness of their number had a result the very reverse of what was expected, by tending to cast doubt upon the so-called 'orthodoxy' of those who did not adhere to them in their action. One practical lesson may be learned from this, and that is, that to ground any action of our churches by regard to what persons of *other* denominations may think of us, or to be over-sensitive to their views of the teaching given in our pulpits, indicates not only great moral weakness, but also lack of confidence in our own beliefs. The reputation of any religious body is in its own keeping, and in the faithfulness with which it adheres to the truths its members profess to believe. The expectation that Congregational polity would be shown to be 'competent to maintain purity of doctrine' was also falsified by the event, if by 'purity of doctrine' be meant the particular views of the Glasgow churches in regard to the work of the Spirit, for the action of these churches only exposed the weakness of Congregational polity when the attempt is made to apply it to cases of doctrinal difference. It has neither the doctrinal 'standards' nor the ecclesiastical machinery requisite for such an application. The fact that the result of the action of the four churches was to sever their fellowship with a few neigh-

bouring churches and to leave the other churches in passive inaction regarding the matter only served to show that, while Congregational polity is quite competent to regulate the relations to each other of Christian men united in their common faith in Christ as their Saviour, it is a clumsy and inefficient instrument in dealing with differences of opinion and belief which do not affect the vital faith of Christian men and women, on which alone their real fellowship must be grounded.

One happy result of the controversies of the time with which we are dealing was that they served to clear the air, and became an education and a warning to the churches in regard to their proper relations to each other. The 'new views' controversy died away in course of time, partly by ministers and churches finding the unprofitableness of such discussions as had disturbed their peace, and partly owing to the increased favour with which the opinions of the 'new views' party came to be held. There was no formal indication of a departure from the Calvinistic position held in former days; but in the pulpits of the churches and among the members it became increasingly evident that the old differences which had never been very pronounced except among the ministers, had ceased to exist, and that, both in regard to the universal atonement of Christ and the work of the Spirit in conversion, the formerly divided parties had become practically one. The truth of this will concern us in a later chapter.

CHAPTER XI

THE EVOLUTION OF THE EVANGELICAL UNION

I

ALTHOUGH John Kirk has not received at the hands of church historians the recognition he deserves as a pioneer of the movement away from Calvinism, the supreme place in that movement belongs to James Morison, who by his Universal Atonement theology gradually leavened the theology of nearly all the churches in Scotland in the nineteenth century with sweetness and light. Morison does not seem to have owed anything important to McLeod Campbell and Erskine of Linlathen. He was rather a spiritual child of McCheyne and the 1839-40 revival. Fergus Ferguson in his *IIistory of the Evangelical Union* connects the immediate awakening of a new life in the mind of young Morison with the perusal of Finney's *Lectures on Revivals*.[1]

The son of a United Secession minister, Morison was licensed to preach in the spring of 1839. In his first efforts he made little or no impression on his hearers. But a remarkable change came over the character of his ministry while he was in charge of a small rural parish in the Cabrach on the borders of Banffshire. Morison is described as setting out for his northern charge with Finney's book in his pocket for reading on the journey and as having at the time a deepening conviction that there was something amiss in his style of preaching. What befell him was later described by himself in his defence before his Presbytery. 'For many years', he said, 'he had laboured under total darkness as to the way of salvation. By patient research and study he had at last found a truth in the Bible, which had the effect of introducing him all at once into a new world. It changed all his views, all his feelings, all his desires, all his conduct. This gracious and glorious truth which he had discovered in the Bible was nothing else than the love of God to him in particular in giving His own dear Son to die for him. This Bible truth he saw clearly stated in many portions of Scripture; and having seen it, he burned with intense desire to make it known to others, that they also might receive the same unspeakable

[1] F. Ferguson, *A History of the Evangelical Union*, p. 7.

peace and joy which it had imparted to his own soul. Animated by this desire he began to preach it everywhere; and he had no sooner begun to preach it than he saw sinners finding peace in believing it, and deriving from it a motive to live entirely to God.'[1]

Morison did not become immediately a fully-fledged Arminian. His theology grew under the discipline of study and experience. The first idea he got hold of was that Christ died in the same sense for all men; and this he preached as his gospel, asserting that all who believe that Christ has died for them will certainly be saved. For a number of years after this he adhered to a doctrine of election which he called one of the most delightful doctrines of Scripture—albeit the view he took of it was apparently not very high. According to his teaching till 1843, 'election in the order of nature comes after the atonement. . . . God foresaw that none of the whole human family would be willing to be saved (through the atonement), and then he elected.'[2]

This doctrine, however, necessitated his continual acceptance of the Calvinist idea of 'effectual calling' by the Holy Spirit, and by-and-by Morison moved still further from the *Westminster Confession*, and taught that election is not a matter of eternity but of time; not an absolute decree, but a selecting process; not an election *to* faith, but an election *through* faith.

These views naturally led to a new estimate of human ability. Original sin was not denied, nor was it asserted that any man has the power, apart from grace, to save himself. But under the economy of the gospel, circumstances have so changed, that salvation is literally within the reach of all who choose to use the ability they now possess. 'When the atonement has been made, and the Holy Spirit has not only embodied the record of it in the inspired gospel, but is himself present to persuade and guide the sinner to the faith of it, the sinner is able to surrender himself to this divine influence and believe and be saved.'[3] Thus he approached the position held by John Kirk outlined in the previous chapter.

II

In the summer of 1840 James Morison received and accepted a cordial invitation to the pastorate of Clerk's Lane Secession

---

[1] F. Ferguson, *A History of the Evangelical Union*, p. 70.

[2] Morison's position at this time was close to the moderate Calvinist's in the Scottish Congregational Churches, led by Ralph Wardlaw.

[3] *Doctrinal Declaration*, Glasgow, 1858.

Church, Kilmarnock. The induction service on the first Sunday of October was marred by an unhappy incident which foretold troubles to come. When ready to enter the church the young minister was severely questioned by members of the Presbytery as to the nature of his faith, in the light of his utterances, and particularly of the small tract entitled, *The Question 'What must I do to be saved?' answered*, recently published by him. As a result the service was long delayed, and before the laying-on of hands promise had to be extracted from the ordinand that he would suppress the pamphlet and be in future careful in public speech. In fact the feeling in the Presbytery was so antagonistic that only one of the ministers remained to the ceremonial dinner which followed the ordination.[1]

On subsequent reflection, Morison felt that he could not be bound by his word to the Presbytery, whereas he did not himself reissue the tract in question, he did not prevent others from reprinting and distributing it. Moreover, he commenced his ministry with a strong and confident proclamation of universal salvation. The vigour of his proclamation and the daring of the young preacher crowded Clerk's Lane Church to the doors on every following Sunday. The Monday Prayer Meeting also soon attracted followers from near and far, and as many as a thousand week by week filled the church. The sermons on the Sunday and Monday were almost invariably expository, the preacher often taking his volumes of reference into the pulpit with him.

These sermons provoked considerable and often acrimonious comment in the neighbourhood. Printers in Kilmarnock and district were kept busy setting up pamphlets in which Morison's pulpit utterances were bitterly attacked. Sad to relate some of the members of his own church, who had favoured a rival candidate at the time of his election, were not slow to seize the opportunity of a heresy-hunt.

There was rarely a Presbytery meeting in Kilmarnock (and the meetings were held in Clerk's Lane vestry) at which Morison was not interrogated as to what he had been saying from his pulpit. There was, moreover, strong feeling that the offending tract had not been suppressed as promised. These criticisms were met with boldness, as they were made from the pulpit, in the vestry, and by means of pamphlets which had a wide circulation.

[1] This section is largely a transcript of three articles by R. F. G. Calder which appeared in *The Scottish Congregationalist* in 1943.

At length the dissatisfaction of the Presbytery grew so great that a committee was appointed to confer in private with Morison concerning his alleged errors in doctrine. The committee met him twice, early in 1841, at Irvine. What was said we do not know, for no notes were published; but there was no settlement. A libel thereupon was published against him, to be heard at a special Presbytery meeting convened for the second day of March 1841.

The trial of James Morison before the Presbytery of Kilmarnock in Clerk's Lane Church, aroused considerable and wide interest. The building was crowded to capacity by an audience whose sympathies were, naturally enough, mostly with the young minister. First of all a letter was read from the congregation affirming their intention to adhere to Morison 'notwithstanding any procedure that might be adopted towards him by the Presbytery'. This was followed by a memorial from forty-one members who professed to be dissatisfied with their minister's doctrine. The charge was then read, based on the report of the Irvine meetings. Seemingly its details were now made known to the accused for the first time. There were eight counts of errors taught and still maintained, and three of disingenuous conduct. In brief, though care was taken to avoid an accusation in these terms, it was objected that James Morison preached Universal Atonement contrary to the Westminster Confession.

It is difficult today to read the lengthy speeches (the defence, for example, lasted fully four hours) with patience. There is an extraordinary amount of sheer quibbling, of appeal to authorities and of concern for theological minutiae aside of the main issues. One detects too, more desire to score points than to make plain the truth, and often on the part of Morison's accusers a spirit akin to that of bear-baiting. But the outcome was that after a prolonged and animated discussion, lasting till close on midnight, a motion was carried 'that the Presbytery shall admonish Mr. Morison and suspend him from the exercise of his ministry and the fellowship of the church; aye, and until he retract his errors and express his sorrow for the offence given to the brethren in the church by the propagation of these errors'. Against this decision Morison appealed to the Synod, tabling his shilling according to custom.

For the three months until the Synod met there was stay of execution and sentence. They were very busy months for the minister of Clerk's Lane. The publicity of the trial brought him literally hundreds of 'anxious inquirers', whom he interviewed individually, leaving himself scant time for any other activity. Of these nearly two hundred joined the church at the quarterly Communion. In that period he also married. And the week before the Synod meeting he published another pamphlet entitled *The Extent of the Atonement*, a booklet of over one hundred pages of no little learning and skill.

The Synod—the highest court in the United Secession Church, which never had a General Assembly—met in early June 1841, in Gordon Street Chapel, Glasgow. The trial of James Morison was the main business, and itself lasted nearly a whole week. All the leading ministers of the Secession Church took part in the discussion. One or two gave evidence that they understood and shared to a degree the defendant's views, but the majority, for reasons theological and ecclesiastical, were strongly opposed. The speech in defence lasted over six hours. It became increasingly evident that the future of the denomination was at stake, and interest and excitement mounted.

An attempt was made by means of a committee to get Morison to change his views, but he declined to be so treated. The Synod, therefore, finally declared 'that he was no longer connected with the United Secession Church', and 'that all ministers and preachers in this Church must consider themselves prohibited from preaching for Mr. Morison, or employing him in any of their public ministrations'.[1] Only one vote was recorded against this decision of the Synod—that of Robert Morison, father of the accused. John Guthrie, afterwards a leading figure in the Evangelical Union, also protested, but failed to have his protest recorded.

A day or two before the final excommunication, when he was under sentence of suspension, Morison deliberately disregarded the will of the Synod by returning to Kilmarnock to receive the host of new members gathered in the last quarter. It was this action which made excommunication inevitable; but, in reality of course, it was his criticism of the commonly accepted Calvinism which put him outside his mother Church. As we shall see, he was in a short time to pass on theologically to a complete repudiation of all distinctively Calvinistic doctrine, but at the time of the trial before the Synod he was a Moderate Calvinist, as were most of the Congregationalists of his day.

---

[1] For a full and detailed account of the trials of James Morison before the Presbytery and Synod, see *History of the Evangelical Union*, by Fergus Ferguson, and *The Life of Principal Morison*, by William Adamson.

At the end of June that same year the Synod's Moderator came to Kilmarnock to preach Clerk's Lane Church vacant. A great crowd prevented him from entering the church. The congregation thus gave convincing proof that it was in full agreement with its minister's position, and in complete loyalty to him.

From the summer of 1841 James Morison and his congregation constituted an Independent church.[1] There can nave been at this time no thought whatever of the formation of a new denomination. Indeed, the young minister felt keenly his separation from his brethren. However, it soon became clear that he was not to stand alone in his protest against a narrow interpretation of the Gospel. From all parts came messages which showed that his case had been followed with sympathy and his works read with approval. But perhaps more significant for the future was the fact that in the next two years three other ministers made public that they too could not hold to the strict Calvinism of the Church to which they belonged.

Robert Morison, father of James, and minister in Bathgate, strongly influenced by his son, wrote a pamphlet on Limited Atonement which drew the attention of his superiors. And when he wrote in no uncertain terms a reply to the Synod's Statement of Principles, formulated to make plain its position after the trial and excitement of 1841, it was no longer possible that he could be ignored. At the Synod of 1842, which met in Edinburgh, Robert Morison was declared no longer a minister of the United Secession Church.

Next year he was followed by two other ministers—A. C. Rutherford of Falkirk, who later returned to the then United Presbyterian Church, and John Guthrie of Kendal, who became 'the Melanchthon of the Evangelical Union'. The churches of the four pastors so far adhered to them, and to them they continued to minister with renewed spiritual power.

III

The controversies through which the four pastors passed led them to take an important step theologically. They found by the arguments brought against them and by systematic study of the Scriptures, that the ground they occupied during their trials before the Synod was not, on the whole, so secure and scriptural

---

[1] See *A Chronicle of the Churches*, below.

as they imagined it was. This was decidedly true of Morison himself and ultimately he was forced to abandon the last distinctive Calvinistic doctrine to which he clung. From Moderate Calvinism he and the others named advanced to the doctrines of universal atonement, universal and resistable grace of the Holy Spirit, conditional election, and limited foreordination. By the proclamation of these doctrines from the pulpit and by the press an extensive interest was excited, more particularly in the west of Scotland. The 'new views' were welcomed by large numbers, who left the churches where the doctrines of the *Confession* were preached, and were formed into groups for the study of the Bible and the preaching of the Gospel. In order that the movement might not run to seed, and might be made permanently useful, some organisation was seen to be necessary.

After much consultation and prayer it was determined to hold a meeting of the expelled pastors and representatives of their churches to consider how best to consolidate the movement. The meeting was held in the vestry of Clerk's Lane Church, Kilmarnock, on the 16th day of May 1843, and was attended by thirteen persons—four ministers, one evangelist and eight elders—representing three churches and two preaching stations. Robert Morison, being senior minister, was called to preside, and John Guthrie acted as clerk. The meeting having been formally constituted, James Morison introduced the business by submitting for the consideration of the brethren a statement of the basis and objects of the proposed association. The statement was examined with the greatest care sentence by sentence, paragraph by paragraph, and as a whole. Finally it was unanimously adopted and agreed to be issued as a manifesto. Its introductory paragraphs run thus:

'We, the undersigned Christian Brethren, representatives of Christian Churches, and others, having met together at Kilmarnock, May 16, 17, and 18, 1843, for the purpose of praying and conferring together about the best means of being useful in the service of our dear Redeemer, have agreed to form ourselves into an association under the designation of "Evangelical Union".

'The objects of our Union are mutual countenance, counsel, and co-operation in supporting and spreading the glorious, simple, soul-saving and heart-sanctifying gospel of the grace of God.

'The nature of our Union is strictly voluntary.

'The members of our Union comprise all brethren who choose to be associated with us, who have "peace with God", and give decided evidence of being "new creatures in Christ Jesus", and who can concur with us in the following great principles, which great principles constitute the basis of our Union.'

Then follows a statement of the doctrines or principles which were to constitute the basis of the Union. These are summed up in the following:

'We hold that the Bible is the Book of God, and that, amongst other important truths, it reveals to us,

'1st, God's character as our Sovereign Governor.

'2nd, Our duty as the subjects of His government.

'3rd, Our state and character as rebels against the authority of His government. And,

'4th, The way of salvation by which we and all our fellow-rebels may be delivered from the penal and demoralising consequences of our rebellion.'

These general principles are explained at some length and the doctrines affirmed of the universality of the atonement, the universality and moral nature of the influences of the Holy Ghost, and the simplicity of faith, which by means of its object, brings peace to the conscience and purity to the heart. Brief paragraphs follow as to the nature and government of a church. From these it is clear that they had departed from the Presbyterial idea of a church and government. This did not prove itself to be favourable to liberty of conscience and brotherly love in their experience, and would have its effect on their views as to what a church should be and how it should be governed. It was therefore declared:

'That in reference to the edification and usefulness of the believer, we hold it to be his duty to associate with other believers in the same locality, for the purpose of securing to one another mutual counsel, exhortation, warning, and edification (Heb. iii. 13).

'Believers thus associated constitute a church (Gal. i. 2).

'Every church thus constituted we conceive to be complete within itself—a separate church of Christ, over which no adjoining church or churches have any other liberty of control than that of Christian counsel and warning.

'Every such church is bound to admit none to its fellowship but such as enjoy "peace with God", and give evidence of being "new creatures in Christ Jesus".'

Prefixed to the whole is a Note which manifests the position occupied by those who put it forth. The Note says:

'We wish it to be distinctly understood that the following statement of great principles is not to any degree, or in any sense, to be regarded as a permanent or present Standard Book in the churches with which we are connected; neither is it to be a test or term of communion in any of these churches. The Bible is the only standard book which we recognise, and to no other standard book whatsoever can we subscribe.'

The position thus laid down, the Evangelical Union ever adhered to. Formal subscription to a creed was never demanded from any of its members. It reserved to itself the power of issuing a doctrinal declaration when it was thought needful to do so in the interests of the Gospel. This power was exercised in the year 1858, when a *Doctrinal Declaration*, written by John Guthrie, and adopted by the Conference, was issued. Care was taken, in the preface of this document, to state that it was not a formal creed but a declaration of the faith of the members of the Conference which sent it forth. It became, however, an exceedingly useful deliverance, being used as a textbook in many Bible classes, and was the means of dissipating much of the darkness which prevailed as to what the churches of the Evangelical Union believed and taught.

From this it will be noticed that it was not originally intended by the founders of the Evangelical Union that it should be a denomination, a sect, or a separate church. Individuals could become members no matter to what section of the Christian Church they might belong. 'We hail', said the founders of the Union, 'as "true yoke fellows" all of every name and denomination who wish the pleasure of the Lord to prosper and who have peace with God, and evidence their possession of this peace by the purity and spirituality of their lives.' In the addresses delivered at this time it was said they could take in the Bishop with his clergy, the Moderator with his Assembly or Synod, and the Congregational Union with all its ministers and members. 'It had room and to spare for them all', said John Guthrie in one memorable address, and his words revealed the sentiment which then commonly prevailed. But this condition of things could not continue long. The logic of events was too powerful for their large-hearted intentions and desires to be unsectarian. Churches were formed to preach and defend their theological views, and these soon became distinct from all others, which necessitated more organisation in the Evangelical Union, which ultimately determined its development into a denomination as clearly marked off from other Christian churches as any in the land.

It was agreed that there should be an annual meeting of the members of the Union to hear reports from churches and to transact what business required to be done. The meeting was designated the Evangelical Union Conference, and was presided over by a President selected by the members. Its membership was to consist 'of delegates from the churches of the Evangelical Union, and Evangelical Union pastors of churches, every church being entitled to send two delegates'. The condition of membership was never changed, and though it was rather peculiar in one or two of its provisions, it was practically a success. Thus, for example, pastors of other churches than those of the Union had a seat in the Conference, and this was found to add to the strength, and not to the detriment of the brotherhood. Indeed, in the circumstances of the churches and pastors it was the wisest course that could have been adopted, and contributed not a little to the growth of the denomination.

The Conference originated all the institutions connected in any way with the Union, and controlled them all, with the exception of the Ministers' Provident Fund, which was managed by its members. These different departments of work, such as the Theological Hall, Home Mission, Augmentation of Stipend Fund, Chapel Debt and Building Fund, Temperance, Sabbath School, Foreign Mission, Publications, and others, were committed to the care of special committees appointed by and responsible to the Conference, to which they reported at the annual business meeting. All financial matters were also under its control, and the detail of income and expenditure was submitted annually for its consideration and approval. It also appointed a Commission as a 'General Committee for taking up any matters that may occur in the interval of the meetings and may not admit of delay, and to watch over the interests of the Union generally'.

Thus it will be seen that the Conference exercised considerable power, and that its organisation was more elaborate than that which obtains in other ecclesiastical Unions composed of Independent churches. This is true; but it is also true that in no single case did the Conference seek to exercise the slightest control over the internal management of any of the churches connected with it.

The principle upon which it ever acted was that of recognising that no one had a right to interfere with the government of a church, with a pastor or its members, though it recognised that, as members of the Union, and in relation thereto, it had a right to interfere if need be. The Commission was on more than one occasion appealed to to adjudicate regarding differences in churches, arising from various causes; but in no case did it accede to the appeal, except when requested to do so by both parties concerned.

IV

Shortly after the first meeting held in Kilmarnock in 1843 an impetus was given to the work of the Evangelical Union by the co-operation of a number of ministers and students who, as we have noticed earlier in this narrative, had been disassociated from the Congregational Union of Scotland for their anti-Calvinist views.[1] Amongst the most prominent of these were John Kirk of Hamilton; Fergus Ferguson of Bellshill; Peter Mather of Ardrossan; and Messrs. Fergus Ferguson (Junior), Ebenezer Kennedy, James B. Robertson, and William Bathgate. Some of these formally joined the Evangelical Union before their churches did so, the latter fearing, if they became members, they would surrender their independency. These churches, however, were in most instances affiliated, and contributed regularly and generously to the various funds, and in the minds of the public were identified with the work and witness of the Union.

In the forties of last century the churches increased rapidly in numbers and strength, notwithstanding that the field was occupied almost entirely by the larger and older denominations. Only eight churches formed before 1843 identified themselves in any way with the Union, and the others had to be gathered in, organised, and provided for until they were able to be self-governing.

The parent churches of the movement numbered thirteen: four from the Secession Church, namely, Kilmarnock, Bathgate, Falkirk, and Kendal; and nine from the Congregational Union, namely, Hamilton, Bellshill, Cambuslang, Bridgeton, Ardrossan, Westhill, Woodside, Fraserburgh, and Forres. Churches were established, mostly in the 'forties, at Kelso, Galashiels, Hawick, Melrose, Jedburgh, and Selkirk. Later attention was directed to

---

[1] See Chapter x, above.

the great centres of population. In the city of Glasgow Montrose Street Church was formed in 1844, North Dundas Street Church, associated with the historic ministry of James Morison, in 1848, and at least four other causes arose before 1875. Three churches were formed in Edinburgh between 1845 and 1866, of which Brighton Street, where John Kirk ministered so long and memorably, was the most influential. The Evangelical Union flag was unfurled in Dundee in 1848, when Reform Street Church was founded, followed by Morison Church some twenty years later. A church was formed in Perth in 1856. The new movement reached the city of Aberdeen early in the 'forties and a church was established there (St. Paul Street) in 1846, of which Fergus Ferguson was the pastor till 1872, when Andrew Martin Fairbairn began his five years ministry of power and distinction. Another church, John Street, was formed in Aberdeen in the 'sixties. A church was founded in Ayr in 1844, and some villages and towns of the county had churches or preaching stations. Paisley saw its first Evangelical Union church in 1845. The movement came to Caithness in 1846, when a church was formed at Wick. Some four years later the most northern outpost of Evangelical Unionism was planted on the island of Shapinsay in the Orkneys.[1]

Time would fail us to particularise the origin and progress of all the churches in connection with the Evangelical Union. Suffice it to say that the original thirteen had by the year 1875 increased to eighty-two, and by 1896 to some ninety churches. They were scattered all over the country, from Shapinsay in the far north to Dalbeattie in Dumfriesshire, in the south; and from Arbroath in the east to Ayr, in the west. In addition, for some time in the period under review, there were churches in Ireland (in Belfast) and in northern England (at Kendal and Huddersfield).[2]

Although there was nothing in the constitution or the stated objects and aims of the Evangelical Union regarding temperance, the furtherance of this good cause, made all the more necessary since the Industrial Revolution, was viewed as part of its mission. In 1843 temperance, with what many good people considered its doubtful and as yet novel adjunct total abstinence, was as yet merely the concern of insignificant societies. The scandal of open

---

[1] See *A Chronicle of the Churches*, below.
[2] Ramsden Street Church, Huddersfield, was formed in 1846 by a group of men zealous to preserve Yorkshire Congregationalism from the invasion of Morisonianism from Scotland.

public-houses on Sundays still existed. Drunkenness was the most manifest national vice.[1] Without any law demanding abstinence from intoxicating drink on the part of the ministers or students of the Evangelical Union, it was soon found that they were all abstainers, and they viewed this as part of their practical Christianity. No licensed seller of liquor was allowed to become a member of its churches. This action was taken on the ground that drink-selling was an anti-Christian trade opposed to the teaching and spirit of Jesus Christ, and should not be treated as a lawful business. Whether a drink-seller was a Christian or not they did not judge—that was a matter between the soul and God—but they had no hesitation in affirming that the trade was not in harmony with the mind of Christ, and was a most deadly foe to the advancement of the Saviour's kingdom in the world. Being morally wrong, they contended that the drink trade could not be politically right, and should be put down as a source of manifold evils by the strong arm of the law. This was the position taken by the fathers of the Union and endorsed by the great majority of the members. To the advocacy of these principles many of the ministers and others devoted much of their time and energy when other churches looked with a little suspicion on the whole temperance movement.

John Kirk, when pastor of Brighton Street E.U. Church, Edinburgh, was the first Grand Chaplain of the Good Templars Order in Scotland, and his church the first in Edinburgh to use unfermented wine at the Communion Service.

A local historian tells us that when the present Congregational Church in Langholm was opened for public worship as an E.U. church, in July 1863, the fellowship, staunch in the temperance cause, bade God-speed to twenty-two of their members who were emigrating to Australia. Not long after their arrival in that distant colony these Evangelical Unionists instituted the first lodge of Good Templars in that land. Such creative work in the cause of temperance might be similarly illustrated from the annals of many of the early E.U. churches.

Because of their temperance advocacy, as well as their theological innovation, the infant fellowships met with considerable opposition and like their Congregational brethren, with cruel

---

[1] 'You go into a house where on your last visit you saw a child very ill, and you see the mother huddled at the top of the bed sleeping a drunken sleep and you know that the child is dead. They baptise with whisky and they bury with whisky.' *Scottish Social Welfare, 1864-1914*, by Thomas Ferguson.

persecution. 'To wear the Morisonian badge in those days,' the historian of Wishaw Church reminds us, 'was to incur social scorn; it was hardly respectable to be an Evangelical Unionist.'

It was from spiritual seed such as this scattered throughout Scotland that the Union came to exert a cleansing social as well as a liberalising theological effect upon Scottish thought and life. By the eighteen-eighties practically the entire organised religious life of Scotland recognised the significance and value of the stand made by James Morison to widen and sweeten Scottish theology. The conferring upon him, in 1882, of the Degree of Doctor of Divinity by Glasgow University was a public testimony that at last his aims and manner of life were being nationally understood and esteemed.

The very constitution of the Evangelical Union which had been formed partly 'for the purposes of training up spiritual and devoted young men to carry on and carry forward the work and pleasure of the Lord', involved the starting of a Theological Academy. It could scarcely have been otherwise, for both in Kilmarnock and in many of the neighbouring towns and villages an eager interest in and enthusiasm for Morisonian teaching had been aroused. Wherever Morison preached multitudes flocked to hear him from miles around. In many places small groups of people rejoicing in the liberty of the gospel preached by him gathered together and formed new churches, and from near and far came requests for preachers able to expound the 'new views', and to take upon themselves the oversight of the causes so rapidly springing up. Accordingly the inaugural Conference of the Union, held in Kilmarnock from 16 to 18 May 1843, thought it advisable that a Theological Academy should be started without delay.

The first session of the Academy met in a room of Clerk's Lane Church manse, Kilmarnock in August and September of 1843. The accommodation proved inadequate, and in the following year a large classroom of the church was put at the disposal of the institution. Here the work of teaching was carried on until 1851 when Morison removed to Glasgow, and a suitable habitat for the classes was found in the halls of North Dundas Street Church, where they continued to meet for thirty-five years. In 1887, through a number of generous gifts bequeathed to the Union, the institution was provided with more adequate premises at 18 Moray Place, Regent Park, Glasgow. Here the Academy, which since 1879 had been renamed the Evangelical Union Theological Hall,

I

remained for the rest of its separate existence, uniting in 1896 with the Hall of the Congregational churches.

James Morison readily undertook, without fee or monetary reward, the arduous task of superintending the Academy, of arranging its curriculum, and of giving the necessary instruction. For half a century he was the principal teacher. In the course of the years several Chairs were founded, but at first there was one tutor only to occupy them all.

In the first session which was duly opened at the beginning of August 1843 the following classes were conducted:

(1) A Hebrew class for instruction in the language and criticism of the Old Testament.
(2) A class for the study of New Testament Greek and the scientific exegesis of the New Testament books.
(3) A class of Systematic Theology, with arrangements for practical sermon-work.

It was further provided that the Academy, which was modelled on that of the United Secession Church in which Morison had been trained, should have a curriculum of five sessions of eight weeks each—these to be held during the months of August and September. The arrangement was not without advantages: it enabled students to attend concurrently the Hall and the University; it shortened the time of training, no small boon to poorer students; it met the needs of an increasing number of churches which were awaiting pastors; and it rendered possible the continuance of the tutors' regular pastoral ministry. For all the teachers of the academy were also pastors of churches.

In the inaugural session seven students, of whom three were private, signed the register. In the second session the number rose to sixteen, and in the third to no fewer than thirty-one. In the fifty-three years of its history, 1843-96, 305 names are recorded in the List of Alumni, among them many illustrious names, like William Adamson, William Landels, William Taylor, Fergus Ferguson, Andrew Martin Fairbairn, George Gladstone, Charles Richardson, and Andrew Ritchie. Many of them did honourable work, not only as ministers of the Gospel at home and abroad, but also in the realms of literature, medicine and commerce.[1]

The impact of Morison's personality and religious passion was the greatest formative influence in the training of the students.

[1] See the present chapter, v, below.

Deeply convinced of the truth of the doctrines which he taught he never failed to inspire his men with a like conviction. A finished scholar himself, he communicated to his classes, not only academic scholarship, but a deep love of learning.

From the circumstances of its origin, it is little to be wondered that Biblical and Theological study had a foremost place in the curriculum, and that some personal experience of evangelism was required of every student during his training. The nature and extent of the Atonement claimed a large amount of attention. Nor was Biblical criticism overlooked, for Morison believed that all their studies were, at the root, Bible studies, and accordingly the exploration and criticism of the sacred texts became a prime necessity.

Evangelistic enterprise was both a tradition and a passion. Every year, at the close of the session in September, arrangements were made for the students in pairs to conduct a week's or a fortnight's mission anywhere where such help was desired. Year after year these evangelistic embassies were sent out. Through them churches were blest and new causes were founded, and many young knights of the universal gospel gained their spurs in the work of soul-winning.

As the years went by other men of scholarship and piety assisted Morison in the work of teaching. In the fourth session John Guthrie began to assist in the Old Testament side of the work, and, in 1857, the teaching of Pastoral Theology was undertaken by John Kirk. Further changes took place in 1867. In that year Guthrie resigned and for a time Fergus Ferguson undertook the Old Testament teaching, while William Taylor became professor of Systematic Theology. Two years later Robert Hunter was installed in the chair of Hebrew. From 1876 to 1879, Morison was obliged, for health reasons, to relinquish his labours in the Hall. Thereupon the Conference appointed Robert Craig to carry out the work of the New Testament Chair. With the Principal's improving health and resumption of duties, Craig resigned in 1879. Alexander McNair succeeded Hunter as professor of Hebrew in 1884, and in 1891 Fergus Ferguson took the Principal's place in the chair of New Testament Exegesis. On the amalgamation of the two denominational colleges in 1897, Taylor and McNair became tutors in the Theological Hall of the Congregational Churches of Scotland.[1]

[1] See Chapter XVII, below.

The Evangelical Union Theological Hall was the first and dearest child of the Union. Every year the closing meeting of the Hall inaugurated the Union's Annual Conference. Every year, too, at a set session of the Conference, the outgoing students were solemnly ordained to the work of the ministry, and the laying-on of hands of the fathers and brethren, representing the Union, made a deep and ineffaceable impression upon all who participated in the service.

V

A modern historian has remarked upon the literary activity of the Evangelical Union, especially through the periodical press.[1] Indeed no Church has had greater faith in the power of the press or used it, so far as its means allowed, more extensively. From the very first, the pen and the press were enlisted in the exposition of the new views of divine truth, and in defence of the new theological position. Innumerable tracts were printed and many volumes were published with these ends in view. Periodical literature was presented with vigour. A monthly, *The Day Star*, was issued, which had a large circulation in all parts of the English-speaking world for nearly half a century. The *Dewdrop*, a juvenile monthly, also had a wide reading public, and continued all the time of the Union's separate existence. The *Christian News*, a weekly newspaper, was started in 1846, and lived long enough to be accounted the oldest religious weekly in Scotland. The *Evangelical Repository*, a quarterly magazine of theological literature, was commenced in 1854, and continued for thirty-four years. *Forward*, a monthly, devoted to the exposition of a liberal evangelical theology, existed for seven years, and had amongst its contributors Andrew M. Fairbairn, George Matheson, and William Robertson Nicoll, and others who rose to foremost places in the world of literature and theology. These periodicals were not official organs, but were carried on by private persons, and on that account were more independent in their treatment of subjects, and reached a larger class of readers. The contributors were generally the pastors of the churches, who rendered voluntary service, and felt that their vocation was not to be preachers of the Word by means of the voice alone, but also through the printed page. *The Evangelical*

[1] J. R. Fleming, *A History of the Church in Scotland*, p. 249.

Union Magazine was started in 1896 as the organ of the minority party who declined to enter into the union of that year.

The Evangelical Union, moreover, made a not inconsiderable contribution to the theological literature of the period 1843-96. James Morison's Biblical Commentaries, *Matthew* (1870) and *Mark* (1873) were among the best of their day; and the works of Andrew Martin Fairbairn with their wider horizons were internationally acclaimed. In the course of his memorable ministry in Aberdeen (1872-77) Fairbairn contributed many important articles on philosophical and theological subjects to the *Contemporary Review*. Subsequently as Principal of Mansfield College, Oxford, he enhanced the prestige of Congregationalism in the world of scholarship. His own published work did notable service in mediating between the historic Christian faith and the newer intellectual positions into which the educated classes were being forced by the progress of science and criticism. Among his significant works were *The Place of Christ in Modern Theology* and *Philosophy of the Christian Religion*. Some students, it is said, found a striking resemblance between the plaster cast of Socrates in the Greek classroom at Aberdeen University and the appearance of Fairbairn, as he delivered there his Gifford Lectures, in 1892, which became the substance of the latter-named book.

The Evangelical Union was one of the first religious bodies of Presbyterian provenance in Scotland to extend its psalmody to include hymns. As early as 1844 *Hymns and Spiritual Songs collected by James Morison* was published in Kilmarnock. The book contained eighty hymns, arranged in two parts, in the second of which two hymns by John Guthrie, the hymnodist of the new movement, first appear.[1] The volume was reissued in 1848. It was superseded in 1856 by *The Evangelical Union Hymn Book* containing 559 compositions, with an interesting preface over the name of John Guthrie. Appended to this book is a selection of forty-five hymns for children and some instructive 'hints as to singing'. Four hymns from Guthrie's pen are included in the body of the book: 'Blood of sprinkling, healing tide' (541), 'How lovely are thy tents' (460), ' 'Tis evening; over Salem's towers' (555), and the once favourite strain in E.U. congregations,

> Ye ransomed of Jesus,
> Come, sing of His love,

[1] See also *Sacred Lyrics: Hymns, Original and translated from German; with versions of Psalms*, by John Guthrie, M.A., 1869.

> He stooped down to raise us
> To mansions above.
> Jehovah on Him our transgressions did lay
> And he bore the huge burden, and bore it away (456).

The book also contained Fergus Ferguson's hymn, included in *Congregational Praise* (1951), albeit in a much abbreviated version,

> He lovéd me, and gave himself for me!
> Amazing love! amazing sacrifice!
> I'll take my harp down from the willow tree
> And bid its notes in praise of Jesus rise (548).

That devoutly breathed and widely repeated stanza explains why the 'Morisonians' were from the first a gospel-singing church.

A desire having been expressed for a more select and adequate collection of hymns, a committee was appointed, in 1874, to prepare a new hymnal; and their work appeared as *The Evangelical Union Hymnal*, in 1878. This consisted of 420 hymns, with names of authors and dates of publication affixed, fifteen doxologies and forty chants. The book also contained an Index of authors, and, what is almost a unique feature, a list of the original readings where the author's text had been altered. These notes were prepared by William Dunlop, the minister of Nelson Street Church, Glasgow, and the editor of the collection, the selection of hymns having been made by the committee as a whole. It is altogether a carefully selected and well edited collection.

After the amalgamation of the Evangelical Union and the Congregational Union of Scotland, it was this excellent hymnary that was adopted as the basis of a new hymnal for the use of the denomination in worship.[1]

---

[1] The new hymn book, *The Scottish Congregational Hymnal*, was produced by adding a supplement of a hundred hymns.

CHAPTER XII

THE LIBERAL ERA

I

CONGREGATIONALISM in Scotland, as we have noticed, was affected in the middle of the nineteenth century by the anti-Calvinist movement in theology. As that century progressed the spread of liberal ideas altered the character and, in some respects, the beliefs of the churches. At first, however, the Congregational Union was guided in its thought and work by the powerful conservative minds of Ralph Wardlaw and Lindsay Alexander. These great men had their place, too, in the phalanx of earnest theologians and statesmen that defended the rights of the Redeemer in Scotland, during the first half of the century. Each turned his pulpit into a throne and, in a city of preachers, held sway over the minds and hearts of multitudes. At the height of his powers Wardlaw was one of the greatest forces in the civil and religious life of the Scottish West country. A mighty pulpiteer, he could, when occasion demanded, deal persuasively, and indeed drastically sometimes, with great social issues, and affect the decisions of magistrates and unruly mobs. For instance, in the eighteen-twenties Glasgow shared in the popular discontent, which generally characterised the manufacturing districts of Britain, excited by commercial embarrassments and exasperated by violent measures of government. Riots and public disturbances broke out in the city. Wardlaw, from his early education strongly prejudiced to the side of authority, enforced in sermon and address the Christian duty of submission to civil government. On one occasion he preached a sermon from I Peter, ii. 13-15, in which he stressed the importance of this duty on the part of the unruly citizen. The sermon was afterwards published and inscribed to the Provost and Magistrates of Glasgow 'in testimony of the approbation which . . . he strongly feels . . . of that happy union of promptitude and vigour, with mildness and forebearance, which distinguished their official conduct during the recent alarms of the city and neighbourhood'. Wardlaw's biographer believes that the preaching and publishing of this discourse was of important service to the cause of law and order, 'as it tended to withdraw from the ranks of the insubordinate those whose character and intelligence alone could give their cause weight'. The magistrates and Council showed their sense of its value by ordering one hundred copies to be sent for their disposal.[1] When Queen Victoria and Prince Albert visited Glasgow in 1849, the Royal Party, in passing along West George Street, were attracted by the simple classic proportions of West George Street Chapel;[2] and the Queen asked, 'What church is this?' 'Dr. Wardlaw's', replied Sheriff Allison. Looking at the Queen, the Prince promptly added—'the distinguished Scottish Dissenter'. West George Street Chapel was the rallying place of multitudes, not only on Sundays. Many of the great questions of the day were discussed there during the week. 'No good cause that needed assistance, no wrong that lacked resistance, but could find in it a gathering place. There was rung the death-knell of many a hoary wrong; there, too, was often celebrated the triumph of many a bloodless victory.' Notably there may be recalled the meetings in connection with the anti-slavery agitation, helping forward, as they undeniably did, the day of emancipation throughout the British colonies. In 1818, Ralph Wardlaw was honoured by Yale University with the degree of Doctor of Divinity.

William Lindsay Alexander, the scholarly and eloquent pastor of Augustine Church, Edinburgh, was perhaps the most prominent figure in the Scottish ministry at this time outside Presbyterianism.[3] He was one of the panel of British scholars chosen to revise the Authorised Version of the Bible in 1870. In 1861 he undertook the editing of *Kitto's Cyclopaedia of Biblical Literature* (left unfinished at the time of Kitto's death), and wrote himself so many of the articles that it might as truly have borne his own name. He wrote, too, on important subjects in the *Encyclopaedia Britannica*. As a member of the Hellenic Society of Edinburgh, better known in those days as the Blackie Brotherhood, Alexander cultivated serious Greek study, and on occasion contributed his share of amusement by turning Scottish songs into very nearly faultless Latin. Some of these were printed privately and sent to members of the Society. On receiving a copy, Dr. John Brown wrote to Alexander saying 'I have read nothing since Lord

[1] W. L. Alexander, *Memoirs of the Life and Writings of Ralph Wardlaw*, p. 195.
[2] See *A Chronicle of the Churches*, below.   [3] *Ibid.*

Macaulay's as good. . . . I must send a copy to Gladstone, to Thackeray, to Stanley, and to Theodore Martin'. Alexander was also a member of the Royal Society, and for eleven years one of its Vice-Presidents. He received the degree of Doctor of Divinity from St. Andrews University and that of Doctor of Laws from the University of Edinburgh.

During Alexander's Edinburgh ministry a large number of that city's great men sat under his preaching. On the roll of members and in constant attendance were Professor George Wilson, James (afterwards Sir James) Marwick, Dr. Matthews Duncan, Alexander Moncrieff (advocate), Admiral Ramsay (brother of Dean Ramsay), and others equally well known. In the long line of deacons who served with him at different dates are— John Gibson, W.S., legal adviser to Sir Walter Scott; Adam Black, one of Edinburgh's M.P.s, when the city returned only two; James McLaren, Master of the Merchant Company; Sir George Harvey, President of the Royal Scottish Academy; and Sir James Donald- son, then Rector of the High School and later Principal of St. Andrews University, a pioneer in Patristic study long neglected in Scotland.[1]

Dr. Alexander's powerful influence pervaded Scottish Con- gregationalism until his retiral from the ministry in 1877. Even after that date his influence continued through his training of men in the Theological Hall of the Scottish Congregational Churches, until the early 'eighties. From 1856 to 1882 he guided that institu- tion, the last five years as its Principal. The classes were held in a room beneath Augustine Church, and the students passed their days, as one of them humorously described it, as 'cave dwellers' in the sunless apartment 'down among the dead men'.[2]

Wardlaw and Alexander represented a conservative and rather aristocratic species of Congregationalism, and their influence upon the life and beliefs of the denomination was very great and all pervasive. However, even in the heyday of their power, there were operative new tendencies, social and intellectual, that were soon to affect the character of the churches. In the middle of the century significant social changes were in progress. Industrialism was beginning to lay hold of quiet rural districts which have since become sites for busy hives of people. Seven hundred thousand of

[1] The first volumes of the *Ante-Nicene Christian Library* of T. and T. Clark were in part edited by Donaldson in 1867.
[2] See II of following chapter.

the entire population of two and a half millions were living, in 1843, in Edinburgh, Glasgow, Aberdeen, Dundee, and Paisley.[1] A visible sign of the change coming over the face of things in Scotland was the incipient railway revolution.[2] Hugh Miller published in the *Witness* of 4 March 1843 a powerful article—'A Vision of the Railroad'—in which he indulged, not without cause, in gloomy prophecies as to the disintegrating effect of the new method of travel on Scottish religious traditions. The Edinburgh and Glasgow line had just been opened, and a trip upon it was regarded as a thrilling adventure.[3] Ideas now had iron wheels. From that time onwards we find the new tendencies arousing reactionary movements. The fear lest the Anglicising process, strengthened by better facilities of transport and communication, should undermine the foundations of Scottish nationality gave birth to the 'National Association for the Vindication of Scottish Rights', which held a great demonstration in Edinburgh on 1 November 1852. Similar movements of reaction are discernible in ecclesiastical quarters, chiefly in the Free Church, where we notice a renewed interest in seventeenth century Scottish Covenant theology and devotional practice.

But these barriers and barricades could not hold back the gathering surge of life. Industry, commerce, shipping, and learning combined to create a democratic spirit and to keep the vast populations of the big Scottish cities and their adjacent burghs keenly alive to new movements in the thought and life of the world. For the most part, even in the 'eighties, the Church of Scotland was conservative in politics and theology. But some of its people were reading Carlyle, Ruskin, and Kingsley. Radicalism and social democracy were spreading through the people outside the churches.

After 1870, under the influence of the idealistic tradition in philosophy, this liberal movement gathered momentum in some quarters of the National Church. Principal Tulloch of St. Andrews and Principal John Caird of Glasgow gave it impetus. In the Free

[1] Edinburgh, 166,450; Glasgow, 274,533; Aberdeen, 64,767; Dundee and Paisley each had had a little over 60,000.

[2] J. Mackinnon, *The Social and Industrial History of Scotland, passim.*

[3] The Railway Revolution supported the mobilisation of ideas. Between 1843 and 1853, 1,000 miles of line had been laid down. All the chief towns, except Inverness, were linked up, and the English Border was only one and a half hours from Edinburgh and three from Glasgow. Two main routes were open to London.

Church, despite the ejection of William Robertson Smith, the critical historical study of the Bible continued. A. B. Bruce was originating the 'Back to Christ' movement through his learned and deeply religious studies in the New Testament. In Glasgow the new temper found its clearest manifestation. The Cairds— John and Edward—were at the height of their influence at the University, and were moulding the youth of that generation in the liberal Hegelian forms of thought. Indeed, John's theology was criticised in orthodox circles as being 'too palpably an impress of the present generation'.

William Pulsford and John Hunter represented the Congrega-tionalists in the Scottish Churches' acceptance of a more liberal theology. They were both ministers of Trinity Church in Glasgow, Pulsford from 1864 to 1884, and Hunter from 1886 to 1901 and, again, from 1904 to 1913. Pulsford during his pastorate exerted a thoughtful and liberating influence. But it was left for Hunter to put 'Trinity' on the map of the English-speaking world as a centre of liberal preaching and spiritual worship.[1] He came to Glasgow at the time when the Cairds were at the height of their power, and often preached at their invitation in the University chapel. It was said that only two preachers could fill the gloomy Gothic Bute Hall, John Caird and John Hunter. Like Wardlaw and Alexander before him, Hunter, because of his consecration and great gifts, made Congregational thought and polity count outside his own pulpit and denomination. Wherever Hunter went the enquiring and intellectually alert followed him. The Sunday services at Trinity Church were a source of inspiration and a mental and spiritual tonic to hundreds—many of whom tramped for miles and thought nothing of standing for an hour in the mud and rain, 'feeling that physical fatigue and discomfort counted as nothing compared with the heartening effect of the preacher's message and the helpful and quietening influence of the beautiful services'.[2] By the close of the century the membership of Trinity Church had risen from 400 to 900, and every seat was let. There-after the demand for seats was always in excess of the supply. For many John Hunter's fame rested on his liturgical labours. He was indeed a pioneer in introducing a liturgical element into noncon-formist worship. While in Glasgow he compiled his now popular

[1] See III of following chapter.
[2] L. S. Hunter, *John Hunter, D.D.: A Life*, to which I am indebted for much of the material in this section.

Devotional Services for Public Worship, which in fifteen years expanded through eight editions, as well as a new hymn-book for the use of his own congregation.[1]

Hunter returned to Scottish Congregationalism at a time when his particular kind of culture and spiritual witness was needed. The old evangelicalism in a new world of scientific enquiry was ceasing to grip men. Besides its ethic, though severe and intimate, was narrow in this new world of wider moral horizons. Furthermore, it had no philosophy except a vague utilitarianism. As we have noticed, new tides of religious thought were sweeping away the harsh accretions of later theology from the primitive Christian conception of God. Maurice and Robertson in England, Erskine, MacLeod Campbell, and James Morison in Scotland, had been engaged in this destructive yet cleansing work. Hunter, liberal in mind and heart, with a wide and humane culture firmly based in the Gospel was able to hold thoughtful people to Christianity, when they were in danger of being alienated from the more orthodox churches. In this important work he was ably supported up and down Scotland by a team of great preachers, pastors and scholars. In Glasgow there was Albert Goodrich at Elgin Place Church. David Macrae and Kerr Anderson laboured mightily for liberal Christianity in Dundee. John Pulsford, the evangelical mystic, of Albany Street Church, Edinburgh, 'cherished a high and hopeful view of humanity not easily reconciled with the stern puritan creed of the period', and made a strong appeal to the student body and seekers after larger truth. Whilst away to the north in Aberdeen Andrew Martin Fairbairn attracted the Christian thinkers of that philosophical city into St. Paul Street Church. These great men won to their churches many who otherwise would have been lost to the Christian enterprise. Rescue work of this kind Congregationalism, with its wider freedoms in doctrine and method, was fitted to carry out in this age of intellectual ferment and religious transition.

Hunter himself fully appreciated the special place and function of Congregationalism in the religious life of the nation. 'Our independency', he once said, 'may have its disadvantages but rightly conceived and used it affords, in the present distress and transition, a great opportunity for truly catholic worship, catholic teaching, catholic work. I hope to see before I die a Church of Scotland thoroughly comprehensive and catholic, but until the

[1] See III of following chapter.

day of such a church dawns we must continue to stand where we can honestly and without compromise.'[1]

With the death of John Caird in 1898, Hunter was recognised as *the* spokesman of liberal Christianity in Scotland. His voice carried far. His courage in stating his convictions, social, political and theological inspired others to speak more boldly. His preaching was the inspiration of much social welfare work done in the city of Glasgow. At a time when the churches were mostly indifferent to social issues, or blindly antagonistic to political and social reformers, it was John Hunter who, with characteristic fearlessness, offered his pulpit to Keir Hardie, the Labour leader.[2] The minister of *Trinity* saw earlier than most that the Church must exert herself to win the workers of the world, or close her doors.

II

In the eighteen-eighties there was evinced a growing impatience with denominational inactivity. It would not do to rest on past achievements, as some felt had been done. New interest and gathering enthusiasm proclaimed the return of something of the denomination's early life and energy. Particularly among the younger men there prevailed an opinion that Congregationalism had marked time long enough and must now reach out in some forward movement. In this period the District Committees, which were to play a leading rôle in the new century, were, for the most part, inaugurated.

Some few years later the attention of the churches was drawn to the place of women in the Christian enterprise. At that time, and for some years afterwards, there were no lady delegates at the annual meetings of the Union. The ministers' wives gathered in the gallery of the church 'watching, listening—and waiting, a charming ecclesiastical Zenana!'[3] John Hunter predicted, 'the nineteenth century has been described as the century of the working man; the twentieth century is going to be the woman's century.' Within Scottish Congregationalism signs of things to come in this regard were seen at a public conference held on 27 April 1893, during the Annual Meeting of the Congregational

[1] L. S. Hunter, *John Hunter, D.D.: A Life*, pp. 122 ff.
[2] *Ibid.*
[3] Margaret H. E. Calder, 'Scottish Congregational Women', *The Scottish Congregationalist*, July, August, September, 1955.

Union in Aberdeen. Mrs. Gregory, wife of the minister of Augustine Church, Edinburgh, spoke on 'Women's Ministry in the Church', and pleaded for 'greater cohesion and communion between the women workers in each Church, and also between the various churches in the denomination, and for the making use of that greatest of all powers, "the power of prayer" '. 'Is it not time', she said, 'that we had a Union of Christian Women to which each church should be affiliated and which should be the means of communication between the churches? How can we pray for each other's work if we have no more knowledge of it than at present is possible? Should we not more clearly approach our ideal Church and be in a truer and deeper sense members one of another and of the Body of Christ?' Five years later the Women's Christian Union was established.[1]

At the turn of the century we notice another of the Union's keen interests coming to the front again, namely its concern for the training of children and youth. One of the denomination's specific duties, said J. R. Sandilands in his address from the presidential Chair of the Union, in 1896, 'is the welfare of the young in our churches. If we fail in this we fail in loyalty to our traditions. . . . We make a mistake it appears to me, in devoting nearly all our attention to the adults of our congregations.'[2] We perceive faintly the beginning of that strong accent which is to be a predominant characteristic of Congregational work and witness in the twentieth century.

[1] Margaret H. E. Calder, *ibid.*, and Chapters XV and XVI, below.

[2] J. R. Sandilands, *Scottish Congregationalism: A Retrospect and a Plea*, 1896.

CHAPTER XIII

WIDENING WORK AND WORSHIP

I

AMONG the various religious agencies in connection with Congregational churches in Scotland none has probably been more influential and useful than its periodical literature. The magazines that have from time to time appeared have done much to keep in remembrance the great truths and principles professed by the churches, to foster a spirit of unity and interest in their common cause, and to supply them with interesting and valuable information regarding each other's work and the progress of religion generally. We have already dealt with the periodicals issued from time to time by the Evangelical Unionists.[1] It remains for us to say something now about the periodical literature associated with the Congregational churches in Scotland.

The first of these periodicals was the *Missionary Magazine*, the original number of which appeared on 16 July 1796. With the single exception of the London *Evangelical Magazine* it was the first religious periodical in Britain, and probably in the world. Originated, as we have seen, to supply information and to excite interest in connection with foreign missions, it became, in the course of a few years, the organ of the Congregational churches, and while it never ceased to give a larger place to the foreign missionary enterprise, it devoted an increasing portion of its space to the operations of the Scottish Congregational churches. Its first editor was Greville Ewing, who for four years continued to edit it, but who, owing to the pressure of other duties that fell to him about the year 1800, had to relinquish his charge.[2] For some years afterwards the magazine was conducted by John Aikman and others, and in 1814 its name was changed to the *Christian Herald*. A further change in its designation took place in 1835 when it became *The Scottish Congregational Magazine*. From 1814 till 1880 the magazine had as its editors men whose names shone as stars in the firmament of the denomination—John Aikman,

---

[1] See Chapter XI, v.   [2] See Chapter IX, above.

George Payne, Gilbert Wardlaw, David Davidson, George D. Cullen, Henry Wilkes, Edward Napier, Henry Wight, William Lindsay Alexander, James Campbell, Robert Spence, James Robbie, James Stark, and David Russell. In 1881 a further change was made in the name; it became *The Scottish Congregationalist*. From that year till the present time [1959] its editors have been James Ross, Robert Auchterlonie, Douglas Mackenzie, David Caird, Alexander Roy Henderson, Alexander Brown and Thomas Templeton, Alexander Brown and W. S. Thomson, Henry Parnaby, Thomas H. Walker, David Farquharson, Andrew James Forson, A. Ireland Robertson, Ralph F. G. Calder, Arthur G. Reekie, and John B. Wilson.

For some years prior to the change of the name of *The Scottish Congregational Magazine* to that of *The Scottish Congregationalist*, in 1881, *The Advance* was originated and conducted by a number of friends connected with churches of the Congregational Union in the West of Scotland. It was the first penny monthly periodical in connection with these churches, and did good service in endeavouring to stir a lively interest in their work and witness. Its editor was Thomas Brisbane. When *The Scottish Congregationalist* appeared as a penny monthly, *The Advance* ceased to exist.

The missionary cause, as we have noticed from time to time in this narrative, was closely connected with the journalistic ventures of the Congregational churches. During the existence of the *Missionary Magazine*—some eighteen years—it continued to advocate foreign Missions and to supply its readers with full accounts of what was happening in the missionary field in various parts of the world. As the magazine was largely circulated in the homes of the early Congregationalists, the perusal of its pages created and maintained an intelligent interest in missionary enterprise. Every church became an auxiliary to the London Missionary Society (which, be it remembered, had famous Scots among its founders),[1] and the monthly missionary prayer-meeting, which was regularly held in nearly all the churches, became one of the most interesting gatherings of the people. Although more attention was given to home evangelism after the *Missionary Magazine* appeared as the *Christian Herald*, yet for many years the pages of the latter had assigned a large place to accounts of work abroad. That interest has continued to the present time, and every district of the Union has a strong missionary auxiliary in con-

[1] See James M. Calder, *Scotland's March Past*.

nection with the parent society. One fruitful result of this missionary interest has been that a large number of missionaries have gone from the churches to the foreign mission field. Including those who have gone from the Theological Hall and the present Scottish Congregational College, and those who have been trained elsewhere, it is estimated that the contribution of men and women to the foreign field from the Scottish Congregational churches has been upwards of one hundred and thirty missionaries in the century and a half and more of the society's existence, some ten of whom are still labouring abroad.

Congregationalism has contributed handsomely to the magnificent rôle which Scotland has played in the missionary enterprise. John Philip, James Legge, James Chalmers, David Livingstone, James Gilmour, Eric Liddell—names such as these shine like the sun in the annals of the World Church. Nor should we forget the illustrious line of the society's district secretaries for Scotland and Ireland who, by their deep consecration to the missionary cause, have kept the challenge of missions before the churches, men like W. G. Allan and Sidney Nicholson. And there was James Macnair who, after twenty-six years work in India, returned home to serve for six years as Scottish Secretary. In the long evening of his life he carried through his monumental labours in connection with the Scottish National Memorial to David Livingstone at Blantyre, and became a world authority on the life and works of that greatest of Scottish missionary heroes.[1] James M. Calder, Dr. Macnair's successor from 1936 to 1951, held a deep and wide place in the affection of all the churches, and bequeathed to them a little literary masterpiece, *Scotland's March Past*, which recounts in warm imaginative words the thrilling story of the contribution the Congregational churches have made for 150 years towards the maintenance and witness of the London Missionary Society.[2]

II

We have traced elsewhere in this book the beginnings and early years of the Glasgow Theological Academy.[3] For over a quarter of a century Ralph Wardlaw and Greville Ewing served

---

[1] See Chapter XVI, below.
[2] Cf. *A Chronicle of the Churches*, 'Morningside, Edinburgh'.
[3] Chapter IX, II, above.

K

that institution as tutors without financial remuneration, with a zeal and devotedness beyond all praise. It was now felt that the churches ought no longer to allow the tutors to labour gratuitously. In May 1839, John Morell Mackenzie was requested to give his undivided services to the academy, and was appointed resident tutor at a salary of £200. Mackenzie was a young man of outstanding Christian character and intellectual gifts, and under his superintendence the Academy enjoyed a season of great prosperity. All too soon, however, the brightness was clouded, first by the death of Greville Ewing in 1841, and then by the sudden and lamented death of Mackenzie himself, who was drowned in the wreck of the *Pegasus* off the west coast, in 1843.[1] The vacancies thus caused were filled by two former students, William Swan and Gilbert Wardlaw, who, before they entered the pastoral ministry, had been associated with Dr. Wardlaw in the tutorial work of the Academy, 1844-45. In 1846 Alexander Thomson, who had succeeded Morell Mackenzie as the pastor of the church in West Nile Street, Glasgow, was appointed to the Chair made vacant by Mackenzie's death and, associated with Dr. Wardlaw, gave great satisfaction as tutor till 1855, when he removed to Manchester. Meanwhile, Dr. Wardlaw had died in 1853. In the year of Thomson's departure for England William Lindsay Alexander was appointed professor of Systematic Theology, and Anthony Gowan professor of Biblical Literature. As they were both to retain their pastoral charges in Edinburgh and Dalkeith respectively, it was found expedient to transfer the Academy to Edinburgh, and to give it the designation of 'The Theological Hall of the Scottish Congregational Churches'.

Dr. Alexander and Dr. Gowan were in the prime of their days and powers when they undertook their task. They brought to it a degree of learning and ability which rendered them distinctly worthy of the title of 'professors', which was henceforth to be given to them and their successors on the teaching staff. Alexander took charge of the Systematic Theology and Church History departments, along with the class for sermon preparation. Possessed of a strong and capacious mind, stored with a full knowledge of Patristic, Augustinian, and Puritan theology, Alexander was also deeply versed in the history and literature of philosophy. These gifts and qualities, enhanced by the effect of a

---

[1] See G. Gilfillan, *Remoter Stars in the Church Sky*, p. 114, for an appreciation of Morell Mackenzie.

commanding personality, gave to his lectures a force and breadth of view which evoked the admiration of the student body.[1]

The classes in Hebrew, Old and New Testament Exegesis and Criticism were conducted by Gowan, who stood in the front rank of Greek and Hebrew scholars in his day. His penetrating insight and reverent spirit made him a wise guide in dealing with the new questions which were then beginning to be raised by Biblical critics in Germany and elsewhere.

The number of students continued to be steadily maintained. In the early sixties of last century there were between twenty and thirty in regular attendance. The session lasted from November to July of each year, classical and literary subjects being studied at the university during the winter, and the special theological subjects during the summer months. Experience in preaching was gained by the fulfilment of engagements for pulpit supply, for which the services of the students were in frequent demand.

Meanwhile, with the advance of intelligence in the country, there had grown throughout the churches a deepened sense of the necessity of as thorough an educational preparation as possible for all candidates for the ministry. The interest thus awakened was shown by the increase of the contributions sent in to the treasurer, and also by the appointment at the Annual Meeting in 1872 of a third professor, in the person of James Mitchell Robbie, minister of Canmore Street Church, Dunfermline, to whom was allotted the department of Old Testament literature.

Several bursaries and scholarships were founded by the donations or bequests of generous friends. One of these—the gift of Miss Baxter of Ellengowan—was the Baxter Scholarship of the annual value of £100, which was designed to be awarded to a student of recognised merit and proficiency, to enable him, after completing the curriculum at the Hall, to pursue his studies at some British or foreign university, as the trustees might sanction.

Another gift by Miss Baxter was the provision of an endowment, amounting to £10,000, the income of which was to be applied to the raising of the Professor of Systematic Theology to the position and status of Principal, entirely free from pastoral work, and charged with the general oversight of the students. Dr. Alexander was formally installed in this new dignity in 1877.

[1] See also I of the present chapter.

The work proceeded steadily and with a fair average of students till 1879, when James Robbie was obliged to resign his professorship owing to failure of health; and the two colleagues, who were now veterans in the service, engaged to conduct the various branches of study as before. The weight of years, however, constrained both to retire in 1882.

After an interregnum of two sessions, filled up by the assistance of several ministers in the neighbourhood, Dr. D. W. Simon, of Spring Hill College, Birmingham, was appointed as Principal and Professor of Systematic Theology, in 1884; and his inauguration synchronised with an incident which claims an important place in this historical record.

Hitherto the institution had possessed no building of its own. The classes had been held in premises connected with one of the churches, first in Glasgow and then in Edinburgh. For many years the most suitable meeting-place available had been a room underneath Augustine Church in the latter city. In 1884, however, a most welcome benefit was conferred through the purchase by Miss Baxter of a commodious house in George Square, Edinburgh, and the handing over of it in due legal form as the entire property of the Hall. This act of thoughtful liberality, following upon others of equal value, from the same source, deserves to be recorded in this history with grateful remembrance.[1]

In the brighter home thus provided, with ample accommodation for the library, and the large number of portraits of eminent ministers and friends of the Hall which had gradually been collected, Dr. Simon began his duties. In the following year [1885], Andrew Findlater Simpson, minister of High Street Church, Dalkeith, a former student and well furnished scholar, was chosen as Professor of Old and New Testament Exegesis and Criticism. The supply of students continued well up to the average, and the power of the new Principal as a stimulating thinker and theologian soon made itself felt. The atmosphere of vitality was revived, and under the influence of such helpful teaching many were prepared for fruitful ministerial service, not only in Scotland but also south of the border and abroad. Some modifications were now made in the curriculum, applicants for admission being required to take the greater part of their Arts course at the university before entering the distinctively theological classes at the Hall. This arrangement was intended to secure a degree of knowledge and

---

[1] See present chapter, i, above.

mental discipline which would fit the young men for prosecuting their theological studies with greater advantage, and it has been found to work with satisfaction up to the present time.

For some time an effort had been made to raise an endowment for the second chair, and such was the measure of success attained that in 1893 it was found practicable to relieve Professor Simpson from the care of a pastorate, and enable him to give his full time and energies to his professorial duties. This desirable object had just been reached when Dr. Simon removed to Bradford to act as Principal of Airedale (now Yorkshire United Independent) College there. His place was filled by James M. Hodgson, who was elected to the office of Principal in 1894.

The work was in the hands of Dr. Hodgson and Professor Simpson when another change occurred which marks the commencement of the modern era of the denomination's ministerial training, which will receive more detailed consideration in a later chapter.[1] In October 1896 the long contemplated union between the Congregational Union of Scotland and the Evangelical Union was formed, and this led, in the following year, 1897, to the incorporation of the Theological Halls of the two denominations constituting the enlarged body. The two separate institutions were combined in one organisation, which found its home and centre of operations in one building, at 30 George Square, Edinburgh.

It should be added that it was largely through Dr. Simon's interest and effort that the Scottish Congregational Ministers' Symposium was founded in 1886. Simon was its moving spirit from the time of its inception to his leaving Scotland in 1893. It is not too much to say that the Symposium has called into prominence the best minds in the Congregationalism of Scotland. Practically all of the men who have made their mark in the denomination at home and abroad have been numbered among its members and officials. A. E. Garvie was General Secretary of the organisation for a number of years before proceeding to his professorship in New College. G. Currie Martin was its secretary previous to his departure to Reigate and his subsequent promotion to a professorship at United College, Bradford. Among those who have been members are to be numbered Principal D. L. Ritchie of Nottingham, Professor R. Mackintosh of Lancashire College, and Dr. James Ross of Glasgow. Today the Symposium consists of four sections which meet once a year at different centres for the

[1] See Chapter XVII, below.

convenience of members residing in the northern, eastern, southern, and western districts respectively. Most of the ministers in the Union are members of it. The late William Gray, minister of Portobello Church, occupied the office of General Secretary for many years, and was a zealous champion of the Symposium's aims and ideals.

The Union and the Theological Hall have been regarded as the leading institutions connected with the Congregational churches in Scotland; but a very brief sketch of the origin of some other societies connected with the churches is given here. In 1820 the Scottish Congregational Ministers' Widows' Fund was originated, and, in 1859, the Scottish Congregational Ministers' Provident Fund.[1] A similar institution, the Evangelical Union Ministers' Provident Fund Society, was formed by the Evangelical Union eight years later. The Scottish Congregational Chapel Building Society originated in 1866. A like institution, the Chapel Debt and Building Fund in connection with the Evangelical Union was formed in 1868. The Pastor's Supplementary Stipend Fund was formed in 1872. A similar fund originated in the Evangelical Union with the designation Evangelical Union Augmentation of Stipend Fund in the following year.

The Conference of Scottish Congregationalists was instituted in 1869 with the view of enabling the ministers and members of the Congregational Union to confer together on important subjects which at the time were not regarded as coming within the scope of the Union. At the meetings of the Conference papers were read and discussed bearing upon various aspects of church life and work. Inasmuch, however, as the changes made from time to time in the constitution of the Union allowed of greater latitude in the selection of topics dealt with at its annual meetings, the necessity for the Conference came to be less felt than in former years, and when the union of the Congregational and Evangelical Union churches took place in 1896 the Conference ceased to exist.

The Scottish Congregational Total Abstinence Society was instituted in 1867, with the object of promoting the practice of abstinence among members and ministers of Congregational churches. In 1879 a Standing Committee of the Evangelical Union was appointed 'to promote the interests of the Temperance Reform'.

---

[1] These ceased in 1957 with the inauguration of a comprehensive Ministerial Pension Scheme; see final chapter in the present book.

Several home-missionary associations have done valuable work in several parts of the country. The Paisley Society for Missions to the Highlands and Islands was instituted in 1817, and supported many itinerant preachers in their labours. The Edinburgh Itinerant Society was formed with similar aims in 1816, and the labours of its agents were conducted mainly during the summer months, and extended over a large part of the Highlands and Islands. There was also the 'Perth, Angus, and Mearns Itinerant Association' and a similar association for Stirlingshire. Early in the nineteenth century there was an association formed in Aberdeenshire for the purpose of prosecuting home-missionary operations, and in 1848 it was revived under the name of the 'Aberdeen and Banffshire County Association', but the name was changed in 1870 to that which it at present bears, the 'Northern Association of Congregational Churches', and its operations extend over the counties of Moray, Nairn, Inverness, as well as Banff and Aberdeen. Meetings are held from time to time in the several districts for the purpose of evangelism and friendly conference on the part of ministers and members of churches. The principal source of income is a fund known as The Farquharson Bequest, which was bequeathed by the late William Farquharson of Keith. The original capital was £1,200. The annual income is about £42, from which grants are made to churches for evangelistic work. The Association also administers the Taylor Bequest, the capital of which is £200. The interest is paid annually to a Congregational minister for services in the Cabrach. The Northern Association is the last surviving society of many that once existed in several parts of Scotland. Many years ago there was also a 'Glasgow Congregational Union', which was instituted for the purpose of bringing into closer union the churches of the district, and for common effort in evangelistic and other work; but it survived for only a few years. A few years before the turn of the century the Union was revived but lasted only a short time. Other associations with similar aims to the Glasgow Congregational Union have since been formed in different parts of the country, and of these 'Airdrie and Coatbridge Congregational Association', 'Ayrshire Association', and 'Greenock, Port Glasgow and District Congregational Association' still function and do good work.

There is also the 'Scottish Congregational Peace Society' which exists to unite in work and witness ministers, students, and members of Congregational churches who believe that War is contrary to the mind and spirit of Christ.

III

Each succeeding wave of revival in the Church Universal has been accompanied by a fresh outbreak of song. It would have been singular had there been nothing akin to this phenomenon in the evangelical revival in Scotland which followed the preaching of the Haldanes and their associates. The Scottish mind, until late on into the nineteenth century, was conservative in matters relating to forms of worship, and at the time of the Haldane movement the *Metrical Psalms* with, and more often without, the addition of the *Paraphrases* were, as a rule, rigidly adhered to in the services of the churches. It is interesting to note that among churches of the Presbyterian order the Relief body, with its Congregationalist associations, was the first Church in Scotland to sanction the use of hymns in public worship.[1]

To supply the need for something more varied and more distinctly evangelical, a book entitled *Hymns for the use of the Tabernacles in Scotland*, probably compiled by John Aikman and George Cowie, was published in 1800. (In the 1807 and later editions the book was enlarged from 320 to 326 hymns, and renamed *A Collection of Hymns for the use of Christian Churches*.)

It was on the whole a poorly arranged collection, prefaced by a page of pious doggerel, set to a tripping measure, thus,

> What think you of Christ? is the test
> To try both your state and your scheme.
> You cannot be right in the rest
> Unless you think rightly of Him, etc.

At the end of the book, after the index, were some verses, beginning

> The Bible is the word of God
> Which He alone could frame;
> A little child may learn to prove
> It answers to its name

and so on, reciting sacred story and doctrine throughout eighty-six stanzas!

---

[1] See also Chapter III and Chapter V, above, for references to Glasite and Berean hymnology.

This early hymn-book, however, is not without historical value. It at least taught many Scotsmen to appreciate and sing gospel songs, and it contained two of the earliest and most popular of Ralph Wardlaw's hymns: 'Lift up to God the voice of praise' and 'O Lord our God, arise'.

Scottish Congregational hymnology in the nineteenth century is linked with the names of three illustrious men, Ralph Wardlaw, William Lindsay Alexander, and John Hunter. Each was a pioneer in hymnological science in Scotland, and all with varying degrees of merit, were writers of original hymns. As a hymn-writer Wardlaw was the greatest of the three. One of the first things he did when he settled as a young Congregational minister in Glasgow was to compile a new hymn book. This he published in April 1803 as *A Selection of Hymns for Public Worship: Intended primarily for the church in Albion Street Chapel, Glasgow.* The book contained 322 hymns, a number that was increased to 493 by a supplement issued in 1817. In the third, [1811] and later editions, the book was re-entitled, *A Selection of Hymns for Public Worship, by Ralph Wardlaw.* It ran to thirteen editions and enjoyed considerable popularity in the churches, until it was replaced by Congregational hymn books in the eighteen-sixties. From a literary standpoint it was a great improvement on the Tabernacle collection. In the preface Wardlaw has some sound remarks on compositions suitable for public worship. In this connection he pointed out that the practice of singing hymns of didactic and exhortative cast originated from a mistaken punctuation of Colossians iii. 16, which he renders, contrary to the customary reading: 'Let the word of Christ dwell in you richly in all wisdom teaching and admonishing one another; in psalms, and hymns, and spiritual songs, singing with grace in your hearts to the Lord.' Eleven of the hymns in the book are of his own composition and some few of them have since found a place in standard collections throughout the English-speaking world.[1] Probably the best known is that beginning, 'Lift up to God the voice of praise', which is the only one of the eleven

[1] In the first edition seven of Wardlaw's hymns appear:

At the time by God appointed (132).
Contemplate, saints, the source divine (168).
Each word of Christ affection breathes (183).
Glad when they saw the Lord (192).
Hail! morning, known among the blest (74).
Lift up to God the voice of praise (48).
Remember thee! remember Christ (163). [*Over*

included in most modern Congregational hymn books. *Congregational Praise*, however, has Wardlaw's two grandest hymns, 'O Lord, our God arise' and 'Christ of all my hopes the ground'. The most popular and most frequently sung of Dr. Wardlaw's hymns was 'A Sabbath Morning Hymn' which, sung to the once familiar tune *Derby* evokes the image of West George Street Chapel, and its worthy precentor, Samuel Barr,

> Hail! morning known among the blest!
> Morning of hope, and joy, and love;
> Of heavenly peace and holy rest;
> Pledge of the endless rest above.
>
> Bless'd be the Father of our Lord,
> Who from the dead hath brought His Son;
> Hope to the lost was then restored,
> And everlasting glory won.
>
> Descend, O Spirit of the Lord!
> Thy fire to every bosom bring!
> Then shall our ardent hearts accord,
> And teach our lips God's praise to sing.

Following Wardlaw's lead, Greville Ewing and George Payne, pastor of the church in Bernard's Rooms, Edinburgh, published, in 1814, *A Collection of Hymns from the Best Authors, adapted both for Public and Family Worship*. The book was first used at West Nile Street chapel on 20 November 1814. An eleventh edition appeared in 1846. The collection contained 647 hymns and doxologies. It was not, however, of great merit.

The second creative hymnologist in Scottish Congregationalism was William Lindsay Alexander, the greatest name in the classical period of the denomination's history.[1] To his other gifts bequeathed to the Church he added that of hymnody. His *Selection of Hymns for Public Worship in Christian Churches*, first published in 1849, was the best collection so far privately compiled. It was commonly called *The Augustine Hymn Book*, and contained 553 hymns and doxologies. Various changes were made in the

---

The other four hymns were added in a later edition:
> O how good the hallow'd union.
> Whence the sounds of plaintive wailing.
> See the Sun of Truth arise.
> Christ of all my hopes the ground.

[1] See 1 of present chapter.

second [1858], and subsequent editions, the fifth edition of 1872 containing 616 hymns, doxologies and anthems. Of the hymns in the first edition seven were original and three others translations by Dr. Alexander himself.[1]

As we should expect his own compositions have a strong theological content. But Alexander also was the possessor of considerable poetic ability and, what is more important in a hymnist, of an architectonic sense. His compositions usually have form, and their thought progresses in an orderly manner to a definite goal. Witness this one on 'Christ—the Brother' (No. 153),

When Thou, O Lord, didst come
From Thy bright throne on high,
To serve and suffer in our room
Thou laidst Thy glory by.

Though in the form of God
Equal with His Thy claim,
As we partake of flesh and blood
Thou didst partake the same.

And now that Thou art gone
To that blest world above,
A Brother's name Thou still dost own,
And bidst us prove Thy love.

Saviour, what love is Thine!
How boundless and how free.
Give us to feel its power divine,
And yield up all for Thee.

In the sphere of hymn translation Alexander excelled. Verbal brevity and delicacy characterised his work in this *genre*. His translation of a hymn to the Trinity by Ambrose is especially striking,

[1] Original hymns:
From distant corners of the land (514).
God of all, we bow before Thee (259).
God of grace and love, the Father (196).
Hallelujah, note of gladness (546).
Saviour, by whom the guilty live (506).
Spirit of power and truth and love (184).
When Thou, O Lord, didst come (153).

Translations:
Bright and blessed Three in One (195).
Redeemer, when Thy work was done (90).
Thrice holy and thrice potent God (198).

Bright and blessed Three in One,
Unity supreme, alone.
While from us the daylight parts,
Pour Thy light into our hearts.

Thee when breaks the morning ray—
Thee when evening shuts the day—
Thee we call on suppliant knee,
Offering endless thanks to Thee.

Alexander's hymn 'Composed for the Anniversary Meetings of the Congregational Union' which runs,

From distant corners of our land
Behold us, Lord, before Thee stand

used to be sung frequently in the fraternal gatherings of the Congregational churches in Scotland. It was the one hymn of Alexander's included, in a truncated form, in the one and only *Scottish Congregational Hymnal*, published soon after the union of the two denominations in 1896. This hymn, we venture to suggest, might be used to advantage at the Annual Assemblies of our own day and age. Indeed Dr. Alexander deserves better treatment at the hands of present day hymnal compilers than he has received.

The last and greatest influence on nineteenth-century Scottish Congregational hymnology, and indeed on the whole field of its worship, was John Hunter, the world-renowned minister of Trinity Church, Glasgow. His *Devotional Services* perhaps did more to raise the standard of Nonconformist worship throughout Britain than any other single influence. The shining ideal of his ministry, he never wearied of saying, was to produce 'a worshipful Church'. To contribute to the fuller realisation of that end he prepared in 1889 a hymn-book for his Glasgow congregation, called *Hymns of Faith and Life*, and in 1895 he issued a new edition of it, carefully revised and much enlarged, and arranged on the basis of the Christian Year. In the preface to the first edition of *Hymns of Faith and Life* Hunter's aims are clearly enunciated, 'In preparing this book I have carefully tried to avoid hymns written to express scholastic and sectarian interpretations of the Christian facts and truths. The hymns most suitable for common worship are those which give expression to the fundamental experiences and persuasions of the soul, and to the largest and simplest aspects of Christian faith and life; whose statements are

so undogmatic and comprehensive that they are not restricted by
private interpretation, but may be sung by the devout and
thoughtful without any strain to the mind and conscience. I have
also sought to avoid hymns unreal, exaggerated, and sensuous in
their sentiment and language. . . . The Christian conception of the
Kingdom of God, as existing now and here, and of the essential
divineness of the present life, has determined the selection of many
hymns.'

Hunter's hymn-book provoked violent criticism from conservative and orthodox circles. But it served as a pioneer work in
widening the *social* horizons of the Church. Moreover, it introduced into insular and orthodox quarters the work of a group of
American hymn-writers who wrote some of the best hymns with
humanistic content of the last century—F. L. Hosmer, Samuel
Longfellow, W. C. Gannett, and J. G. Whittier. Hunter's religious,
rather than narrower theological, interest allowed him, in his
choice of material, to draw freely—too freely his critics considered
—from the minor poets of the century—Jean Ingelow, George
Macdonald, Stopford Brooke, and others. He did in fact cast his
net so widely as to enmesh a hymn from the pen of the Scottish
national bard,

> O Thou unknown, Almighty Cause
> Of all my hope and fear!
> In whose dread presence, ere an hour,
> Perhaps I must appear! . . .
> (Hymn 235)

Hunter's pioneer work sponsored not a few hymns which have
since become popular, for example J. A. Symond's 'These things
shall be!' His book contained also several anonymous compositions,
written by Hunter himself. Amongst these are two quatrains entitled 'Dream and Deed' included as hymn 263,

> Dear Master, in whose life I see
> All that I would but fail to be,
> Let Thy clear light for ever shine
> To shame and guide this life of mine.
>
> Though what I dream, and what I do,
> In my weak days are always two;
> Help me, oppressed by things undone,
> O Thou whose deeds and dreams were one!

The Methodist Hymn Book (1933), *Songs of Praise* (1951), and
Congregational Praise (1951) all include this devotional gem from
Hunter's pen.

In 1899, extending still further the frontiers of his reform of public worship, Hunter published a contribution to a much neglected children's hymnody, *Prayer and Praise for Children.* This too was printed for use in Trinity Church.

In addition to the above triad of hymnologists of distinction, Scottish Congregationalism in the century under review produced three other significant collections of hymns. C. H. Bateman, the minister of Hope Park Church, Edinburgh, and the author of the well-known children's hymn 'Come, children, join to sing', published, in 1846, *The Congregational Psalmist; or, a Selection of Psalms and Hymns specially adapted for the use of the Congregational churches of Scotland.* Seven years later S. T. Porter, pastor of Bath Street Church, Glasgow, edited and issued *A Selection of Hymns, chiefly Watts's for use in Public Christian Worship.* The book contained 800 hymns. In 1861 appeared *Hymns and Passages of Scripture for Divine Worship Selected and arranged by John Hutchison.* The compiler was minister of Canmore Street Church, Dunfermline, 1859-65. This was a commendable collection, with 479 hymns, 16 doxologies, 51 Scripture passages, and 5 ancient hymns.

Whilst these compilations and those by Wardlaw, Alexander, and Hunter were used by the churches of which their editors were pastors, and perhaps by a few other congregations, the churches of the Congregational order in Scotland generally remained conservative in their attitude to public praise, with a strong leaning towards the use of *The Psalms of David in Metre.* This predilection is illustrated in the case of the church at Perth. Robert Little, an English Congregationalist, was minister there from 1802 to 1806. A bitter quarrel was provoked when he expressed dissatisfaction with the Scottish Psalter as being unfit for use in Christian worship, and suggested that it should be replaced with his own *Abridgement of Watts' Psalms and Hymns, with Corrections.* Each side of the congregation, in the ensuing dispute, was adamant in its opposition to the other, and the parties abused each other in terms unworthy of members of a Christian church. However, Little was determined to have his way, and his opponents were equally determined that they should have theirs. In the end the innovating pastor carried the majority of the congregation with him, and at a meeting held on 22 February 1804, seven members were solemnly excommunicated from the church.

There was a like animosity in the Scottish Congregational churches to the use of an organ in church worship.[1] In January 1856 while the new building of Elgin Place Church, Glasgow, was under construction, a proposal was made at a church meeting that 'the propriety of introducing an organ to lead the psalmody' be considered, but on account of the strong measure of dissent elicited, it was withdrawn. The proposal was again brought forward in March 1865, when it was discussed at two church meetings. Considerable feeling emerged in the course of the proceedings. One of the arguments of those who supported the proposal was the familiar one that for the sake of the young people, the innovation should not be opposed, else they might leave for churches where more brightness characterised the service. A conservative stalwart replied with a dissertation on the text 'Do thyself no harm: we are all here'. Another pointed out that at the annunciation to the shepherds by the heavenly choir at Bethlehem, no instruments were employed, surely a time of all others when their use might have been expected were they really an aid to spiritual praise. At a point when some heat was engendered, and the emotional mercury was still rising, a worthy deacon interjected, in pawky Doric, 'Mr. Chairman, I think we've had aneuch o't', an expression that at once restored all to good humour. The proposal to introduce the organ was formally agreed to with thirty-five dissentients.

A similar attitude to organ accompaniment to public praise is found in the annals of Augustine Church, Edinburgh. For nearly twenty years Dr. Alexander had advocated the introduction of an organ into the church, which aim was not accomplished till October 1863. When he first began to speak to his congregation on this subject there were some who decidedly objected to the practice he was so zealous to introduce. One of Dr. Alexander's best stories was of two interviews he had with one of these objectors. Seated in his vestry between Services one Sunday, the doctor heard a knock at the door, which was slowly opened by a well-known 'character', a member of the church, who, putting no more than his head within the room, said in wrathful tones, 'Doctor, I hear ye want to bring an organ into the kirk. Noo, I just want to tell ye, if she comes in, I'll tak' a stick an' brak her!' whereupon the head was withdrawn, and the door was shut with a

[1] The first organ to be used in Scottish Presbyterian or Congregational churches was probably in North Dundas Street E.U. Church, Glasgow, 1851.

bang. About a year after this fierce gesture of defiance, the same member came to his minister in the vestry, and, in a very different mood, asked if he might have a little conversation. 'Dae ye mind, Doctor', he asked, 'aboot a year ago I said to ye that if ye brought an organ into the kirk I wad tak' a stick an' brak' her? Weel, I want to tell ye I have changed my mind on the subject. Ye see, I gaed to see my son in Birmingham a short time ago, an' on Sabbath I gaed wi' him to Mr. Jeems's Kirk, where my son has a seat.[1] Ye ken, I had aye a great admiration for Mr. Jeems, and expectit a great treat in hearin' him preach. I hadna been lang in my seat when I heard a great bum-bummin' and then the organ began to play: I hadna expectit that, and so I startit up, determined I wadna sit and hear sic desecration in the hoose o' God. But reflectin' a wee, I sat doon, thinkin' maybe I was rash, and then I concluded to sit still for several reasons. First, I didna want my son to think shame o' his auld faither, if I made a steer and gaed oot. Secondly, I didna want to lose Mr. Jeems's sermon, though I didna expect muckle good even frae him, aifter the organ. And, thirdly, I thocht it was just possible I micht be wrang. So I concluded to sit still, an' protest in my ain conscience. I got some quieter in my mind when Mr. Jeems cam' in—he was sic a fine sauntly-lookin' man. Then he gaed oot the hymn, an' the organ began bum-bummin' again, and the congregation stood up to sing, but I determined to keep my seat, an' let them bum awa' wi' their organ.   But they sang sae heartily that before they had finished I began to think it micht be real praise aifter a'. Then Mr. Jeems gaed a gran' prayer, an' put a' thochts o' the organ oot o' my head. When the second singing cam' on I was in sic a fine frame o' mind that I stood up wi' the rest, though I wadna sing. Then cam' the sermon—and sic a sermon! It was gran', gran'! When the next hymn cam' on, I just thocht that if a holy man like Mr. Jeems could see nae hairm in the organ, I wasna gaun to haud oot against him, an' sic as he. An' I sang the hymn wi' a' my heart, an' I really thocht it was a' the better o' the organ. So, Doctor, if ye bring an organ into the kirk, I'll sae naethin' against her!' The long-awaited instrument was duly installed on 23 October 1863 at a large meeting in Augustine Church. Dr. Alexander's church ultimately reached the distinction of being 'the best sung congregation'—a rather singular expression—in Edinburgh.

[1] John Angell James, minister of Carrs Lane Congregational Church, Birmingham.

From the middle of the century most of the churches which had departed from the use of the metrical psalms as the entire content of public praise, adopted one or other of the hymnals produced by the Congregational Union of England and Wales: mainly *The New Congregational Hymn Book* (1859); and the *Congregational Church Hymnal*, edited by G. S. Barrett (1877). On the amalgamation of the E.U. and the Congregational Union of Scotland in 1896, the necessity for a new hymn-book was raised and discussed on several occasions. At the Annual Meeting of 1902 it was moved that a supplement of eighty hymns be added to future editions of the erstwhile *Evangelical Union Hymnal*, and that the resulting compilation be used as the official hymn-book of the Congregational Union.

During the first fifty years of the present century most of the Congregational churches adopted hymn-books of English provenance. *The Congregational Hymnary* (1916) is gradually being replaced, in the town churches at least, by *Congregational Praise* (1951) which, by reason of a strong Scottish representation on its editorial committee, has included some of the best things in Scotland's psalmodic tradition, as well as from the pens of Scottish Congregational hymn-writers.

L

PART FIVE

THE UNION OF 1896

CHAPTER XIV

HOW THE TWAIN BECAME ONE

I

FOR many years the Congregational and Evangelical Unions, because of theological differences, and consequent ecclesiastical and personal tensions, some of which have already been mentioned, were alienated, and had little intercourse with each other. However, in the course of time it became evident that churches and ministers alike on both sides were disposed to regard each other with more friendly feelings than in former times, recognising the fact that they belonged to one body of Independent churches, and that their similarities were greater than their differences. This change of heart was due to several causes. The men who had been leaders in the divisive movements of earlier years were now dead. Their places had been taken by younger ministers of the churches, who did not attach the same importance to the points of dispute that had separated their fathers. In regard to the preaching of a full and free Gospel the churches of the two sections of Independents were now practically at one. A change had taken place, too, in the attitude of the members of the churches of both bodies. They had no longer the same interest in discussing doctrinal grounds of difference between Calvinists and 'Morisonians'. Besides the more liberal tendencies in the thought and conduct of the age, which have been alluded to in a previous chapter, encouraged the rapprochement of the two religious bodies.

Although the feeling in favour of a closer approach to each other had often been expressed by individual ministers and members, it was not until 1867 that any formal indication of it was given. In that year there appeared a correspondence in the *Christian News* in which ministers of both denominations strongly advocated union. The proposal, however, was strenuously opposed by several correspondents on the Evangelical Union side, and notably by the editor of that periodical, and it became evident that the time was not yet ripe for any overt action. Nevertheless discussion of an unofficial character continued, for we find the Western Association of Congregational Ministers considering a paper on the subject in March 1877. They noted the similarities between the two bodies. Both were Voluntaries, Independents, and generally Congregational in their practice; both admitted members on the same conditions; both repudiated human confessions of faith, and were more or less in agreement about doctrine.[1] The advantages of union were considered to be: economy in man-power and money; more effectual evangelism; and the possibility of church extension over a much wider area. At the Annual Meeting of the Congregational Union in that year [1877], moreover, the movement towards union took a practical and official form by the appointment of David Russell, the minister of Eglinton Street Church, as a delegate to the Evangelical Union Conference. The following year the good feeling of the Congregationalists was reciprocated by their friends in the E.U. camp, when they nominated Fergus Ferguson, the distinguished minister of Montrose Street Church, to represent them at the Annual Meeting of the Congregational Union. From that time there continued to be a yearly exchange of delegates from both bodies of churches, until their ultimate union in 1896.

In May 1881 the following comment on the Annual Meetings of the Congregational Union appeared in the *Aberdeen Free Press*: 'How near the two Unions are to one another was strikingly shown in Aberdeen not long ago when Dr. Fairbairn was taken from the pastorate of an E.U. church in this city to fill the responsible office of Principal of an Independent College. It may be said that there is no great object to be served by the inclusion of two sets of churches under such a loose confederacy as either of the existing Unions. The Unions, however, admittedly serve a highly useful purpose within their own well defined limits, and to maintain them as two when one would suffice seems to be neither valuable nor desirable.' That same year Bailie Maxwell, representing the Congregationalists at the Evangelical Union Conference, expressed the view that, whereas there were some few unimportant points of disagreement between the two bodies, their points of agreement were numerous and fundamental. He hoped the time was not far ahead when the two Unions would see their way clear to amalgamate. In the following year [1882], much the same thing was said from the E.U. side by Robert Finlay, minister of Perth E.U. Church, who was delegate at the Annual Meeting of the Con-

[1] A. C. Ashcroft, 'The Pros and Cons of the 1896 Union', *The Scottish Congregationalist*, September 1956, p. 197.

gregational Union.[1] And so the discussion went on both at unofficial and official levels.

In 1884 James Stark, the scholarly minister of Belmont Street
Church, Aberdeen, was the delegate from the Congregational
Union to the E.U. Conference. In his address he urged that the
continued division of the two denominations was pointless and
needless. The Evangelical Unionists thereupon attempted to set
up a Committee, but the motion was defeated at the instigation of
William Adamson, pastor of Buccleuch E.U. Church, Edinburgh,
who objected that the Congregationalists were no nearer accepting
the 'three universalities'.

Nevertheless real progress was made in this movement towards
union when at the Annual Meeting of the Congregational Union in
1885 a favourable reception was given to a paper at the Conference
of Scottish Congregationalists on 'Union between the Churches of
the Evangelical Union and Congregational Union'. The discussion
which followed resulted in the adoption of a resolution instructing
the committee to consider by what means fellowship and practical
co-operation could be promoted between the two sections of
churches, and also to make inquiries of the Evangelical Union on
the whole subject of union. At the same time the deacons of the
Congregational churches attending the meetings took action on
the same lines, and appointed a committee to confer with the
office-bearers of the Evangelical Union churches, and to endeavour
to ascertain whether a feeling in favour of union existed in that
body, and if so to take what steps might be deemed necessary to
promote the same. Accordingly, a joint meeting of the office-
bearers of both denominations was held in April 1886, with the
result that a resolution was passed to the effect that it was desirable
that a union should take place, and a committee was appointed to
consider matters of detail in connection with the proposal.

The Committee met in February 1887, and, as the result of its
deliberations, it was agreed to ask each of the churches of both
Unions to state:

(1) whether it was in favour of the proposed union;
(2) whether it approved of the proposed draft of union sub-
    mitted; and
(3) whether it had any suggestions to make on the whole
    subject.

[1] A. C. Ashcroft, *ibid.*

The draft basis was briefly, (1) that the name of the united body should be the Congregational Evangelical Union; (2) that there should be no more limited doctrinal basis of union than the great principles of the evangelical faith and the congregational independence of the churches, and that special doctrines as to the mode of Divine operations or the Divine methods by which the blessings of the Gospel are conveyed to men, ought to be left to individuals and churches, and have no place as a doctrinal formula or theological creed in the constitution of any association of Independent churches; (3) that the united denominations should continue their efforts for the suppression of intemperance; and (4) that in regard to finance there should be one common purse, but that the details of this question be left for future consideration and adjustment.

Sixty of the churches of the Congregational Union and 43 of the E.U. churches, sent replies to the queries. To the first, whether they were in favour of the proposed union, 38 C.U. and 30 E.U. churches sent favourable replies; 3 C.U. churches replied in the negative, 29 C.U. sent no reply. To the second, whether they approved of the proposed draft of union, 30 C.U. churches sent a favourable reply, 2 C.U. churches were unfavourable and 28 sent no reply, and 2 E.U. churches replied in the negative and 27 E.U. churches sent no replies.

From the response made by the churches, and the remarks made by some of them, it was evident that they were not prepared to deal with the question of union in a decided way, owing, as was stated by some, to the lack of sufficient information, and of time for careful consideration.

A further step in the direction of fraternal co-operation was taken at the C.U. Annual Meeting of 1887, when the committee was instructed to consider the desirability of holding a conference between the committees of both Unions, for the purpose of arriving at an understanding with regard to the appointment of agencies and the distribution of funds, so as to avoid unnecessary waste of resources, and also to arrange with the committee of the Evangelical Union for holding such a conference. Moreover, in 1887 the matter was taken up by the Evangelical Union ministers of Glasgow, apparently under the leadership of Fergus Ferguson, who suggested that the E.U. Conference should receive suggestions submitted by a joint-meeting of the ministers of the two unions. The suggestions were relevant to finance, inter-church co-operation and the elucidation of the strength or otherwise of the desire expressed by some Congregationalists for union with the Congregational Union of England and Wales. This aroused a great deal of opposition, in which the lead was taken by William Adamson the staunch temperance advocate who again was much concerned about the 'three universalities', and the temperance question.[1] The outcome was that at the Conference of the Evangelical Union in 1888 a resolution was passed to the effect that 'in view of the differences of opinion which the discussion at last Conference brought to light, and of the interests of our churches, the commission unanimously recommend that discussion of the subject of union with the Congregational Unionists should not in the meantime be further prosecuted.

During the next four years the subject of union did not cease to engage the attention of many of the ministers and members of both Unions, and was repeatedly discussed in the pages of *The Scottish Congregationalist* and the *Christian News*. At length, at the Annual Meeting of the Congregational Union in 1892, a resolution was adopted to appoint a special committee for the following four purposes: '1. To inquire thoroughly whether the proposed union is desirable and practicable; 2. to invite the Conference of the Evangelical Union to appoint a similar committee to confer with the committee of this Union on the matters aforesaid; 3. if the result of the said Conference be in favour of union, said committee of this Union shall carefully, and, if possible, in conference with said committee of the Evangelical Union, study the steps which must be taken towards the consummation of the proposed union; and 4. that a report from said committee shall be presented at next Annual Meetings of the Congregational Union.'

At the next Annual Meeting the special committee reported that the proposed union was deemed desirable; that in order to discover its practicability eight members had considered and reported on doctrinal, legal, financial, institutional, ecclesiastical, and temperance questions in their bearings on the matter of union; and that the committee had invited the Conference of the Evangelical Union to appoint a similar committee to confer with them on the whole subject of union, which that body had cordially agreed to do. The committee further reported that a meeting of the joint-committee of both Unions met on 27 March 1893, and after friendly discussion it was agreed to appoint a sub-committee consisting of members of both committees, to draw up a short

[1] A. C. Ashcroft, *ibid*.

doctrinal statement for the consideration of a future conference of the two committees, and another sub-committee to investigate the institutions of both bodies. It was also agreed to adopt the following resolution: 'This meeting of joint-committees of the Evangelical Union and Congregational Union finds that the proposed union is desirable, and expressed its confidence that all practical difficulties can, with care and patience, be overcome.' The report was adopted unanimously, and the special committee reappointed to study further the details of a scheme of union, in conjunction with a similar committee of the Evangelical Union, and report. At this meeting a statement was submitted by several ministers of the Congregational Union in the west of Scotland to the effect that, without in any way expressing disapproval of union, they wished it to be recorded that, in the event of the amalgamation interfering with the financial position of their churches, they held themselves free to take such action as the circumstances might warrant.

At the Annual Meeting of the Congregational Union in 1894 a further report of the joint-committee was presented and adopted, and the committee reappointed with special instructions to co-operate with the members of the Evangelical Union in joint-committee in preparing an Explanatory Statement based on the report of the joint-committee of all the facts bearing on the proposed union, and the form it should take; to send a copy of the same to each church of the Congregational Union, with the request to transmit a statement of its views on the whole question of the advisability of union; to arrange in joint-committee for the calling of a joint meeting of the pastors and delegates of the Congregational Union and the Evangelical Union to consider the reports of the churches; to obtain the opinion of legal counsel as to the relations of the Congregational churches to the Ferguson Bequest Fund in the event of union; and to consult with the trustees of the Ferguson Bequest Fund as to any possible effect union might have on the administration of their trust in relation to the Congregational churches now on the list of beneficiaries. The Explanatory Statement was prepared by the joint committee, and 35,000 copies were issued to the churches for distribution among the members. Along with the Statement there was sent a request to each church to return answers to the following queries: '1. Are you in favour of the union of the churches of the Congregational and Evangelical Unions? 2. If so, do you approve of the union of the churches on the basis of the recommendations of the joint-committee now submitted to you? 3. If you answer the foregoing queries affirmatively, do you leave to the annual meetings of the two Unions the work of adopting the constitution, and of taking all steps requisite for the consummation of the union?'

A joint meeting of the two Unions was held in Glasgow in March 1895, to which scrutineers, who had been appointed to examine the replies of the churches, reported as follows:

CONGREGATIONAL UNION CHURCHES

					Queries	
				1	2	3
67 churches have voted				Yes	Yes	Yes
2 ,, ,, ,,				Yes	Yes	—
2 ,, ,, ,,				Yes	No	No
1 ,, ,, ,,				Yes	—	Yes
1 ,, ,, ,,				Yes	—	—
1 ,, ,, ,,				Yes	No	—
11 ,, ,, ,,				No	—	—
8 ,, ,, ,, for delay						
3 ,, remain neutral						
—						
96						

EVANGELICAL UNION CHURCHES

				Queries	
		1	2	3	
60 churches have voted		Yes	Yes	Yes	
5 ,, ,, ,,		Yes	No	—	
20 ,, ,, ,,		No	—	—	
2 ,, not formally connected have voted		Yes	Yes	Yes	
1 ,, not formally connected remains neutral					
2 ,, have not voted					
—					
90					

The joint meeting adopted resolutions to the effect that it found that the replies of the churches to the queries addressed to them indicated that the judgment and desire of the majority of these churches were in favour of union; that, inasmuch as it was extremely desirable that the judgment of the churches should be unanimous, the meeting appointed a committee to address a letter to, or otherwise approach, each of the churches voting either against the union or for delay of proceedings, requesting them to reconsider their decision, and expressing the hope that they would see their way to fall in with the decision of the majority of the churches; that it be recommended to the next annual meetings of the Congregational and Evangelical Unions respectively to take all further steps required for the accomplishment of the union; and that special resolutions should be adopted by both annual meetings to this effect.

The Annual Meeting of the Congregational Union was held in Dundee in April 1895, when the foregoing resolutions, together with the replies of the churches, were submitted. After considerable discussion a resolution was unanimously adopted to the effect that, though the judgment and desire of a large majority of the churches of both Unions had been expressed in favour of union, yet, in view of the extreme desirability of arriving at a more nearly unanimous vote, the supporters of union had consented to the postponement of any vote thereon until the next annual meeting of the Congregational Union, on condition that the opponents of union then present pledged themselves to accept individually, and to use their utmost efforts to induce the churches they represented to accept, whatever decision might then be arrived at by the majority of the meeting; and that the minority having so pledged themselves, the meeting resolved to delay the discussion of the report until April 1896. At the same time a committee was appointed to continue consultation and conference with a similar committee of the Evangelical Union, and to take such action as might appear desirable in connection with the proposed union until next meeting. Owing to this decision, the Evangelical Union Conference also delayed further action.

The consummation of these long and fitful deliberations came in April 1896 when the Annual Meeting of the Congregational Union was held in the Christian Institute in Glasgow. The galleries were crowded with visitors—shrewd men of commerce, Presbyterian clerics, and a host of E.U. pastors—who had foregathered to watch the fray in the arena below. The following resolution was proposed by James Ross, historian and ecclesiastical statesman, the man who did most from the Congregational side to further the rapprochement of the two denominations:

'That in view of the judgment of the Congregational Union given in favour of the union of the two denominations, and in view of the resolutions adopted at last meeting of the Conference of the Evangelical Union, expressing its willingness, in name of the churches thereof, to unite with the churches of the Congregational

Union under the name and designation of "The Congregational Union of Scotland, comprising the Evangelical Union and the Congregational Union as existing in 1895", and on the basis of a constitution indicated in the Explanatory Statement sent last year to the churches of both denominations, provided a resolution of similar import be accepted by the Congregational Union, this meeting, in name and by authority of the churches of the Congregational Union expressed in the answer to the third of the queries submitted to the churches, hereby agrees to unite with the churches of the Evangelical Union, under the name and designation, and on the basis of a constitution aforesaid.' It was agreed that the following rider to the resolution should be made: 'At the same time, in so agreeing to unite with the churches of the Evangelical Union, this meeting, desiring to emphasise what is contained in the Explanatory Statement, declares that the Union shall not be in any sense an ecclesiastical court or corporation claiming to interfere with the independence of the churches, and that under the new constitution no theological test shall be imposed on any member, minister, or professor, the Bible alone being regarded as the standard of faith and life.'

The motion in favour of union was appropriately seconded by John Hunter of Trinity Church, Glasgow, whose name as an exponent of liberal Christianity sounded forth to the ends of the earth. Thereupon followed a battle of argument. The most eloquent of the opponents of the resolution was the Welshman, Eynon Davies, minister of Elgin Place Church, Glasgow. There were others who believed that the time for organic union was not opportune. Professor John Glaister, of Glasgow University, representing this view, moved an amendment in the following terms:

'That the report of the Congregational Union committee on union with the Evangelical Union be received, and the committee cordially thanked for their labours and diligence in carrying out the remit of the annual meeting of 1894; and that this meeting, while prepared to welcome heartily and to co-operate in any measure which will promote and increase fraternal intercourse between the churches of the Unions, such (1) as more frequent and more general pulpit exchanges by the ministers of the Unions, (2) by a working mutual eligibility to pulpit charges, (3) by the formation of a council appointed with powers, and which would be equally represented by and representative of both Unions for the purpose of promoting Christian work, the preventing of overlapping, and the planting of new churches, and (4) by means adapted to produce closer fellowship generally, hereby resolves not to proceed further in the meantime with the proposals for union on the basis proposed by the joint-committee.'

At long last the vote was taken and the result announced—for union 144; against 33. Twenty members did not vote. The result of the vote having been intimated, fourteen ministers and delegates protested, declaring that the carrying out of the resolution would involve a secession from the Congregational Union and that on such secession taking place the remaining churches of the Union would alone belong to and represent the Congregational Union of Scotland, and have right to its whole assets and estate, powers and privileges. A resolution was then passed declaring the motion carried to be the finding of the meeting.

It was agreed that a joint meeting of the two unions should be held in October following for the purpose of declaring the union, and that the meeting of the Congregational Union should be adjourned until the day appointed for such joint meeting. It was also agreed that the committees of the Congregational Union should hold office only and until the amalgamation of the two Unions, and that thereafter the affairs of the united body should be conducted in accordance with resolutions passed by the joint meeting for that purpose. Thereafter the following resolution was adopted: 'That in agreeing to enter into union with the Evangelical Union this meeting declares that, notwithstanding such union, the churches of the Congregational Union of Scotland do not mean or intend that there shall be any departure from the principles or objects for which this Union has hitherto existed, and that for all essential purposes it will continue to exist under the proposed designation as if no such union of the denominations had taken place.' A final resolution was adopted, to the effect that, in the first instance, the following branches of the work be taken up by the Union under the care of committees: A General Committee to manage the general business of the Union, a Church-aid Committee, a Home Mission Committee, a Foreign Mission Committee, a Sunday School or Welfare of Youth Committee, a Publications Committee, and a Temperance Committee; that provision be made for including the following branches of work among the operations of the Union at as early a date as may be found practicable: the Theological Hall, Ministers' Widows' Fund, Ministers' Provident Fund, and Chapel Building and Manse Fund; and that a committee be appointed to act conjointly with the committee appointed by the Evangelical Union for the purpose of entering into communication with the last-named societies, with the view of arranging for their inclusion in the Union at as early a date as possible, preparing a draft constitution to be submitted to the joint meeting of the two Unions, and to take such action as might be needful to carry out the foregoing resolutions.

On 1 October 1896, the adjourned meeting of the Congregational Union was held in Glasgow, and the various resolutions and draft constitutions, which were subsequently submitted to the joint meeting of the two unions on the same day, were considered. The first resolution (see below) was carried by a vote of 93 to 17. Fourteen pastors and delegates thereupon protested in terms similar to those of the protest made at the annual meeting in April. The other resolutions were unanimously adopted. The draft constitution was also considered, and several amendments having been made, it was agreed to submit the draft as amended to the joint meeting.

On the same date and at the same place a meeting of the Evangelical Union was held, at which the following resolution was proposed: 'That in view of the judgment of the churches of the Evangelical Union and Congregational Union in favour of the union of the two denominations, and in view of the decision of last annual Conference, this Conference, as representing the Evangelical Union churches, hereby resolves to unite with the churches of the Congregational Union under the name and designation of "The Congregational Union of Scotland, comprising the Evangelical Union and the Congregational Union as existing at 1896".' An amendment was proposed in the following terms: 'That, while recognising the duty of co-operation with all Christians in common Christian work, and of cultivating the spirit of brotherliness and unity in relation to other denominations, Conference is solemnly convinced that in the meantime the Evangelical Union can best promote the Master's work by keeping intact its distinctive denominational position.' The motion was carried by 140 votes to 14 for the amendment.

Following up this Conference of the Evangelical Union, the united assemblies met on Monday afternoon, 1 October 1896, about 300 ministers and delegates in all, for declaration of union between the two denominations. William Taylor presided and the historic motion was proposed by James Ross:

'That the churches of the Congregational and Evangelical Unions having expressed their readiness to unite, and the annual meetings of both Unions having passed resolutions to the same effect this meeting of pastors and delegates declares the union of the churches of the two bodies, as from 1st January 1897, under the name and designation of "The Congregational Union of Scotland, comprising the Evangelical Union and the Congregational Union as existing at 1896".'

Fittingly the motion was seconded by George Gladstone, the Nestor of the Evangelical Union who had laboured untiringly for the amalgamation of the two unions, and passed amid much enthusiasm, the audience afterwards singing the Doxology.

A second resolution, in the following terms, was also unanimously adopted: 'That this meeting desires to express its fervent gratitude to the great Head of the Church for the spirit of brotherly love and unity in His service which, it believes, has moved the churches to seek this union, and which it gratefully recognises as the operation of His gracious Spirit among them, and prays that the union may be for the greater glory of God.' The draft constitution, as amended by the Conference of the Evangelical Union and the adjourned meeting of the Congregational Union and also by the joint meeting of both, was then adopted. Other resolutions were adopted giving directions as to the business and other arrangements required to give effect to the decisions of the joint meeting.

II

A comparison between the principles involved and the methods adopted in connection with the union of sections of Congregational churches on the one hand and Presbyterian churches on the other would bring into prominence the distinctive features of Congregational and Presbyterian polity. It may be sufficient, however, to point out that the ultimate decision in vitrue of which the churches of the Congregational and Evangelical Unions became united was given by the members of the churches; that church functionaries, whether ministers or other office-bearers, had their share in the negotiations and ultimate decision, not in any official capacity, but as members of the churches; and that the various committees and the Union meetings of both bodies had no determining voice in the proceedings, but acted only in an executive capacity in carrying out the instructions of the members of the churches and giving effect to their decision.

On the first day of January 1897, the union of the two bodies came into operation, and all the office-bearers previously appointed assumed office.[1]

Dating from the exchange of fraternal greetings on the past of both Unions by the appearance of David Russell as delegate from the Congregational Union to the Evangelical Union in 1877, twenty years elapsed from the first approach towards union until its consummation in 1897. The first attempt of a more practical kind in the direction of union was made in 1885, when the office-bearers of the churches arranged to obtain an expression of the mind of the churches in regard to union; so that about twelve years were spent in conference and negotiation with a view to union.

At an early stage of the proceedings in connection with union the question of its practical bearing on the pecuniary interests of certain churches was forced upon the attention of the Congregational Union by the action of the pastors of churches in the west of Scotland, who (at the annual meeting in 1893) claimed freedom to take such action as the circumstances might warrant, in the event of the union taking place. This was the beginning of a movement which resulted in troublesome litigation in the Court of Session, which continued over some years. By the will of the late John Ferguson of Cairnbrock, Ayrshire, who died in 1856, he directed his trustees to hold the residue of his estate as a permanent fund 'and to apply the annual income for the maintenance and promotion of religious ordinances and education and missionary operations, in the first instance, in the county of Ayr, Stewartry of Kirkcudbright, and counties of Wigton, Lanark, Renfrew, and Dumbarton, and thereafter, if the trustees think fit, in any other counties in Scotland', by means of payments for the erection or support of churches and schools (other than parish churches and parish schools) belonging to quoad sacra churches connected with the Established Church of Scotland, the Free and United Presbyterian churches, the Reformed Presbyterian Church and the 'Congregational or Independent Church', in supplement of the

---

[1] In the foregoing account the steps taken by the Congregational Union are given in more detail than those of the Evangelical Union, in order to avoid needless repetition. The ultimate results of the proceedings of both Unions were the same, but in the case of the Congregational Union they were more complicated and protracted than in the case of the Evangelical Union, and are therefore narrated at greater length.

M

stipends of the ministers of these churches. Grants to Congregational ministers in the counties mentioned had been given by the
trustees of the Fund from the beginning of its operations, in their
belief that the Congregational Union represented the body of
churches designated 'The Congregational or Independent Church'
of Ferguson's Will. When, however, the union of that Union with
the Evangelical Union began to be considered the questions arose
as to whether the new body of united churches would come under
the designation of 'The Congregational or Independent Church',
and so be entitled to claim grants from the Fund, and whether the
union might not endanger the interests of the churches already
aided by the Fund. These, along with other questions bearing on
the legal position of the enlarged Union, were submitted to counsel
for their opinion, when the subject of the *name* of the proposed
Union was under consideration. The answers given were such as
encouraged the Congregational Union to proceed with the negotiations for union. The protest and claim of the minority of the
Annual Meeting of the Congregational Union in 1896 to be the
'Congregational Union of Scotland', while that designation was
also given to the united body which came into existence in January
1897, created a difficulty for the trustees of the Ferguson Bequest
Fund, and accordingly they presented a petition to the Court of
Session on 25 June 1897, asking 'which congregations ought the
petitioners to recognise as eligible to participate in the benefits of
the Ferguson Bequest Fund provided to the Congregational or
Independent Church in Scotland', and also asking the guidance
of the Court. Pending the decision of the Court they requested its
authority to continue the payments to each of the twenty-two
Congregational churches in receipt of grants at the date of the
union of the two bodies. Answers were given on behalf of 'The
Congregational Union of Scotland, comprising the Evangelical
Union and the Congregational Union as existing at 1896', to the
effect that 'congregations or churches composing the existing
Congregational Union, including alike those attached to the Congregational Union as existing prior to 1897, and those originally
attached to the Evangelical Union, or at all events the former,
together with the dissenting or protesting Congregational churches,
are now "the Congregational or Independent Church" in the sense
of the Ferguson Bequest, and are all alike eligible as recipients of
the benefits thereof'. Answers were also given by the minority
party, to the effect that 'the churches of the Congregational order

which have amalgamated with the Evangelical Union have lost
the distinctive quality of Independent churches', inasmuch as
'they had not only united themselves with churches professing a
creed which, besides, was at variance with the religious belief of
many Congregationalists, but they had themselves adopted as a
basis of union with these churches a form of creed which was set
forth in the constitution of the new body', 'that the constitution of
the new body differed essentially from that of the Congregational
Union as it existed prior to 1896', and that 'the churches which
had amalgamated had lost all title to be considered as "The
Congregational or Independent Church" in the sense of John
Ferguson's settlement'. The minority party did not object to the
continuance of grants from the fund until the settlement of the
questions raised, but they submitted that none of the churches of
the enlarged Union was entitled to participate in the funds of the
trust. The majority party, on the other hand, stated in their
answers that they did not desire that any of the dissenting minority
should be excluded from the benefits of the trust.

On 19 October 1897, the case came before the Court of Session
(First Division), and after a short debate, and the counsel for the
Congregational Union having stated that he did not know that the
petition and answers contained all the facts that the Court should
have before it, a proof of the averments of the parties was ordered
to be taken by Lord Adam. On 5 and 6 July 1898, Lord Adam
heard proof. The witnesses examined were, on behalf of the
Congregational Union, James Ross, George Gladstone, A. F.
Simpson, and W. H. Davison; and on behalf of the minority party
John Glaister and John Graham. The evidence ranged over a
variety of subjects, but, from the amount of attention which it
received, it was evident that the 'Prefatory Note' to the constitution
of the enlarged Union was felt to be the crucial point, so far as
the minority party were concerned. This note was recommended
by the joint-committee of the two bodies to be prefixed to the
constitution of the Union, as 'explicative of the purposes of the
Union and of the chief grounds on which the union of the churches
has been sought'. In the note it is stated that 'while the churches
now entering into union do not require formal subscription or
assent to a doctrinal creed from their ministers or members; they
have been moved and encouraged to seek this union, (1) in the
belief that they agree in holding as the ground and condition of
church-membership confession of personal faith in Jesus Christ

as Saviour and Lord; (2) in the desire to hold fellowship one with another in the worship and service of God; and (3) in order to achieve effective co-operation in extending the kingdom of God and proclaiming the Gospel of Jesus Christ, through whose person and work as God incarnate, and the saving and sanctifying grace of God the Holy Spirit, God the Father, in His love, has made provision for and is seeking the salvation of all men'. The last clause of the note, as had been frankly acknowledged in the course of the negotiations for union, was inserted in order to meet the desire of the Evangelical Union churches for some record being made of the special doctrinal testimony they had given concerning the universality of the Divine love, especially in regard to the work of the Holy Spirit. It was found that the Congregational churches had no objections to such a statement being made, seeing they were in virtual agreement with the Evangelical Union churches on this head, and this agreement had been confirmed by the vote they gave in favour of union and of the constitution and prefatory note recommended by the joint-committee of both bodies. The chief contention of the witnesses for the minority party was that the last clause of the note was a 'form of Creed', while the witnesses for the Congregational Union held that it was simply a statement of the general belief of the churches of the Union, but that it was not a creed in the sense that assent or subscription to it was or could be required on the part of any minister or church in order to connection with the Union.

In May 1898, a 'Joint Print of Documents' admitted by both parties was drawn up and submitted to the Court. This contained extracts from church title-deeds, and various other documents bearing on the use made of statements of doctrine by Congregational churches. In September 1898, the 'proof' taken before Lord Adam was also printed, along with an appendix containing various supplementary documents similar to those given in the 'Joint Print'.

On 9 and 10 November 1898, the case was debated before the First Division of the Court of Session—the judges being the Lord President (Robertson), Lord Kinnear, Lord Adam, and Lord Maclaren. The counsel for the enlarged Union were Charles Guthrie, Q.C., and Mr. Craigie; and for the minority party, Mr. Ure, M.P., and Mr. Maclure. The case was taken ad avizandum, and on 6 December 1898, the following interlocutor was pronounced by the Court:

'Find, in answer to the question submitted by the petition, that the congregations which the petitioners are entitled to recognise as eligible to participate in the benefits of the Ferguson Bequest provided to "The Congregational or Independent Church in Scotland" are the congregations which prior to 1896 belonged to the Congregational Union of Scotland, irrespective of whether they have or have not joined the new Union called the "Congregational Union of Scotland, comprising the Evangelical Union and the Congregational Union as existing at 1896", and also the congregations which have been formed since the formation of the last-mentioned Union, and belong to that Union; but that the congregations which before the formation of the last-mentioned Union belonged to the Evangelical Union are not so eligible, and decern; appoint the expenses of all parties in the proceedings . . . to be paid out of the trust funds.'

It is pleasant to record that almost all the minority churches on both sides came into the newly-constituted Union in the first decade of the twentieth century.[1] And, unlike some other unions which have taken place in Scotland, there are no remnants of these dissenting churches still extant.

III

We close this part of our narrative with an observation that is most necessary, if one wishes to understand Scottish Congregationalism. Historically discerned, it is a double dissent from Presbyterianism rather than a system of church-government adopted for its own sake. Had the early Congregationalists found sympathetic support for their views regarding the membership of the church as a spiritual fellowship, and had church-courts not interfered with their efforts by means of lay-preachers and others to carry on the work of evangelisation, Congregationalism would not have found a footing in Scotland at the time it did. So far indeed from adopting the Congregational system in its entirety, the early Congregationalists shed so only much of their former

---

[1] Ward Chapel, Dundee, resumed fellowship with the Union in 1899, Emmanuel, Wardlaw, Great Hamilton Street, Elgin Place, Parkhead Churches, Glasgow; Elder Park Street Church, Govan; Sannox Church, Arran; Albany Street, Edinburgh; Wishaw E.U. Church; Thorniehall E.U. Church, Selkirk all between 1900 and 1903. East Fountainbridge E.U. Church, Edinburgh joined the U.P. Church in 1899, and Bank Street, Falkirk joined that body in 1898.

Presbyterianism as proved a hindrance to them in their desire to realise their new ideas of church life. For a considerable time after their origin many of the churches retained Presbyterian usages, and many of them to this day (to the puzzlement and embarrassment of their friends from over the Border) have some of the elements of Presbyterianism in their practice. These hybrid features of Scottish Congregationalism were heightened by the Union of 1896. The churches with an E.U. provenance brought with them more decided Presbyterian elements, such as the 'Session', consisting of elders, whose functions were substantially identical with those of the same class of officials in Presbyterian churches, the only distinctive feature of their Congregationalism being that in all important matters the sanction of the congregation is required to give effect to their decisions.

Even in regard to 'Church-courts' there would have been no objection taken to them either by the early Congregationalists or the Morisonians if they had been only 'consultative meetings rather than legislative and executive assemblies'. The leaders of the Evangelical Union had no special objection to church-courts as such, but only to the abuse of their functions. When James Morison in proposing the formation of the Evangelical Union said, 'Let all ecclesiastical cases be thrown back into the several churches, and chained there by the sound and scriptural principle of Congregationalism',[1] it was not because he was opposed to church-courts as ecclesiastical institutions, but because he knew that men were so liable to abuse them, as he had himself discovered, that he and those who acted with him sought what they considered the more excellent way of Congregationalism.

[1] W. Adamson, *Life of Principal Morison*, p. 237.

PART SIX

OUR DAY AND AGE, 1900-1958

CHAPTER XV

THE CENTRAL FUND

I

CONGREGATIONAL history in the period 1900 to 1958, which we now seek to trace and evaluate, unfolded itself against a background of social revolution that coloured the life of the denomination, even altering its structure in some significant ways. From a personal viewpoint Scottish Congregational history in this half-century (with a slight alteration of Carlyle's definition of general history) was 'the essence of *a few* biographies'. It is perhaps too soon to evaluate the work of its thinkers and leaders, and to set them by the side of the Congregational Fathers of whom we have written, and who have been finally delineated by the criticism of time. Whereas we shall have cause to appraise the labours of not a few men and women who have impressed their learning, spirituality or administrative gifts on the malleable life of the denomination,[1] our main standpoint will be that the holders of the Union secretaryship, elected by the churches themselves, have revealed at one and the same time the social tensions and pressures of the hour, and God's word to it. For this reason their tenures of office will for the most part form the framework of the unavoidably discontinuous story which we now endeavour to tell.

The appointment of Charles Richardson, a distinguished student of James Morison's, and minister of Montrose Street Church, Glasgow, as Union secretary in 1900, was a decision momentous and wise. He was the man for the hour, and indeed for the age, for he was to occupy this responsible office, with only a short break, for thirty-five years, the first eighteen as a part-time appointment. The facts that the 'Union office' in this initial period was his own manse study, and the appointment an honorary one, point alike to the zeal and heroism of the man, and the denomination's rudimentary organisation.

Richardson brought to his task a warm pastoral sense and a flair for administration. In the prosecution of his duties over so

---

[1] Cf. Chapter XVIII for a supreme illustration of this fact.

long a period he acquired an unmatched knowledge of ecclesiastical life and affairs. Moreover, his own experience and love of the pastoral office constrained him to enter intimately into the life of all the churches great and small, near and afar, making him the brother and confidant of their ministers, especially in times of stress and difficulty. It was this passion for the ministry that made him one of the chief protagonists in the inauguration of the Central Fund.

The democratic side of his character was perhaps expressed by the fact that he never wore clerical dress. For ecclesiastical millinery of any kind he had no liking. He was the least ecclesiastical in appearance of all ecclesiastics. But an ecclesiastic he doubtless was and in this half-century Scottish Congregationalism's greatest. Inside the denomination he had an air of authority that could not be disputed; outside of it, he won the regard of all Church leaders.

Though a man of ecumenical vision he was, most likely because of his Evangelical Union provenance, a keen champion of the Scottishness of the Congregational churches. And it was he, more than any leader before or since his time, who gave Scottish Congregationalism a place on the ecclesiastical map.

Richardson's task in this century was not dissimilar, in general outline, to Greville Ewing's at the beginning of the last. As Ewing was called to be the architect of the old denomination, so Richardson was raised up to be the main architect of the new. Both leaders saw clearly that a church can be no better and stronger than its ministry. It was largely from this insight that the Congregational Union of Scotland evolved, as we have seen. From a like intuition in the early years of Richardson's secretaryship, issued the Central Fund, that other fount of blessing, which ever since has been a source of strength to weakened churches and their economically embarrassed ministers. More than any other material agency it kept the denomination in fair health during the economic troubles at the end of the First World War and in the aftermath of industrial unrest. Many a church in the far north, or on the fringes of the densely-populated industrial belts in the south, would have had to close its doors but for the encouragement and sustenance that the Union was able to disburse through the Central Fund.

At the Annual Meeting of the Union held in Glasgow in May 1910, an appeal was made by the Church Aid Committee to bring the deserts and needs of the aided churches sympathetically before the denomination. Clearly something required to be done to put the Fund on a sounder foundation. At Greenock, where the Annual Meeting assembled in April 1913, D. S. Smith of Dundee, in supporting the Church Aid Report, urged the Union to inaugurate a Central Fund, such as had been promoted by the Congregational Union of England and Wales. The motion was cordially adopted.

Before anything could be done in this connection the First World War began with drastic effects upon the life and work of the churches. Richardson's Report to the Annual Meeting of May 1915, in Edinburgh makes sad but not uninspiring reading: 'Since the last Annual Meeting our beloved land has been passing through a grave crisis which has tried the faith and resources of all classes. It is, however, a matter of devout thankfulness that during this time our churches have sustained their spiritual power and usefulness.' Returns from the churches reveal, the report continues, that nearly 4,000 men were already serving in the Forces, and five of their ministers were officiating as chaplains. By the close of 1915 7,000 men had gone from the churches and four ministers. This was the commencement of a long period of austerity and testing throughout the entire denomination.

The situation would have been considerably more distressing than it was but for Richardson's hopeful leadership. From the first he kept his fingers on the spiritual pulse of the churches. By constant visitation he kept them in good heart, and his own zeal and courage did much to heal their hurts.

In this work of shepherding and strengthening the churches, he had the much blest co-operation of George Wolfe of Bathgate, Union treasurer, 1912-24. Wolfe realised more than most laymen of his day the absolute necessity for the churches to keep near to one another and in closest touch with the Union. He preached his doctrine during his visitations of the churches, and taught them by precept and example that finance, commonly considered a terrestrial concern, might have celestial implications as well. It is heartening to notice that in 1915, despite the financial stringency caused by the War, the contributions from the Churches to Union funds had increased and indeed credit balances appeared in the General Purposes and Church Aid Funds.

Largely through Wolfe's advice, the District Committees that were now coming into greater prominence, were fired with a vital concern for the churches under their supervision. From this time onwards systematic visitation of the congregations within their respective areas was realised as a primary need.

At the Annual Meeting held in Glasgow in 1914 the District Committees were advised to discuss the advisability and possibility of launching a Central Fund. The following year, in the shadow of war, the majority of the districts intimated to the Annual Meeting in Edinburgh that they thought that the exigencies of the hour precluded the possibility of setting out with any degree of success on such a venture. In the teeth of much opposition, Andrew Ritchie, the minister of Dundas Street Church, Glasgow, thereupon moved 'That a Committee be appointed, consisting of five members from each of the three chief Committees of the Union, to consider the question of forming a Central Fund, and to report to next Assembly Meeting'. D. F. Chalmers seconded, and the motion was carried.

The Committee, who had in the meantime inquired into the ministerial stipends paid by churches of the Union likely to be affected by the proposed Fund, urged upon the Annual Meeting at Glasgow, in 1916, the necessity of doing something on a large scale to augment those meagre stipends. Their investigation brought to light some hard and bleak facts. The pastors of seventy of the 180 churches then in the Union were receiving, including grants, not more than £150 per year, while thirty-four of the seventy were 'maintaining' themselves and their dependants on an annual income of less than £110! The Committee thought that, all things considered, the Union would require to raise an additional £1,200 a year to provide a minimum stipend of £120 a year, and £1,500 to ensure a £150 minimum. The Committee's main recommendations were that a Capital Central Fund should be organised, amounting to £30,000 or £40,000, its chief object being the securing of a minimum stipend for pastors, and that the scheme should be inaugurated at the end of the War.[1]

It speaks volumes for the courage and devotion of the Union leaders in that dark hour of Church and nation, and for the concern and consecration of the Congregational churches themselves that the scheme was adopted there and then, without tarrying for more auspicious days, and at its higher target of £40,000. Indeed at the Annual Meeting of 1917 in Glasgow, the

---

[1] Other objects of the proposed Fund were Church Aid, Home Missions, and Church Extension.

chairman for that year, Provost John Orr of Airdrie, intimated that £5,450 had been already donated or promised to the Fund.

Charles Richardson put his spiritual and indeed his physical energy at the disposal of the scheme from the beginning. His business and administrative gifts were completely dedicated to its success. So were those of George Wolfe and John Orr and other laymen, who regarded their time and substance as a trust from the Lord, and who were prime movers in the heroic venture. For heroic it was to work with hope of raising £40,000 for religious purposes under the shadow of war. The secretary or his coadjutors visited all the District Committees, and within them local committees were formed to promote the interests of the Fund in the churches. Central meetings in support of the Fund were held in Edinburgh, Glasgow, Greenock, Motherwell, Dundee, and Aberdeen. Everywhere interest was aroused.

It should not be forgotten that one reason for the success of the venture was that almost from its start it enjoyed the enthusiastic support of the Women's Union. It was doubtless, in a time of war, this feminine support that led the congregations in increasing numbers to take up the scheme with growing heartiness.

By 1918, when the Annual Meeting assembled in Dundee, under the chairmanship of Thomas Templeton, £17,000 had been subscribed or promised. And on the strength of the scheme's success bonuses were voted to pastors, and it was further agreed, with George Wolfe's warm advocacy, that the Capital sum of the Central Fund aimed at should be increased to £50,000.

At this momentous hour, Charles Richardson after nearly nineteen years of strenuous and wise leadership of the churches and the Union retired from the office of Union secretary. Much of the onus of the Central Fund venture had rested on his shoulders, and not a little of the glory of its success crowned his head. With his demission from office, difficulties began to raise their heads, some of them due to the new social situation caused by the cessation of hostilities in 1918.

II

A. G. B. Sivewright succeeded him as secretary and held the office till 1924. Sivewright had entered the ministry at St. Andrews in 1896. He had held pastorates in Oban and Partick. He was a courteous and genial man and brought to his duties as Union secretary a keen interest in the local churches and a conscientious and thorough regard for his work. The beginning of his appointment synchronised with the close of the War. With the signing of the Armistice in November 1918 the country was troubled with a spirit of unrest that only increased with the years. The general note of disillusionment is detected in Sivewright's official utterances. Addressing the 1920 Annual Meeting of the Union, in presenting the Report of the General Committee he said: 'the times through which we are passing are still as troubled as the years of war, and the Church cannot but be profoundly affected by the general state of affairs. We cannot be blind to the fact that many of the high hopes entertained from both war and peace have not yet been realised.'

The Congregational churches had their own share of the difficulties arising out of post-war unrest. Around them and sometimes within them, there was an ominous lowering of moral tone. In some quarters there was a regrettable failure on the part of congregations to attract and hold the returned servicemen. And more ominous still, in the light of subsequent history, there was a falling away of the working and artisan class from association with the churches, because of their dissatisfaction with the general attitude of the Church towards political and industrial questions.

It is no surprise, therefore, that the response to the Central Fund was now small and slow. A little less than £4,000 was added between the Annual Meetings of 1919 and 1920. At the latter date the Fund stood at a little over £32,000. We find the Committee expressing the feeling 'that the majority of our churches do not realise their responsibility'. The need for the Fund was never more apparent, as the cost of living was ever soaring. Emotionally charged voices were raised in concern for financially harassed pastors. How they managed the domestic budget in those days must be left to the imagination. We read that 'little is heard of actual deprivation, because the spirit of independence has elected to suffer in silence. That is heroic, but it is a reproach to the churches.'

It was proposed at the Annual Meeting in Edinburgh in 1920 that Richardson, who was still secretary of the Central Fund Committee, should, with the consent of his congregation, be set free for three or four months to visit the churches in order to stimulate interest in the Fund. But the times were out of joint. The black clouds thickened over the social life of the nation and the churches. The 1921 Annual Meeting at Dundee gathered under threatening clouds. 'It is only too apparent', Sivewright told the delegates, 'that the bright millennial expectations of many hearts have been antedated.' Since last year there had been an unprecedented trade depression. There were also uncontestable evidences of a serious recrudescence of crime, aggravated undoubtedly by the encroachments of the liquor trade. 'Whether we look at home or abroad', the secretary said, 'we are painfully aware that men have not learned and laid hold of the Life that is life indeed.'

The grim situation constituted a fresh demand on the loyalty of the churches to the Lord Jesus Christ, and on their intelligence, zeal and endurance. Strength would come, the hopeful in Israel believed, as the churches struggled, for through struggle life and growth alike emerge.

The time was opportune for such a message, for the Congregational churches had now reached the quarter century of their enlarged fellowship, and the hour for a fresh summons to consecration had come. In Ward Chapel on 5 May 1921, Thomas Templeton, sensing the opportunity the situation offered, moved 'That the Congregational Union of Scotland do record its gratitude to God for His blessing on the first 25 years of its united existence. It would reconsecrate itself to His service in the Gospel of its Lord and Master Jesus Christ. It would urge all its members to re-think and ratify the principles and events that led to its formation, to celebrate in deep inward fashion the approaching semi-jubilee anniversary, and resolve that triumphant completion, and perhaps extension, of the Central Fund would be the best memorial of the occasion.'

At the 1922 Annual Meeting of the Union in Glasgow the Central Fund was still £10,000 short of its target. It was decided to keep the Fund open until the £50,000 target at least had been reached. Definite regulations as to the character and administration of the Fund were now drawn up, and Charles Richardson was warmly thanked for his long and arduous labours as secretary of its Committee. It is, however, sad to narrate that the other zealous protagonist of the Fund and its aims, George Wolfe, did not live to see the dream of its completion realised. After serving the Union as treasurer with singular devotion for twelve years, he died in 1924. It was in large measure due to his heroic championship of the scheme that a more adequate minimum stipend was

enjoyed by the pastors of the Congregational churches. It is well
that Congregationalists, who possess a blest tradition of the importance of the lay apostolate, should remember the ministry
of men of the calibre of George Wolfe. Moulded in early years by
the preaching of A. M. Fairbairn, Wolfe sought Christian service
in his own church in Bathgate eventually becoming its president.
But his greatest work was done as Union treasurer. During the
twelve years of his tenure of office he learned to know the churches
of the Union inside out and loved his way into their hearts. In the
interest of the Central Fund he travelled from Kirkwall to Garlieston and from Oban to Peterhead, and everywhere he won the
affection of the people. He was a brother beloved by every aided
pastor. His ready wit, his ever-flowing humour, the twinkle in his
eye when about to crack a joke, the warm humanity of the man
never failed to secure the attention of his audience. There are still
a few amongst us who can picture him on the floor of the Assembly
or on its platform making earnest and effective appeals on behalf
of the smaller churches and their ministers, pleading with his
contemporaries to take their part in the task of helping them to
bear their burdens.

Wolfe's successor in the Union treasurership was Henry
Brown, an office-bearer of Morningside Church, Edinburgh. He
held the office from 1924 to 1933, and under his capable direction,
assisted by a steady improvement in the nation's industry and
commerce, the £50,000 Central Fund target was reached by the
time of the 1926 Assembly. In the Central Fund Committee
Report of that year we read: 'The Committee has been gratified
by the testimonies borne by ministers, and especially by their
wives, to the benefit received from the Central Fund. It is well
worth all the effort and sacrifice involved in building up the Fund
to know that burdens have been made lighter for those who receive
too little remuneration for their labours on behalf of the Kingdom
of God.'

III

The story of the inauguration, progress, and completion of the
Central Fund has occupied the focus of our attention so far in this
chapter. It is now necessary in the interest of a full and true record
of matters pertaining to the life and work of the Congregational
churches to retrace our steps and consider some other things.

At the commencement of the century the traditional fervour for evangelism, which had characterised both streams of Scottish Congregationalism, manifested itself in campaigns up and down the country. Evangelistic work was carried out in Wick, Aberdeen, Newburgh, Kilmarnock, and Edinburgh. The names of missioners were sent to churches desirous of guidance in the conduct of revival services. The recommendation of the Annual Meeting of 1901 that a simultaneous mission be held in February of the following year met with the support of all ten districts of the Union, from Lerwick and Kirkwall in the northern isles to Annan, Langholm, and Hawick in the south. In the city of Aberdeen, where the mission was more thoroughly organised, all the churches participated with great blessing. In all, about seventy churches of the Union engaged directly, and quite a number indirectly in what contemporaries regarded as 'the greatest of our evangelistic efforts'.

In Greenock in 1902-3 Congregational, Baptist, and Methodist churches conducted an exceedingly successful mission under the leadership of Gipsy Smith.

In the period under review new churches were formed at Ayr (Morison, 1897), Glasgow (Broomhill, 1897), Dunoon (1899), Pollokshields, Glasgow (1899), Greenock (Martyrs, 1899), Rutherglen (1901), Clydebank (Radnor Park, 1908), Cathcart, Glasgow (1911), Brisby Memorial, Glasgow (1916), and Rosyth (1918). Among the churches closed between 1900 and 1924 were Stuartfield, Victoria Place (Wick), John Street (Aberdeen), Sidney Hall (Edinburgh), Regent Street (Rutherglen), Ebenezer (Glasgow), Keptie Street (Arbroath), Harray and Sandwick (Shetland), Culsalmond, Greenlaw, Overnewton (Glasgow), John Street (Montrose), Dunoon, Manse Street (Fraserburgh), Great Hamilton Street (Glasgow), Murray Place (Stirling), Brechin, and Lindsay Street (Dundee).[1]

As the century progressed an increased interest in and concern about social problems is clearly noticeable, especially in the years immediately following the close of the First World War. Prior to that time the Temperance question, important as it was and still is, had been in the focus of the attention of the Churches, to the exclusion of other clamant problems of men and women in their social relations. However, as early as 1908, we learn that two members of the Temperance Committee of the Union had attended

[1] Cf. *A Chronicle of the Churches*, below.

a National Conference on Sweated Industries. In that year, it is significant to notice, some members of the same committee expressed the opinion that the scope of the Temperance Committee's work should be extended 'so as to include generally the questions of public morality'. At the Annual Meeting of the Union, in Aberdeen in 1908, the designation of the Committee was altered to 'Temperance and Public Morals Committee'.[1]

Without soft-pedalling their hatred of the drink traffic and ceasing to exert their utmost energies to wipe it out, or at least alleviate its evils, the newly-named Committee directed their attention also to political questions and social welfare. For instance, in 1912, they deprecated the action of the War office in sanctioning gun practice and the movement of troops on Sundays, and called upon the Government to issue orders for the discontinuance of these practices. On another occasion the members of the churches were urged to do all in their power to secure a worthier observance of the Lord's Day. The shape of things to come is discernible in the Committee's concern about the growing encroachments upon the sanctity of the Lord's Day. Sunday concerts, 'cinematograph exhibitions', and other public amusements are some of the things that are criticised. On another occasion it is the opium traffic in India and the Chinese ports that comes to their notice, and the Government is admonished 'to restrict the growth of the opium poppy'. At the Annual Meeting of the Union in Glasgow in 1917, we hear the Committee expressing its horror at the bombardment of open towns in Germany by allied aircraft. They urged the British Government 'to maintain the proud, clean record of Britain by ceasing to imitate the practices of the enemy'.

From 1918 onwards the Committee is concerned with post-war problems of one sort or another. From now on industrial questions come to the fore. Equitable distribution of the fruits of industry; easier access to the land; better housing; education for life and not just for work—are some of the questions that arise for discussion. At the Annual Meeting of 1919 in Glasgow the Committee put forward a notice of motion with a very modern ring about it: 'The Congregational Union of Scotland declares its profound sympathy with all just social aspirations; and pleads that in the effort to readjust industrial conditions, employers and employees will be prepared to sacrifice vested interests wherever these stand in the way of legitimate social evolution.' In 1920, it is 'the moral laxity

[1] Now designated 'Temperance and Social Questions Committee'.

revealed in recent Divorce-Court proceedings' that fills the Committee with concern. They maintain 'that the well-being of the family and of society depends upon the sanctification of this vital relationship'.

Sufficient has been written to show that in the years 1900-24 there was evinced in the work of the Congregational churches and their Union an increasing interest in and concern for the problems of man in a society disrupted by war, an interest and concern that were to grow infinitely greater in the second quarter of the century, as is symbolised in a further change in the designation of this Committee to 'Temperance and *Social Questions*'.[1] Indeed in 1921, when the Annual Meeting met in Dundee, and again in 1922 at the Glasgow Annual Meeting, it was thought by some that the gradual widening of the Committee's interests had concealed its traditional concern with Temperance, and that, partly as a result, the churches were responding slowly to any appeal for aggressive temperance work. The estimated national expenditure on alcoholic beverages in 1924 was £315,858,000 yet only two Temperance societies had been formed during that year in the churches of the Union, despite the gravity of the situation.

During this quarter century we notice the beginnings of two emphases characteristic of more recent times—the granting to women of official status in the churches and Union, and the realisation of the paramount importance of work with youth. The first was hardly thought of in the last century. Femininity never graced the courts of the church. It was a thing unheard of to see a lady delegate at the Annual Meeting of the Union. In 1903 a male delegate had the temerity to ask whether it was in order that churches should be represented by lady delegates at the Annual Meeting! But at least one of the Congregational Fathers away back in the masculine nineties, the liberal John Hunter, had predicted that 'the twentieth century is going to be the woman's century'. And so in fact it has proved to be. The use of the bicycle in the late years of the nineteenth and the granting of the franchise to women after the First World War in the twentieth century, combined with other factors to bring about the emancipation of women. Today women have an assured place in industry and all the professions.

---

[1] See the excellent *Report on the Moral Use of Power and Freedom in a Planned Society*, as an example of the realistic and penetrating work that this Committee was later to do. This Report was presented to the Autumn Assembly at Motherwell in September 1950.

The first sign of this growing significance of women in the Scottish Congregational churches was in 1917 when, at the Annual Meeting in Glasgow, the womenfolk of the churches were invited to co-operate in the raising of the Central Fund. 'Believing that valuable help can be given by the women of the churches,' the Central Fund Report reads, 'we invite the co-operation of the Women's Union in furthering the scheme.' The wisdom of that move was attested by the fact that by 1920 the women had raised £600 by a special effort for the Central Fund, in addition to their customary support for the venture through the local churches.

In the previous year (1919) the gradual process by which women have won *official* status in the churches and the Union may be said to have begun, when at the Annual Meeting in Glasgow the Women's Union was recognised as an integral part of the Congregational Union of Scotland.[1] Thereupon a Committee was appointed 'to promote fellowship and co-operation among the women of the churches and to enlist the interest and energies of young women in the manifold forms of present-day Church and social service'. One of the members of the original Committee, Mrs. Fitzgerald of Glasgow, addressed the Autumnal Conference of the Union, held in School Wynd Church, Paisley, in October 1921, on 'Women's Place in the Church'.

The second emphasis, that on youth[2] was, in a sense, a return, with added knowledge and organised vigour, to primitive Congregational tradition. Christian education had occupied a prominent place in the evangelistic programme of the Haldanes. Furthermore at the end of the nineteenth century J. R. Sandilands, one of the denomination's most devoted laymen, had said in his address from the presidential chair of the Union, that one of the specific duties of the Congregational churches was the welfare of youth. He considered that the churches devoted too much of their attention to the adult needs of their congregations. He, therefore, called them to a loyalty to a tradition they were in peril of neglecting.

But it was war with its aftermath of social unrest and relaxing of moral standards that recalled the Congregational churches to put a stronger emphasis on youth in their programmes and policies.

---

[1] Cf. M. H. E. Calder, *Year Book of the Congregational Union of Scotland, 1919-1920*, and 'Scottish Congregational Women', *The Scottish Congregationalist*, and Chapter XII, II, and Chapter XVI, IV, below.

[2] Cf. Chapter XVIII, IV, below.

Throughout the quarter-century the Sunday schools were on the whole numerically strong and in a thriving condition. But the exigencies of war and wartime industry depleted the Bible classes. The bad effects of war service and the laxity of moral control in the home, with parents serving either in the forces or industry, rendered it imperative to stress the religious instruction of Youth.

At the Annual Meeting of the Union in Glasgow in 1917 a request was received from the Church of Scotland's General Assembly's Committee on the Religious Instruction of Youth, that delegates be appointed by the Congregational Union to attend a Conference of representatives of the Scottish churches to consider the religious instruction of youth in schools.

Round about this time, we find the Sunday School and Welfare of Youth Committee of the Congregational Union 'deploring the growing menace to the young life, especially in our large cities, of the automatic gaming machine in ice-cream saloons and other places of child resort'. The Committee attributed to the introduction of these machines, designed to 'foster gambling and a spendthrift spirit' a large measure of the 'recent alarming increase of juvenile crime in all parts of the country'. It was felt, too, that Government action was imperatively called for 'to procure the removal of this aggravated form of temptation from the environment in which our children live'.

In this period practically all the churches in Scotland turned their attention to more scientific and imaginative methods of the teaching of religion in Sunday schools. There was a general feeling that the content and method of teaching usually adopted, in the light of modern advances in education, were alike outmoded. In October 1916 Sunday school workers in Edinburgh and Leith held a meeting in Augustine Congregational Church and listened to a paper given by G. Smissen, minister of the Congregational church at Annan, on 'Suggestions in Sunday school methods drawn from the War'. The Annual Meeting of the Union at Glasgow in 1917 included in its programme a Conference on Sunday School work, at which the leading speaker was Dr. Garvie, and his subject 'Lesson Grading in the Sabbath School'.

In the immediate post-war years in the churches, we notice, in addition to the customary meetings for youth, the emergence of a brave array of Y.P.U.s, Girls' Auxiliaries, Girl Guides, and Brownies, Boys' Brigade and Boys' Life Brigade Companies, and Boy Scout Troops.

Some other matters of interest strike the student of this period of Scottish Congregational history. In the early years of the century, the traditional friendly rapprochement of the Scottish Union and the Congregational Union of England and Wales plainly manifested itself. United Autumnal Meetings were held in Glasgow in September 1902, when the address from the chair was given by A. M. Fairbairn on the Education Bill. At a subsequent meeting of the Congregational Historical Society, James Stark of Aberdeen spoke on 'Historical Points of Contact between English and Scottish Congregationalism'.

In the last quarter of the nineteenth century the English churches had received from their Scottish brethren two of the most influential minds in the world of theology, Fairbairn and Forsyth. The latter has only quite recently been appreciated as the creative religious thinker he undoubtedly is.[1] South of the border Forsyth became the leading protagonist of orthodoxy in the New Theology movement which was an English, and only sporadically a Scottish phenomenon. In the twenty-five years of the present century under review, A. E. Garvie was called south in 1903 to the Chair of Ethics, Philosophy and Comparative Religion in Hackney and New College. England reciprocated, supplying the Scottish pulpits with men of spiritual fire and preaching gifts, like Ambrose Shepherd of Elgin Place Church, and teachers of real scholarship and deep spirituality, like A. T. Cadoux, minister of Broomhill Church, Glasgow.

There was a joint meeting of the English and Scottish Unions at Manchester in October 1901, and in September of the following year the Congregational Union of Scotland invited the sister Unions of England and Wales and of Ireland to meet in joint assembly in Glasgow. Thus A. M. Fairbairn's wish, expressed in 1896, to see British Congregationalists getting together was, in some measure, fulfilled. The General Committee Report of 1903 states: 'In arranging for these meetings the Committee looked forward with much hope and satisfaction to the realisation of a dream which had long been in the hearts of many of our brethren.'

During the Education controversy in the south, at the beginning of this century, the Congregational Union of Scotland expressed on more than one occasion its sympathy with the English Nonconformists and particularly with the Congregationalists in their resolute stand for efficient education and their just rights in

---

[1] Cf. H. Escott, *Peter Taylor Forsyth, Director of Souls*, pp. 3-33.

schools assisted out of public funds.[1] In fact the General Committee of the Union did appoint a Committee with powers to co-operate with their English brethren. At the Annual Meeting of the Union, in 1903, Robert Craig, presenting the Report of the Committee on the English Education Bill said: 'The discussions in Parliament were followed with much interest by your Committee through all the stages of the Bill until it became law, and their desire is that soon a better measure may take its place. By correspondence your Committee considered a form of petition which was published in *The Christian News*, with the request that the members of the churches who desired to protest against the injustice done to the Nonconformists might sign such a petition, and draw the attention of their Members of Parliament to the serious infringements of the rights of conscience.' Again, in 1908, when the Education Bill for England and Wales passed the Commons, the Scottish Congregationalists showed their concern for their brothers in the south and petitioned Parliament 'to secure a system of education which shall give equality of opportunity to all teachers, and equality of teaching to all scholars'.

In this connection, the Report of the Education Committee of 1908 reminded Scottish Congregationalists that the principle of religious equality had not yet been acknowledged as it ought to be in democratic Scotland. It is imperative, the Report continued, 'for members of Congregational churches to seek to be representatives of the citizens on the School Boards, in order that the rights of Congregational teachers and pupils may be respected and protected'. In reviewing other regions of the educational landscape, the Report recounted with gladness that in that very year (1908) action had been taken in the General Council of Glasgow University to secure that the academic chairs in all the faculties should be open to all competent teachers, so that in future Congregationalists, who cannot conscientiously subscribe to the Westminster Confession of Faith, may not be excluded by law. Nevertheless, the Committee thought that public attention needed to be drawn to the fact that certain restrictions of an invidious kind were still in force, restrictions which could not be removed except by Act of Parliament. Since the Universities are national and not denominational colleges, Congregationalists desired as citizens equal rights for all students and teachers. In national education they asked for nothing which they were not prepared to grant to all. Their claim,

[1] Cf. Albert Peel, *These Hundred Years*, pp. 362 ff.

which they backed up by strong words and hard work, was for religious equality in all educational institutions supported by the State, without respect of persons.

In the first twenty-five years of the twentieth century, especially in the years following the Armistice of 1918, there were glimmerings of an ecumenical vision, a vision that expanded to fill the thoughts of almost all Christian communions in the century's second quarter. The ravages of war at home and abroad compelled the churches to forget their historical and theological prejudices in the common task of sweetening the bitterness of social life, and releasing the tensions between the nations.[1] The Congregational Union of Scotland, along with other Protestant Communions, gave its wholehearted support to the principle of the League of Nations which had been approved by the Peace Conference in Paris in January 1919. A Resolution of the Annual Meeting of that year, in Dundee, expressed the view of all the churches: 'Convinced that the only security against the arbitrament of war in international disputes lies in the promotion of relationships expressive of the spirit and teaching of Jesus Christ, we agree to exert all our influence on behalf of the establishment of a League of Nations for the peace of the world, and urge the Government to make this a part of the peace settlement to be arranged.' Two years later, we find the leaders of all the Churches expressing their thankfulness that Christian people in Scotland, of all communions, were not deaf to the summons for succour from the famine-stricken areas of Europe and Asia Minor. But in the speeches of them all there is the note of regret that America is holding herself aloof from the League.

About this time a Scottish League of Nations Council was formed on which the Congregational churches had three representatives. Its main object was to quicken the Christian conscience of the land in international relations. Branches of the League of Nations Union were formed in all the congregations.

The conviction was slowly dawning in the soul of practically every Protestant communion in Scotland that only a united Church could help heal a divided world. At the Union Assembly Meeting in Aberdeen in 1923, H. Moffat Scott moved a special resolution that the Congregational churches offer their zealous support to the proposal to form a Scottish Churches' Council. By the time of the Dundee Assembly in May 1926 the Council had

[1] Cf. Chapter XVI, v, below.

been formed. It represented all the Scottish Protestant Churches, with one exception. Its main function was twofold: (1) to suggest when concerted action on questions of national importance, or moral, spiritual, and social problems is necessary, (2) to conduct inquiry on matters affecting the moral, spiritual and social conditions of the people. The Congregational churches were represented on the original committee by Robert Rae, Charles Richardson, H. Moffat Scott, and Henry Brown.

Thirty Scottish delegates attended the Third International Congregational Council held in Edinburgh in the summer of 1908, a fair number of whom were drawn from the Congregational churches. Five members of the Union addressed the Council. One of the subjects treated was 'The Witness of the Congregational and Free Churches'. Twelve Scottish Congregationalists attended the Fourth International Council held at Boston, U.S.A., in June 1920. On that occasion valuable contributions to the deliberations of the Council were made by Dr. Grieve on 'Current Problems of Christian Education', A. C. Hill, the eloquent minister of Elgin Place Church, Glasgow, on 'Continuing the Fight for Freedom', and Dr. W. L. Walker, a theologian of international repute, on 'The Spiritual Import of Congregationalism'.

CHAPTER XVI

THE TENDENCY TOWARDS CENTRALISATION

I

THE completion of the Central Fund in 1926 ended something like an heroic age in the history of the denomination since the union of 1896. In the quarter century, moreover, nearly all the Fathers, who as men in their prime had participated in that union, had passed to their rest and reward. Among them were William Adamson, George Gladstone, James Ross, Alex. Brown, William Taylor, James Stark, Kerr Anderson, great names and great souls. With the departure of these strongly independent minds who had tested their ecclesiastical principles in the fires of life, and found them, so they sincerely believed, to be absolute, a milder day was dawning, but a day of wider horizons.

This new era in Scottish Congregationalism may be said to have begun when Charles Richardson accepted full-time employment as the secretary of the Congregational Union in 1924. He remained in office till his death seventeen years later, in 1941. In this momentous period Richardson was elected president of the Union for a second time, received a doctorate in Divinity from Glasgow University, and was accepted by the National Church and the other Communions in Scotland as a great ecclesiastical leader and statesman. His name was sometimes linked in conversation and in the columns of the religious press with Dr. John White, a student contemporary of his at the University of Glasgow. He has been described also as the J. D. Jones of Scottish Congregationalism. Such encomiums were not out of place, for Richardson was the master builder of the denomination in the present half-century. More than any of his contemporaries he dovetailed the E.U. and C.U. elements in the Congregational Union together, and made the local congregations conscious of one another, assisting them in the creation of a pervasive feeling of interdependence. In the carrying out of this task he had, of course, the example of the closely-knit framework of the Church of Scotland, and his Evangelical Union origin did not render him critical of Church Courts as such. Furthermore, his second tenure of office as Union secretary coincided with a growing tendency towards greater centralisation in secular affairs and institutions.

For better or for worse the most obvious tendency in Scottish Congregationalism from 1924 onwards was the growth of a tighter organisation as a denomination.[1] It began with Richardson's full-time appointment as secretary in that year. It was continued in 1936 by the renting of a Union office at 92 Bath Street, Glasgow.[2] Whereas in 1900 the secretarial work of the Union had been done by a part-time official in his own house, in 1958 it occupied two or three full-time officials, and that with fewer churches to deal with, though with departments of government and local authorities who demanded to deal with a headquarters rather than with a local congregation. Furthermore, by a gradual process the duties of the Union Secretary were extended beyond the General Committee to several other committees, and this resulted in a certain concentration of activity into a narrower circle of people. Moreover, as we shall notice later on, with the large growth of inter-war building schemes in the cities a new conception of Church extension emerged. It was felt to be no longer possible to leave the building of new churches to the initiative of local groups, but that the Union as such should undertake the planting of churches in housing schemes, whether there was a local group in existence or not. Of the ten or so churches formed since 1900 seven were definitely formed as 'church extension schemes', and three were groups which had formed themselves, and these last all fall into the period 1901-11.[3] In all seven cases a fully organised church was 'laid down' with buildings and minister, built and maintained, in the first instance, by the Union, and with a minister appointed by the Union, although, be it said, accepted by the congregation when effectively formed.

A further illustration of this tendency towards centralisation is discernible in the growth and increasing power of the Settlements and Ministerial Recognition Committee, resulting in a careful grip on admission to the ministry, and ensuring a public avowal of responsibility to the Union in the approved form of Ordination questions as passed by the Annual Assembly of 1949, and the reiterated assertion of the place of the Union in ordination in the By-laws since 1951.[4]

[1] Cf. v in the present chapter.
[2] Later (in 1946) situated at 217 West George Street.
[3] Cf. *A Chronicle of the Churches*, below, for details, and Chapter XVIII, iii, below.   [4] This was resolved at the 1926 Assembly. Cf. *Year Book*.

It has been felt also that the creation of a new office of chairmanship by the Annual Assembly of 1945 tended towards the building of a central 'authority'. The multiplication of committees is a further example of the modern tendency towards centralisation.

It is outside the province of the historian (so some consider) to pass judgment one way or another on events and tendencies. But one can say as a statement of fact that the problem facing Scottish Congregationalism, as the second quarter of this century progressed, was to resolve the tension between the independence claimed in Christ's name by the local congregation and the responsibilities of interdependence within a Union. That will become increasingly the problem of Congregationalism in the modern world.

The social historian of a century hence, in reviewing the work of all the free churches in this period, will probably have to admit that some sort of centralisation, such as we have suggested developed within Congregationalism, was essential to keep the churches open, and in order that they might have more than a merely pious impact upon the society amid which they existed.[1]

II

The beginning of Richardson's second period of office as Union secretary was grim and dark enough in all conscience. True, the Central Fund had been safely gathered in, at least all except a moiety.[2] But the fields of industrial Scotland were black unto harvest. Emigration was fast emptying the glens and impoverishing the towns of some of the best Scottish stock. The gambling habit was demoralising both sexes. 'It was ruining personality, undermining home life, crippling industry and becoming one of the most prolific sources of crime ordinary and violent.' It was a deplorable fact (we read in a Report of the Temperance and Public Morals Committee) that the popular press had ceased to be 'the guide of the citizen and had become the organ of the book-maker'.

The General Strike of 1926 struck a mortal blow at the heart of industrial Scotland. Most of the Congregational churches were situated in the industrial belts and many of the workers in

---

[1] It is interesting to notice that as early as March 1923 Harry D. Bedford had written a plea in *The Scottish Congregationalist* for 'The Need for Denominational Organisation'.   [2] It was completed in 1925.

dockyard, factory, and mine were associated with them. These congregations were adversely affected. Losses in membership were caused by removals, and especially by emigration.

Edwin Muir in *Scottish Journey* draws a harrowing picture of the industrial west and of the bored workless men lolling at street corners. 'The effect of one, or two, or five, or ten years of waiting for work can be seen in their attitudes as they stand at the street corners; the very air seems empty round them, as if it had been drained of some essential property; they scarcely talk, and what they say seems hardly to break the silence: the strongest impression I received of Glasgow was one of silence. In the centre of the city people are still busy or seem to be so; but when one goes down the Clyde, to what used to be the busy shipbuilding quarter, there is hardly anything but this silence, which one would take to be the silence of a dead town if it were not for the numberless empty-looking groups of unemployed men standing about the pavements. I noticed that even the children seemed to make less noise than they used to do, as if silence had seized upon them too, or it may have been simply that they were insufficiently fed.'[1]

The industrial depression continued almost to the eve of the Second World War; and its effects were a blearing of moral distinctions, and a religious scepticism that shaded imperceptibly into atheism.[2] The newly-formed Scottish Churches Council set out in 1926 to investigate the Home Mission problem, hoping to formulate a scheme whereby the churches might find it possible to take common action. Their first Report revealed a state of things that staggered Christian leaders. 'The fact that 36 per cent of the total adult population, approximately 1,100,000 men and women of Scottish birth and of mainly Protestant ancestry are wholly non-churchgoing, and to that extent out of all living relation to the Faith, constitutes a challenge and a task which the churches cannot, and dare not, ignore.' Consecrated and energetic measures were demanded of all the churches. A more intensive culture of their spiritual life and their distinctive witness; a closer co-operation in local effort; a more sustained and intensified evangelism; an earnest call to their youth to Christian teaching in the educational system of the country—were some of the measures which were considered to be of paramount importance.

[1] Edwin Muir, *Scottish Journey*, pp. 138 ff. See also C. L. Mowat, *Britain between the Wars*, pp. 284 ff. and *passim*.
[2] Cf. G. S. Spinks (editor), *Religion in Britain since 1900*.

A few years later the churches, including the Congregational Union, were represented on the Northern Area Religious Advisory Council of the B.B.C. and also on the local Councils. Doubtless this new and ubiquitous organ of Christian propaganda aided the churches in their task of reaching the unchurched multitudes with the Gospel.

Under the guidance of Charles Richardson the policy of the Congregational Union followed this extra-denominational urge towards spiritual renewal in the local churches, and evangelism to those outside their fellowship. The District Committees were encouraged to take a more active interest in the congregations of their respective regions. The important lay element in these associations—the veritable life and breath of traditional Congregationalism[1]—under God's hand, worked wonders of grace in the churches, and gave inspired and practical leadership in a new Church Extension Movement of which we shall have more to say in the present and a later chapter of this book.[2]

The formation in the nineteen-twenties of Office-Bearers' Associations considerably strengthened the districts of the Union in their spiritual task. By 1933 these were to be found in Mid-Lanark, Glasgow, Dundee, Aberdeen, and border districts; but it was not until April 1935, at Glasgow, that the Office-Bearers' Federation was formed. Its chief aim was in complete alignment with the need of the time in Congregationalism: to increase the efficiency and spiritual influence of the laity, with the object of strengthening the individual churches in their task of evangelism.[3] Of its many interests and activities we have space only to mention two: namely, its emphasis on denominational propaganda, revealed in the arrangement of pilgrimages to places and sites of historical importance to Congregationalists, and its publication from time to time of Congregational literature. It is interesting to notice that it was the Office-Bearers' Federation that first requested that a new and up-to-date history of Scottish Congregationalism be produced, away back in 1941. The virtual founder of the movement was W. Stewart Smith, a son of the manse, and a most ardent supporter and apostle of Congregational principles and polity. Not a few leading personalities in Scottish life and affairs have

---

[1] Chapter XVIII, IV, last para. below.

[2] Cf. Chapter XVIII, III, below.

[3] Cf. *Year Book of the Congregational Union of Scotland, 1929-1930,* and J. M. Borthwick 'The Union's Debt to its Laymen', *The Scottish Congregationalist.*

been members of the Federation, men of intellectual and spiritual calibre like Ex-Lord Provost E. W. Watt, M.A., LL.D., J.P., Aberdeen; George Blatch, F.I.B., F.R.ECON.S., Glasgow; A. E. Walker, O.B.E., Aberdeen; James McLay, Glasgow; all of whom have been Presidents of the Union; and David Carruthers, Lockhart W. Hutson, O.B.E., F.R.I.B.A.; James Davidson, M.D.; J. M. Borthwick; J. R. Darling; Thomas Kemp, J.P., F.J.I.; George R. Green, M.A., C.A.; John McBryde, M.A., F.E.I.S., who have served the movement with wholehearted loyalty in other capacities.

The first move in the matter of church extension was made by the Glasgow District who, at the 1926 Assembly in that city, intimated their decision to establish a church in the Mosspark suburb of Glasgow. At the subsequent Assembly in Edinburgh the Report of the General Committee of the Union reminded the churches that an entirely new situation had been created all over the land by the new housing schemes. The District Committees were asked to rally to the opportunity that the situation offered, for it was one, the Report stated, on which the future vitality of the Union depended. The members of the Assembly were urged to take note that if Congregationalism was not adequately represented in the new districts which were rapidly springing up it would be considerably weakened in its life and witness. A Church Extension Committee was formed with representatives from the General, Home Mission, Central Fund, and Chapel Building and Manse Committees.

The Glasgow District was the first to respond in a practical manner to this urgent appeal. A church hall was built at Mosspark and a church subsequently formed, in 1929, with Thomas S. Loudon as minister. The Union had its eye on suitable sites for church extension work in Edinburgh, and in 1929 the Church Extension Committee, largely through the Edinburgh District Committee, were directed to the spiritual needs of the Saughtonhall district of that city, and in November of that year a church was constituted, of which A. F. Simpson became pastor in 1930. An effort was made round about this time to acquire a site in the Knightswood suburb of Glasgow and a church was formed there in 1933, in which year Walter Gerrard was inducted to the pastorate.[1]

This venture in church extension and all the other advances made by the denomination at this time owed a considerable debt

[1] See *A Chronicle of the Churches*, below, for details. In this period the churches at Croft Street, Dalkeith, and Sullom were closed.

to A. J. Forson, the editor of *The Scottish Congregationalist*, whose zeal and literary gifts over a decade (July 1922 to May 1932) extended the influence and promoted the success of the official organ of the Union. Forson was a trained journalist and an able propagandist of Scottish Congregationalism, and turned his attention to the instruction of youth in the Congregational heritage. During his editorship he wrote an excellent series of brief articles on Congregational history which he called 'Little Chapters for Young Folks'. These were later collected and published in booklet form in 1929 with the title *The Story of our Union and What we Stand For*. Forson's Foreword to the booklet was most timely, especially in view of the controversy as to the necessity or irrelevance of the Congregational churches, which was soon to sound forth from the pages of *The Scottish Congregationalist*.[1] 'The future of our Union', the foreword begins, 'is very much in your hands (i.e. the youth of the churches). In another generation some of you will be the office-bearers of our churches and the officials of our Union. These pages will explain to you what Congregationalism is and what we stand for. The religious life of our country would be very much the poorer if our distinctive witness were withdrawn at this time. We are, it is true, a comparatively small body, but our influence in the past has been out of all proportion to our numbers, and it may be the same in the future. That, however, depends upon the young people in our churches today.' Arthur Mee the journalist used to say that there was an air of briskness and variety in the magazine during Forson's editorship. He retired from office through illness in 1932 and his death not long afterwards was mourned by the whole family of Congregational churches.

The sudden spurt in church extension drained the financial resources of the Union—at least the funds allotted for work of this sort. *The Scottish Congregationalist* for June 1932, after outlining the completion of the little slice of extension work in Glasgow and Edinburgh, ends with something like a moan: 'Unfortunately, the financial resources for Church extension are now almost exhausted.' Union Committee Reports reveal the same undertone of financial anxiety. True, the Union thanked God for the Central Fund, which in these lean years enabled it to increase the meagre stipends of ministers. During 1930, for instance, the sum of £1,990 was distributed among forty-three

[1] See Chapter XVIII, below.

pastors, providing a stipend of £195, £205, and £215, according to the size and situation of the pastorate. But the Report of the Church Aid Committee had the now customary lugubrious strain: 'The finances of the Committee are not satisfactory. It is significant that since the installation of the Central Fund the income of the Church Aid Fund has steadily declined. It would seem as if the churches need to be reminded every year that the Central Fund was not intended to take the place of the Church Aid Fund.' It was a case of robbing Peter to pay Paul. It was, perhaps, not so much a failure in sacrifice as a result of the general economic depression.

Similar financial difficulties faced the Missionary Societies. The L.M.S. for example, in 1931 reported a serious deficit. The previous year had been disappointing enough with its deficit of £18,929, but 1931's figure was £21,421. The Scottish contribution, £5,969, was nearly seven hundred pounds down on the previous year.[1] These figures must be read in the light of the stringent industrial conditions and wide unemployment, not only in Scotland, but throughout the world.

III

The full history of the London Missionary Society has been recounted elsewhere, and the honourable place that the Congregational churches of Scotland have occupied in its long and glorious testimony has been described in James M. Calder's *Scotland's March Past*, to which we have alluded earlier in this narrative. To what has been said in previous chapters about the close affiliations of the churches and Union with the L.M.S., we wish to add just one or two things. It is interesting to note that two of the honoured sons of Scottish Congregationalism, who in recent years have occupied positions of responsibility in native Congregationalism, J. H. L. Burns and Adam Black, left for the foreign field in 1923. On 17 June of that year Burns was ordained in Morningside Church, Edinburgh, and sailed in October for South Africa. About the same time Black, a member of Dundas Street Church, Glasgow, was appointed a treasurer to the L.M.S. and Baptist Missionary Societies in China. Eric Liddell sailed in July 1925 for Tientsin, China.[2]

---

[1] In 1933, however, Scotland's contribution was £6,290 4s. 5d., an increase of £495 18s. 7d. and the Missionary Committee noticed with pleasure the increasing interest in the Missionary cause among the younger generation.

[2] Cf. Chapter XVII, para. 14, below.

O

A Conference was held in Glasgow on 10 November 1925 to inaugurate a Five Years' Campaign to further Missionary work in Scotland. Representatives numbering over fifty, drawn from Auxiliaries, the Union officials, the Scottish Directors, and the District Committees were present. W. H. Somerville represented the L.M.S. The methods adopted were educational and spiritual. The Conference pledged itself to ask each church to enquire whether the support it had hitherto given to the great enterprise of the Kingdom in human material of dedicated lives, and in consecration of means had been proportionate to the need and to its own ability.

In 1926 missionary enthusiasts heard with dismay that the house at Blantyre, in which David Livingstone had spent his early years, was in danger of being demolished. A movement was started which aimed at the purchase and restoration of the property and the establishing, either in the building or near it, of a museum in which it was hoped to gather Livingstone relics. A meeting to launch the scheme was held in Glasgow on 22 January 1926. Dr. John White, Moderator of the General Assembly of the Church of Scotland, presided. The scheme was explained by James I. Macnair, and was warmly supported by Dr. Donald Fraser and representatives of other Churches. The Scottish National Memorial to David Livingstone was opened on 5 October 1929, when before a large concourse of people, Master David Livingstone Wilson, great-grandson of the missionary, presented the key to Her Royal Highness the Duchess of York, who opened the door of the Missionary's old home. James I. Macnair, chairman of the Executive Committee, to whose initiative, vision, and constant labour the memorial largely owed its existence, was honoured at the opening ceremony by a presentation. More than £12,000 originally asked for the memorial had been received, and good progress was thereafter made with the Endowment Fund.[1]

The L.M.S. Summer Schools at Bonskeid House, Pitlochry, which have been a fruitful means of Christian fellowship and missionary learning, began in August 1929, when the subject for study and discussion was 'Christ and the World Confusion'.

In 1930 an event occurred which had the effect of strengthening even further the ties which bound the Congregational churches and the London Missionary Society. In that year James I. Macnair succeeded Sydney Nicholson as the Society's District secretary

[1] Cf. Chapter XIII, 1, above.

for Scotland and Ireland. The appointment met with utmost satisfaction throughout the churches. Macnair had been trained in the Edinburgh Theological Hall (now the Congregational College), and as a L.M.S. missionary he had given twenty-six years of his life to India. Moreover, he was a past president of the Union and chairman of the Livingstone Memorial Executive Committee. It would have been difficult to find anyone more suited to the office which he held with success and distinction till 1935.[1] The next year he was succeeded by James M. Calder, who carried on the work with distinction till 1951.

IV

In the period immediately under review the Women's Union, which, as we have seen, became an integral part of the Congregational Union of Scotland in 1919, grew apace. By 1932 there were ninety affiliated branches, which number had increased to 110 by 1940. Doubtless the extension of the political franchise in 1928 to all women over twenty-one years of age was a contributory factor. The women often had a moralising effect on the churches. For example, in 1932 we find them deploring the growth of the gambling spirit. They called on 'the women of the churches to refuse to adopt raffling as a means of raising money'.

Mrs. A. Trevelyan Smith, who joined the Women's Union Committee in 1917, became convener of the committee which formed the Girls' Auxiliary. She was an inspired leader and counsellor of that organisation till 1947, when it transferred its affiliation to the Youth Committee.

Between 1920 and 1930 the Women's Union raised at least £1,038 for the Hall of Residence Fund of the Scottish Congregational College. Much of the onus of this work rested on the shoulders of Mrs. T. S. Loudon, the able treasurer.

The Women's Union gave full support to the growing ecumenical movement. Since 1933 they have invited to their Annual Meeting delegates from all the Protestant Churches. And these invitations have been as warmly reciprocated. Since 1937, moreover, the Women's Union have taken part in the Women's World Day of Prayer, attended inter-denominational services, and been

---

[1] For his devoted labours in the missionary cause Macnair received the Doctor of Divinity degree of Edinburgh University, and in 1954, the research medal of the Royal Scottish Geographical Society. He died in 1955.

represented on the Central Committee for Scotland. They have also been supporters of overseas Christian work through the L.M.S., C.M.S., and other missionary agencies. Truly ecumenical work and witness!

During the war years the Women's Union was represented on the Scottish Churches Committee for work among women in the forces, and on the Committee for Women's Social Welfare.

Among the excellent personnel of the Women's Union in this period the following deserve special mention: Mrs. James Donald, secretary, 1923-28; Miss McKinlay, secretary. 1928-33; Mrs. A. S. Guild, secretary 1939-48; Mrs. R. T. Stevenson, treasurer 1930-38; and of the presidents: Mrs. Baxter, 1932-34; Mrs. Sivewright, 1934-36; Mrs. T. G. Ogilvie, 1936-38; Mrs. William Kirk, 1938-42; and Mrs. D. Cook, 1942-45.[1]

The growing official status of women in Scottish Congregationalism in the half-century is illustrated by the increasing number of women delegates representing the churches at the Annual Assembly of the Congregational Union. Whereas in 1910 there were only 4 women delegates, in 1925 there were 53, 148 in 1945, and as many as 162 out of a total of 300 in 1955.

At the Annual Assembly held at Glasgow in 1929, an exciting new chapter opened in the ministerial history of the Congregational churches in Scotland and, indeed, of all the Scottish Churches, Protestant and Catholic alike. Miss Vera Mary Muir Findlay applied for recognition as a minister of the Congregational Union of Scotland. Miss Findlay, a double graduate of Glasgow University, a daughter of the famous Trinity Church in that city, and a distinguished alumnus of the Congregational College, Edinburgh, had been for several months prior to her application the well-loved pastor of Partick Church, to whose services of worship she had drawn admiring crowds.[2]

In the months prior to Miss Findlay's application for official status as a Congregational minister, many letters had appeared in the religious press, some supporting her in her phenomenal rôle as preacher and pastor, others frankly and occasionally rudely critical.[3] Perhaps Thomas Templeton did more than anyone else by writing and debate to turn the wavering and undecided in favour of admitting a lady amid the fathers and brethren. In *The Scottish Congregationalist* of March 1929 Templeton had written:

[1] See Chapter XV, III, above.   [2] Cf. Chapter XVII, below.
[3] Cf. *The Scottish Congregationalist*, February, March and April 1929.

'We are considering a phase of the long slow progress of woman in the course of civilisation. A progress which the Lord Christ and His Church have mightily accelerated. Will you set a throne at the entrance to the ministry, like Canute's, and say to the tide "No further!" Don't! You will be more like Mrs. Partington. And if a call to the ministry comes to a woman—and the Salvation Army has shown that it often does—who are we, to bar the way? Haply, we might be found fighting against God. Our Church boasts its freedom. Let us use it to give full opportunity of survival to the woman ministry.'

Miss Findlay (now Mrs. Colin Kenmure) was duly accepted as a minister of the Congregational Union of Scotland, on 29 April 1929, after a motion by T. Berrie, seconded by Thomas Templeton.[1]

In the course of the years other women have been ordained to the ministry of the Congregational churches of Scotland, and served them faithfully and well: Helen E. Woods (1934); Beatrice D. Bonnar (1941); Jean I. Thomson (1946); Isabel G. D. Shedden (1949); Dahlia M. S. Grigor (1950); Jean B. Robson (1957). Mary W. Marks (*née* Hutson) was trained for the ministry but did not take up a pastoral charge. Nancie Ward, and Phyllis M. Martin, though trained and ordained in England, have served the Scottish churches and Union.

V

We conclude this chapter with a few references to changes suggested or effected on the administrative side of the Union's work in the second quarter of the century.

It is interesting to note that as early as 1929 the question of ministerial superannuation was claiming the attention of some concerned and far-seeing people in the Union. In May of that year at the Glasgow Assembly David Russell Scott moved on behalf of the Edinburgh District Committee, 'That the Assembly appoint a representative Committee of ministers and laymen to consider the whole question of Superannuation and report to next Assembly. The consideration of the question to include: (1) the position of those outside the present scheme; (2) the position of those inside;

---

[1] Cf. *A Chronicle of the Churches*, below, under Partick, Christ Church, Glasgow; Hillhead, Glasgow; and Pollokshields, Glasgow for the record of her subsequent ministry. She was President of the Union 1951-52.

(3) the position of ministers transferring from one Union to another; (4) the advisability of amalgamation with the scheme of England and Wales; and (5) any other relevant matters.' For twenty-eight years this important matter seems to have fallen into abeyance: not until 1957 was a Scottish Congregational Ministers' Pension Scheme successfully launched.[1]

Two changes of designation were made in 1922. Up to that time the yearly gathering of Congregationalists was referred to as the *Annual Meeting*. From then on, probably reflecting Presbyterian influence, it was designated the *Annual Assembly*. The annually elected leader of the Union's proceedings had been to this date referred to as the Chairman of the Union. His designation was altered to President of the Union.

The marked development of denominational life to which reference has already been made necessitated the creation of new Union Committees; and to deal more speedily and cheaply with the growing financial work of the Union, Henry Brown, its treasurer, outlined in 1927 a plan for unifying the trusteeships of Union Funds. The plan was accepted and carried into effect by the formation of the Congregational Union of Scotland Nominees Limited, which was registered 7 January 1928.[2]

At the Annual Assembly of 1934 a special Remit Committee were asked to consult the Districts as to the formation of three new Committees—on Education, a Settlements, and a Finance and Law Committee. No useful purpose, the Districts thought, would be served by an Education Committee. A Settlements Committee, however, was regarded with favour by almost all the Districts. But its function within Congregationalism, they said, must be limited to the *recommendation* of ministers to churches. The Remit Committee accordingly recommended that a Settlements Committee be appointed, consisting of the secretary of the Union, the chairman of the Church Aid and Home Mission Committees, and the Principal of the College.

As the Union now had large financial interests most of the Districts considered that it was advisable to have a committee whose object would be to conserve the Union's finances. This Committee, they thought, should be small and composed of experts. The Remit Committee accordingly recommended that

[1] Cf. Chapter XX, iv, below.
[2] Cf. *Year Book of the Congregational Union of Scotland 1930-1931* for its aims.

the Finance and Law Committee consist of the treasurer and secretary of the Union, the Union trustees, the treasurer of the College and three others.

These two committees, the Settlements Committee, and the Finance and Law Committee, were added to the existing Committees of the Union at the 1934 Annual Assembly.

At this Assembly also important alterations were made in the 'Machinery of the Assembly'. A new regulation by which the president-elect was chosen by ballot a year in advance of his entering upon his duties, tended to make the election of president much more decorous than hitherto.[1] The president-elect was now enabled to prepare for his office and when the time came for him to assume it, he was formally inducted by the retiring predecessor.

The increasing interest in social and political issues, to which we have elsewhere referred, was evinced by the inclusion of the following words in the Union's regulations: 'One session of the Assembly shall be devoted to the discussion of subjects of public interest.'

The growing ecumenical interest was also manifested at the 1934 Assembly by the insertion in the Regulations of, 'The Assembly may appoint representatives to the annual and other meetings of other religious bodies, or the meetings of any society with whose objects it is in sympathy'.[2]

The Union and the churches suffered a very deep blow by the death of Henry Brown in 1933. He had been a well-known figure in Scottish Congregationalism for forty years. He had occupied many distinguished offices in the Union. He had been its chairman (i.e. president) in 1920. Brown possessed exceptional business gifts, deep religious convictions, and a thorough grasp of Congregational principles. Nine years as Union treasurer had made him familiar with the aided churches and their needs. And his passing was mourned by all.

He was succeeded as treasurer of the Union by Daniel McLay who served the churches in that capacity faithfully and with distinction till 1941. McLay's acceptance of the treasurership synchronised almost with the inauguration of a Church Extension Fund, and this venture benefited from his forthright and consecrated leadership, as we shall see later on.

[1] Previously he had been elected in the year of his office, by open vote.
[2] Cf. Chapter XV, III, above.

CHAPTER XVII

MINISTERIAL TRAINING, 1897–1958

I

THE time has come to complete to date the story of the denomination's ministerial training, instalments of which have appeared in earlier chapters.[1]

In 1897, the students of the two united institutions began their happy association, at 30 George Square, Edinburgh, under the Principalship of J. M. Hodgson. William Taylor and Alexander McNair, of the E.U. Theological Hall, took their places on the teaching staff.

Associated with Principal Hodgson in 1911 were A. F. Simpson, Professor of New Testament Exegesis and Criticism (Interim Principal, 1916-17), who resigned in 1920, after a period of thirty-five years' service; and Alexander McNair, Professor of Hebrew and Old Testament Exegesis and Criticism, who also resigned in 1920.

Alexander J. Grieve succeeded Hodgson as Principal in 1917, when the institution was largely depleted by the First World War. Under his active and scholarly direction the situation was soon changed for the better. In 1919, Grieve was appointed a lecturer in the University of Edinburgh and a member of its Board of Post Graduate Studies in Theology.[2] He instituted, among other things an end of session Speech Day. When the premises of the Theological Hall were transferred, in January 1921, to Mount Grange, 29 Hope Terrace, Edinburgh, he was mainly instrumental in raising the sum of £5,000 to put the building in habitable repair. Grieve left Edinburgh in 1921 to become Principal of Lancashire Independent College, Manchester. During the last year of his principalship of the Hall its name was changed to that of 'The Scottish Congregational College'.

[1] Chapter VII, VI; IX, II; XI, IV; XIII, II. The present writer owes much of the substance of this chapter to the kind co-operation of the Rev. J. H. L. Burns, M.A., the Secretary of the College Committee.
[2] Thus starting a precedent, the Principals since his day have occupied this position.

In 1920 David Russell Scott, minister of Castle Street Church, Dundee, was appointed Professor of Biblical languages, Criticism and Exegesis. Scott was a man of great intellectual ability, wide culture, and Christian brotherliness. In 1923 he was awarded the degree of Doctor of Philosophy by St. Andrews University for a thesis on the Atonement. Fifteen years later the same university conferred upon him the degree of Doctor of Divinity. From 1941 to his retiral in 1944 during the trying period of war, he served as Principal of the College.

T. Hywell Hughes followed Grieve in the principalship in July 1922. His tenure of office, which unfortunately closed for health reasons in 1936, was marked by distinction and success. It was largely through his efforts that the College course was recognised as qualifying for the B.D. examination in all the Scottish universities. In 1934, the University of Edinburgh recognised his scholarship through lectures and publications, when it conferred upon him its Doctor of Divinity degree.

In 1930 the United Free Church of Scotland had established a college in union with the Scottish Congregational College, Allan Barr of the former institution becoming Professor of New Testament Studies to the combined students. On Dr. Hughes's retiral it was desirable to appoint a principal who should suit the two colleges. H. F. Lovell Cocks, a member of the teaching staff of Yorkshire United Independent College, Bradford, was appointed in 1937, and remained till 1941, when he left Edinburgh to become Principal of Western College, Bristol.

From 1941 to 1944 Dr. Scott was Principal, but in the latter year he requested to be relieved of the burden of the principalship.

His successor was Charles S. Duthie, a brilliant scholar who had been a resident tutor at Paton College, Nottingham, and came to his arduous task in the prime of life, with a valuable knowledge of men acquired as a chaplain to the Forces in the Middle East. He became Principal, in 1944, at the comparatively early age of thirty-four. As other Principals before him, he was appointed a lecturer in the Post Graduate School of Theology in Edinburgh University. From 1947 to 1951 he served as chairman of the Forward Movement Committee of the Congregational Union of Scotland.[1] and for the year 1952-53 he was President of the Union. During his presidency his Alma Mater (Aberdeen University)

[1] Cf. Chapter XIX, below.

conferred upon him the honorary degree of Doctor of Divinity. This honour was given partly because of his wide interest in Congregationalism, which included a share in the activities of the International Congregational Council. At the Wellesley, U.S.A., Meeting of the Council, in 1949, he was one of the leading speakers and in the preparations for the St. Andrews Meeting of the Council, in 1953, he played an active part.

During a distinctive tenure of office, which it is hoped will continue for many years to come, Dr. Duthie has resuscitated, in fuller measure than any of his immediate predecessors, the evangelistic traditions of the institution.[1] Linked with a careful superintendence of the devotional life of the students has been his leadership of united Student Evangelistic Campaigns in towns and cities throughout Scotland, campaigns which have afforded to the students valuable practical experience.

From the commencement of his principalship, C. S. Duthie recognised the necessity for a vigorous and long term campaign of recruitment of candidates for college training, with a view to the ministry and other Christian work. Articles from his pen, speeches and, in 1950, the start of an annual Pre-Candidates Conference all contributed to bring the number of students to a post-war record of twenty-four, in 1954. When the need for a Capital Fund for the College became imperative he gave himself heart and soul to the planning and launching, in 1954, of a campaign to raise a sum of £15,000 to stabilise the College finances. By 1956, £500 over that amount was contributed by the churches and friends of the College at home and abroad.

In order to sustain the academic status of the College in relation to the universities, and to meet the gradual increase of students, it was decided in 1946 to arrange for the appointment of a second professor. In the following year James Wood, minister of Belmont Street Church, Aberdeen, was appointed to the Chair of Biblical Languages, Criticism and Exegesis, an office he still occupies with success and distinction.

For twenty-five years of the period under review Pastoral Theology, too often the Cinderella of nonconformist training-colleges, was taught by two men of learning and piety, whose names will be long revered in the history of the College. The first was George McHardy, who was appointed Honorary Professor of Pastoral Theology in 1919, and was a member of the teaching staff

[1] Cf. Chapter VII, vi; IX, ii; XI, iv; XIII, ii.

until his death in 1930. A year later George S. Stewart, who was appointed by the U.F. Church of Scotland College Committee, succeeded Dr. McHardy. Dr. Stewart's death, in 1945, was a great loss to the College. In recent years Henry Cook, Harry Escott, J. G. Mackenzie, and W. B. J. Martin have from time to time served the College as extra-mural lecturers.

Amongst its 239 alumni of this half-century shine many names of renown. Vera M. M. Findlay (now Mrs. Kenmure) entered the theological course in 1926 and was the first woman minister to be trained for the ministry in Scotland and to settle in a Scottish charge.[1] The most outstanding of the seven missionary students was Eric Liddell who distinguished himself as a world's record-breaking runner at the Olympic Games in Paris in 1924, and died in a Japanese internment camp in China in 1945. It is of interest to note that a young man, Peter Marshall of Buchanan Street Church, Coatbridge, who was accepted as a student in 1924, at the same time as Eric Liddell, resigned three years later, emigrated to the U.S.A. and eventually became Chaplain to the Senate in Washington.[2] Dr. John Short, minister of St. George's United Church, Toronto, Shaun Herron, late Editor of the *British Weekly*, and Dr. Duthie himself were all trained at Hope Terrace.

II

The story of an educational institution is mainly that of its head and teachers. But the work would soon come to a standstill without the support of the officers and Committee of Management. This Committee and the three officers appointed by it stem from the District Councils[3] of the Union, and behind the Councils are the churches without whose prayers and generosity the work of Christian education would cease.

The College owes much to those who have acted from time to time as chairman of the Committee. But the onus of the work has fallen upon the treasurers and secretaries of the Management Committee. During the period under review the following have served in these important offices:

[1] Cf. Chapter XVI, iv, above.
[2] Cf. *A Chronicle of the Churches*, under Buchanan Street Church, Coatbridge, below.
[3] Originally designated 'District Committees'.

Treasurers

John Orr, 1900-14	E. F. Barron, 1933-52
W. Malcolm, 1914-21	Walter A. Brotchie, 1951-
Henry Brown, 1921-33	

Secretaries

W. Hope Davison, 1890-1901	G. B. Shepherd, 1920-25
A. R. Henderson, 1901-2	J. Pickthall, 1925-26
George McHardy, 1902-10	James I. Macnair, 1926-47
Henry Parnaby, 1910-12	J. H. L. Burns, 1947-
J. B. Allan, 1912-20	

It has been the privilege of the present writer to know from personal experience of the work of the more recent officers of the College Committee—of E. F. Barron so assiduous in his duties as treasurer, of Walter A. Brotchie without whose administrative gifts and leadership the Capital Fund Campaign could not have been the success it was, and last but not least J. H. L. Burns who has served his Alma Mater as secretary for a decade with such distinction and zeal.

Burns's appointment in 1947 coincided with the need to bring the work of the College to the closer attention of the churches. He immediately gave himself to the larger task—organising the new 'Friends of the College' scheme, editing *College News*, recruiting new supporters, producing an annual Syllabus for the students and, in general acting as secretary of the College itself. It is in no small measure due to the untiring faithfulness and enthusiasm of J. H. L. Burns that the College has won through to the place it now occupies in the affection of all the churches and at the heart of the Congregational Union of Scotland.

III

The process of bringing College and Union into such intimate rapprochement was long and often beset with difficulties. Indeed during this half-century the relationship between them gave rise to keen and sometimes heated discussion. Occasionally a proposal was made that the College should be brought under the control of the Union, but the Baxter Trust, to which we have referred in an earlier chapter, made that impossible without extremely heavy legal costs.[1] The next best thing was to bring the College into as

[1] Chapter XIII, II.

close association with the Union as possible. A step in that direction was taken in 1917. From 1897 to that date the Annual Report of the Committee and the Annual Financial Statement of the treasurer of the (then) Theological Hall were submitted for adoption, first to a Session of the Annual Meeting of the Union, and secondly to the Annual Meeting of the Hall, which was held after the Union meeting was ended. This arrangement with its duplication of business called for improvement, so it was decided at the Annual Meeting of the Hall, in 1917, after joint consultation between the Hall Committee and the General Committee of the Union, that the two annual meetings dealing with the business of the Hall should be united, and that the Annual Meeting of the Hall should be held during one of the Sessions of the Annual Meeting of the Union instead of after its close.

Another step bringing College and Union closer together was taken when the following suggestions, made in 1925 by Henry Brown, were approved by the College Committee and Union: (1) that the Principal of the College should be *ex officio* a member of the General Committee of the Union, and (2) that the secretary of the Union should be *ex officio* a member of the College Committee.

Later, in 1945, the inclusion of the secretary of the College Committee *ex officio* as a member of the General Committee brought the two bodies into still closer association.

The relationship between the College and the Union was further strengthened when, in 1949, the Annual Meeting of the College agreed to the following additions to the College Committee of Management: two members nominated by the General Committee, two members, one from the General Committee and one from the Settlements and Ministerial Recognition Committee, to be added when matters specially affecting the Union have to be dealt with.

CHAPTER XVIII

THE 'PERISCOPE' CONTROVERSY

I

THE most significant spiritual event within the Union, in the years between the Wars, was the appearance in *The Scottish Congregationalist* of a series of articles by J. G. Drummond under the pseudonym of *Periscope*. The first appeared in January 1928, and in it the writer championed the democratic character of Congregationalism, and its adaptability as a vehicle of divine revelation. 'If any church endeavours to be a church of the people', he wrote, 'it is our own. . . . We do not need to fear new ideas: they can be the voice of the Holy Spirit.' The second article in the March issue of the magazine further developed the theme of the intellectual adaptability of the Congregational churches: 'The Haldanes and Dr. Morison made us what we are by a revolt against traditional belief. Their work was that of re-interpreting the old truth to the modern mind of their day. That is our origin, and that is our genius.' The May article affirmed that Congregationalism 'has repeatedly suffered for some religious revelation which has later become the possession of all the churches'.

So far Drummond's 'credo' had been innocuous enough, and stirred up no dust in the denominational arena. However, in the article of July 1928, written on the eve of the union of the Presbyterian Churches of Scotland, a note of judgment upon Scottish Congregationalism, as it is tending is clearly heard: 'The endeavour to establish the Church as an organ of the social system', he considers, 'may produce a great institution, but it will never stir the heart of humanity to the real heights of religious zeal.' He asks, 'Are we (Congregationalists) in any better state? When we report progress, it is in terms of the success of individual churches. When we think of advance it is in terms of strong churches growing in membership and affluence throughout the land. . . . When we meet for combined effort, the atmosphere is readily vitiated by the poisonous suggestion of inter-church rivalry. At our Assembly we rejoice if we can show a record of general prosperity. That may be comforting to ourselves, and we may attract a few more into our churches by the signs of prosperity. If this is all we are doing, we are merely maintaining in isolation from the main stream of spiritual advance back-waters of foam-flecked religiosity, with a lazy swirl within ourselves in pretence of movement.' With prophetic insight Drummond saw the peril inherent in big national churches: 'it will be a soul-destroying event', he wrote, 'if a united Presbyterian Church in Scotland should succeed in *administering* religion to the community.' He considered that the function of Congregationalism was to prevent any such spiritual tragedy from happening. 'Each individual church should be a centre of spiritual activity and investigation to meet the need of the hour.'

The discussion of the place of the Congregational churches within the wider ecclesiastical framework in Scotland, and their contribution to the spiritual life of the nation, took a new and controversial turn after the International Council of Congregational Churches, which met in Edinburgh in the summer of 1929. Dr. J. D. Jones had been the honoured guest of the Council, and at a luncheon given in his honour at the Cockburn Hotel, he had 'tested Scottish feeling with regard to the advisability of a union between Scottish and English and Welsh Congregationalism'. Such a union had been desired by some at the beginning of the century as we have noticed, when joint assemblies of the two Unions had been held.

J. G. Drummond, who had been present at the International Council, made Dr. Jones's suggestion, which apparently he did not favour, the subject of Periscope's next article in *The Scottish Congregationalist*. In it he argued, convincingly we think, for the *Scottishness* of Congregationalism north of the Border, but in the fervour of his patriotism, he expressed the view that Congregationalists in Scotland 'have the right to consider themselves as belonging to the Church of Scotland', an argument, perhaps, not equally convincing. He believed that there would be 'in the course of time such a union in Scotland as will include (the Congregational churches) without destroying our individuality'. He further added, 'in view of Scottish national feeling might it not be unwise of us to throw over our honoured national heritage for the sake of the comfort which union with England would bring us?'

Drummond reminded English Congregationalists, and the Church of Scotland which looked upon Scottish Congregationalism as an importation from the south, that in actual fact, in both its branches which interlocked in 1896, it was 'born of Presbyterianism and native to the soil'.

This outburst of ecclesiastical patriotism almost synchronised with the historic union of the Established Church and the United Free Church of Scotland.[1] That event stirred the imagination of the Scottish people generally, and some Congregationalists were not unmoved by the great occasion and its colourful spectacle.[2] The re-union was in fact the consummation of a process of Presbyterian re-union which began in 1900, in which year 293,000 Free Church members had united with the United Presbyterians who numbered 196,000, to form the United Free Church of Scotland—1,112 congregations in all. The earlier of these two Scottish re-unions had, moreover, encouraged other re-unions of Presbyterian bodies, notably in South Africa, Australia, India, and New Zealand, while in England these reunions were not without effect upon negotiations proceeding between the Methodist bodies.

The 1929 reunion of the Presbyterian Churches in Scotland was considered to be necessary because of the changing social situation. The number and distribution of congregations had failed to keep pace with the enormous increase of population. It was estimated that at least one million were unconnected with any form of institutional religion, while the social problems in the large towns constituted an inescapable challenge to the churches. The situation, it was believed, needed an undivided Presbyterian Church. Furthermore, such a closing of the churches' ranks seemed to be demanded by the phenomenal growth of the large immigrant Roman Catholic population introduced from Ireland at the end of the last century, which had coincided with the emigration of Protestant Scotsmen and seriously altered the centuries-old religious balance.

Church union was called for also, it was very generally thought within Presbyterianism, by the growing secular temper of the time.

But to return to domestic affairs. In *The Scottish Congregationalist* of May 1929, J. G. Drummond in his increasingly provocative Periscope article does 'not see any reason why we should not be ready to enter into negotiations with the Church of Scotland. . . . As Christian people, however, we have the duty to discover why we are standing apart. It would be an act of grace on

---

[1] With the exception of some churches that dissented, the present U.F. Church.

[2] Cf. *The Scottish Congregationalist*, November 1929, p. 3.

our part to be prepared to enter into negotiations before the opportunity arises. . . . Let us try to discover if our principle will permit us to unite with the larger body of Christian opinion in the land.'

This conviction that the time was ripe for reunion with Presbyterianism was strengthened in Drummond's view by a speech by Nathaniel Micklem, Vice-Principal of Mansfield College, Oxford, delivered at the Centenary Celebrations of the Congregational Union of England and Wales held at Manchester, in October 1931. Micklem suggested, Drummond said in *The Scottish Congregationalist* in November of that year, 'that the real and effective liberty of the individual congregation is not incompatible with membership in a great national Church; that Congregationalism must, for the sake of a larger mission, resile from its somewhat intransigent individualism, and that the time would come when we may decide that Congregationalism as a sect should cease to be. Can we accept that point of view in Scotland?'

In January 1932 continuing his articles in *The Scottish Congregationalist* Drummond said: 'It would almost seem as if (as Congregational churches) we had done our work as a separate body, and that, if we are to do more, we must do it in closer association with those we have helped to influence.'

Henry Brown, treasurer of the Union, writing in its official organ in February 1932, shows that the dust of battle was being raised by Drummond's views: 'there have been quiet rumblings in certain quarters indicative of some unrest.' Indeed as the months went by indignant voices were raised by the champions, laymen, and ministers alike, of the Congregational principle. W. Stewart Smith cited eminent Presbyterians who had become Congregationalists for freedom's sake, like A. E. Garvie and Robert MacIntosh. He quoted the latter as saying: 'I fled to Congregationalism as a means of escape from outworn dogmas and creeds. How immensely the central things gain by being disembarrassed of association with secondary and questionable elements. Christianity as a polity, when trimmed of superfluous fat and reduced to its innermost essence, is Congregationalism.' Smith believed, he said, with Dr. C. J. Cadoux, that Congregationalism is the true Catholicism.

That redoubtable warrior in the Congregationalist cause, A. F. MacRobert, then minister at Uddingston, entered the lists, his trusty spear being the freedom of Congregationalism from State

P

endowment and patronage. He asked, 'Are we to emulate the majority of the United Free Church by resiling from our faith in free church principles?'

There were voices too on the other side, mostly from those with an Evangelical Union provenance. Chief among them was John Safeley, then minister of Canmore Street Church, Dunfermline. In March 1932 he wrote in *The Scottish Congregationalist*: 'The main question with us is—Is there a future for Congregationalism at all in Scotland, standing by itself? . . . A considerable proportion of our ministers (he lamented) have come from south of the Border, and know but little of our Scottish history, traditions, character and religion. . . . Our denomination has just about fulfilled its specific mission. . . . Something daring and decisive in the way of union must be faced if it is not simply to peter out or to become a mere northern annexe or outpost of England. Personally I am constrained to hold that our true line of destiny leads towards the re-united Church of Scotland.' Safeley thought too that the pressure of the terrific problems confronting the Christian Church and the stimulus of the various reunion movements at home and abroad would perhaps soon decisively influence Scottish Congregationalism.

A. F. Simpson, the scholarly pastor of Saughtonhall Church, Edinburgh, and of honoured Congregational parentage, came out boldly, and with wise counsel, on the Congregationalist side.[1] 'Experience of the greater union in Scotland', he said, in April 1932, 'is already causing much disappointment and heart-searching within the united body itself. It is found that the one denomination is not serving Christ's Kingdom any better than the two. The amalgamation has nothing to show in the way of an increase in the spiritual vitality of the people. . . .' He goes on to say: 'It is futile to imagine that the opinions of Congregationalists (i.e. in the event of re-union with the National Church) on such vital issues as Orders, the Creeds and the Sacraments will have any more weight with ecclesiastical authority than similar opinions of many Presbyterian Christians who surrendered their convictions on these matters in view of what appeared to them the greater cause of Union.' Simpson's final word was one of defiance. 'Such a surrender some of us will refuse to make; because we know that to stifle conviction is to stifle the soul of Christ's Church.'

[1] Cf. also Andrew Ferguson Simpson, *Congregationalism and the Church: a message to the Congregational Churches of Scotland*, 1946.

MacRobert came back to the fray defending the Congregational principle of liberty of thought and worship. Surely, he argued fiercely, a denomination which gave us John Philip, Livingstone and Gilmour, Wardlaw and Lindsay Alexander and, in more recent times, progressive thinkers like A. M. Fairbairn, P. T. Forsyth, John Hunter, A. E. Garvie, and W. L. Walker can claim to be a pioneer school of Christian thought in Scotland.

J. M. McGaulay thought that Congregationalism with its lay and democratic traditions stood a better chance of winning the workers—a spiritual advantage it might lose if reunion was sought with the Church of Scotland.

The controversy, which had raged mainly in the correspondence columns of *The Scottish Congregationalist*, came to an end, in that periodical at least, in May 1932, when its newly-appointed editor, A. Ireland Robertson, wrote a leading article on 'The Future of Congregationalism', in which he assured the readers of the magazine that the views so vehemently expressed through its pages in recent months did not represent the policy of the Union. Every communication on this topic, he said, 'had been spontaneous'. Two months previously, Drummond himself, apparently dumbfounded that his views should have disturbed so much dust, had confessed that his desire had not been to disrupt. Indeed he believed Scottish Congregationalism *had* a future and 'that our work is not yet done. We require, however, the sense of a definite mission.'[1]

In the years between the wars, J. G. Drummond was unmistakably one of the denomination's ablest thinkers and, at times, the possessor of spiritual insights which he declaimed fearlessly (if not always wisely) in unforgettable phrases. We have felt in re-reading the Periscope articles that it was his desire to keep unsoiled the *Scottishness* of his native Congregationalism that made his words sound in some ears like disloyalty. Doubtless he did force the denomination to look within itself, and then out and around upon the Scottish scene to discover its 'definite mission', as we shall now try to show.

II

At the Annual Assembly of the Union held in Dundee in May 1932, Drummond moved that a Commission be appointed to

[1] *The Scottish Congregationalist*, March 1932.

consider the question of the Witness of Congregationalism in Scotland. After debate and discussion the Assembly unanimously resolved:

> THAT the District Committees shall consider—
>
> 1. The function of our Churches as independent units within the Church of Christ;
> 2. The function of the Union of Congregational Churches in Scotland; the possibility of some development of the same; and
> 3. The importance of our freedom from doctrinal bondage in dealing with the problems of faith and conduct.
>
> THAT a small committee be appointed to arrange the discussions and co-ordinate the work of the District Committees, and prepare a report for a Conference at next Annual Assembly.

The following were appointed to the Union Committee: H. Moffat Scott, Charles Richardson, J. G. Drummond, J. A. Lees, William Crombie and E. Y. Harrison. Immediately after appointment the committee met and decided to send suggestions to the District Committees for their guidance in considering the Assembly Remit. These suggestions were not intended to be exhaustive or to set limits within which the discussion should be confined. Thereafter the District Committees dealt with the suggestions with enthusiasm, insight and thoroughness. They all felt the challenge of the hour and were anxious to meet it. Their reports show that the investigation had been amply justified, and they constitute a valuable record which should be preserved.

J. G. Drummond distinguished himself at the Edinburgh Assembly in 1933 in skilfully piloting the completed Report through Assembly. And at the request of the Special Remit Committee, the General Committee of the Union decided to publish the Report on 'The Witness of Congregationalism in Scotland' for general study.

This published Report makes instructive and inspiring reading. It is the most masterly explanation of the meaning of Congregationalism that has issued from north of the border in this century. We have room in this narrative only for a mere outline of its contents.

As to the contributions of Congregational churches as independent units within the Church of Christ, the Report affirms the spiritual idea of the Church as expressed in the words of Christ 'where two or three are gathered together in my name, there am I in the midst of them'; it holds that this spiritual life demands obedience to the Lordship of Christ; and also freedom from external control in order to nurture and develop this obedience. Apropos the function of the Union of the churches and the possibility of some development of the same, the Report advocates fellowship for mutual guidance; organisation for mutual help; and association for united witness to the world. In its examination of the implications of spiritual freedom, the Report states what it considers to be the obligations of church membership and also the social responsibilities of members, and what their attitude to present-day problems should be. In the final section on suggestions for a revival of religion, the Report relates the Gospel to present-day needs, mentions some methods of stimulating churches and of reaching the non-church-going, and finally posits the possibility of co-operating with other Churches.

The two most valuable insights of this Report are its stress on the 'receptive function' of Congregationalism in every generation, which it is the duty of churches and members to maintain, and its emphasis on common obedience to the Lordship of Christ as the only key to Christian unity.[1]

III

In the previous chapter we stated that in common with other communions, in the years between the wars, the Congregational Union of Scotland turned its attention to the question of church extension.[2] The Periscope controversy did much to intensify this interest within Congregationalism.

The new suburbs which were growing around the great centres of population called unmistakably for church extension. Some erstwhile strong causes in town and city were in process of becoming 'down town' churches. There was need to follow the population. The last venture of the Church Extension Committee at Knightswood in the west of Glasgow, where a church had been formed in 1933, showed that, if the opportunity of worship were provided, the people would respond. A twofold suggestion was made, that churches in depopulated areas should be transferred to more promising districts, and that a union might be affected between neighbouring congregations which were finding it difficult to maintain and justify their separate existence. This suggestion

---

[1] *The Witness of Congregationalism in Scotland*, pp. 5, 7, 11.
[2] Cf. Chapter XVI, ii, above.

was in alignment with the denomination's practice in days gone by. Last century, and in the early years of this one, unions of local churches had been effected, and indeed *all* church extension work was regarded as the responsibility of the congregations themselves. Hope Park and Buccleuch Churches in Edinburgh had amalgamated in 1908, and Hillhead Church in Glasgow, which originated as a congregation in the city centre, had made several moves westwards with the migrating population. The adoption of this policy in the 'thirties bore fruit eventually in some wise amalgamations of churches, such as those of Bristo and Augustine congregations in Edinburgh (1940) and Dennistoun and Wardlaw Churches in Glasgow in 1946. The destruction of church property through bombing in the Second World War rendered this kind of amalgamation the most realistic policy for some congregations to adopt.[1] The present church at Giffnock, Glasgow, is the best and happiest illustration of the adoption of the traditional method of church extension within living memory. Formerly it was designated Eglinton Street Church and worshipped in that district from 1825 till 1936 when it began to meet in its present habitat in Fenwick Road, Giffnock. Lloyd Morris Memorial Church, Glasgow, which moved out to Castlemilk, in 1957, promises to be yet another shining example of the wisdom inherent in the older method of church extension.

J. G. Drummond submitted the Report on Church Extension when the Annual Assembly met in his own church of Dundas Street, Glasgow, on the memorable afternoon of 2 May 1934. He pleaded that the times were not propitious for collecting money, but, he added, for the purpose in hand the times were extraordinarily propitious for spending money. He suggested that the General Committee should bring forward at next Assembly a proposal for the constitution of a Church Extension Committee. Some desultory conversation ensued. Thereafter, Thomas Kemp of Dalkeith sprang to his feet. 'I propose', he said, 'that here and now we resolve to open a Church Extension Fund of £25,000.' E. Y. Harrison seconded. Then came proposals about setting up a Committee. At this stage, Daniel McLay took the Assembly by storm, 'What's the use of talking about setting up a Committee?' he exclaimed, rising to his feet, 'Let's *do* something right away. I'll give £50 to the Fund. Who will follow me?' 'I will', replied E. Y. Harrison promising the same amount. 'Put me down too,

---

[1] Cf. *A Chronicle of the Churches*, below, for further illustrations.

for £50', said Thomas Kemp. The excitement increased as one delegate after another called, 'Put me down for £50, £20, £10, or £5', as the case might be. A. C. Hill, the President of the Union that year, was no less moved than the others. 'This is really the best thing we have done so far', he exclaimed excitedly. 'Put me down for £20.'

On the call of members of Assembly, slips of paper were sent round, and in less than a quarter of an hour from the time when the treasurer opened the Fund, £750 had been subscribed. By the following morning McLay announced to the Assembly that the Church Extension Fund had reached £1,125.

During the following year the Fund inaugurated with such feverish enthusiasm had the earnest but sober consideration of the General Committee. A special representative committee was formed to stimulate interest in the new financial venture. The co-operation of the Women's Union was sought and obtained. The District Committees were requested to take steps to arouse interest in the Church Extension Fund in their respective areas. And largely on the strength of the earnest of the Fund's success, a site for a new church was secured at Granton Mains, Edinburgh; a new building was erected for the congregation at Cathcart, Glasgow; and the foundation stone of the new church at Saughton-hall, Edinburgh, was duly laid.[1]

But the Church Extension Fund, so dramatically launched at the Assembly of 1934, was hatched out in a psychological hot-house. Soon snell winds from the outside world blew upon the delicate thing and almost slew it. By the 1938 Assembly in Glasgow the amount raised had been alogether disappointing and unsatis-factory, and enthusiasm had almost evaporated. Indeed the Committee had decided that the target should be, not £25,000, but £10,000.

The times were unpropitious in the churches for raising large sums of money, outwith their customary domestic budgets. The hope was expressed that the Fund might be completed by April 1940 by the launching of a 100,000 Shillings Fund. The ministers responded to the appeal, and gave a heroic lead by contributing ten shillings per £100 of their stipends. Yet by the appointed time the balance had not been donated. Meanwhile the heavy hand of war had again come down upon the economy of the churches. In one sense the horizons of the congregations were narrowed under

[1] Cf. *A Chronicle of the Churches*, below.

the demands of war, in another sense considerably widened, as we shall see in the section of the narrative that follows.

IV

In surveying such a crowded landscape of events and describing it within the compass of a few chapters, a certain discontinuity in the narrative is unavoidable, and the narrator must be forgiven if the chronology should sometimes appear like the bandying about of a tennis ball, and he weary the reader with repetitions or disappoint him by omissions.

All the churches in the thirties, especially in the large towns, had to put up a tremendous fight against secularism. Roderick G. Davies, minister of Morningside Church, Edinburgh, said at the Dundee Assembly in 1932, 'that the world at the present time was offering a serious challenge to the Christian Church. They were told by some writers that there was no need for religion; that the Church had outlived its usefulness, and should be scrapped. Quietly, but nevertheless really, psychologists, biologists, and philosophical writers were propagating pernicious ideas. Men had lost the vision of God. They were being offered the religion of Nature, Beauty, Patriotism, or Creative Evolution.'

In reporting on the previous year's work, Dr. Richardson (in 1938) alluded to the national 'Recall to Religion', and the urgent need for it. He mentioned some of the great changes which were taking place throughout the world—ominous changes as we were all too soon to see. Among domestic problems, he listed the increasing desecration of the Lord's Day, and the enormous spread of gambling in its various forms. There was on all sides a growing paganism, and the churches were harassed by economic problems within, and outside by indifference.

At this time the churches were re-awakened to the necessity of making a more determined and better organised attempt to win the youth of the land for Christ and His Church.[1] An entire session of the Annual Assembly of the Union of 1938 was devoted to a Conference at which 'the many-sided problem of the Youth of today in relation to the Church' was discussed. *The Scottish Congregationalist* for July of that year was a Special Youth Number. In its editorial, 'The Child in the Midst', Ireland Robertson

---

[1] Cf. Chapter XV, III, above.

said 'that the churches of all denominations are awake to the tragic significance of the fact that a large proportion of the rising generation are growing up without any religion beyond what may be acquired through the Bible lesson in the day school. Here and there individuals and congregations have been grappling with the problem, but too many of our churches are still content to jog along in a free and easy way on the beaten track, expressing at times their regret that the number of children attending their Sunday school is diminishing, and sorrowing, almost to tears, that so many children who pass out of Sunday school are subsequently lost to the Church—yet doing nothing practical.' This pressing problem was thoroughly dealt with a few years later as part of the Forward Movement programme of the Union.

The ominous worsening of the international situation is reflected in the Report of the Temperance and Social Problems Committee at the Glasgow Assembly of 1938. D. Gordon Livingston, the secretary of the Committee, in submitting the Report, strongly criticised the attitude of the British Government to the Abyssinian oppression.

J. G. Drummond was elected president of the Union for 1938-39, an honour truly deserved. 'It is noteworthy', wrote the editor of *The Scottish Congregationalist*, in this year, 'that in the volume of sermons published some time ago under the title *The Scottish Pulpit* Congregationalism is represented by A. C. Hill and J. G. Drummond.'

Drummond's philosophy of the development of Congregationalism in Scotland, which he outlined about this time in *The Scottish Congregationalist*, is full of interest. He held that its contribution had been greatest in the river valleys and those geographical areas that had facilitated community life and free movement of people. Congregationalism, he maintained, had not been able to settle where life was static. He believed that this fact bore its lesson to the present policy of the denomination. 'We cannot continue in strength', he said, 'simply by isolated conviction or traditional loyalties, but only by a closer association with one another through common helpfulness and sympathetic interest.' Congregationalism, he considered, had met the spiritual needs of the industrial areas because it had been more in line with the psychological character of the workers. 'Industry that is carried on by means of nerve-racking machinery, acting on stubborn metals, demands quick decision and ready adaptability. A frame of mind rebellious of old restraints and impatient of outworn methods, is the result. It is important to note that it is in such a spiritual atmosphere that we have our most crowded areas.' He further pointed out that the Congregational churches had been least successful in the Celtic regions of the west and north-west, and in those parts of the country where 'the landed interest is strong. There we find that conservatism which does not respond readily to spiritual adventure.' He and Richardson believed that it was necessary now, more than ever before, to develop the machinery of the Union for, as Drummond said, the Union was another means of association of churches than those provided by river valleys and the intimacy of industrial life. A strong Union, he believed, was absolutely vital to the future of Congregationalism.

J. G. Drummond's presidential year was marked by many splendid appeals by him from pulpit and press for a return of the traditional pioneering spirit of Congregationalism. That the other communions in Scotland owed a debt to the Congregational churches he never tired of saying. In some places, 'because we have proved ourselves, the old antagonisms of denominations, which were so hateful, have been broken down, and there has come to be a co-operation for the good of the community which is introducing a new conception of inter-denominational life in Scotland'. 'We know not what lies before us', he wrote in November 1939, 'but we can see by what we have been, and we can determine by what we are, that we must approve ourselves as efficient to proclaim our part in the Universal Church of our Lord Jesus Christ.'

Two months before Drummond wrote those words the second war of the half-century had began, and gradually the customary pattern of the churches' life was dislocated and their activities restricted. Before the 1941 Annual Assembly in Glasgow at which both the secretary and treasurer of the Union closed their periods of office, and their successors were appointed, the smaller countries of Western Europe had been overrun, France had fallen, and the first Battle of Britain had been fought and won. Some churches in the Clydeside area had been destroyed or damaged in the barbarous aerial attacks. Members of the churches were among the victims. Many were rendered homeless. Dr. Richardson's last public service to the Union was when he viewed the desolation of Clydebank and Radnor Park churches after the raids.[1] He was not really

---

[1] Morison Church, Clydebank; Radnor Park Church; Lloyd Morris Memorial Church; and Knightswood Church suffered in the bombing.

physically fit for the ordeal, but he walked amidst the ruins and felt the desolation in his heart.

The 1941 Assembly constituted an Emergency Committee to deal with the bombed churches in the Clydeside area. At that Assembly, Albert Peel, the delegate from the English and Welsh Union, came with the sad news of the plight of the sister churches in the south. Three hundred had been damaged, ninety of which were unusable. The terrible situation brought the churches closer together. E. W. Watt, of Aberdeen, addressing that Assembly, as its retiring President said: 'The war has drawn the churches closer together. There was more co-operation between denominations than would have been possible a few years ago. We have seen the two Archbishops of the Church of England, the Roman Catholic Cardinal Archbishop of Westminster and the Moderator of the Free Church Federal Council uniting in signing a letter on *The Foundations of Peace*. That is a remarkable combination and could only have been achieved through the compelling stresses of war.'

Yes, indeed, the churches did come closer under the all-embracing shadow of war, and the ecumenical movement, faint streaks of whose light we have already marked, rose higher on the rim of the once dark horizon, to shine, when the day of darkness and storm was past, with meridian light and warmth. A World Church was growing up into maturity amid the desolation of war. 'The blight of narrow nationalism', Dr. Watt said in the same address, 'could be overcome only by the World Church, and if the problems of peace and post-war construction were to be solved, the only way was to build up in every nation a community which worshipped the one God and Saviour of all nations.'

The Women's Union under a grand team of officials did wonderful service in these dark days. 'A shining example of cheerful courage', writes Margaret Calder, 'was Mrs. D. Cook, President, 1942-45.' The Women's Union was represented on the Scottish Churches' Committee for work among Women in the Forces, and on the Committee for Women's Social Welfare.[1]

At the 1941 Annual Assembly of the Union some important changes were made in the personnel and function of the District Committees. Churches were now entitled to elect one, two or three delegates (according to the size of membership) in addition to those appointed to the Annual Assembly. The number of

[1] Margaret H. E. Calder, 'Scottish Congregational Women', *The Scottish Congregationalist*, July, August, September 1955.

representatives from the churches on the District Committees was thus doubled, and the influence of the laity increased. Moreover, the new arrangement afforded an opportunity to the younger members, who could not attend the Assembly Meeting, to take a more active interest in the affairs of the Union. In addition to the duties hitherto discharged by the District Committees, they were authorised now 'to act as intermediaries between the General Committee and the individual churches, by discussing beforehand business to be brought forward at Assembly; sending reports of the decisions to the General Committee, generally acting in co-operation with the General Committee in a consultative capacity, and having the opportunity of considering locally, prior to Assembly, business contained in the Agenda'.[1]

[1] *The Scottish Congregationalist,* June 1941.

CHAPTER XIX

THE FORWARD MOVEMENT

I

CHARLES RICHARDSON was succeeded in the Union secretaryship in 1941 by Thomas Carlyle Murphy, minister of Cathcart Church, Glasgow, which by 'vigour and geniality' he had built up from a congregation of 192 (in 1927) to 440 (in 1941). His keen pastoral sense and knowledge of conditions of life in the forces (for he had been an army chaplain in the First World War) were considered to be qualities chiefly needed now in the Secretary of the Union. Moreover, by nature and nurture, Murphy was a democrat with a warm affection for the under-dog, and courage to confront realities.

The successor of Daniel McLay in the treasurership was George R. Green of Glasgow, a man of distinction in his profession of accountancy. These two consecrated and able men were to pilot the denominational ship safely through the deep waters of the remaining war years, Murphy to 1951, Green to 1955.

In August 1942, before the new officials of the Union got into the full sail of their work, Dr. Richardson died. His death was universally lamented. Right to the end of his life the joys and cares of the Congregational churches had been engraved upon his heart. That the Union, which he had shaped by his administrative genius, should be an efficient instrument of Christ's Church and Kingdom, had been Richardson's chief concern. He was a great man and a good. One of his most memorable and self-revealing utterances was spoken in his second term of office as President of the Union, in 1939, to the new ministers. In it he said: 'You will be disappointed in the ministry if you regard it simply as an opportunity for study, for public standing, or as a social utility; but if you will seek to comfort two sisters who have lost a brother, speak to a lonely woman at a well, share the truth with a troubled man at night, confront a rich man with the peril to his soul, pass through an agony of soul to deliver another—then you will truly do the work of Christ and find satisfaction for your own soul.' Charles Richardson was a true *pastor pastorum*.

II

The war had disastrous effects, not only upon the material fabric of the churches, but also on the spiritual fabric of the whole denomination. In the black harvest of war all communions shared. There was, of course, real heroism in places, as there always has been under stress of difficulty, and ever will be. But the overall picture of church life was of spiritual inertia. With his characteristic forthrightness, Carlyle Murphy described the situation in the Congregational churches, in the autumn of 1942: 'Even the so-called fine "voluntary" members are anywhere up to fifty per cent. "paper" members, and the office-bearers half-timers at best. Members have been received into the church fellowship on easy terms, and office-bearers induced to take office on the assurance of how little it would demand of them. And the young have been slipping away out of the church's orbit. . . . We have made the Church so cheap, we have made it so low in the estimation of the outsider, that many who are turning from the materialist view of life, and groping towards a spiritual view, will not turn to the Church for guidance and help.'

About this time, or a little before, an effort was made on a nation-wide scale to revive the religious life of Scotland by a call to an intensified Christian witness. Its chief aim was to make clear the striking growth of the World Church as a unifying power in that day of disintegration.[1] But it became also a call for unity amongst the various churches in Scotland, and a clearer witness of all professing Christians. The movement was a distinct success, though its effectiveness varied in different parts of the country. One marked result, however, was a growth of unity and fellowship among ministers of different religious bodies.

In the dark days of 1944, there began what has been called 'the Reformation of Scottish Congregationalism' through its Forward Movement, which provides one of the most thrilling chapters of Congregational history during the half-century; when the structure of the common life of the churches, reflected in numerous committees dedicated to specific tasks, was revolutionary in combining the values of responsible fellowship with the traditional master passion for spiritual freedom.[2] At the time of the Movement's inception the denomination was numerically small

---

[1] Cf. Chapter XVIII, above.
[2] James M. Calder's Secretarial Survey, *Year Book*, 1953-54, p. 79.

and financially embarrassed. There were 158 churches, with 38,991 members. Much that the churches had witnessed to had now become the common heritage of other communions. But the hearts of the churches still beat true to the great notes of their forefathers in the faith—evangelical; missionary; brotherliness; and the spice of adventurous pioneering. It was felt, moreover, that the World Church needed the essential witness of Congregationalism 'unfettered either by state control or ecclesiastical domination'. The social and spiritual situation in Scotland rendered such a movement imperative, if the denomination were to survive and play its part in the religious awakening. Like all churches in the last thirty years, the Congregational Churches had 'felt the drift and the draught'; the decrease in membership and finance. The Second World War had seriously affected all the work of the churches. But in these black times keen Congregationalists had been praying, planning and longing for brighter times and new vitality.

The real beginning of the Forward Movement of the Congregational Union of Scotland was in the concern felt by a number of Glasgow ministers and laymen. It was soon found that this concern was shared by others outwith the Glasgow area. We proceed now to give a brief factual report of its inauguration and progress.

The Union *Year Books* revealed that the peak years, numerically speaking, in Scottish Congregationalism were those of the middle 'thirties. From then onwards there had been a general decrease in the number of church members, Sunday school scholars and Bible Class pupils. It was felt that the Congregational churches had no longer sufficient life to reproduce themselves and something required to be done in the denomination as a whole. Accordingly the suggestion was made to the General Committee of the Union that a Forward Movement be undertaken and a Commission appointed to consider its nature. This was agreed to and was brought before the Annual Assembly of 1943. That Assembly agreed and remitted it back to the General Committee to consider the launching of a Reconstruction Scheme 'to overhaul our organisation and to think of it in terms of new life and power for reconstruction and revival'. The General Committee appointed a sub-committee to choose from the membership of the Union a number of men and women whom it judged fitted to deal with the matter. This constituted the Commission and consisted of sixty-nine members, 'chosen without fear or favour'. The then president of the Union, George Forges Morgan, minister of Dalmarnock Road Church, Glasgow, was elected chairman of the Commission and led it till the completion of its task, roughly a period of five months.

The Commission was divided into eight panels, embracing Evangelism; Youth; Students, College and the Ministry; District and Union Committees; Assembly Business; Finance; Propaganda and Publications; Ecumenical. Each panel appointed a chairman and a secretary reporter, and eventually drew up its final Reports. Thereupon the Commission as a whole discussed, amended and passed all the Reports on to the Annual Assembly of 1944 for judgment.

Along with this Report there was also brought to the notice of the 1944 Assembly the need for raising a Forward Movement Fund of £100,000. This was to be used for Home Mission work, Youth work, increasing the minimum stipend of ministers, and Church Extension. However the vastness of the sum terrified the Assembly, and it finally agreed to the attempt to raise £50,000. Some slight alterations were made in the Commission's Report but generally it was accepted and passed. The Report was subsequently published under the title *Reconstruction and New Life*. A shorter and more popular pamphlet, outlining the aims of the Movement, was written by Ernest James, minister of Elgin Place Church, Glasgow, and was deservedly popular. A New Life Crest designed by John T. George, then minister of Ebenezer Church, Airdrie, was superimposed on all the literature of the Movement and added to its propaganda value.

In 1944, George Forbes Morgan, who had led the Commission so ably, was appointed salaried Commissioner for three years, and set apart at a service held in Elgin Place Church, Glasgow. The choice was a happy one for Morgan, by grace, temperament and training was an evangelist, and a persuasive and powerful one. From 1925 he had ministered to Dalmarnock Road Church which at the time of his Union appointment had the largest congregation in the denomination. Morgan was popularly known as 'the Bishop of Bridgeton'. He gave splendid leadership and unstinted service to churches and Union alike at this time when new life was stirring throughout the land. He and Carlyle Murphy were the national leaders of the Movement and, whatever success it had, was due in large measure to them, not forgetting the support they received from George R. Green, who placed his gifts of heart, mind, and business so completely at the disposal of the Union in this new venture.

An honorary Commissioner was appointed for each District and it was endeavoured, but without complete success, to have a Commissioner within each church. Thus the Movement enjoyed the support of many laymen of ability who contributed much to its success. A panel of special speakers was drawn up which proved of very great assistance.

For three years Forbes Morgan moved about among the churches, keeping the aims of the Forward Movement before them and seeking to stimulate their interest, especially in the Fund. Through the generosity of some business men, in each of the districts, two ministers' conferences were held on the deeper issues of the Movement, one at Wiston Lodge, Lanarkshire, and one at Cove on the Clyde. The summer conference at Wiston Lodge for young people was a direct outcome from the Forward Movement.

The Commissioner's main task was the raising of the money and here the target was not reached. With a few private donations, and £1,000 from the American Congregational churches, plus the giving of the Home churches, the half-way mark was reached with £25,000, a creditable sum when all the circumstances are taken into account.

It was the writer's privilege to discuss the Movement with Forbes Morgan just before his lamented death in 1958. It appeared to him as he went amongst the churches, that, between the two wars, they had lost the evangelistic impulse, and life within them seemed at low ebb. In numerous instances it was difficult to stir up interest in the churches because they contended that 'the principles for which their Congregational Forefathers fought no longer existed, at anyrate in the same degree. They said we have now nothing for which to fight separately.' Moreover, Morgan considered that the Movement began at a difficult time, during the closing stages of the war. Some of the ministers were on service as chaplains and the source of student-supply had dried up. Besides, many of the most enthusiastic among the young were away with the services and the interests of those at home were naturally much divided.

Economically, too, the time was not propitious. As the war drew to a close, churches that had been stimulated by the Movement were starting to consider their domestic needs. Some felt

Q

they needed a new organ, others a new hall, and where the accommodation was sufficient the property had deteriorated. The putting right of these needs was real Forward Movement work, though it did not add anything directly to the Fund.

Whilst the raising of the Minimum Stipend commended itself to the churches, there was not the same eagerness for Church Extension. It was held that many of the ministers were then aged and there would be vacancies soon. There would not be a sufficient number of ministers for the churches already existing, without worsening the situation by creating new causes. The Commissioner answered these difficulties fully and he believed satisfactorily; but, in many cases, it seemed to him that the mind of the congregation was made up before he had the opportunity to visit it.

It is perhaps too early to view the Forward Movement in historical perspective. Its function was threefold:

1. The rebirth of the Congregational Churches to face the conditions of the new day and age.
2. The development of the family spirit amongst them.
3. The raising of £50,000 in three years to do the work envisaged.

None of these things was accomplished fully, but something of them all was achieved, as in recent years has been shown by the large number of students that entered the Scottish Congregational College,[1] the new churches built, the minimum stipend raised, and new and worthwhile reconstruction carried through by many of the long-established churches in the Union.

Yes indeed it was a 'Reformation of Scottish Congregationalism'.

III

As we have noted above, the Forward Movement Fund made possible a new programme of Church Extension in the 'fifties. New causes were founded and churches erected at Priesthill, Glasgow (1950), Saughton Mains, Edinburgh (1951), Mastrick, Aberdeen (1953), Drumchapel, Glasgow (1953), and East Kilbride (1955).[2]

A new impulse was given to the Youth work of the Union which has been mentioned from time to time in these annals. As we have noticed, the Wiston Week was started. The entire

---

[1] Cf. Chapter XVII, above.
[2] Cf. *A Chronicle of the Churches*, below.

organisation of the Union's Youth activities was gradually improved. Money was now available to send delegates to national and international Conferences. In 1947 the Union appointed George Renton Brown as Youth Organiser—a most happy appointment, all too soon cut short by mortal illness. In September 1950, Miss Mary Blatch of Hillhead Church, Glasgow, was appointed as full-time Youth Adviser of the Union for a period of three years. A recognition service was held in Elgin Place Church, Glasgow, at which she was set apart for her task. Teaching gifts, coupled with a gracious Christian character, rendered her period of service a real ministry to the churches and Sunday schools, and a tower of strength in their work of Christian education. Miss Blatch was re-appointed for a second period of office, and when she retired from this work, in 1955, the Youth activities of the Congregational Union of Scotland were built upon sure foundations.

CHAPTER XX

GREETING THE ECUMENICAL AGE

I

ONE manifest outcome of the Forward Movement of the Union was a stronger emphasis on ecumenicity. The spiritual challenge of the war years, as we have seen, tended to bring the churches together and widen their horizons.[1] The Women's Union, which incidentally had raised £1,310 for the Forward Movement Fund, was active also in the Ecumenical movement. It was in at the commencement of the Scottish Churches Ecumenical Association Conference at Dollarbeg in 1947, and indeed the S.C.E.A. caught the imagination of an increasing number of its members.

A new statutory committee of the Union—the Ecumenical Committee—which henceforth played a large and significant rôle both in the domestic affairs of the denomination and its inter-church relations, was formed in June 1945, itself an outcome of the Forward Movement.

Its aims were 'to further interest in the World Church movement among the churches of the Union; to take appropriate steps to secure more intimate fellowship with other Congregational Unions at home and abroad; to further closer co-operation with other communions in Scotland; in general to act as a liaison between the Union and national and international movements on behalf of the Kingdom of Christ'. Some names that have since assumed prominence in the ecumenical movement in Britain and abroad appear on the original committee: James M. Calder, J. G. Drummond, J. T. Hornsby, R. F. G. Calder, and A. F. Simpson, the committee's secretary and treasurer in its formative period.

II

The first major task of the Ecumenical Committee was to assist the churches of the Union in framing a Statement of Belief, which appeared as a denominational document in 1949.

[1] Cf. Chapters XV, III; XVI, IV; XVIII, IV; XIX, II, paras. 2 and 10.

This statement had its origin in a recommendation by the Ecumenical Panel of the Commission on Reconstruction and New Life (1943-44).[1] 'That there should be a restatement of our credal position as a Union of churches containing the substance of the things most surely believed, thus enabling us to subscribe to a common declaration of the Evangelical Protestant Faith' (Sect. I (2)). When the Report was presented to the Annual Assembly on 2 May 1945 it was suggested that the Union already had such a statement in the Prefatory Note printed yearly in the *Year Book*, and that it would be sufficient to bring that Note up to date. Accordingly the Assembly determined: 'That a Committee shall report to the Districts upon the reasons for, and the desirability or otherwise of a revision of the Prefatory Note to the Regulations of the Union, and shall endeavour to bring forward some suggestions towards a restatement.' It was further agreed that this Prefatory Note Committee be nominated by the Ecumenical Committee, and this was done on 12 September 1945, the members being D. Cook (Helensburgh), R. Dobbie (Glasgow University), C. S. Duthie (Scottish Congregational College), C. F. Graham (Westhill), J. T. Hornsby (Arbroath), A. May (Castle Street, Dundee), T. C. Murphy (secretary of the Union), H. G. Newsham (Morningside, Edinburgh), A. M. Price (Perth, chairman), and A. F. Simpson (Fraserburgh, secretary).

The Committee decided that it was impossible to revise the Prefatory Note, since it was the basis of union between the Congregational and Evangelical Unions in 1896, so that as a record of historic fact it could not be amended. Therefore they recommended to the Ecumenical Committee that they should be empowered to produce a completely new Statement of Belief along the lines of the original recommendation by the Commission. The Ecumenical Committee reported accordingly to the Annual Assembly of 1946, which thereupon resolved 'That the Prefatory Note Committee be asked to continue for another year, and formulate a short statement embodying the fundamental principles of our Beliefs for consideration by the Union'.

In carrying out this remit the Ecumenical Committee recommended to the Prefatory Note Committee that the Statement of Belief be (1) brief, about two thousand words; (2) clothed in language that would be understood by the ordinary man; and (3)

[1] Cf. Chapter XIX, II, above.

framed so as to meet, as far as possible, the varied shades of conviction in the churches.

Work was started immediately. It was decided that there should be fourteen headings or paragraphs, and four of the members were asked to draft provisional statements on the various subjects. The main work fell upon Principal Duthie, who indeed carried the main load throughout. He undertook the paragraphs on God, Jesus Christ, The Holy Spirit, Revelation, The Authority of Scripture, God and the World, The Nature of Man; the Rev. Alex. May those on The Kingdom and the Church, The Christian Life, and The Church and the Social Order; the Rev. A. F. Simpson those on The Ministry and The Sacraments; and the Rev. A. M. Price that on The Life Everlasting.

Consideration of these drafts was continued through the winter of 1946-47, partly by the Committee as a whole, partly through a sub-committee consisting of C. S. Duthie, A. May, and A. M. Price. It was apparent that the Statement could not be ready for presentation to Assembly 1947, and so it was reported in the Ecumenical Committee's Report with the promise that the final draft would be ready by 1948. A draft drawn up in the autumn of 1947 was submitted to the Ecumenical Committee, who suggested certain emendations, after which a final draft was made and submitted to the General Committee of the Union. This was printed and sent down to the District Councils, and emendations either by the Councils or individual members, were sent back to the Statement of Belief Committee, as it had come to be known without any official alteration in its title, for consideration before the draft was presented to Assembly on 4 May 1948. It was there resolved that the Committee should take back the Statement, with several emendations presented at the same time, and report to a Conference Session of Assembly the next year. This was duly done. A thorough revision was made, and some quite considerable alterations in wording were introduced, with an additional section on The Last Things, making fifteen sections in all, to which was added a Preamble and Epilogue explaining the purpose and recognising the limits of such a Statement in Congregational Churches.

The Statement so revised was presented to Assembly on the evening of 2 May and the morning of 3 May 1949 by the Chairman of the Committee, and duly passed with only three amendments carried by Assembly, and one accepted by the

Committee. It was printed at the beginning of the *Year Book*, 1949-50.

In the following year (1950) the Youth Committee of the Union drew up a Syllabus with appropriate Scripture passages to aid the systematic study of the Statement, which was published in August 1950. Dr. A. M. Price in a Foreword to this pamphlet, while pointing out the necessity in every age to set forth intellectually the implications of the Christian Faith, is careful to insist that for Congregationalists 'the desire to follow Christ is the sole requirement of Church membership' and not subscription to a credal statement.

III

We have already in the course of this narrative alluded to the growth throughout the half-century of a tighter organisation of the Congregational churches as a denomination. This tendency is further traced in the creation of the office of chairmanship by the Assembly of 1945 which has become a more permanent office than that of president and in some ways (some presidents themselves have considered) a more important one for the Union as a Union. Be that as it may, the new office has brought order and decorum to the conduct of Assembly business and enabled the Union to benefit from the service of Masters of Assemblies such as Hassal Hanmer 1946-49, George Kirk 1949-53, Arthur Morton Price 1953-56, George R. Green 1956-58, and James L. Proudfoot 1958-.

We have mentioned in other places the meeting of the International Congregational Council at Wellesley, U.S.A., in 1949 and at St. Andrews, in 1953, and the important contributions made at these ecumenical fellowships by Scottish Congregationalists.[1] Also in the period under review there was evinced a new emphasis on evangelism both in the churches and in the training of the students in the Scottish Congregational College.[2] This was the age of sea-side missions, day-school, and industrial chaplaincies. The outreach of the Congregational churches into the intellectual life of Scotland was revealed in the appointment of chaplains to Congregational students at colleges and universities: John Fullerton (Aberdeen), H. T. Donaldson (Dundee), W. B. J. Martin (Edinburgh), Harry Escott (Glasgow), and Helen E. Woods (St.

[1] Chapter XVII and elsewhere.   [2] Chapter XVII, above.

Andrews), have assisted the Union in this important extension of its work.

IV

T. Carlyle Murphy relinquished the office of secretary of the Union in 1951 and undertook the pastoral charge of Montrose Street Church, Glasgow. His death in 1953 was mourned in all the churches. He was succeeded in the secretaryship by James M. Calder in 1951. The new secretary, who had been president of the Union, 1945-46, brought to his task personal, intellectual, and administrative gifts. A successful tenure of office as district secretary of the London Missionary Society for Scotland and Ireland, 1936-51, had familiarised him with the conditions and problems of the individual churches, and his kindly disposition had endeared him in their affections. The newly-appointed secretary was equipped by character, learning and experience to lead Scottish Congregationalism into the full light of the Ecumenical Age. Moreover, his long training as a servant of the World Church had given Calder a standing in the courts and assemblies of sister communions, which in recent years has done much to bring the Congregational Union into close rapprochement with the other religious bodies.

For all that, James Calder remains a staunch champion of the Congregational principle of the autonomy under Christ of the local church. The real headquarters of the Union, he never tires of saying, are the churches themselves. What he deplores and exerts all his energies of mind and heart to alter is the selfish isolationism which in some quarters palms itself off as Congregationalism. Under his leadership not only have the denominational horizons widened but there has been a growing family spirit among the churches of the Union. 'We are a fellowship of churches', he said in his first Secretarial Survey, at the Aberdeen Assembly of 1952, 'and only as the fellowship grows have we anything to contribute to the Ecumenical Movement.'

'Gratitude for past blessings, consecration to the tasks of today, and confident hope for the future' of Scottish Congregationalism were expressed and strengthened at the Diamond Jubilee Assembly in celebration of the union of 1896, which was held in Glasgow, 1 and 2 October 1956. Some 500 ministers and delegates met on Monday afternoon, 1 October, in the Christian Institute where, as we have seen, the historic decision to unity had been taken sixty years previously. The most moving feature of the afternoon's proceedings was 'the naming and reception of a wonderful company of veterans'. Of the surviving ministers, who in 1896 were students or in pastorates, Andrew Ritchie and Donald Grigor were present, and addressed the Assembly with vigour and conviction. Another unforgettable moment of these anniversary celebrations was when at an evening meeting in Elgin Place Church, Dr. R. F. V. Scott, Moderator of the General Assembly of the Church of Scotland, made a passionate plea for church unity. One felt that these historic proceedings were not just backward-looking but indicated the shape of things to come.

During the first four years of his office Calder enjoyed the continued loyal support of the treasurer of the Union, George R. Green, in the financial and spiritual work of the denomination. Green demitted office in 1955 after fourteen years of dedicated leadership. His gifts of heart and brain contributed not a little to the success of the Forward Movement. As a reorganiser and rationaliser of the Union's finances he is worthy of a place of honour in these annals. 'His treasurership was one long administrative triumph.'

In the closing years of his treasurership Green was assisted by a young and virile Glasgow accountant, John K. Templeton, a member of Pollokshields Church, a man of Congregational lineage and conviction, and a missionary enthusiast. In 1957 he succeeded Green in this important Union office. Before taking upon his shoulders the full onus of the treasurership Templeton travelled through the length and breadth of the land with the purpose of persuading the churches to initiate a pension scheme for ministers of the Union—a much needed and too long delayed undertaking.[1] At the 145th Annual Assembly of the Union held in Elgin Place Church, Glasgow, in May 1957, a scheme for the setting up of a Central Pension Fund for the benefit of ministers was heartily approved. The present writer will not forget the inspiring spectacle of young Templeton fighting in Assembly for high views of finance. It is not likely that time, for all its cruelty, will deface from the minds of many the image of John K. Templeton when, after the success of the Pension Scheme, he exclaimed with a full heart 'This is the Lord's doing; it is marvellous in our eyes'.

One need not despair of the future of Scottish Congregationalism's testimony within the Church Catholic, when such sons

[1] Cf. Chapter XVI, v, above.

and daughters are born of its principle. Its wider power of self-adjustment to the changing needs of changing days, moreover, assures the Congregational churches of Scotland of a continuing mission in the religious life of the land. With all her sister Communions the Congregational Union of Scotland greets the Ecumenical Age.

PART SEVEN

A CHRONICLE OF THE CHURCHES

THE CHURCHES

A NOTE ON ORIGINS

SCOTTISH Congregationalism manifests itself to the historian of its origins and evolution as three streams.

The earliest had its source in the independent study of the Scriptures by individuals like Glas, Smith, Ferrier, Barclay, and Dale. It is now extinct.

The middle stream which rose towards the close of the eighteenth century was fed from several sources, of which four are singled out for special consideration.

In the first place, at least one Congregational church originated through the ministrations of one who had no connection with any of the religious bodies in Scotland. This was so in the case of the church at Annan, which was formed at the end of the eighteenth century and whose first minister was Andrew Carnson, a native of Ireland.

A second class of churches arose through the narrow and despotic action of Presbyterian Church Courts, which compelled members and ministers of Presbyterian churches to seek elsewhere the liberty denied them in their own denomination. They left it without in the first instance having any clear idea of Congregational principles, which were intelligently adopted only at a later period. To this class belong the churches in Huntly, Perth, Paisley, and other places mentioned in the ensuing chronicle. Although their formation as Congregational churches did not take place until the last few years of the eighteenth century, they had in spirit and practice adopted almost unconsciously the principles of Congregationalism prior to that time.

A third class consisted of churches which appear to have been constituted by groups of pious men who, having made an independent study of the Scriptures, came to the conclusion that the 'Congregational Way' was most in accord with New Testament teaching and example. Accordingly they were moved to seek a purer Christian fellowship than they could find in the churches existing at the time. To this class belong Belmont Street Church, Aberdeen, and the church in Montrose.

A fourth, and the most numerous class of churches in this middle stream, consisted of those whose origin is traceable to the great evangelistic movement that took place during the last few tempestuous years of the eighteenth century, and with which the names of Robert and James Alexander Haldane and their colleagues are connected.

The later stream of Scottish Congregationalism had its source in the new theological insights of James Morison, and the resultant formation of the Evangelical Union in 1843. This ebullient movement mingled with the middle stream of Congregational witness in 1896, and added some ninety churches to the newly-constituted Congregational Union of Scotland.

Since the end of the nineteenth century other churches have been formed from time to time largely as a result of the Church Extension work of the Union and the evangelistic ventures of the District Councils.[1]

[1] In the Chronicle of the Churches that follows, churches marked thus with an asterisk (*) are now extinct.

NORTHERN COUNTIES

ABERDEEN

BELMONT STREET (formerly GEORGE STREET) is the oldest Congregational church in the north of Scotland, if not in the whole country.[1] It owes its origin to George Moir, a hosier in Aberdeen, who, on reading King's *Inquiry into the Constitution, Discipline, Unity and Worship of the Primitive Church*, became convinced that the first Christian churches were Congregational, and set his heart upon seeing such a church in Aberdeen. He took council with two friends, and after 'occasional interviews and conversations', the three held their first formal meeting on Friday, 15 September 1797 to consider what action should be taken. They were subsequently joined by six others. Whilst seeking a suitable site on which to build a chapel, they worshipped in a hall. A place of worship to seat 1,200 was erected and opened in George Street, 2 September 1798. On 16 September the church was formed, nine brethren standing up 'and avowing the Congregational discipline, and their relation to each other as church members by giving each other the right hand of fellowship'. The first minister was William Stephens of Bingley, who began his ministry on 25 May 1800. He remained only

[1] See note on School Wynd Church, Paisley, below.

some three years. In April 1804 Stephens became James Haldane's colleague at the Edinburgh Tabernacle and one of the tutors at the Theological Academy in that city. John Philip succeeded him in the Aberdeen pastorate in 1804. Prior to Philip's settlement there had been trouble in the church, and matters were made worse in that a minority of the members had objected to the call to him. To test the strength of the dissentients Philip adopted a very drastic course. In May 1806 he dissolved the church! Out of a membership of 277 only thirty declined to come forward and sign in favour of the new order. Evidently the minority had been more noisy than numerous. From that time until the close of his ministry in 1819 the church enjoyed a period of uninterrupted peace and prosperity. John Philip left Aberdeen in 1819 to become one of the agents of the London Missionary Society in South Africa, where he laboured for thirty years, and became a figure of international importance. 'Belmont' has played no small rôle in the history of the denomination and the religious life of Aberdeen under the leadership of distinguished ministers like Alexander Thomson, David Arthur, James Stark, Henry Alexander Inglis, and James Gilmour Drummond. The present building was opened for worship in 1865.

FREDERICK STREET.* Early in the nineteenth century this, the second Congregational church in Aberdeen, was formed. A malt barn used by the first body of seceders who set up in Aberdeen in 1756, was adapted by the Haldanes as a preaching station. Thither went a few of the dissentients from George Street Church when Philip dissolved that church in 1806. David Russell, who had previously conducted the services, was recalled from Montrose, and, after some weeks, the church was formally constituted on 8 February 1807 with a membership of seventeen, four of whom came from George Street Church. David Russell's ordination followed on 11 March. After a brief ministry of two years he was called to Dundee, and for some six years thereafter there appears to have been no settled ministry. The church, which was never numerically large, suffered by the departure of several members who, along with others from George Street Church, formed a new church in BLACKFRIARS STREET (now SKENE STREET CHURCH), in 1820. Prominent among the original twenty-five members of Blackfriars Street Chapel, which was opened for public worship on 26 August 1821, was Peter Taylor, the name-father of the distinguished theologian, Peter Taylor Forsyth. The members remaining in Frederick Street Church removed first to DEE STREET* and then in 1871 they united with Blackfriars Street Church. Some years before this date an 'unattached' congregation, of which for many years Hugh Hart had been minister, settled in the old building in Frederick Street, and in 1865 this congregation and its minister, John Hunter, became connected with the Congregational Union; but the church ceased to meet in 1882. Blackfriars Street Church had a line of distinguished ministers of whom

John Kennedy, 1836-46, was the chief. His work was memorable, particularly among the young. The church's two Sunday schools had 800 children on the roll, and the minister's Bible class was crowded, especially by young men from the university. George Macdonald, the poet and novelist, was a member of the class for 1843. Among other notable men who came under Kennedy's influence were Principal James Donaldson, Professor Alexander Bain, and Walter C. Smith, the poet-preacher of Edinburgh. Kennedy's interests extended far beyond his church and city. He moved a resolution at the great Anti-Slavery Convention in London in 1840, was an ardent temperance advocate, urged the repeal of the Corn Laws, and helped to found the Liberation Society. Sheriff Wilson secured his help for his Aberdeen School of Industry, the precursor of the Ragged Schools.

Kennedy was a very strict Sabbatarian. On one occasion he reproved his young wife (a sister of John Stuart Blackie, then Professor of Greek at Marischal College) for breaking the Sabbath by taking their first-born infant for an airing on that day. Deacon Peter Taylor shared his pastor's prejudice. He used to draw the blinds of his house on Saturday night and keep then down until Monday morning so that the Sabbath might be honoured. George Macdonald, who with his brother Charles lodged with the good deacon, found this habit highly inconvenient, but Taylor would not change his ways. The only light permitted came from the back door which young George used purposely to leave open.

Another famous ministry at Blackfriars Street was that of Joseph Vickery (1871-82). During his time current political and social questions were discussed from its pulpit and platform with fearless energy. 'Blackfriars' was then the Mecca of the intellectuals of Aberdeen. William Robertson Nicoll, the founder-editor of the *British Weekly*, attended Vickery's services. Sometimes Robertson Smith was seen in the congregation. The office-bearers of that day included several prominent Aberdeen citizens, among whom were Dr. Barker, Principal of the Gymnasium, John Leith, the founder of the P.S.A. movement in Aberdeen, and William Watt of the *Free Press*. Sir James Murray was a member of the congregation, and P. T. Forsyth was active in the junior ranks of the church.

His command of straight-forward and direct language made Vickery a powerful force in the pulpit. In 1874 when horse-racing was much in vogue in Aberdeen, he condemned that sport most vehemently in a sermon. In revenge a horse named after him was entered for a race at the next meeting. 'Joseph Vickery', however, apparently endorsed the views held by his namesake, and made his protest by bolting off the course. Horse racing soon afterwards was brought to an end in the city.

The present attractive building in Skene Street was opened for public worship in October 1886, since when the designation of the church was changed to Skene Street Congregational Church.

ALBION STREET Church was formed in 1856, as a result of the evangelistic labours of James Hall Wilson, who since 1847 had directed a mission in the East end of the city. He and his people were pioneers in home mission work and enjoyed the support of Queen Victoria. Owing to the increase of members the majority of the congregation left and formed TRINITY CHURCH in October 1878, its first minister, John Duncan, exercising a famous ministry of twenty-three years. WOODSIDE CHURCH was formed 13 March 1821 by members of the other Aberdeen churches to meet the requirements of a growing population in a newly industrialised area. ST. PAUL STREET Church was formed in June 1846 mainly by members of Blackfriars Street Church, who were dissatisfied with the attitude of that church and its minister towards the Morisonian movement. A. M. Fairbairn ministered to St. Paul Street Church, 1872-77, and helped it to acquire its reputation as a centre of scholarly evangelical preaching. The congregation joined with Albion Street Church to form ALBION AND ST. PAUL'S in 1938. JOHN STREET* Church was an Evangelical Union cause formed in 1863 by members of St. Paul Street Church. It was closed in 1913. BON ACCORD* Church was formed by seceders from Trinity Church in 1897. It was admitted into the Congregational Union in 1899. It was closed in 1937.

MASTRICK Church was constituted on 3 March 1953, as a part of the Church Extension programme of the Forward Movement of the Congregational Union. The present building was opened for worship 28 May 1954. Andrew G. Jenkins was the first pastor.

ABERDEENSHIRE

HUNTLY Church was formed in 1800 by George Cowie (who had been deposed from his ministry in the Anti-Burgher church there for supporting James Haldane and his colleagues) and some of his original congregation who shared their minister's enthusiasm for the missionary preachers and their aims. The first Congregational church was opened for worship in 1802. The present building was erected some fifty years later. The Huntly church from its commencement has been famous for its contribution of dedicated life to the cause of missions. It has given to the Church Universal men like John Philip, apostle to the Hottentots; William Milne, coadjutor with Robert Morrison of China; James Legge, missionary to China, 1839-73, and Professor of Chinese Language in the University of Oxford, 1875-97. Scotland's great mystic, George Macdonald, was a son of this church.

STUARTFIELD* Church was formed in 1802. Three members of the Anti-Burgher church at Clola, who declined to submit to ecclesiastical discipline for having gone to hear William Stephens preach at Belmont Church, Aberdeen, joined with nine converts of a neighbouring

R

Episcopalian divine to form a prayer meeting and later a congregation. They erected a chapel in 1801 and formed themselves
into a church the following year. They called James Robertson to be
their pastor, who laboured among them for thirty years. The church
ceased in 1900.

FRASERBURGH—MID STREET Church was formed in 1803, as a
result of the preaching of James Haldane in the town and neighbourhood. In the same year Udney Anderson became pastor, and served the
church for twelve years. It was from the fellowship of this church that
Charles S. Duthie, the present Principal of the Scottish Congregational
College, came. A second church, MANSE STREET,* was formed in
1845 by Archibald Duff, the minister of Mid Street Church, and three
deacons and fifty-six members of that church, who avowed their
sympathies with the Evangelical Unionists. A small chapel was erected
in Manse Street. The congregation joined the Evangelical Union in
1865. The church was closed in 1916.

In 1805 a small church began at WESTHILL, largely through the
efforts of friends in George Street Church, Aberdeen. In 1845 the
church ceased to be connected with the Congregational Union, and
ultimately in 1862 joined the Evangelical Union with which it remained
connected until the union of 1896. One of its ministers, William Cran,
1901-32, was a botanist with a national reputation. In or about 1805
churches were formed in BUCKSBURN* and ST. FERGUS* but they
seem to have ceased after a few years. At PITSLIGO* a struggling
church formed in 1803 existed for three years under the pastoral care
of John Beattie. He left because of the inability of the congregation to
support him and his family. The members subsequently became the
nucleus of a Baptist church in the village. In June 1808 the church in
DUNCANSTON* was formed by members of the Huntly congregation,
who carried into the new cause some of the Presbyterian practices of
the mother church. Their chapel, a building of stone and turf, was
erected almost entirely by their own labour. Under their first minister,
Donald Morrison, who remained with them till his death in 1846, the
cause prospered greatly. One of its pastors, Andrew F. Simpson, later
occupied the Chair of Biblical Language and Literature in the Congregational Theological Hall, Edinburgh. Some of the members of
Duncanston Church formed a sister church at CULSALMOND* in 1824,
of which John Rennie was minister for many years. They also formed
another sister church at INSCH* in 1874, though Alexander Wilson,
a native of Insch and a member of the Huntly Church, had as early as
1812 founded a Sunday school there, which he conducted in the
Mason's Hall, at Insch. The church is now closed. The Congregational
church of RHYNIE has a complex history. It was formed in 1804, as
the end result of a visit of the Missionary preachers to Cabrach in the
closing years of the eighteenth century. The Secession Church at Old

Town, Cabrach, gathered largely by the probationary labours of George Cowie of Huntly, had been perplexed by the question of the legality of giving countenance to the itinerants. The minister resigned and the congregation split. The result was a more or less 'unattached' church, meeting first in Cabrach, and then alternately there and in Lesmoir, a hamlet two miles from the village of Rhynie. Ultimately, on Cowie's advice, the fellowship applied to the Congregationalists for pulpit supply. The preacher sent was George Cruickshank who laboured among them for some time, and was then ordained pastor of the church in 1804. From that date the church considered itself connected with the Congregational order of churches. In 1808 a church building was erected on a brae eastward from Mains of Lesmoir. The little chapel was often in need of repair. Its roof was of thatch, and under rigorous winter conditions far from weatherproof. After a time it was decided to seek a site for the erection of a new building in the village. The new church was opened in Rhynie village in 1829. It had three galleries, on the west, north, and south ends. On the east side stood the pulpit with the precentor's desk between the two windows. From its inception the little church was deeply dedicated to all missionary and philanthropic movements. In 1815 it formed the Rhynie Auxiliary Bible and Missionary Society. One of the honoured sons of the congregation, Robert Harvey Smith, was instrumental in forming the Aberdeen and Banffshire Mutual Instruction Union in 1851—the first 'W.E.A.' in the north-east of Scotland. The Rhynie church has a long roll of honour of sons given to the ministry of the Church at home and overseas. In 1822 the church at INVERURIE was formed as the result of the evangelistic labours of William Brown, who became its first pastor.

PETERHEAD Church owed its formation in 1823 to James Anderson, a merchant in that town. He and his family were members of the church at Stuartfield, about ten miles distant. Anderson was the means of bringing its pastor, James Robertson, periodically to Peterhead, and secured the Masonic Lodge as a place of meeting. After a lapse of some years, Anderson purchased the chapel in Windmill Street which had been built by the Anti-Burgher body. The first minister of the Peterhead Church was James Scott, 1823-31. Several of the members of the congregation formed the church in PORT ERROL (now CRUDEN BAY) in December 1882. It met first in a mission hall. The present building was opened for worship in November 1884. A church was formed in ELLON* in 1828, and at BANCHORY* in 1830. When a congregation of the Free Church of Scotland was formed at Banchory at the time of the Disruption, the remaining members of the Congregational church united with it. In 1861 the church in NEW PITSLIGO* was formed by members from neighbouring Congregational churches. The church ceased in 1927. In 1879 the church in NEW DEER was formed by members who had seceded from the Established church of the parish.

BANFFSHIRE

BANFF* was visited by James Haldane on his first preaching tour in July 1797, when on the bank of the Deveron he preached to large and interested crowds. But it was not until 1809 that a church was formed. Members of a Relief Church which had been dissolved purchased their old building and sought a Congregational minister. The church split in 1820 and formed the U.P. Church. The most famous minister of Banff Congregational Church was John Murker who was a household name with Congregationalists of the old school. When he died in 1879 many members left to form the church at MACDUFF, and in 1886 the Banff church ceased to meet. There was a church in KEITH* formed in 1801, of which Mr. Japp was pastor, but it seems to have had only a brief existence. The church in MILLSEAT was formed in August 1830, largely as a result of the labour of Joseph Morrison, who became its first minister. The congregation was mostly composed of members and adherents of the church in Banff. After a site for a place of worship had been promised by the proprietor of Craigston, and the foundation of the building had been dug out and some portion of the stones laid, the proprietor withdrew the agreement, verbally made, and intimated in the most decided manner his determination not to allow them to erect a church on his property. This intimation produced 'a sort of panic in which all hands were feeble and all hearts faint'. However, the Millseat Congregationalists determined not to abandon their design, but to look to God for guidance and help for this emergency. Nor did they look in vain. The Earl of Fife allowed them a site on his property and the church was built on the spot where it still stands. It was a very homely and unpretentious edifice thatched with the heather among which it stood. A new chapel was opened in December 1858. The church in Millseat has had many distinguished sons, among whom were John Duncan, the famous pastor of Albion Street Church, Aberdeen; Professor A. F. Simpson; David Duncan, Professor of Moral Philosophy in Madras Presidency College, and the biographer of Herbert Spencer; and Principal A. R. Henderson of Paton College, Nottingham. In CULLEN* a church was formed in 1846 by members of the church in Banff. Charles A. Piper was the first pastor. The church ceased to meet after the retirement of its fourth pastor, John Taylor, in 1877. The church building is now occupied by the Episcopal Church. There was a preaching station at PORTSOY* early in the nineteenth century, of which George Douglas, of the Society for Propagating the Gospel at Home, was in charge. But no church was formed there till 1862, when one was constituted by members of the church at Banff. Robert Bell became pastor in 1871, but after his retirement in the following year the church ceased to meet. Congregationalism in MACDUFF can be traced to Joseph Gibb, minister of Banff

Church, who conducted Sunday evening services in the old Town Hall of Macduff in 1826. When Gibb emigrated to America, he was succeeded by John Murker, who continued the services with such success that in 1862 it was decided to form a church, which was accomplished in June 1879. The present church building was opened for worship in March 1881. Macduff Church is remembered far and wide as the scene of the first ministry of A. E. Garvie, whom John Morley once met there in his journeyings in the north, and described as 'a genius and a scholar shut away in a cold dour town'. Garvie commenced his ministry at Macduff in 1893. Many years later, he related of this period how at the ordination luncheon, one of the deacons extolled the Rev. John Murker of Banff and expressed the hope that the mantle of Elijah would fall upon Elisha. The new minister was 'irreverent enough to suggest' that he would prefer a mantle of a more modern cut. And it would seem (added the narrator with pawky humour) that he wore the modern mantle during his stay in Macduff, for to some of the older people of that time the young minister's presentation of Christian truth appeared to be 'another Gospel than that they had previously known!' In April 1895 A. E. Garvie was called to the charge of Montrose Church, from which he went some years later to begin his life work as a teacher of theology. The church at Macduff paid tribute to Dr. Garvie when he left them for Montrose in these prophetic words: 'From your brilliant gifts as a scholar, and from your exceptional qualifications both as a preacher and a teacher, we are confident that you have a distinguished ministerial career before you as well as an important work to do for Scottish Congregationalism; and we are proud that the church here should have been, even for a brief period, the scene of your earliest labours in the ministry.' Dr. Garvie's successor was Adam Drummond, a hard-working, self-sacrificing pastor whose attractive lectures on Buchan characters are still remembered as an outstanding contribution to the cultural life of the town. His son, J. G. Drummond, has been for many years now one of our ablest denominational leaders.

MORAYSHIRE

The church in ELGIN* was formed in January 1804 with William Ballantine as the pastor. The circumstances of its formation were somewhat peculiar. In 1801 Ballantine, who had formed a Congregational church at Thurso, came to Elgin to minister to a numerous body who called themselves 'A Free Presbyterian Congregation'. 'Finding them a very mixed and ill-assorted body, he began to apply discipline, and gradually touched upon Congregational principles.' His people were not prepared to submit to this, and after much contention and confusion they dismissed him. Some of the members, however, followed him, and to these he began to preach in a garden, and afterwards in a hall. From among these Elgin Congregational Church was formed. A meeting place for the church was found in the Tabernacle which Robert Haldane had built. The cause, however, did not prosper. The building had a seating capacity of 1,300 but only a handful of worshippers gathered week by week. At the end of 1806 Ballantine, who had adopted Glasite views, resigned. His immediate successor, Alexander Stewart, soon after his coming to Elgin adopted Baptist views, and the Haldanes doing likewise, the congregation was deprived of a meeting place. A small chapel, that had originally belonged to the Episcopalians, was rented and proved more suited to their needs. Neil McNeil, one of the Edinburgh students, took up the work and attained considerable success. He was repeatedly urged to assume the office of pastor from his arrival in 1808, but he declined to do so till 1815, when his induction took place. He remained as minister until 1854, a year before his death. During his time the church at Elgin was the centre of widespread evangelistic work. McNeil conducted regular services at Knockando. One of the results of his labours was the conversion of John Mackenzie who subsequently became High Commissioner in South Africa. His son was W. Douglas Mackenzie delightfully known by all Scottish Congregationalists. One of the most renowned and honoured sons of this church was James Ross, a pioneer historian of Scottish Congregationalism and one of the denomination's most revered statesmen and leaders in the last quarter of the nineteenth century. The church ceased some ten years ago. Occasional visits to FORRES* were paid by various itinerant preachers at the beginning of last century. Regular preaching was first provided by David Sutherland who was followed by John Martin in March 1802. Much excitement and blessing followed his labours in the district, and two years later in 1804 a church was formed over which he presided for thirty years. He was followed in the pastorate by Robert Weir who remained until 1843. In the following year Nisbet Galloway, who was connected with the Evangelical Union, became pastor, with the principles of which body the church and its succeeding ministers continued to be sympathetic, though the church was never formally connected with the Evangelical Union. The church ceased in December 1939. In the rural district of KNOCKANDO* some earnest folk 'who valued the Gospel and were willing to travel for it' formed the nucleus of a church which was formed in 1804 'by prayer and fasting'. John Munro was the first and only pastor. After his death in 1853 the church gradually languished, and ceased round about 1860. The church in NAIRN was formed in 1806, when James Dewar became pastor. For some years before his settlement Dewar had done fine work as an evangelist in Argyllshire. In 1804 he came to Nairn and such blessing attended his preaching there that a call to remain permanently was given to him, and in July 1806 he was solemnly ordained to what was to prove his life work. The extent of James Dewar's and his brother

Alexander's (of Avoch) evangelistic work is thus stated by the latter: 'From Fort William in Lochaber to John O'Groats and round Cape Wrath, we proclaimed the glorious gospel in every parish where Gaelic is spoken but three.'

INVERNESS-SHIRE

In 1804 there were several preaching stations in the district of Strathspey, at some of which the people met in fellowship, but without ministers. When the dispute on the Baptist question arose in 1807 most of the members adopted Baptist views, and formed the Baptist Church in Grantown (Moray). There was a Congregational church at ROTHIE-MURCHUS* formed as a result of the preaching of James Haldane. Here people gathered from Strathspey and Badenoch to sit under the ministry of Lachlan Mackintosh, a man of outstanding gifts and character. This church became Baptist in 1807. There was a preaching station at FORT WILLIAM* at which John Campbell of Oban and McKillican of Acharan occasionally preached, but no pastor appears to have been settled. In the town of INVERNESS* a church was formed in 1818. By the middle years of the century the church had become almost extinct, and was re-formed in 1871. It ceased to meet in 1875.

ROSS AND CROMARTY

No part of Scotland was less accessible to the evangelistic labours of the Haldanes and their colleagues than the counties of Ross and Sutherland, in both of which Presbyterianism held the field more exclusively than in any other part of the land. They do not appear to have been visited by James Haldane; but every year from the beginning of the nineteenth century till many years thereafter they were visited by Congregational ministers who preached the Gospel in various parts of the county. Neil McKechnie, minister of Woodside Church, Aberdeen (1821-38) made it a condition of his accepting the call to the pastorate that he be allowed six or eight weeks free from his pastoral work every summer to preach the gospel to his countrymen in their native glens and mountains. The earliest date at which anything like a movement in favour of Congregational principles took place was in 1802, when, through the preaching of a Mr. Rae, a student of divinity, many persons in the town and neighbourhood of FORTROSE* received spiritual blessing. As a result of his earnest labours Rae was invited to become the pastor of a number of Christian people in the district, and was ordained by Cowie of Huntly and Ballantine of Elgin. A place of worship was in process of being built when the people found they were unable to complete the work. Soon afterwards Rae became a Baptist and many of his followers joined him in the adoption of his views. The church in AVOCH was formed early in 1808 as the result of the evangelistic labours of Alexander Dewar. He became the first pastor of the church and was the means of gathering a large and prosperous congregation in Avoch which, almost 150 years later, still holds a leading place in the district as a centre of evangelistic life and activity. In addition to his pastoral labours Dewar was a zealous evangelist and for many years an itinerant preacher in many parts of Ross and Sutherland. He died in 1849.

CAITHNESS

Wick and Thurso were among the first places visited by James Haldane and John Aikman in the memorable tour of 1797, and in no part of the land were their labours ultimately more successful. 'The state of religion in that country was then most deplorable. Thurso, that is Thorstown, had not been catechised for forty years, a circumstance which then implied great neglect, and in all the shire of Caithness, consisting of ten parishes, there was scarcely an instance of the gospel being fully preached.' Tract distribution, open-air preaching, and the opening of Sunday schools were the methods adopted by the evangelists. At first they had audiences of a few hundred but soon numbers increased to four and five thousand, and conversions followed the preaching of the gospel. The result was that soon forty of the converts at WICK formed themselves into a church in 1799, and invited John Cleghorn to be their minister. His ordination took place on 17 March 1799. For nearly fifteen years he laboured there with great success. There was also an E.U. church in Wick, VICTORIA PLACE,* formed in 1846. It ceased in 1902. At THURSO a meeting place was built, and in the beginning of September 1799 James Haldane and John Aikman 'separated the brethren and united them in church fellowship'. William Ballantine was the first pastor.

ORKNEY AND SHETLAND

On his first preaching tour in 1797 James Haldane exercised a memorable ministry in KIRKWALL, thousands listening to his preaching on many occasions. As a result of his labours and those of the preachers who followed him, a congregation was gathered, and a church formed in 1806. John Black became pastor in that year. He stayed only a short time and was followed by David Ramsay in 1807. He was joined by George Robertson in 1815 and together they did a great work not only in Kirkwall but throughout all the islands. The present church building in Palace Road is the fourth used by the congregation since its constitution in 1806. It was opened for public worship in November 1876. In the early years of the church's history John Ireland, the composer of many old Orkney psalm tunes such as 'Barray', 'Ronaldshay', 'Deerness' and 'Elwick', was precentor. A church at WESTRAY* was also the fruit of the spiritual revival brought about by the labours of James Haldane. During Haldane's 1797 visit to Orkney he was so impressed by the earnestness and ability of William Tulloch, a catechist who was one of his guides through the islands, that he engaged him immediately afterwards for extended work. Tulloch, a native of North Ronaldshay, thereafter evangelised through the numerous islands. Westray responded to his preaching, and a company of Christians came together for edification. In various parts of the island meetings were held in barns and other places. Subsequently, it was proposed that they should form themselves into a Congregational church. Separation between Church and State was a new idea to all of them, and the more influential part of the company opposed the proposal. However, despite the opposition, a church was formed about the year 1806 and Tulloch was its first minister. The formation of the church led to such bitter opposition that all accommodation for indoor services was denied them. Refusing to be hindered in their obedience to the Lord, they met and worshipped in the open air until permission was granted them to hold their meetings in the large hall of Noltland Castle. The accommodation was unsuitable, being dark and damp. They decided to build a church. Money was scarce but they gave what they could and everyone had a mind to work. The fruit of their sacrifice they gathered the following year when a little chapel was opened free of debt. The church grew and multiplied, but after a few years was in troubled waters in the controversy over the nature of baptism. They ultimately adopted the Scots Baptist system. A church was started in HARRAY* in 1810 through the labours of Ramsay and Robertson of Kirkwall, but no minister was settled there till twenty-five years later. A chapel was erected in 1817, and the labours of visiting preachers were much blessed. In 1823 a church was formed in RENDALL* through the labours of George Robertson of Kirkwall. James Russell became pastor in 1835, but the church ceased in 1882, on the removal of its pastor, Alexander Whyte. The church building was purchased by the U.P. Church in 1883. In SHAPINSAY a church was formed in 1852 by persons who had adopted Evangelical Union principles. The meetings at first were held in a barn, then in a joiner's shop, and subsequently in different parts of the island. A building was opened for worship in September 1853. The church joined the Evangelical Union in 1855, and Thomas G. Salmon became its pastor in the same year.

In 1799 James Haldane and William Innes visited SHETLAND and spent six weeks in an itinerating tour, preaching to large congregations. Their good work was continued by James Tulloch, who had attended the classes of the Theological Academy conducted by Greville Ewing in Glasgow. He returned to his native Shetland in 1803, where, in the region around Lerwick, he preached the Gospel. While thus engaged Tulloch was 'impressed' and hurried on board a warship, but was soon liberated through the influence of friends, who were more conversant with the toleration laws than his persecutors. However, having no adequate means of support for his family he was compelled to seek secular employment, but continued his evangelistic labours. He took the pastoral oversight of a church at BIXTER* which was formed in 1808 largely of people from Walls. When Tulloch died in 1863 the church was almost extinct, and was ultimately united with the church in Walls. The church in LERWICK was formed in 1808, as the result of the combined labours of George Reid and Isaac Nichol, who had been sent to Shetland in 1805 as evangelists by the Society for Propagating the Gospel at Home. Reid had been a student in the theological class conducted by William Ballantine in Elgin. He became pastor of the church in Lerwick in 1808, where he remained until his death in 1845. The church in WALLS was formed in 1812 as the result of the united labours of George Reid of Lerwick and Alexander Kerr. The latter became pastor of the church in 1825. Kerr, while pastor at Walls, acted as pastor of several other churches in the islands, which had been originated through his labours. In 1817 a church in FOULA* was formed through the labours of Reid of Lerwick. It ceased in 1918. A church was formed in SAND in 1835 through the labours of Alexander Kerr, and John Nicholson became pastor in 1837. A few years later Nicholson moved to SULLOM* (Northmavine), where a church had been formed through Kerr's labours. It ceased in 1930, when the Home Mission Committee of the Church of Scotland assumed spiritual oversight of the district. The church in REAWICK with which the church in Sand ultimately united, appears to have existed early in the nineteenth century, but it was not until 1842 that a pastor was settled. In that year James Stout took the pastoral oversight of the church and remained until his death in 1862. Up to that date Sand seems to have been the central church, with Reawick and Bixter as sub-stations, but gradually Sand declined in importance and Reawick became the main church. A church in SANDWICK* appears to have been formed as early as 1812 by George Reid of Lerwick. The church ceased to meet after 1882. The church in SCALLOWAY was formed in January 1840. In 1865 Samuel Sinclair became pastor of a church in WHITENESS* the members of which had been connected with the church in Sullom. Subsequently, Whiteness became a branch of the church in Scalloway. It has now ceased to meet. There were several small churches in the Shetland Islands which never had settled pastors and now have ceased: SANDNESS* (connected with the church in Walls) was formed by Alexander Kerr round about 1830. SEAFIELD* (or Mid Yell) was formed by Kerr in 1835. UNST* (or Norwick) was formed by Kerr in 1824. It ceased to meet in 1863. There was a preaching station at

NESTING* where James Pottinger laboured for many years. The services were held in the Wesleyan Methodist Church. The congregation joined with Lerwick in 1864.

EASTERN COUNTIES

KINCARDINESHIRE

SAUCHIEBURN.* About 1809 under the ministry of Thomas McKinnon this church, which was originally the mother church of the Bereans, and as such was started in 1773, appears to have become definitely Congregational. McKinnon was the one and only minister in that connection, for after his death in 1854 the church ceased to meet. Three miles north of BERVIE,* at Fawside, a church was formed in 1803 as the result of the occasional preaching of George Cowie of Montrose. Adam Paterson, one of Robert Haldane's students, was the first minister. The church, at an early stage of its history, was much injured by the pastor and a large section of the members adopting Baptist views. These withdrew and the remnant called James MacKenzie, who settled as minister in 1806. The church ceased in 1848. A church was formed in LAURENCEKIRK* in 1842, as the result of the evangelistic labours of David Moir, and was joined by members of the church in Sauchieburn. Moir became minister in 1842. The church was closed in 1915.

DUNDEE

The church in WARD CHAPEL is the oldest Congregational church in Dundee. It originated in the union of three churches which existed in the town at the opening of the nineteenth century.

1. Members of the Anti-Burgher congregation in 1769 left that body on the deposition of their minister, Andrew Scott, and formed a church on the plan of the Old Scots Independents. On the death of Scott's colleague and successor in the pastorate, the church became Congregational, and William Maxton, one of Robert Haldane's students, was ordained and inducted as minister in June 1803.

2. In the West Port a chapel was erected for the Relief denomination to which Neil Douglas was called as pastor. His induction took place at the opening of the chapel for public worship in January 1793. On his departure towards the end of 1797 the congregation, many of whom had adopted Congregational views, secured supplies of that denomination from England. In November 1804 John Campbell, pastor of the Congregational church at Dunkeld, accepted a call to the West Port Church and remained there until 1810.

3. In October 1800 the Tabernacle, which had been built at Robert Haldane's expense, was opened in Dundee, and in January of the following year a church was formed with William Innes as pastor. Differences of sentiment very soon began to appear and the controversy of 1808 rent the church. The majority were opposed to the Baptist views but Robert Haldane, to whom the building belonged, favoured the minority. A new place of worship had therefore to be found in a hall in Barrack Street, and later in the Sailors' Hall. While they were meeting there David Russell, minister of Frederick Street Church, Aberdeen, was called to the pastorate, and, the call being accepted, his induction took place in August 1809. Shortly after Russell's settlement William Maxton of the Old Scots Independent Church died and many of the members joined the Sailors' Hall congregation. In October 1810 the West Port pastorate became vacant and almost immediately the members of that church made a proposal of union to David Russell and his people. This proposal being accepted, the union took place on Christmas Eve 1810. The West Port Chapel was the place of worship till 1833 when the present building was opened and the designation Ward Chapel adopted from the name of a field in part of which it was erected. Ward Chapel has had a long and glorious history. In the first decade of the present century the Chapel with its 950 sittings attracted large congregations from all quarters of the city. They came not only to sit at the feet of the celebrated liberal theologian, Kerr C. Anderson, but also to enjoy a service of worship which in taste and dignity was second to none in Scotland. Ward Chapel has nurtured men of pulpit power like Charles Short and William Major Scott. One of its more recent ministers, Thomas Samuel Taylor, became the revered Principal of Paton College, Nottingham. LINDSAY STREET* Church was formed in 1840 by members of the local Wesleyan Methodist Church and their minister D. K. Shoebotham, who seceded from that body. The church ceased in the early twenties of the present century. PRINCES STREET* Church was formed in October 1839 by members of Ward Chapel residing in the district. TRINITY Church was formed in 1848 by members of Ward Chapel and others who had adopted the principles of the Evangelical Union. The church joined the Evangelical Union in 1849. PANMURE STREET Church was formed by members of Ward Chapel in January 1853. The congregation met in the old Episcopal Chapel, Nethergate. In the early years of the present century Panmure Street Church had a strong and influential congregation and maintained extensive mission premises in the Hilltown, with the largest institutional church in the county. During the ministry of Thomas Templeton, 1907-22, a thousand men were associated with Panmure Street P.S.A. CASTLE STREET* Church was constituted in January 1855 by 'parties who had on the previous day (December 31) retired from the fellowship of Princes Street Chapel', leaving only fourteen

members. Alexander Hannay was appointed minister. Their departure from the mother church 'did not arise from any difference of opinion about Divine truth, or from any want of confidence in the Christian character of the members of the church as it now exists, but simply from our wish to have a more eligible place of meeting, than Princes Street Church'. The church building adopted had been erected in 1812 by the Scottish Episcopal congregation in Dundee and was purchased for the members of Princes Street Chapel by Neil Street, Esq., in March 1853. Castle Street Chapel was perhaps the most unique of all the Congregational churches in Dundee in the first quarter of the twentieth century, in that 'it was the home of those who loved to combine the cultural in life with the aesthetic in worship'. For long this church under the ministry of Joseph Vickery (1893-1913) and later of Andrew Ferguson Simpson (1921-30), maintained a service of responsive worship led by a choir which would have regarded it as a personal insult to themselves had the singing of the prose Psalms or the Anthem been omitted from the service. Castle Street never had a very large membership. It fluctuated between 300 and 400. By 1949 it had dwindled to about 150. In the summer of that year the members combined with Ward Chapel. MORISON Church was formed in 1864 by members of Trinity Church, and in the same year joined the Evangelical Union. There was a preaching station at BROUGHTY FERRY from 1813 to 1824, with Messrs. Fraser and McWilliam in charge. The present church was formed in July 1864 by members of the Congregational churches of Dundee. The opening service in the present building was held on 31 July 1864. There was a split in the congregation in 1871 which was healed the following year. RUSSELL CHAPEL* was the result of mission work carried out by Ward Chapel in the middle years of the nineteenth century. It was formed by members of that church and others in Hawkhill district in May 1866. At the beginning of the present century Russell Chapel served the west side of the city and had a church roll of over 300 members, and two Sunday Schools. Decreasing membership compelled the church to close down on 31 December 1950, the members dispersing to various churches, quite a number returning to the mother congregation of Ward Chapel. GILFILLAN MEMORIAL CHURCH. In 1879 David Macrae was called to the pastorate of the United Presbyterian Church, Dundee, of which George Gilfillan, the literary critic, had been minister. For some time Macrae had been engaged in an agitation with the view of securing a revision of the Westminster Confession of Faith and Catechisms, the doctrinal standards of the U.P. Church, especially in regard to the question of everlasting torment. The Synod not only refused to sanction any change in the formula of subscription but expelled Macrae for demanding it, whereupon his congregation left the U.P. body along with him, and organised an independent movement in

Dundee with David Macrae as its head. 'The Presbyterian form of church government was retained, with modifications, that gave the constitution of the church more of the democratic character.' The affairs of the church are under the management of a session and managers, but in all matters concerning the church the ultimate appeal is to the congregation. Gilfillan Church is not included in the Congregational Union but has always been closely associated with the other Congregational churches of Dundee. Harry Andrew, the minister of Gilfillan Church from 1928 to 1955, was President of the Congregational Union of Scotland, 1950-51.

ANGUS

MONTROSE. The church in BALTIC STREET was gathered in 1800 by the labours of George Cowie, who had resigned his licence as a Church of Scotland minister in July 1799. Cowie was dissatisfied with the National Church both in its administration and constitution. For some time he worshipped with a company of Old Scots Independents who met in a garret room. On the death of one of the pastors of this congregation their meetings broke up, and half of the members placed themselves under Cowie's pastoral care. Some others being gathered by his evangelistic work in the district, he was ordained pastor on 28 August 1801. He remained until his removal to Edinburgh in 1805, when he became a tutor of the theological classes held there. Cowie returned to Montrose in 1814 and started his second pastorate in the church, which lasted till 1824. The present building was erected and opened in 1841. During its long history Baltic Street Church has had some notable ministers, among whom appear illustrious names like James Ross, William Douglas Mackenzie, A. R. Henderson, A. E. Garvie, and David Russell Scott. A second church, JOHN STREET* was formed in 1847 as the result of a movement in favour of the doctrines of the Evangelical Union. The church joined that Union in 1859. The church ceased in 1916.

ARBROATH—QUEEN STREET Church probably had its originating impetus in the visit to the town of James Haldane and William Innes on 21 May 1799, and that of Rowland Hill and Greville Ewing in the following month. There is, however, some uncertainty as to the precise date of the church's formation, owing to the unfortunate destruction of its records by fire in 1849. Most probably Queen Street Church dates back, as some have suggested, to 1800 or 1801, when certain individuals connected with a fellowship meeting, and who had confidence in each other as Christians, united to form a church 'since they could not find food for their souls in any of the places of worship in Arbroath'. Services were held in the Masons' Hall by preachers from Dundee. Thomas Smith settled in 1801 but there is no record of his ordination. Richard Penman succeeded him in 1803. The present building was opened in January 1866. In recent years the church has been enriched by the cultured ministry of J. T. Hornsby. Dr. Hornsby received a doctorate in Philosophy from the University of Edinburgh for a scholarly thesis on the life and work of John Glas. He was President of the Congregational Union of Scotland in 1948. Keenly interested in the Ecumenical Movement he has represented Scottish Congregationalism on several national and international committees. He was one of the original members of the British Council of Churches. In 1864 a second church, KEPTIE STREET* was formed in Arbroath. It met in a hall in John Street till a building was opened for public worship in January 1879. It joined the Evangelical Union in 1866. It ceased in 1908. The church in FORFAR was formed in 1832 by members of the church in Letham. William Low, of Banchory, was settled as pastor in 1837. At BRECHIN* a preaching station was started in 1831 by David Russell of Dundee, who formed a church in October 1839. It ceased as a church some ten years later, but continued as a preaching station until 1862. A new church was formed in Brechin in 1867 by sympathisers with the principles of the Evangelical Union. It met in the Temperance Hall and then in the New City Hall. A church building was opened in August 1888. The congregation joined the Evangelical Union in 1869. The church closed in 1920 when the congregation appears to have amalgamated with Bank Street U.F. Church, Brechin. A church in COUPAR-ANGUS* was originated by members of the Relief Church there in 1848, who sought connection with the Evangelical Union. As a Relief congregation, its origin goes back to 1789. The occasion of its separation from the Relief Church arose from the discovery that the minister of the Secession Church in Coupar-Angus had been trying to dissuade preachers from accepting a call to the Relief Church, because he wanted the church to unite with his own denomination to form the United Presbyterian Church of 1848. The members of the Relief Church were averse to this amalgamation and accordingly applied to the Evangelical Union for preachers. It became connected with the E.U. in 1848. Its first minister was James Frame who was settled in May 1850. The members of this church met for the last time in church fellowship on 24 November 1954, when it was decided that the church be dissolved and its assets made over to the Congregational Union's Church Extension Fund. It was further agreed that part of the Communion Plate (dated 1791) be lodged in the Abbey Church, Coupar-Angus, and part in the Congregational Church at Perth to provide some memorial within both branches of Christ's Church in Scotland of a fellowship with far-reaching roots. A church at LETHAM* was solemnly constituted in October 1803. Preaching for some time previously had been given by students from William Innes's classes. William Lindsay was the first pastor and held the office for nearly forty years. The cause proved a struggling one. Lindsay had to turn to teaching and also to keeping a shop to augment the pittance the people were able to give him. The church ceased at the end of the century. A church was formed at LOCHEE* in May 1803 from the preaching of Alexander Thomson, who in June of the same year became its first pastor. The church ceased in 1829. In the year 1803 a church was formed at WHITELEY* (now Invergowrie). Here during the years 1803 to 1805 there was a fellowship of some fifteen members. No pastor was settled although David Davidson and Walter Balfour preached there for several years. The smallness of the population prevented the continuance of the cause. A church at KIRRIEMUIR* was formed by certain members of the Relief Church who, on that body giving up their cause in Kirriemuir, had associated themselves with the Congregational Church in Dundee. For a time the church was supplied by students of William Innes's class in Dundee, and in 1804 David Dunbar, a student from Greville Ewing's class in Glasgow, was settled as pastor of the small church which had just been formed. He was succeeded in the pastorate by A. Collins, who remained until 1824. Robert Machray was the third pastor. When he left the church in 1829, the membership was so reduced that the church ceased. A church at BALFOUR* was formed in 1806. It met in a chapel erected for Robert Haldane round about 1800. The church was under the pastoral care first of John Campbell and thereafter of Thomas McKinnon, and ceased to exist on the removal of the latter to Sauchieburn in 1809.

FIFE

There was a church in NEWBURGH in 1778, the pastor of which was Alexander Pirie, who had been connected with the Relief Church. This Newburgh Church, the church in Barrack Street, Dundee, and the Berean congregations in Sauchieburn, Stirling, Dundee, Arbroath, and elsewhere were all Congregational, though each of them had its own peculiarities in church order and doctrine. After Pirie's death the Newburgh Church appears to have been dissolved, but another church was formed in May 1841 of which Andrew Yuill became the minister. This church ceased to meet in the seventies of last century. The origins of the presently existing church in Newburgh are rather complex. They can best be seen in three stages:

1. As a Relief Church,
2. Which united with a Secession Church to form a second U.P. Church in the town in May 1847,
3. Which church became E.U. when a 'proposal was made for union with the other U.P. congregation' (1873).

Rather than unite this congregation decided to form an Independent church and, after consulting Robert Wallace, the pastor of the Coupar-Angus Church, they decided to attach themselves to the Evangelical

Union, which they formally did in 1893. At one time Robert Haldane had a tabernacle in CUPAR* in connection with which a Congregational church was formed in 1800. Here Francis Dick ministered for some time with much acceptance, but partly because of the Tabernacle being sold by Robert Haldane to another body, and partly because of the unpopularity of the pastor, Peter McLaren, who was ordained in 1809, the cause gradually sank. There is no mention of the church after 1830. It most likely became Baptist. In 1802 a church was formed in PITLESSIE* with some thirty-three members. A man by the name of Currie, a farmer in the neighbourhood of Airthrey, after concluding a course of study under Greville Ewing, settled as pastor. He was the first and only minister. The church broke up at his death, and united with the church at Cupar.

KIRKCALDY—WEST END Church was formed in 1800. Some time in the year 1798 a few individuals of various religious bodies in Kirkcaldy who had become dissatisfied with the coldness and indifference of their own denominations, heard of the work that was going on at the Circus, Edinburgh, and, having attended the preaching there, they agreed to unite in observing the Lord's Supper as observed in that place. Becoming acquainted with each other they met weekly for prayer and reading the Scriptures in the upper flat of a flax-dressing warehouse near to the beach. There was no formal constitution of the church. The members who had been admitted to the Circus Church admitted others in whom they had confidence. The new church was warmly and familiarly known in the district as the 'Tow Kirk'; but in 1803 a site was obtained on the corner of Charlotte and Cowan Streets and a plain high-windowed chapel erected. The church became universally designated as the 'Tabernacle', and for more than fifty years the people worshipped and witnessed there under the guidance of several worthy ministers. Archibald McLae was the first pastor. The present church building was opened for public worship in April 1874, and in 1896 when the C.U. and E.U. amalgamated the name of the church became the West End Congregational Church. The church in PATHHEAD was formed in 1867 by friends of the Evangelical Union. The church joined that body in 1871. Ebenezer James E. Boon became the first pastor in 1870. A church in ANSTRUTHER* came into being about 1800 through the missionary labours of Messrs. Haldane and Rate in 1798, who both preached with great acceptance and success. Their converts were 'anxious to hold fellowship with each other and to have the ordinances of the Gospel statedly administered among them'. Accordingly a church was formed. It met in a weaver's shop known locally as the 'Tabernacle'. Preachers from William Innes's class at Dundee supplied for a considerable time. W. Hastie became settled pastor in 1802. For a time the church prospered, but secessions to the Baptists and the Bereans in 1812 and 1830 much reduced its

S

membership. The church became E.U. in 1844 and joined the Evangelical Union in 1861. The church ceased in 1919. A few earnest persons at DUNFERMLINE 'having been desirous of enjoying what they esteemed a pure and Scriptural communion, and of having a place opened for the use of any faithful Gospel minister who might visit them, in 1801 united in fellowship for these purposes'. They built a chapel capable of holding nearly 500 people, and for a time they had preaching from the students under Greville Ewing's direction. On 22 December 1801 Peter Grant, who had laboured among them for some months, was duly inducted to the pastorate. Two years later he left owing to their inability to pay his salary (£40 per annum). From this time till 1805 they were without a pastor, but in that year they chose two of their number for the office. But a short time after this almost all of them became Baptists. Attempts were made to revive the cause but without success till 1840 when the present church in CANMORE STREET was formed. In 1839, according to a contemporary record, 'a few individuals of the United Secession Church, having become impressed with the evils of promiscuous communion, began to examine into the system of church government and discipline under which these evils were permitted; and after the most anxious enquiry, and a careful comparison of the different forms of church government with the Word of God, they came to the conclusion that the Congregational or Independent form of government and worship is the most conducive to purity of communion and is in accordance with the practice of the primitive Churches as recorded in the New Testament'. Thereupon they entered into correspondence with William Lindsay Alexander of Augustine Church, Edinburgh, and George D. Cullen, of Leith Congregational Church, who later visited Dunfermline and arranged for the holding of services. A hall in the Maygate was rented and services conducted by Cullen were commenced on Sunday, 15 December 1839. By February of the following year the fellowship numbered thirty-eight and the desire was expressed that they might be formally recognised and constituted as a Congregational church. Services of recognition were accordingly held on 6 March 1840 and Canmore Street Church was added to the number of churches of the Congregational order in Scotland. George Thomson was the first pastor. In January 1842 the church began to worship in a building on the present site. In 1851 the Evangelical Union Church at Dunfermline (BATH STREET), now designated NORTH Congregational Church, was formed. It originated about 1848 in the secession of several members of Chalmers Street United Presbyterian Church who were attracted by the doctrines of the Evangelical Union. One of their early meeting places was the Yellet Farm, whose proprietor, Robert Husband, was a founder member of the church with which his family's name has never ceased to be honourably linked. For a time the group existed as a branch of Brighton Street Church, Edinburgh, of which they actually became members. In January 1851, however, they established themselves independently as 'The church worshipping in Mason's Hall, Maygate'. George Wisely, a student at the Theological Hall, undertook to act as minister, though he was never ordained to that office in Dunfermline. In 1853 the congregation moved to the Masonic Hall in Guildhall Street. The present church building, which belonged to the Episcopal Church, Bath Street, was bought and, after extending the seating and adding galleries and a hall, was opened for public worship in May 1891. The First World War saw the building of the Garden City of ROSYTH* and the Congregational Union proposed establishing a church there to meet the needs of the growing community. An appeal to support the venture was made to Canmore Street Church, Dunfermline, then under the vigorous ministry of W. Selby Stein. Congregation and minister immediately took the new cause under their care. In addition to financial assistance, the members of Canmore Street Church made a personal canvass of the district. However, with the change in the status of the Dockyard on the termination of the War, the new church saw many of its members leave the district, and when a disastrous fire destroyed the building, the cause was abandoned. John Elder went to LEVEN* in 1802 on behalf of the Society for Propagating the Gospel at Home and as a result of his labours a church was formed there in 1804. The cause was a small and struggling one, and throughout his entire ministry of thirty years the pastor had to keep a stationer's shop in order to augment his income. The church ceased to meet in 1860. A church was formed in NEWPORT in 1801. It originated in a Sunday school held at 'Waterside' by three brothers, Thomas, George and David Just. They were subsequently joined by a few men and women 'attracted by the new spirit in religion'. They kept in touch with the Congregational churches in Dundee, and on the last Sunday of November 1801 fourteen men and women crossed the Tay and were constituted a Congregational church by their Dundee brethren. From 1803 to 1806 the church was under the pastoral care of Thomas Taylor. Thomas Just then assumed the pastorate and did good work for close on forty years. The congregation met in part of his father's house. The room became too small to accommodate the growing membership. Accordingly Thomas Just and his brothers built a chapel in West Newport which they called the 'Upper Room'. Here the young church worshipped and grew until their building also became too small. The erection of a new church was decided upon but until it was ready the congregation gathered in a building called the 'Granary'. In 1866 sixteen members of Ward Chapel joined the fellowship, and at a subsequent church meeting it was decided 'to call a minister and to build a church in an inviting situation and inviting in interior and exterior appearance, although the great power and attraction will ever be the glorious Gospel preached from the pulpit, and the consecrated and holy walk of the members'. The new church free of debt was opened for worship in April 1868. There was a church at KELTIE BRIDGE* in 1804, but it seems to have had a very brief existence. No mention of it or even indirect reference to it is to be found in Kinni-burgh's MS. which gives a full account of the other churches of Fife. A church was started in ELIE* in 1802 but had no settled pastor till 1805 when J. Gilbert was inducted. Ill-health compelled him to resign in 1808. The cause progressed for some years under a succession of faithful pastors. The church ceased to meet round about 1870. ST. ANDREWS was one of the places selected as a preaching station by the Society for Propagating the Gospel at Home. Here James Haldane and Rowland Hill and others preached from time to time. Thomas Paton, 'who had received religious impressions while in the Army', was ordained as pastor in October 1805. The church appears to have been formed some three months previously. Paton gave a long and faithful ministry. In 1841 there was a secession of Baptists who had hitherto worshipped with their Congregational brethren. The present church building was opened in December 1854. The present pastor, Helen E. Woods, was one of the first women ministers of the Congregational Union of Scotland. She has exercised a long and useful ministry in St. Andrews. She is also a Justice of the Peace and Chaplain to Congrega-tional students at St. Andrews University. A church was started in FALKLAND* in 1806 and ordained James Garden as its pastor in October of the following year. He resigned in 1810 and became a parochial teacher under the Established Church. The cause seems to have lapsed after his departure, but was revived round about 1840 when John Elrick became pastor. The church ceased in 1854. There had been round about 1865 a preaching station at ST. MONANCE con-nected with the church at Elie. A church was formed at St. Monance in 1877, in which year John W. Lockie was settled as pastor. The church was admitted into the Congregational Union in 1897.

CENTRAL COUNTIES

CLACKMANNANSHIRE

ALLOA.* This church was formed in 1810, in which year William Howden was settled as pastor. Of its early history nothing is known. Later it adopted Morisonian views. Early in 1846 the members from Clackmannan split off in an attempt to form a separate church. Being unsuccessful they returned as a body in January 1847. The church ceased in 1855. A preaching station was formed in TILLICOULTRY in

May 1850. In September 1851, it became an E.U. church, ANN STREET, of which George Anderson became ordained pastor in August 1853. The church joined the Evangelical Union in 1862. A second church, HIGH STREET, was formed in 1872 by members of the U.P. Church who had adopted Congregational principles, of which Enoch D. Solomon became pastor in 1873. In 1911 the two churches amalgamated under the ministry of Alexander F. MacRobert. Ann Street Church building was sold to a branch of the Plymouth Brethren, and the Congregational Church, High Street became the place of worship of the united congregations, under the designation Tillicoultry E.U. Congregational Church.

PERTHSHIRE

The beginnings of Congregationalism in PERTH are not easy to trace. The historian of the present church there claims that some thinking men became Congregationalists as early as 1794, and purchased Paul Street Chapel about that time, and looked around for a suitable man to act as pastor. One of their number, William Gardiner, Master of King James VI Hospital, wrote to John Campbell, an Edinburgh ironmonger and a leading spirit in the Home Mission movement, asking if he could recommend anyone to fill this important office. As it happened Campbell has just heard of James Garie, a Scotsman from Tynninghame, East Lothian, formerly chaplain to Lady Harriet Hope and Lady Glenorchy, who had been trained for the ministry at a dissenting academy in England. Garie was at that time pastor of a Congregational church in Dublin, but feeling that his labours there were complete, he had written to John Campbell asking whether there was any opening for him in Scotland. Campbell recommended him to William Gardiner, and he was duly requested to supply the Paul Street Chapel for one month. Garie's preaching was so acceptable that at the end of the month a unanimous call was extended to him, which he accepted and was settled in his pastorate in October 1794. Garie was most eager to have the chapel linked up with the Church of Scotland as a Chapel of Ease, but the proprietors were opposed to such a step, and so, after a ministry of eighteen months, Garie resigned. He endeavoured to enter the Church of Scotland but without success. The old Chapel meantime had been sold, but some of his former members invited Garie to return. This was in 1798, in which year there appeared in the *Missionary Magazine* the announcement of the re-purchase of Paul's Chapel for the use of 'Mr. Garie and a congregation of Christian people'. The actual date of the constitution of the church has been lost, but we do know that it took place before December 1798 when Greville Ewing records several visits to 'Paul's Chapel'. James Garie appears to have been a man of much ability, energy and devotion. The Church flourished under his guidance and influence; and, besides the work of the pastorate, he was engaged in a great deal of itinerating work in the surrounding district, and took a not inconsiderable part in the building up of the new Congregational churches which were springing up all over Scotland as a result of the missionary labour of the Haldanes. The historian of the Perth Church informs us that the oldest surviving plate bears the inscription 'Perth Union Chapel, 1798'; whether this was the title of the Church right from the start, and why it should have been so called, he is not prepared to say. However, the oldest communion cups carry the better-known and less ambiguous legend 'Congregational Church, Perth, 1798'. Not long after James Garie's settlement in the pastorate Robert Haldane built a Tabernacle in South Street to which the congregation moved, having disposed of the Paul Street property. After Garie's death in 1801 Ralph Wardlaw, then fresh from college, and others were in charge of the Church for longer or shorter periods; and in the spring of 1807 William Orme was sent from the Edinburgh Theological classes. In 1808 he was settled as pastor along with two of the brethren who were to share the oversight of the church with the minister. Orme had the idea, then prevalent in Scottish Congrega-tionalism, that there should be a plurality of elders or pastors in every church, and that the Sunday morning service should be devoted to the spontaneous exhortations of these elders. This arrangement continued in the Perth congregation for about a year, but in practice was found not to lead to good results. In 1809 the two lay pastors followed the example of the Haldanes in adopting Baptist principles, and, with the support of about twenty more members, left the church and formed a Baptist congregation. Orme and his people were later evicted by Robert Haldane from the Tabernacle that the Baptist congregation might occupy it. The remainder of his ministry was spent in a long search for a suitable place of worship. For some months the church found a not too comfortable home in a hired hall, but at the beginning of 1810 the fellowship determined to build a chapel. This was done speedily in 'the upper part of a tenement in Canal Crescent'. As the church increased other places of worship were secured. Ultimately in 1824 we find the congregation domiciled in MILL STREET which became the name of the church, in which year also William Orme terminated his ministry. Orme may be regarded as among the fathers and founders of modern Congregationalism. He was the author of some dozen books of renown in their day, including *A Catechism of the Constitution and Ordinances of the Kingdom of Christ* (1817) which for a long time was accepted by the Scottish Congregational churches as the authentic statement of their particular views of church membership. Orme also took a leading part in the establishment of a Scottish Theo-logical College. And again in September 1812 when a meeting was held to discuss the formation of a Congregational Union, William Orme took a prominent part among the twalve men who drew up the scheme for the union. In later years he became Foreign Secretary of the London Missionary Society. In 1851 a new church was formed in CANAL CRESCENT* by members of Mill Street, and John Pillans was the first pastor. It was never a strong congregation but its people were intensely loyal. In 1872 it closed down and its members scattered. In 1855 a number of earnest men in Perth had come to accept the teaching of James Morison on the universality of Christ's atonement. They applied to the Home Mission Committee of the Evangelical Union to establish a preaching station in the city. Through the good offices of Sir Wilfred Lawson and John Kirk of Edinburgh, Fergus Ferguson formed such a station on 23 March 1856. This was raised to the status of a church designated PERTH E.U. CHURCH on 12 November of that year. William Adamson was the first pastor. On 16 December 1896 this church and Mill Street Church united, thus anticipating the union of the C.U. and E.U. by a fortnight. In April 1899 the united church entered their new and lovely sanctuary in KINNOULL STREET where the congregation has increased under some memorable ministries. Its present minister, A. Morton Price, is one of the more youthful statesmen and scholars of the denomination. He has served the Union as its Chairman for several years and has occupied the Presidential Chair. The church in ABERFELDY originated from an earlier preaching-station in 1800 while Hugh Ross, a catechist, laboured in and about the village. Three of the students from the theological classes in Edinburgh preached in rotation. Later Daniel Dewar (who became Principal Dewar of Aberdeen) was for a time there, and received a call to the pastorate, which he declined. James Kennedy settled as first pastor in 1806 and remained nineteen years. During the early years of the church's history both pastor and people encountered much opposition and persecution. On several estates in the district farmers were deprived of their farms for daring to associate themselves with the Congregationalists. An illuminating story is told of the Baronet of Weem of that time. He had been extending his kindly Highland hospitality to a number of his friends at Castle Menzies one fine Sunday evening in early summer, within a mile or so of an assembly of an entirely different sort gathered on his property in a field on the banks of the Tay. Here James Kennedy of Aberfeldy, who had crossed the river, was preaching to a large concourse of people. During the preaching a Strathtay Laird passed up the Weem road on horseback and, on reaching Castle Menzies, up-braided Sir Neil Menzies for allowing 'that fellow Kennedy' to preach on his estate. The Baronet's pride and anger got the better of his reason, and, in a state of considerable excitement, he hurried off to the scene of the service. Kennedy was all unconscious of his danger till he found himself collared by the irate aristocrat. A staff which the latter held up in his trembling right hand was, luckily for the preacher, snatched away from Sir Neil by a sympathetic onlooker close by. That staff was preserved for many years afterwards as a souvenir of an interesting and significant occasion. The preacher was forced across the field to the public highway, but there he pulled himself up and would be dragged no further. 'I am now on the King's highway, Sir Neil,' Kennedy definitely asserted, 'so you had better take care what you do.' 'What will you do, Sir?' asked the Baronet. 'Oh, I'll just go over there', Kennedy replied, pointing to the other side of a burn which separated the Menzies and Killiechassie estates, 'and I'll just continue my preaching there.' 'I'll roar, Sir, that the people can't hear you', threatened Sir Neil. 'You'll very soon tire of that' was the preacher's retort. The Baronet realising that discretion was the better part of valour then returned to his castle. The little story has a most satisfying ending. Not many years after this incident Sir Neil Menzies came to know the Aberfeldy Congregationalists better and to learn of the good work they were doing in the district, and James Kennedy and his people received much kindness at the good laird's hands. Kennedy was a conspicuous figure in the 1817 revival in Breadalbane under the preaching of the Church of Scotland minister, John McDonald, of Urquhart. Kennedy was most active and successful in it, particularly in Glenlyon. The revival may be traced to a period somewhat more remote from the preaching of McDonald. As early as 1800 John Farquharson, supported by the Society for Propagating the Gospel at Home, of which the Haldanes were founder members, had preached in the Breadalbane district. His converts did in fact communicate instruction to the new converts of 1817. James Kennedy had no church to worship in when he was ordained to the pastorate of Aberfeldy in 1806. He and his faithful followers met in a house in the same corner of the Square where the present church stands. This small house served both as manse and chapel, the ground floor being used for public worship, while the upper floor was the minister's house. In 1817 the old Independent Chapel was built in Chapel Street and was the first place for public worship to be erected in Aberfeldy. Indeed for twenty-six years it was the only church in the village. During the faithful ministry of John McLaren, 1836-70, there were more than a dozen preaching stations served from the Aberfeldy Church. The closing services in the old chapel, where the congregation worshipped for over sixty years, were held in July 1878. The present church in the Square was opened for worship in August 1878.

In the year 1802 preachers were sent by the Society for Propagating the Gospel at Home to BLAIRGOWRIE.* Their preaching attracted considerable attention. Some regarded them as vagrants, but a few welcomed them. Some of their converts after a time desired to form a church on the Congregational plan, for this they considered in accord with Scripture. The church was formally constituted by William Innes

of Dundee in 1803. Peter Grant became the first pastor in 1807. Towards the end of the century the church seems to have dwindled. By
1921 its few remaining members were associated with the church in
Coupar-Angus. In 1869 a church was formed in CRIEFF by members
of the Relief Church who refused to join with the Anti-Burgher body.
William Davidson Black became first pastor in 1870. There were
several churches formed in the lowland and highland parts of Perthshire, all of which were extinct long before the close of the nineteenth
century. The preaching of Greville Ewing, David Bogue, John Aikman
and others in DUNKELD* and district in the closing years of the
eighteenth century so impressed the people that a petition was sent to
the Society for Propagating the Gospel at Home for a regular supply
of preachers. The result was a visit of some weeks' duration by James
Haldane when much good was done. Prayer meetings were held and
the building of a chapel was commenced. A church was formed in 1800
and the following year John Campbell, one of Greville Ewing's first
students, was ordained and inducted. Campbell accepted a call to
Dundee in 1804, and the same year J. McLeod was settled as his
successor. He 'found the church in a state unfit to endure the exercise
of discipline, the majority of the members having only the form of
godliness without its power', and therefore McLeod proceeded to
dissolve the church. Those who wished for fellowship had to wait upon
him that he might examine them as to their fitness. A number did
submit to this ministerial discipline and some were re-united, but great
offence was taken by others, 'and the heart-burnings and hatred to the
cause, thus excited, long continued'. Shortly after the reconstitution of
the church the pastor embraced Baptist views and left. A succession
of preachers followed but none was ordained till 1809, when Robert
Kinniburgh, the first historian of Scottish Congregationalism, believed
to be the last individual whom Robert Haldane sent out as a preacher
to any of the Congregational churches of Scotland, was set apart for
the office of pastor. Kinniburgh found that most of the leading members
had adopted Baptist views and further that McLeod by frequent visits
to Dunkeld was encouraging others to take the same attitude. At
Christmas 1810 Kinniburgh left for Edinburgh, having found it
impossible to continue. The church ceased to meet until 1813 when
John Black settled in Dunkeld and a fresh start was made. He laboured
from that year until his death in 1857, after which the church ceased
to meet. A church was formed in DOUNE* in March 1843 by members
of the church in Stirling. A chapel was opened on 24 December 1843.
George Wight became first pastor in June of the same year. The
church ceased in 1864. A church in CALLANDER* was formed in 1805
and by the end of 1806 the number of members was thirty-six. The
preaching of students from Glasgow and mission work by John Farquharson of Breadalbane led to its formation. Unfortunately from the

first there was division. The members could not agree as to the choice of a pastor, and the majority took the drastic course of excommunicating ten of the minority. Eventually they agreed on Peter McLaren, whose settlement took place on 13 April 1808, but before the close of that year there was another division on the question of Baptism. The number remaining being unable to support a minister, McLaren had to take up teaching and continued to do so till the formation of the Congregational Union of Scotland, when a grant from its funds enabled him to devote his whole time to the pastorate. In 1826 McLaren was succeeded by Archibald McEwen, who remained until 1835. Some short time after that date the church appears to have ceased. Several of the members afterwards joined the church at Doune. In the Highlands of Perthshire a remarkable religious movement began in connection with the evangelistic labours of John Farquharson, catechist and preacher. He was a 'man of slender parts, but of great zeal, piety, and perseverance'. In 1800 he visited the district of Breadalbane and began his labours in the village of KILLIN* where a church was subsequently formed in 1801. Being deprived of the place of meeting there Farquharson removed to a village on the south side of Loch Tay. There he was joined by several earnest young men: James Dewar, afterwards pastor of the church in Nairn, John Campbell, who became pastor at Oban, and John Ferguson. The result of their labours was a great revival of religion which extended over a wide district of country.

While many professed to be converted, and manifested great earnestness in their adherence to the Gospel, much opposition was experienced by the preachers and converts. Farquharson was imprisoned in Aberdeen, at the instance of a Highland laird, who gave him in charge for preaching on his estate, but the preacher was liberated soon after. A young and zealous preacher was sent three times to Perth jail on similar charges. So strong was the opposition of the Established church ministers and the landed proprietors to the preachers and their work, that only three families in the wide Breadalbane district would receive Farquharson into their houses. Norwithstanding all this opposition Farquharson's labours were signally successful, and in 1802 a church of seventy members was formed 'on Congregational principles' in ACHARAN* (or Tuar), a village near Loch Tay, of which in that year Farquharson became pastor. The church soon increased to 100 members, the membership being drawn from the Loch Tay district, Glendochart, Glenlochy, Glenlyon, and Glenquaich. In 1804 Mr. McKillican, a student from Ewing's class in Glasgow, became pastor of the church, while Farquharson continued his labours as a preacher in and around Killin. The church was then divided into four branch churches, the mother church being at Acharan, and the other three being at Lawers, Killin, and Glenlyon. In ministering to these churches and in the work of evangelisation in the district McKillican was assisted by Alexander Dewar, who afterwards became pastor of the church in Avoch, Ross-shire, James Dewar, John Campbell, James Kennedy of Aberfeldy and Peter McLaren of Callander. In 1807 Farquharson left the country for Canada, where he continued his missionary labours. In 1816 McKillican also left the district for Canada, owing to the emigration to that country of many members of the churches whom he resolved to follow to the land of their adoption rather than remain with the rapidly decreasing population of the district in which he laboured. For some years prior to this time the once flourishing churches in Breadalbane had not only suffered from the emigration of many of their members but from the troubles that arose in connection with the Baptist controversy. Many of the members became Baptists, others joined the church in Callander, and others were scattered among various churches. The few who remained faithful to their principles as Congregationalists were too poor to support a pastor or pastors, and the aid they had received from the Haldanes and others having ceased after the rupture among the churches caused by their new doctrines, what were the pastors to do? Had the Congregational Union existed at that time there is every reason to believe that there would have been flourishing churches in Breadalbane. Only one preacher was sent to that district after the formation of the Congregational Union, but he soon joined the Church of Scotland; and this last discouragement so affected the members who remained that they ceased to meet as churches.

EDINBURGH

Modern Congregationalism in Edinburgh stems from the missionary labours of the Haldanes and their colleagues, of whom John Aikman was perhaps the most prominent. James Haldane and he often preached in the city and district in the closing years of the eighteenth century. There was at first no church, their meetings for the most part being held in the Circus at the foot of Little King Street, which had been opened for public worship by Rowland Hill on 29 July 1798. The first Congregational church in Edinburgh was formed in the CIRCUS* in January 1799, of which James Haldane was ordained pastor on 3 February of that year. John Aikman assisted him in preaching and pastoral duties, and he too was ordained on 17 May 1800 in the Circus in the presence of an immense congregation. On 9 July 1801 the Circus church moved to the TABERNACLE, LEITH WALK* which had been built for its use by Robert Haldane. This was a commodious edifice with a seating capacity of about 3,000. For some years it was filled almost every Sunday, and often crowded in all parts. 'The under part rose like a gallery from within a short distance of the pulpit; and there were two large galleries immediately above. The upper gallery, which could accommodate upwards of 800 worshippers, was the meeting place of the church under the pastorate of Mr. Haldane, for many years.' The membership of the Tabernacle grew rapidly, and John Aikman decided to form a new church. At his own expense he erected a building for the purpose, which was opened for worship in May 1802. The interesting record of the ceremony is found in the *Missionary Magazine* for June of that year : 'On Lord's Day the 30 May was opened a new chapel lately erected in the street leading to Argyle Square, Edinburgh. This chapel has been built upon the same principle as the Tabernacle in this city, and in the most perfect harmony with those connected in that important institution. . . . A church has since been formed of persons in communion with the Church at the Tabernacle for the observance of ordinances in this chapel, to be under the pastoral care of Mr. Aikman.' The new church was formally constituted on Wednesday evening, 2 June 1802, when after an introductory address on the nature and order of a Christian church, James Haldane commended congregation and pastor to the Divine blessing in prayer. The church was first known as NORTH COLLEGE STREET CHAPEL:* but after 1840 as ARGYLE SQUARE CHAPEL*, the latter designation being taken from a square situated to the west of the church. The chapel was built by Mr. Black, father of Adam Black the publisher, who was for many years a prominent member and office-bearer of the church. It was a severely plain structure both within and without. It is said that one of the instructions given to the builder was that not a penny had to be spent on ornamentation. William Lindsay Alexander, one of Aikman's successors in the pastorate, described this puritanical erection as a 'dark, dingy, comfortless place'. From the opening of the chapel till his death in 1834 John Aikman acted as minister gratuitously, never seeking or receiving a penny of remuneration for his services. He was a capable man and a consecrated servant of the Gospel. His wide knowledge of the French language enabled him to preach to the French prisoners who were incarcerated in Edinburgh Castle. He also spoke fluent German. When in 1815 he visited Hamburg and preached to the British residents and seamen there, one result of his visit was the formation of a Congregational church in that ancient town. Perhaps he may be regarded as the first president of the Congregational Union of Scotland in that he presided at the meeting at which the Union was formed in 1812. The most renowned minister of Argyle Square Chapel was William Lindsay Alexander, a scholar, preacher and theologian with a European reputation. His memorable ministry is associated with AUGUSTINE CHURCH, George IV Bridge, to which the congregation of Argyle Square removed in November 1861. The name of the new home of Edinburgh's second Congregational church was suggested to Dr. Alexander by Mr. Sloan his 'minister's man' for thirty-five years, and one of the very worthiest of that class of 'characters' which one is tempted to believe Scotland alone can produce. Sloan was proud to tell that 'ae Sabbath, when I took in the Doctor's lunch, we were hawin' a crack, and he telt me that they couldna hit on a richt name for the new kirk. I said, Doctor, there's a man ye spoke o' in your sermon the day, and ye often quote him, and ye aye approve o' him, Augustine. Would his name dae? The Doctor lookit at me, and then he lifted up his haund, and when he brocht it doon a' the dishes dirled, and says he, Mr. Sloan, Augustine it will be.' We have recounted elsewhere in this narrative the golden days of 'Augustine's' history under the mighty ministry of Lindsay Alexander, and indicated the high quality of intellect and culture that characterised the congregation. Alexander was the great protagonist of the earlier aristocratic species of Congregational churchmanship. It is on record that one Sunday afternoon he was proclaiming from his throne in Augustine Church when a barn fowl in a neighbouring yard every now and again began to crow. At last the Doctor became quite exasperated, and in the middle of one of his expressive sentences when the bird excelled himself in shrieking, he stopped, shook his leonine head, and said, 'You wretched creature!' Of the subsequent ministries since Alexander's day there are those of A. R. Henderson, a steady thinker, a gifted ecclesiastical leader, as big in soul as in body; Henry Parnaby, keenly active to modern problems; A. D. Martin, who had a true theological insight; Joseph Pickthall, persuasive and scholarly; C. T. Rae, a rare combination of liberal theologian and mystic, and the present minister, W. B. J. Martin, who has brought to his work, in the changed circumstances of church life, Welsh passion and culture and a sure grasp of the social and psychological situation of the present time. Recently a friend worshipped in Augustine Church and found it changed from the quieter more sedate days of the early twenties. On the whole the changes, he thought, were for the better. There were far more children in the congregation. In fact, one felt that it was no longer just a great preaching station but more of a family. All honour is due to more recent ministries, the present one amongst them, that have guided the church in this direction. From its inception the church has shown an active concern for the needs of those around its doors. In 1828 John Cleghorn its second minister was among the founders of the Edinburgh City Mission. In 1845, with the formation of a 'Christian Instruction Society' the church started home mission work. A missionary and later a Bible woman were engaged, and in 1878 premises at Simon Square were secured. The work done at 'the Mission'—including Sunday and week-night services, Sunday School activities with 250 children and nearly fifty teachers, a sewing class, a saving's bank, a brotherhood, and men's club—served the needs of the poorer and more crowded districts of the city, until its discontinuance in 1939. Augustine has always been a great missionary church. In fact at one time there seemed to be a competition between it and Morningside as to which could send the greater number of missionaries into the field. Augustine Church united with Bristo Place Church on January 1 1941. Andrew Graham was appointed Interim Minister of the united congregation which was designated AUGUSTINE-BRISTO Congregational Church. C. T. Rae became its first pastor.

The Church in ALBANY STREET* was a continuation of the first Congregational church in Edinburgh. It was formed by members of the Tabernacle who adhered to their former views of baptism, when James Haldane adopted Baptist opinions. They met for worship, outwith the Tabernacle, on Sunday, 26 March 1808, in Bernard's Rooms, Thistle Street, and in the summer of the same year William Innes of Dundee became pastor. The church building was erected in 1816. During its history, which terminated in 1954, Albany Street Church witnessed some memorable ministries. That of William Pulsford, 1856-65, was particularly significant. In his time the apparent antagonism between Religion and Science was exercising the minds of many. Pulsford had the courage to denounce not only scepticism but also the panic among the 'professedly Christian portion of our people, as if the truth of the religion of Jesus had anything to fear from the fullest freedom of inquiry'. He also supported 'the establishment of an intelligent and defensible principle of Biblical interpretation, which, while it would be in a genuine sense religious and would involve no risk to orthodoxy, must fearlessly demolish superstitions that have grown up around Holy Scripture in the course of centuries'. John Pulsford followed his brother in the pastorate in 1867, and for over a decade carried on a ministry distinguished by ability, originality and saintliness. Though a good deal more of a mystic than his brother William he soon attracted equally large congregations. While minister of Albany Street Church he wrote several books couched in a poetical prose style ranked by some not much below Ruskin's in eloquence and richness. He received the degree of Doctor of Divinity from Edinburgh University. Among John Pulsford's regular hearers were persons of note such as Sir Henry Littlejohn, Dr. Pryde, Professor Blackie and Professor Sims Woodhead. Among the distinguished ministers of Albany Street Church of less remote times was John Murphy, 1907-12, who for many years was Professor of Comparative Religion at Manchester University. HOPE PARK Church originated in an unconventional manner. Round about 1830 Henry Wight, a member of the Scottish Bar, a man of good social position in Edinburgh and an elder of Trinity College Parish Church, feeling a call to propagate the Gospel, began to visit the homes of the people of the district where his church was situated. He also began to engage in street-preaching, and his high natural gifts soon attracted crowds. His efforts led to trouble with the Edinburgh Presbytery. They decided that lay-elders should confine themselves to private exhortation and prayers and desist from preaching in public. Wight, however, felt he had a Divine call to the work to which he had set his hand and refused to obey the ruling of the Presbytery. Accordingly he relinquished the office of elder and continued to preach. Before this time, he had been holding religious meetings in a room in Society Close, Netherbow, in the vicinity of John Knox's House, and after his retiral from the eldership of Trinity College Church a company of two dozen persons who had attended his meetings invited him to become their pastor. This he did, a church having been constituted immediately before in December 1832. The congregation grew rapidly and in March 1834 removed to Richmond Court Chapel. At this time the church had no denominational connection, but in 1837 it applied for admission into the Congregational Union of Scotland. On 21 April of that year the church was received into the Union. Again the congregation grew too large for its place of meeting and a site was secured at the top of Adam Street where a large building was erected and named Richmond Place Congregational Church. In 1876 this building was sold to the Pleasance Free Church and a new church was built in Hope Park Terrace, and named Henry Wight Memorial or Hope Park Congregational Church. It was opened for worship on 16 June 1876. One of its ministers, C. H. Bateman, 1843-46, was a pioneer of children's praise and the compiler of a Sunday School Hymn Book which for a time was widely used. On 3 June 1908 the church united with Buccleuch E.U. Congregational Church under the new designation HOPE PARK AND BUCCLEUCH Congregational Church, and it was agreed that the united congregations should meet in the Hope Park Church building. On 7 July 1880 some of the members of Hope Park Church seceded and formed RICHMOND PLACE* Church of which Andrew Noble Scott became pastor in 1884. The church ceased to meet in 1897. In July 1845 the church in BRISTO PLACE (formerly BRIGHTON STREET) was formed with seventy-five members, as a result of the evangelistic labours of John Kirk, minister of Hamilton Congregational Church, and others, who had adopted the principles of the Evangelical Union. Kirk became its first pastor in October of the same year. The church met at first in Roxburgh Terrace Chapel and then in the Waterloo Rooms. In March 1846 Brighton Street Chapel was purchased from the Relief Church and opened for worship in July of that year. By 1850 the membership of the church had risen to 667. John Kirk was a man with a national reputation as scholar, preacher and healer. He was 'an original and independent thinker, but it was especially as an evangelist that he excelled. He understood human nature and how to deal with men's doubts and difficulties. So crowds flocked to hear him not only in church but when he preached, as he often did, in the open air. . . . But he was not only a great preacher and a prolific writer, he was also an inspirer of preachers. He organised over a score of preaching stations in Edinburgh and neighbourhood, worked by his own young men. Altogether during the thirty-one years of his pastorate, twenty-three men from his church became E.U. ministers. Kirk was a tireless worker. In addition to his evangelistic labours, he served for many years as Professor of Pastoral Theology in the E.U. Hall. . . . He also took a leading part in Temperance work. He was the first Grand Chaplain of the Good Templar Order in Scotland and his church was the first, or one of the first, in Edinburgh to use unfermented wine at Communion.' It was during the ministry of Robert Craig, in 1900, that a new church in Bristo Place was erected. In the nineties at least four members of the church were to be found in the Town Council and this tradition of local public service persisted into the present century. In wider fields of service, mention should be made of such men as Sir David Hunter of Natal and Sir John Macpherson, Governor of Nigeria. Bristo Place Church united with Augustine Church in January 1941 to form Augustine-Bristo Church, with Andrew Graham as Interim Minister. C. T. Rae became the first pastor of the united congregation in 1941. With a view to advancing the witness of the Evangelical Union in Edinburgh a second church, BUCCLEUCH, was formed about 1857. The members met for a time in the Calton Convening Rooms, Waterloo Place, then in the Tabernacle, Leith Walk, and afterwards in the Masonic Hall, George Street. The first ordained pastor was George T. M. Inglis, who was inducted in 1859. In that year the church removed for a time to the Waverley Rooms, Waterloo Place. Inglis embraced Baptist views and resigned from the pastorate in February 1866. In 1874 a place of worship was built in West Crosscauseway and named Buccleuch E.U. Church. Thither the congregation moved in September of that year. The church witnessed the long and highly successful ministry of William Adamson. When he was inducted to the pastorate in 1868 only twenty-two persons were present at his first Communion service : when he resigned in 1895 Dr. Adamson left a strong and well-attended church. Buccleuch Church united with Hope Park Church on 3 June 1908 to form Hope Park and Buccleuch Congregational Church. The services of the united congregation were held thereafter in the Hope Park building. In 1870 a movement was commenced to establish a church in the DALRY district of Edinburgh, and at the end of May 1872 the present church in Caledonian Road was opened for public worship. Of the fifty-one original members, thirty-seven came from Augustine Church, five from Elgin Congregational Church, three from Albany Street Church, and six from other places. The church building was erected from the proceeds of the sale of John Aikman's chapel in Argyle Square, when the Government confiscated its site for the building of the National Museum of Industry (now the Royal Scottish Museum), in Chambers Street. There is a memorial tablet to John Aikman in the vestibule of Dalry Church. Perhaps the

Church should more appropriately be designated the John Aikman Memorial Church. Among its ministers appear the names of two of the denomination's foremost literary men: James Stark, author of *John Murker of Banff*, and Robert Auchterlonie, poet-preacher, who for a number of years was editor of *The Scottish Congregationalist*. Both men occupied the Presidential Chair of the Union. The church which met in SYDNEY HALL* was formed subsequently from a group who seceded from the Cowgate Free Church in 1874. It was admitted into the Congregational Union in 1878. The pastor for the whole of its existence was Alexander D. Robertson, 1877-97. The church ceased in 1901. The last two decades of the nineteenth century witnessed the suburb of MORNINGSIDE, Edinburgh, which had been a delightful rural area, fast becoming an attractive residential neighbourhood to which many were moving from the more crowded districts of the city. Among these new residents were several Congregationalists who found that the distance to their own churches in the city now prevented them from continuing their former activities in those churches. They began, therefore, to discuss the possibility of forming a Congregational church in Morningside. They decided to hire the Morningside Athenaeum, which had been built in 1863 for the U.P. church, and had been used by that church for public worship till 1881; and Inaugural Services were held there on Sunday, 7 November 1887. The new Congregational church was formally constituted on Tuesday, 27 December of that year by twenty-five persons. Principal Simon of the Congregational College was elected president. The first minister was W. Douglas Mackenzie, who was inducted to the pastorate on 17 March 1889. The Athenaeum buildings were purchased by the church in January 1890 and were the home of the congregation until the end of 1927, when the church began to worship in its present commodious church hall. In October 1929 the present beautiful church in Chamberlain Road was opened and dedicated. The church from its inception grew rapidly. By 1900 the membership numbered 282, and there were 239 children in the Sunday School. A few years later the congregation undertook home mission work in some of the crowded areas of the city, and for a time the C.E. Society conducted evening services in a lodging-house in the Grassmarket. Morningside Church will be remembered mainly for its long and faithful support of the London Missionary Society. It claims to have sent more missionaries to foreign fields than any other church in Britain. Forty-three names appear on its Missionary Roll of Honour, including the name ever glorious of Eric H. Liddell. Four of the six secretaries of the L.M.S. in Scotland: W. G. Allan, Sidney Nicholson, J. I. Macnair, and J. M. Calder, have been members of Morningside Church. Of the immortal names among its ministers are Douglas Mackenzie who in 1903 became principal of the Hartford Theological Seminary, U.S.A.; David Caird, some time editor of *The Scottish*

T

Congregationalist ; and Roderick G. Davies who graced the Presidential Chair of the Union, 1941-42. Of the laymen of the church we single one for special mention, Charles Price, Sunday School superintendent and leader in every department of church life, who was elected a Member of Parliament for Central Edinburgh, a seat which he retained from 1906 until 1918. In 1890 the KIRK MEMORIAL Church was formed in Abbeymount. It joined the Evangelical Union in 1891. John Adam became pastor in that year. A church in PICARDY PLACE* was formed in 1897 as an Independent Evangelical Union church. John Anderson was its first pastor. A church in NEWINGTON* was constituted as an Independent Evangelical Union church in 1899. It met in the Literary Institute, its first pastor being Lewis C. Hammond. In 1891 a church in MURIESTON CRESCENT*, Dalry, was formed by members of Fountain-bridge E.U. Church of which John Kirk had become pastor in 1875. John Kirk became pastor of the new church in 1891. The church was received into the Evangelical Union in 1893.

EAST FOUNTAINBRIDGE* Church was formed in 1866 and joined the Evangelical Union in the same year. Its first pastor was William Dunlop. It was received as a U.P. church in 1899. TRINITY* Church was formed about 1892 and Andrew H. M. Sime became pastor in September 1894. The church ceased in 1898, and the church building was sold the following year. SAUGHTONHALL Church began with the holding of Sunday evening services in the district in 1928. In November of that year these were held in Westfield Hall, Gorgie, and were conducted by T. E. Sandeman. They continued regularly and with astonishing success until February 1929. On 17 February 1929 regular services were inaugurated by David Russell Scott under the auspices of the Congregational Union of Scotland in a hall situated in Saughtonhall Drive, which was rented from the proprietor. These services were conducted with most encouraging results by ministers of Edinburgh and district Congregational churches. A Sunday School was started. The Congregational Union then effected a purchase of the building. J. Massie Milne, then a student at the Congregational College, was appointed to carry on the work for the summer months, and at the close of his engagement Andrew Ritchie undertook to act as Interim Minister until the settlement of a minister. On 21 November 1929 a meeting was called to form a church and the following resolution was passed: 'We, a community of Christian people, confessing our faith in Jesus Christ as our Saviour and Lord, and accepting the belief and polity of the churches forming the Congregational Union of Scotland, resolve to unite in forming a church to be known as Saughtonhall Congregational Church, and to seek admission to the aforesaid Union.' Forty-six applicants upstanding responded to the call of their name and were formally acknowledged as the first members of the church. On 31

January 1930 A. F. Simpson of Dundee was inducted as first pastor of the church. The present church building in Saughtonhall Drive was opened for public worship on 22 November 1935. The GRANTON Church was formed in 1936 to meet the spiritual needs of the new Granton Mains housing area. The present church was opened and dedicated on Wednesday, 9 September 1936. Its first pastor was D. S. Sutherland who was inducted in the same year. The church in SAUGHTON MAINS resulted from the Forward Movement of the Congregational Union, and owed its formation in 1951 to three years of gallant evangelistic effort by J. Stanley Perkins, of Glasgow, who became its first pastor. The present building was opened and dedicated on Friday, 11 December 1954.

FORTH VALLEY AND LOTHIANS

A church was formed in Leith, CONSTITUTION STREET, in 1805 as the result of the evangelistic labours of students from Robert Haldane's Academy from 1800 to 1803. In the latter year a meeting place was acquired for the small fellowship, about forty-eight persons in all, in the Malthouse, Yardheads. Here on 17 February 1805 the Congregational church in Leith was formally constituted. The first pastor was John Pullar, 1805-17. During his ministry (1807) the congregation moved to more commodious premises in a large hall of a tenement at Yardheads which was converted into a chapel, largely at Robert Haldane's expense. In consequence it was known for many years afterwards as Tabernacle Land. During the pastorate of William Henry, 1818-22, the church, though small numerically, became a spiritual power in the community, and played a considerable part in the founding of the Leith Religious Tract Society. Henry was also instrumental in forming the Seamen's Friend Society at Leith. During the ministry of George D. Cullen, 1822-56 the church grew to such an extent that larger premises had to be sought. In 1825 a site was acquired at the centre of the town near the foot of Leith Walk, and the present chapel in Constitution Street was built and opened for public worship on 4 June of the following year. In 1890 the building was altered to meet the developing needs of the church and district. In the year 1841 a certain James Douglas came to Leith and with the help of several young men he began to hold a series of revival meetings in the 'Tower' on the shore which was furnished as a meeting house. When Douglas left Leith, the work was continued by John McDougall, a divinity student. The interest in the meetings and the attendance at them so increased that in 1843 the mission was moved to a house in Morton's Entry in the Kirkgate, a spot nearer the centre of population. The cause flourishing still more, it was necessary to move to a larger place of meeting. The 'Old Seamen's Academy' was chosen, which had been purchased and fitted out as a chapel by the Wesleyan Methodists in 1815. Here the mission continued to thrive and to attract notice, especially as amongst the frequent visiting preachers were some of the best known of the first ministers of the newly-formed Evangelical Union. When, therefore, John McDougall, early in 1844, accepted a call to the pastorate of the Congregational church at Anstruther, it was not surprising that his successor was chosen from among the Evangelical Unionists. He was Ebenezer Kennedy, one of the nine students just expelled from the Theological Academy of the Congregational Union of Scotland for holding Morisonian views and was therefore an enthusiastic witness for the 'universal Gospel'. It was now decided that the time had come for the members of the mission to form themselves into a church. Accordingly on Tuesday, 19 November 1844, twenty-eight men and women were solemnly united to form a church. The new body was designated 'the Second Congregational Church in Leith', now known as DUKE STREET. The church joined the Evangelical Union in 1853. The present church building in Duke Street was opened for public worship in December 1867, and from that time to the First World War the church may be said to have grown in numbers and influence. Perhaps its 'golden age' were the years 1902 to 1908, when under the inspiring leadership of Hugh Jenkins, its eighth minister, the membership increased to over 400 ; the interests and agencies of the church multiplied ; and its reputation grew greatly in the district. In 1903 a Mission Sunday School was formed and missionary interest was stimulated by the starting of a Watchers' Band in connection with the London Missionary Society. The following year saw the enthusiastic beginnings of the P.S.A. or Brotherhood which was phenomenally successful and added many members to the church. Within a few months of its inauguration in November 1904 the attendance of men was averaging nearly 600. By 1912 the Brotherhood had reached a membership of 1,200. Unfortunately industrial disputes between 1912 and 1914 followed by the war affected the movement most seriously. Throughout its history the church has had a line of distinguished ministers ; men of learning and consecrated life like Hugh Jenkins, David Hislop, Robert Hunter, Alexander McNair, Charles Richardson, David Beale, and Ralph Calder. The church has sent over a dozen of its sons into the Christian ministry, among whom are Arthur Reekie and John B. Wilson, editors of *The Scottish Congregationalist*, Andrew Fairbairn, theologian of world-wide renown and John Short, whose preaching gifts are recognised throughout the Commonwealth.

A church in Wellington Street, PORTOBELLO was opened as a preaching station in August 1835 by the Congregational Union. For several years prior to that date Congregationalists from Edinburgh and elsewhere had conducted regular open-air services in the town and a schoolroom had been rented and used as a place of worship. Chief among the evangelists were John Watson, of Musselburgh, and James Cameron, a student of the Glasgow Theological Academy. On 15 September 1836 a church was constituted, when 'about twenty gave to one another the right hand of fellowship'. The following year James Cameron was ordained first minister of the pastorate. The church has had some distinguished ministers among whom we notice William Hope Davison, who in 1897 became associate secretary of the new Union ; J. B. Allan, who left the pastorate in 1926 to become Professor of Hebrew and Old Testament Criticism at the Yorkshire United Independent College, Bradford. Early in 1798 a few earnest Christian people invited Rowland Hill the Evangelist to visit MUSSELBURGH. On the day appointed indisposition prevented his coming and James Haldane was substitute for him and addressed a meeting in the Millhill Burgher Church. As a result forty persons decided to meet regularly every week for fellowship. These weekly meetings were addressed by James Haldane, John Aikman, and others ; and when eventually the premises of the Burgher church were refused the itinerant preachers, the meetings were held in a barn, when Sunday services were now added. Early in 1800, Robert and James Haldane, John Aikman and others were appointed as trustees and authorised to purchase a site and proceed with the building of a place of worship, which was opened in 1801. In November 1800 Peter Grant, one of Greville Ewing's students, was student pastor of the church at a salary of £30 per annum. The first ordained minister was John Watson (1806-40) who in 1812 became the first secretary of the Congregational Union of Scotland. It would appear that Musselburgh Church was formally constituted in 1806 when Watson commenced his ministry. But we cannot be certain on this point. The present church building in LINKS STREET was opened in 1894. A second church was formed in Musselburgh, VICTORIA PLACE*, in connection with the Evangelical Union, but it was dissolved at the suggestion of its first minister, W. G. Moncrieff in October 1846, in the hope that a new church would be formed of a purged congregation. The new church was formed on 18 December 1846 with Moncrieff as minister. A third church was formed in Musselburgh TOWN HALL*, on 13 December 1885. It joined the Evangelical Union in 1888. Alexander D. Anderson was its first pastor. The church ceased in 1897 or 1898. Towards the end of 1799 a house 'for the preaching of the Gospel by ministers of Christ of every denomination' was opened in Abbey Road, DALKEITH. Considerable interest was aroused and 'many triumphs of the Gospel over the powers of darkness were achieved'. This happened at the time when the Haldanes were conducting open-air meetings in the town, and it would appear that a Congregational church resulted from these combined evangelistic ventures, round about 1804, the church now known as

HIGH STREET. In that year Alexander Arthur, who was later to take an active part in the formation of the Congregational Union, became its first pastor. In 1805 a new place of worship was acquired at the junction of Tait and Back Streets. It was reached by a stair in a neighbouring close, and known in the town and district as the Tabernacle. The present church in High Street was opened for public worship in April 1868. The Somerville family, who up to modern times have been active workers in the church, serving also as missionaries abroad, appear on the membership roll as far back as 1840. Throughout its history the church has been served by pastors who have also been illustrious teachers at the Congregational College, men like A. F. Simpson, David Russell Scott, and James Wood. A second church, CROFT STREET*, was formed on 24 November 1847 in connection with the Evangelical Union, and joined that body in 1855. It met first in the Mason's Hall. Its first pastor was John Hamilton, 1855-57. The church was dissolved in 1928 and the building sold.

HADDINGTON. In 1804 a church was formed in HADDINGTON* by some sixteen members of John Aikman's church in North College Street, Edinburgh, who, because of the distance from that church, were able to attend but seldom, and so desired a similar church in their own locality. Services had been conducted in the town by students from 1801 onwards, and several of their converts united with the church at its commencement. James Hill was settled as pastor in 1804 and laboured faithfully till his death in 1812. The congregation worshipped in a chapel in Hardgate Street. The church ceased to meet in the eighteen-seventies. An Evangelical Union church was also formed in Haddington in December 1848. In 1804 a small church was started in the village of GARVALD*. The original members came from the church at Haddington. John Dunn was elected pastor and a small chapel built. Dunn's stay was very brief, for he left in 1806. He was followed by George Forrester, who was 'succeeding beyond the most sanguine expectations' when the 1808 controversy wrecked the cause. The church ceased to meet in that year.

LINLITHGOW. A cause in the town of LINLITHGOW* began with the preaching of John Campbell of the Grassmarket, Edinburgh, in the first year of the nineteenth century. In 1803 or 1804 a barn was taken and a succession of preachers sent from Edinburgh. Mr. Cullen, one of Robert Haldane's students, settled as preacher and began to build a chapel, but when the work was only half-completed, it was stopped for lack of funds. Robert Haldane financed the venture with the result that the building was finished and opened for worship in April 1806. Cullen, however, was soon accused of heterodoxy and was compelled to leave. Under his successor Alexander W. Knowles, a small church of sixteen members was formed in July 1807. The fellowship grew slowly and suffered much from the removal of members to other parts.

The church ceased in 1883. A new church was formed on 27 May 1887 as the result of the labours of agents of the Evangelical Union and was supplied by Charles Richardson and John Ure as student pastors. Ure became its first ordained pastor in 1890. The church joined the Evangelical Union in the following year. From 1887 onwards the congregation met in the old Congregational church building. The church ceased in 1940. A church was formed at KIRKLISTON* in 1803 with William Ritchie as minister. At one time the membership was fully sixty and the congregation Sunday by Sunday considerable. The controversy of 1808 affected the church adversely. Many withdrew and, the pastor becoming disheartened accepted a call to Haddington in 1813. Soon after his removal the church ceased. A church was formed in BLACK-BURN* in 1824, when John Hamilton became pastor. The building was sold in 1851 and the church dissolved in 1853. In 1807 the members of Craigmailen Anti-Burgher Church, associated with the preaching of Ebenezer and Ralph Erskine, residing in the Bathgate district erected a church in Marjoribanks Street, BATHGATE, of which in 1812 Robert Morison became the first minister. When the Evangelical Union was formed in 1843 Bathgate Church (whose pastor was the father of James Morison the founder of the E.U.) was one of the original four churches which constituted that body. The present church building was erected in 1895. Bathgate E.U. church has had among its ministers men of deep piety, learning, and preaching power, such as A. M. Fairbairn, Charles Richardson, John Short, and C. S. Duthie. During the ministry of Alexander Wilson, 1873-88, an annual sermon was preached on the site of the old historic church at Craigmailen. 'The scene was a most impressive one and deeply reminiscent of Covenanting times. With what feelings of tenderness one recalls the picture as on a sunny Sabbath afternoon, amid the stillness of the encircling hills, the eloquent voice of the preacher discoursed to his congregation on the hillside from the suggestive text—"Our fathers worshipped in this mountain".' By the Union of the C.U. and E.U. the Bathgate congregation became part of the Congregational Union of Scotland. The church in AVON-BRIDGE was formed in 1844 by members of Bathgate and Falkirk E.U. churches, though many of its members came from the Burgher Church. It was reconstituted in 1867. In 1869 it was under the care of the Bathgate Church. 'The lengthy list of its ministers and the shortness of their stay tells its own sad tale. However, in spite of many ups and downs and much poverty in the past the church gives thanks to God in 1954 for newness of life.' The church in that year was 150 strong and, for the first time in its history, financially secure.

STIRLING. A church in STIRLING* was formed in August 1804 by eleven persons who had been meeting together in fellowship and prayer, and had adopted Congregational principles. From 1807 to 1812 they met in the Trades Hall and then for a short time in the Guild Hall. From

1812 to 1842 the congregation worshipped in a property in Friars Wynd, and from 1842 in a church building. For a time the church was served by various preachers, but when in July 1807 it had attained a membership of forty, William Henry was settled as pastor. Visits from agents of the Society for Propagating the Gospel at Home were responsible for the starting of a Congregational church at FALKIRK in 1803. It was known later as BANK STREET* Church. Robert Caldwell, a student from the Glasgow Theological Academy, became its first pastor in November of that year. A church building in Bank Street was opened in 1822. The church ceased to meet at the close of the century. A second church, BANK STREET E.U.* was formed in May 1843 by members of Erskine Burgher Church who with their minister, Alexander C. Rutherford, had adopted Evangelical Union principles. In January 1844 a church was opened for worship in Bank Street. Alexander Duncanson became Rutherford's colleague in 1846. The two pastors disagreed and a split took place in the congregation. The majority of the members became Congregationalist under Duncanson's ministry. The minority departed under Rutherford, but soon ceased to meet as a church. In May 1852 the church remaining in Bank Street was admitted to the Congregational Union of Scotland. When union between the C.U. and E.U. was expected, the Bank Street congregation preferred to enter the U.P. church and with their pastor J. D. Buchan were received into that body in 1898, and formed the church that subsequently became St. James U.F. Church. It was not until 1871 that another attempt was made to resuscitate the E.U. cause in Falkirk, which later resulted in the formation of the church now known as TRINITY. About a dozen persons, some of whom had been associated with the earlier E.U. cause in Bank Street, had been meeting for worship every Sunday morning in Johnston's Temperance Hotel, High Street. They induced the Home Mission Committee of the Evangelical Union to reopen a preaching station, and this was accomplished in July 1871, when William Dunlop preached in the Corn Exchange. Week by week E.U. pastors carried on the work in a far from weather-proof building, 'the snow or rain dropping upon the heads of the worshippers from the glass roof'. John Guthrie, Fergus Ferguson, Alexander Nairn and Robert Hislop were among the ministerial evangelists sent to Falkirk. After seven months of marked success, the Evangelical Union resolved to give the meeting the status of a congregation. This event was consummated on Sunday, 20 January 1873, in the Corn Exchange, when Robert Hunter of Leith conducted the services and the church was formed. In June 1874 the congregation began to worship in a recently purchased Baptist Chapel in Howgate, which was the home of the church for nineteen years, till the present building in Meek's Road was opened in June 1893. George Bell was the first pastor. During the ministry of Robert W. Jackson, 1885-96, there was an attempt to persuade the church to seek admission to the Church of Scotland. Jackson was of the opinion that the National Church now 'preached the same full Gospel as did the E.U. Churches' and there was no reason for their separate existence. The church was divided and seriously disturbed by this question. In May 1896 Jackson resigned and he and those who agreed with his views were received into the Church of Scotland and formed what came to be known as St. Modan's Church. Alexander Pollock (1896-1904) was the first minister of Trinity Church after the amalgamation of the Congregational and Evangelical Unions. A church was formed in KILSYTH in September 1838 by several people in the town who had adopted Congregational principles, and in 1842 Charles A. Piper became pastor. The church soon ceased to meet. In 1848 the present church, CRAIGENDS, was formed by members of the United Presbyterian Church, but it was not until 1858 that a pastoral settlement took place. A small church was formed in GRANGE-MOUTH* in 1806 as a result of the preaching of students from Greville Ewing's classes. William Watson was ordained to the pastorate in August 1807 and for a period there was promise of a strong church, but after a time the cause declined and seems to have ceased by 1822.

GLASGOW

The oldest Congregational church in Glasgow is the Old Scots Independent Church which met in the early years of the present century in OSWALD STREET* and more recently, though infrequently, in the Christian Institute. The church is now extinct. An account of it and its sister churches will be found elsewhere in this book. The church at HILLHEAD is the oldest of the Haldanite Congregational churches in the city. Its origin may be traced to Robert Haldane's scheme to have in each of the large towns in Scotland a 'Tabernacle' intended to be a centre of evangelistic work in a large population. The first of these was in Edinburgh of which James Haldane had charge, the second in Glasgow, the third in Dundee, and the fourth in Elgin. As each of these buildings was intended not for a particular church exclusively but for large meetings of people expected to attend the preaching of the Gospel, it was made larger than most of the other buildings in which Congregational churches usually worshipped. The one in Edinburgh, for example, seated 3,000 people and that in the small town of Elgin had a seating capacity of 1,500. The Glasgow Tabernacle was opened in July 1799 in a building in Ann Street, off Jamaica Street, that had originally been a circus or riding school. Greville Ewing, a Church of Scotland minister, who had seceded from that communion for conscience sake in 1798, was at first 'missioner' in the Tabernacle and later its pastor when it was constituted a church in August 1800. When Robert Haldane adopted

Baptist views the building was confiscated by him, and in 1809 the congregation had to find accommodation elsewhere. In May 1810 the congregation began to meet in a newly-constructed building in the present West Nile Street, which was named Nile Street Chapel. The church could accommodate 2,000 people. At that time there was no West Nile Street in existence. The new chapel was situated at the corner of the present thoroughfare bearing that name at Drury Street. 'There was no regular street lighting and paving, and a burn at the bottom of a deep and open channel required to be negotiated by way of planks laid across it before worshippers could enter the chapel.' Sometimes, a contemporary tells us, the assistance of a man with a lantern was necessary to prevent accidents on leaving and entering the sanctuary Nile Street Chapel was, with the exception of St. George's Church, the only place of worship in the vicinity. There was not a single chapel belonging to dissenting bodies between Anderston and George Square when Greville Ewing began his memorable ministry. In addition to his duties as pastor Ewing was in charge of the Glasgow Theological Academy which he was largely instrumental in forming in March 1811, and which had its home at first on the premises of Nile Street Chapel. On 3 August 1837 John Morell Mackenzie, a man of learning and preaching power, was inducted as Ewing's colleague in a church that daily increased in numbers and influence. Glasgow's first Congregational church, owing to private circumstance and the movement of the city's population, has had a nomadic existence. The closing services in Nile Street Chapel took place in March 1857. Pending the completion of a new place of worship, the congregation met first in the Merchants' Hall, Hutcheson Street, and then in the session house of Wellington Street U.P. Church. A new church named Ewing Place Chapel, situated at the corner of West Campbell and Waterloo Streets, was opened in March 1859. Here the church continued its beneficent witness till the migration of the population further still westwards compelled it to move out again, this time to its present habitat in the Hillhead district. On 26 September 1890 the lovely sanctuary at the beginning of University Avenue was opened for public worship at a memorable service conducted by R. W. Dale of Birmingham. Here the mother church of Glasgow Congregationalism has continued for over sixty years to serve the community at its door and the wider life of the denomination. The church enjoyed for a season the notable ministry of Vera M. M. Kenmure, 1936-45, at a time when it was a strange and wonderful thing to see and listen to a lady in a Scottish pulpit. Its Primary Sunday School is second to none in the Union and, not surprisingly, it was the nursery of the first Youth Adviser of the denomination. The president of Hillhead Church, George Blatch, has graced the presidential chair of the Union, and is known and respected throughout the denomination as a dedicated and scholarly layman. The second Congregational church in Glasgow, ELGIN PLACE, had its origin in circumstances similar to those in which Augustine Church, Edinburgh, began. The latter was brought into being through the success of the Edinburgh Tabernacle, the former likewise through that of the Glasgow Tabernacle. The first meeting-place was in North Albion Street and Ralph Wardlaw, a convert to Congregationalism from the Associate Synod, was its first minister. In February 1803 the triple event took place of the chapel being opened, the church formed and the young pastor ordained. The original members, many of whom came from the Tabernacle, numbered sixty-two. Despite careful examination of those who applied for membership the congregation rapidly increased, and in fifteen years the chapel became so crowded that a new building had to be erected in West George Street, which was named West George Street Chapel and opened for public worship on Christmas Day 1819. An amusing anecdote is connected with the erection of the new chapel. It appears that the site upon which it was built was the bed of an old freestone quarry, where, strange to relate, a writer in *Glasgow Past and Present* records that he had often fished! St. George's Established Church in Buchanan Street had been built twelve years before and the rubbish from it dumped into the excavation. All this had to be removed in order to get a good foundation. One of Wardlaw's Presbyterian friends said to him one day in good-humoured banter, 'You see now how difficult it is to find a foundation for Congregationalism in Presbyterian Scotland'. 'Yes', replied Wardlaw, in equal good humour, 'it was not till we dug out and carried away all the Presbyterian rubbish that we could find any secure foundation'. We have written elsewhere in this book of Wardlaw's greatness as ecclesiastical leader, hymnologist and theologian. He was honoured by Yale University with the degree of Doctor of Divinity. He continued in his charge till his death on 17 December 1853. Alexander Raleigh followed him in the pastorate in 1855, and about that time the North British Railway bought the West George Street Chapel, which is now the office of British Railways at Queen Street Station. A new site for the church was fixed at the corner of Pitt Street and Bath Street and the present building, named Elgin Place Church, was opened on Sunday, 3 August 1856. Many princes of the modern Protestant pulpit have reigned as ministers of Elgin Place Church: Henry Batchelor, 1859-75; Albert Goodrich, 1876-90; Ambrose Shepherd, 1898-1914; and in more recent years Arthur C. Hill, 1915-36 Maurice Watts, 1937-42; and J. Ernest James, 1943-45 used the opportunities afforded them in pulpit and on platform to carry the theological and social battles of their day and generation right into the enemy's country. The church at GIFFNOCK (formerly EGLINTON STREET) was formed in April 1825, and like the older city churches, has had a migratory existence. It met first from 1825 to 1830 in Fraser's Hall, King Street. From 1830 to 1841 in Brown Street, Anderston.

From November 1841 till 14 February 1866 the congregation worshipped in Nicholson Street, Laurieston. Thereafter in Kingston Free Church from 15 February 1866 to 20 August 1866; whence it moved to Eglinton Street and worshipped there from 23 August 1866 till 11 November 1936. On 15 November of that year it began to meet in its present habitat in Fenwick Road, Giffnock. Edward Campbell became the first pastor of the church at the time of its formation, and carried on his ministry until his death on 29 February 1836. During his pastorate the church in a large measure catered for the spiritual needs of Highlanders who were exiled in the city, and services were conducted in the Gaelic language. The Gaelic services were discontinued, no longer being considered necessary, on Campbell's death. It was during the ministry of David Russell, 1839-89, that the church grew in numbers and influence. In January 1868 a home mission was started in a school in Victoria Street, Port Eglinton, under the care of five deacons who in turn took charge of the meetings. In 1873 William Fish of Perth was appointed the first missionary in charge. It is of interest to note that Arnold Foster, who afterwards served the London Missionary Society so well in China, and Hope Davison, who was secretary of the Congregational Union of Scotland from 1891 to 1899, both occupied the post of missionary and temporary assistant to David Russell in later years before being ordained to the ministry. The energy of the Eglinton Street Church deacons was not confined to Port Eglinton. They devoted themselves to home mission work generally, and in 1874 arranged a Gospel mission in the Assembly Rooms, Crown Street. Later the work was carried on in premises in Commercial Road. From that mission there ultimately was formed the Lloyd Morris Memorial Church, in 1879. On completing fifty years as minister of Eglinton Street Church, sixteen of which had been also devoted to the Union secretariat, David Russell retired from the pastorate in March 1889. Two years later the degree of Doctor of Divinity was conferred upon him by St. Andrews University. Russell died in March 1892. His successor in the pastorate was James Ross who, both spiritually and intellectually, was one of the giants of the denomination at the turn of the century. Of the five pastorates he held in his day, Eglinton Street was the last and longest, being of twenty-four years duration. Like his predecessor, Ross served the Union as secretary during his ministry at Eglinton Street. His broad sympathies, his unfailing charity, his soundness of judgment, his insight into the spiritual condition of his people, and his unaffected love for men, raised James Ross to a position of influence in his congregation and denomination which few ministers acquire. In recognition of the undoubted value of his historical and literary labours, he was awarded the degree of Doctor of Divinity in March 1905, by the University of St. Andrews. He died in June 1912. As the years passed Eglinton Street Church became a down-town church with the congregation

moving further and further away. After much thought and discussion under the wise guidance of its ninth minister, George Kirk,
it was decided in October 1936 to transfer the church to a growing
district which offered a wider field of service and where the support
of the majority of the members might be retained. After consultation
with the Congregational Union Church Extension Committee and the
corresponding committee of the Church of Scotland, the present premises were built in Fenwick Road and opened and dedicated on
20 March 1937. George Kirk successfully maintained the worthy
ministerial record of the church. He was president of the Union in
1947-48 and in the following year entered upon a three years term as
Chairman of the General Committee and of the Business Sessions of
the Union's Annual Assembly. He also represented the Union at the
International Congregational Council held at Wellesley College,
Boston, U.S.A., in June 1949, and was subsequently elected a member
of the Executive Committee of the Council. A former deacon of the
Church, J. R. Sandilands, was the president of the Congregational
Union in 1897 and a distinguished treasurer from 1897 to 1900. A
church in NORTH HANOVER STREET* was formed 27 November
1834 by members of Elgin Place Church, who in May of the same year
rented a Baptist chapel in North Albion Street. The building in North
Hanover Street was opened for public worship on 28 September 1847.
The church ceased in 1878 when the majority of the members transferred to PARKGROVE* Church, Paisley Road. The church in Parkgrove also dissolved as a Congregational church at a later date, owing
to the financial difficulties caused by the erection of too expensive a
building. The congregation went over to the Church of Scotland in
1886. It became Titwood Church and, in 1941, Pollokshields-Titwood.

HOOD MEMORIAL (formerly MUSLIN STREET) Church was
formed in January 1843 as a result of open-air revival meetings conducted by twenty-five persons led by Thomas Pullar. It met first in a
hall in Franklin Street. A chapel was opened in May 1844. In 1844 the
church became E.U. in sympathy and joined the Evangelical Union in
1861. Its first pastor was Robert Simpson. During the memorable
ministry of Robert Hood, 1862 to 1894, the church increased enor-
mously in influence, and reached its peak membership of 800. Hood
was a man deeply esteemed by the poor of the East end of Glasgow.
He was 'everybody's body', as homely Scots folk used to say. His
charity began in Muslin Street chapel but never ended there. He was
known throughout the city as *the* Bridgeton pastor. In 1886 he was
elected president of the Evangelical Union. After his death the
designation of the church was changed from Muslin Street to Hood
Memorial. From some curious items recorded in the church minute
books we select this one. 'On 9 February 1858 the Rev. Nisbet Galloway
appeared in the pulpit wearing a gown. Thirty-five members, who were

opposed to this innovation, resigned their membership—one of them
being the Precentor.' From the membership of Hood Memorial Church
some useful pastors have gone to man the ranks of Congregationalism.
Among them we note Robert Kidd, T. H. Walker of denominational
literary fame, and Charles Cammock, the present Pulpit Supply
secretary. The church in MONTROSE STREET* owed its beginnings
to a secession of members of the Congregational church in North
Albion Street, who sympathised with the nine students who had
accepted E.U. views and were expelled from the Theological Academy.
This small group of members were alienated by the unsympathetic
attitude of their minister in this matter and decided to form a new
church. Accordingly in June 1844 a series of meetings were started in
the Trades Hall, Glassford Street, conducted by leading ministers of
the Evangelical Union and the nine expelled students. At the conclusion
of the meetings eighty persons expressed the desire to be formed into
a church and on a certain Sunday at the end of July James Morison
formally constituted the church and Holy Communion was celebrated
in the presence of a congregation which crowded the hall and adjoining
rooms. Fergus Ferguson, after serving the new church for some months
in the capacity of missionary, was called to the pastorate, and was
ordained as the first minister in April 1845 in the City Hall. In June
1845 the congregation moved into a large chapel in Blackfriars Street
which had been built ten years previously. Here the church worshipped
till the close of 1875, when the U.P. Church in Montrose Street was
bought and re-opened for public worship on 6 February 1876. The
church did not formally join the Evangelical Union until 1863, as there
was a very definite Congregational element in its membership for some
years after its foundation. In 1850 Ferguson and the majority of the
members considered that the time had come when it was their duty to
join. But a small minority opposed this action, thinking that their
principles would be compromised thereby. Indeed so vehemently did
they oppose it that the dispute was carried to the Sheriff Court and
thence to the Court of Session to secure £850 of a Building Fund. After
a long and distressing period of litigation from 1852 to 1857 the Court
came to the decision that the pastor and members who remained were
the *bona fide* church and entitled to all the funds and property. Thereupon most of the 'Protesters', as they called themselves, left in a body.
The ministry of Fergus Ferguson is one of the immortal memories in
the annals of Scottish Congregationalism. In addition to assiduous
pastoral duties (the membership was close on 700 in 1864) and preaching
work both in his own church and throughout Scotland, he served on
the Glasgow School Board from 1882 to 1888, was Professor of New
Testament Exegesis in the Evangelical Union Theological Hall from
1891 to 1896, president of the Union in 1853, 1884 and 1894, and
of the combined Unions in 1897, the year of his death. He was also the

historian of the Evangelical Union and one of its hymnists. In 1875 the church started a Mission in East Miller Street which in 1877 was formed into a separate church named Dennistoun E.U. Church. In the latter year Montrose Street Church attained its peak membership of 800, with close on 900 children in four Sunday schools. From its inception Montrose Street Church was the nursery and training ground of some of the greatest and noblest of the denomination's leaders. Chief amongst these in the last half-century stands Charles Richardson who succeeded Fergus Ferguson as minister in May 1898, and maintained the great tradition of the church for over quarter of a century. Richardson added to the onerous work of a large pastorate his duties as secretary of the Union from 1900 to 1918, and in 1916-17 he was the Union's honoured president as well. In 1924 he was appointed full-time secretary of the Union, which office he held with distinction for seventeen years. Glasgow University conferred on him the degree of Doctor of Divinity in 1930. In 1939-40 he was again president of the Union. Worthy successors of Charles Richardson to the Montrose Street pulpit and pastorate have in the providence of God not been lacking: Harold Newsham (1925-31), Ralph Calder (1933-43), Stanley Perkins (1944-50), and Carlyle Murphy (1951-55) have, each according to his gifts, maintained the high tradition of the church. Twelve of the church's sons have gone into the ministry and its laymen have served the Union with distinction. James McLay (president of the Union, 1955-56), his father, Daniel McLay, and George R. Green (treasurers of the Union) are typical of the gifted and consecrated laymen who have brought in more recent times valued leadership to the cause of Congregationalism in Scotland. The steady migration of the people from around its doors, and the setting up of extension charges in the new districts have, during the last fifty years or so, depleted the membership of Montrose Street Church. This fact, together with the Glasgow Corporation's readiness to purchase the building to facilitate a city development scheme, led the members to dispose of the building and to dissolve the church so that other churches in the district might be strengthened. The church closed 2 October 1955. At the Communion service about 250 worshippers attended. Leaving the church for the last time they were confident in the Lord's assurance: 'I will be with you alway, even unto the end of the world.'

The church in DUNDAS STREET, for many years known as North Dundas Street E.U. Church, was the only purely Evangelical Union church in the city of Glasgow in the middle of last century. It was formed 16 November 1848, and had its origin in the Cowcaddens Society for Propagating the Gospel which had been inaugurated in the spring of the previous year. The object of the Society was the extension of the knowledge of Jesus Christ by means of sermons, Sunday School instruction, and distribution of tracts. The members of the Society thought it desirable that regular Sunday services should be established and it was agreed to approach James Morison, of Kilmarnock, to provide preaching supply. At its formation the church had twenty-two members. John Guthrie was the first minister, and was inducted on 30 November 1848. The little church experienced some slight friction over the framing of its constitution. Some members favoured the Congregational practice of having deacons who should look after financial and spiritual affairs alike on the instruction of church meeting; but the majority preferred the appointment of elders to attend to spiritual matters and managers to look to the financial side. Because of the acceptance of the latter practice five members resigned; but the policy then adopted, common to all E.U. churches, has been followed through the intervening years. For eighteen months the church met in the Mechanics' Hall, North Hanover Street, and then, from 1850 to 1852, in the Athenaeum Assembly Room, Ingram Street. The present church was opened for worship in February 1853. At the first annual business meeting of members soon after John Guthrie's coming as pastor, the reports submitted include one from the Total Abstinence Society which shows that, from its earliest days Dundas Street, like all E.U. churches, took a keen and practical interest in the temperance cause. On Guthrie's leaving the pastorate in 1851 the members invited James Morison of Kilmarnock to become their minister, urging the claims of Glasgow and promising a stipend of £200. Morison accepted, and was inducted in the City Hall on 5 October 1851. Within a month of the commencement of his remarkable ministry, which was to last well over thirty years, the site of the present church was secured, and the money to build it speedily found, even during a period of economic scarcity. The historic sanctuary in North Dundas Street became the home of the church in February 1853. The congregation was most liberal in its attitude to the use of instrumental music in public worship and an organ was soon introduced—the first, perhaps, in Scottish Presbyterian or Congregational churches. Dundas Street Church from 1853 became the nerve centre of the Evangelical Union, not only the main platform for its gospel, but also the place where its future preachers and teachers were prepared for their life's work. For when James Morison moved thither from Kilmarnock the Theological Academy moved with him to find a home for thirty-five years in the halls of Dundas Street Church, he himself being the principal and main inspiration of the institution. In 1862 Morison received a Doctorate in Divinity from Adrian University, Michigan, U.S.A., and from the University of Glasgow in 1883. During his memorable ministry James Morison had several colleagues in the pastorate, chief of whom was George Gladstone who, on Morison's resignation in 1884, became minister of the church and its greatest leader and orator in the ensuing period of its history. Dr. Morison died on 13 November 1893,

having witnessed four months previously the removal by the United
Presbyterian Church—the successors of the Secession Church—of the
ban which had been imposed on him and his teaching in 1841. During
the last thirty and more years Dundas Street Church has flourished
under the pastoral leadership of J. G. Drummond, a past president of
the Union, and one of its foremost statesmen and thinkers. It was an
honour to himself and his church alike when in 1951 his own University
of Aberdeen conferred on him the degree of Doctor of Divinity. In
1850 a church was formed in BATH STREET*, Glasgow, by members
of the church in West George Street (now Elgin Place) under the
ministry of S. T. Porter, but it ceased to meet after 1873. The building
was purchased by James Baird of Cambusdoon and given by him to
the Church of Scotland who formed in it Blythswood Parish Church.
The church in GREAT HAMILTON STREET* originated in 1849 as
the result of the labours of David Johnstone, who, on 13 March 1850,
became its first pastor. The church was closed in December 1917.
SOUTH SIDE (Nelson Street)* Church was formed in 1849 by members
of Montrose Street Church and others. The first minister was Samuel
Chisholm, who was inducted in October 1851. The church formally
joined the Evangelical Union in 1855. At first the congregation met in
a hall in Nelson Street, later in a hall in Norfolk Street, and then in the
church which was opened for worship in June 1877. The church ceased
to meet in 1938. The church in DALMARNOCK ROAD was formed in
April 1858 in McLaren's Academy, Wellington Street, by members
of Southside and Bridgeton Congregational churches. The original
membership numbered sixty-one. The first pastor was Robert Anderson,
who was inducted in June 1858. In the early years of the church's
history open-air services, which helped to increase the membership,
were frequently held on Glasgow Green. From March 1859 to 1869
the church worshipped in the Mechanics' Hall in Canning Street. In
the latter year the congregation removed to a little chapel in West
Street, Calton. In 1862 the congregation was admitted into the Evangelical Union and thereafter was designated the Calton E.U. Church.
When in 1899 the building in West Street was condemned as being
unsafe, the congregation gathered first in the Albert Halls, Main Street,
and later in the Bridgeton Working Men's Club. The present church in
Dalmarnock Road was opened in September 1902. In recent years
the membership of the church has increased to be the largest in the
Union. This was due in great measure to the evangelical ministry of
George Forbes Morgan, from 1925 to 1944. In the latter year the
membership reached the peak figure of 1172. Forbes Morgan was
president of the Congregational Union 1943-44, and in 1944 was elected
Commissioner of the Forward Movement. WARDLAW (Bellgrove
Street) Church was formed on 28 December 1857 as the result of the
labours of Gilbert McCallum, who from 1851 had worked in the

U

district as a missionary of Elgin Place Church in connection with the Dovehill Mission. The church was named after Ralph Wardlaw the minister of Elgin Place Church. McCallum became its first pastor in 1857. The chapel in Bellgrove Street was built in February 1865. A vigorous work was carried on for many years, the Sunday School being one of the largest in the city. However, a change in the character of the locality caused many members to move out to other districts, and the membership was much depleted as a result. In the Second World War the church suffered from the blitz and the condition of the structure considerably handicapped congregational activities. The idea of uniting with the well-equipped sister church in Meadowpark Street was cordially received by the members of Wardlaw Church. Accordingly April 1946 the two churches united to form Dennistoun-Wardlaw Church.

TRINITY Church, Glasgow, was formed in May 1862 by members of Elgin Place Church, and William Pulsford became its first pastor in February 1864. This church is remembered chiefly as the scene of John Hunter's historic ministries, 1887-1901, and 1904-13. At a time when the Scottish churches in general were conservative in politics and theology Hunter breathed from his pulpit an air of liberalism. His beautiful services had a helpful and quietening effect upon the thousands that regularly attended them. Hunter was a power in the intellectual and social life of the city and a pioneer of liturgical and hymnological reform in Scotland. Since 1915 the liberal tradition of Trinity has been maintained under the cultured ministry of H. S. McClelland, who has not been afraid of innovations, the hospitality of his pulpit being extended to preachers of all denominations and religions, as well as to distinguished representatives of literature and the arts. McClelland retired from the pastorate in 1956. NEW CITY ROAD* Church was formed in 1862 by members of Elgin Place Church. In 1870, through the liberality of J. H. Watt, a wooden chapel was built in Garscube Road. The congregation moved from there to New City Road Chapel, which had been purchased from the U.P. church, in December 1873. John Douglas was the first ordained pastor. The church closed in 1947, some of the members joining Hillhead Church. BETHANY Church, Glasgow, was formed in 1870 as the result of mission work in Bernard Street district conducted by J. H. Watt and members of Elgin Place Church. A small corrugated iron building served the requirements of the congregation until 1872, when the present large church was built on the same site and gifted to the congregation by John H. Watt. In 1874 the church was dedicated and opened for public worship. EMMANUEL* (Overnewton) Church originated in 1871 through the labours of James McLean, a missionary connected with Elgin Place Church. McLean became its first pastor in 1872. The church was closed in 1913. PARKHEAD Church, Glasgow, was formed in May

1873, chiefly as the result of mission work promoted and supported by John H. Watt of Elgin Place Church. The founder members worshipped in weavers' sheds. The present church was opened in May 1879. The first minister was David Gardner, who was inducted in 1873. The dramatic and unorthodox preaching of George Sharpe, the third pastor of the church, caused a stir in the district. 'His doctrinal preaching of Perfection was strongly resented by the Church management'; a church meeting was called, and Sharpe was asked to leave the pastorate. He subsequently founded the first Church of the Nazarene in Scotland, now known as Sharpe Memorial Church. Parkhead Church increased in numbers and influence under the long and scholarly ministry of Henry Wallace, from 1906 to 1937. Its present pastor, W. Nelson Gray, is exerting a great influence both in the pastorate and denomination by his forthright evangelical preaching and writing. FORSYTH MEMORIAL (formerly Govanhill) Church was formed in April 1876 by members of Evangelical Union churches on the south side of Glasgow. The church joined the Evangelical Union in the same year. Robert Wallace was the first pastor. In 1881 the congregation purchased the U.P. church in Cathcart Road. GUTHRIE MEMORIAL* Church was formed in 1876. It met first in the Mechanics' Hall, Canning Street. It was admitted into the Evangelical Union in 1877. William Halliday was the first pastor. The church building in Moncur Street was opened for public worship in 1880. The church closed on 17 February 1952. DENNISTOUN Church was formed in 1877 by members of Montrose Street Church, and joined the Evangelical Union in the following year. William Arnott who was inducted in December 1877 was the first pastor of the church. In 1875 when Dennistoun estate was being developed as a residential district of Glasgow, Fergus Ferguson and his office-bearers had been quick to perceive an opportunity for church extension in the area. In December of that year a mission was begun in East Miller Street (now Millerston Street) in the old Rutherford U.F. church, which later was constituted a church. The church and halls in Meadowpark Street were opened in May 1889. The church united with Wardlaw Church in April 1946 to form Dennistoun-Wardlaw Church, and worships in the Meadowpark Street premises. WATERLOO STREET* (Ebenezer) Church was formed in 1877 by a union of the E.U. churches in Waterloo Street and West Campbell Street. The former had been founded in 1845 when William Scott and many members separated themselves from Free St. Mark's Church. They met first in the Trades Hall until the erection of Ebenezer chapel in November 1848. The church never entered into formal connection with the Evangelical Union, although it was always closely attached to E.U. principles. The church in West Campbell Street was in connection with the Evangelical Union under the ministry of John Guthrie. The first pastor of the united congregations was Robert Hislop, who entered on his work in June 1877. The united church entered the Evangelical Union in the same year. The church ceased to meet in December 1906. LLOYD MORRIS (Hutchesontown) Church was formed in 1874 and in that year Thomas R. Atkinson became pastor. The church originally met in the Assembly Rooms, Crown Street, later in Commercial Road, whence the congregation moved into an iron church situated in Rutherglen Road. During the pastorate of its most outstanding minister, E. Lloyd Morris, 1894-1929, the present church was opened (1902). Under the enterprising ministry of the present pastor, Leslie Newton, the church moved out in April 1957 to the populous Castlemilk district of Glasgow. FERGUSON MEMORIAL Church, Springburn, was formed in December 1890 by members of Montrose Street Church from a mission commenced in the district some years previously. Alexander Peat was the first pastor. The congregation entered the Evangelical Union in 1892. The present church was opened for worship in December 1897. The church in PARTICK originated in the secession from Emmanuel Church of the minister, James Grant, and a number of members. These and a few others convened a meeting in the Mulberry Bank Hall, Finnieston, in January 1891, when it was agreed to form a new church with Grant as pastor. The church met first in the Mulberry Bank Hall and later in a larger hall situated at Partick Cross. In 1893 the success of James Grant's ministry warranted the building of an iron church in Stewartville Street. The present church, built on the same site, was opened for worship in January 1910. Partick Church proudly recalls that Vera M. M. Kenmure began her pioneer ministry there. BROOMHILL (Whiteinch) Church was formed, after a period of experimental services, in Whiteinch Burgh Hall early in 1898. James Bell was the first pastor. The congregation moved to the Broomhill district in 1900. The present attractive church in Victoria Park Gardens was opened for worship in November 1907. In its comparatively brief existence Broomhill Church has witnessed some notable ministries; chief among them will rank that of Arthur Temple Cadoux, 1920-48, who will be long remembered within and outside the denomination as an important theological thinker and writer. The present minister, Geraint V. Jones, the secretary of the Ecumenical Committee of the Union, maintains the high traditions of this church as scholar and preacher. At the end of the nineteenth century the rapidly growing district of Pollokshields contained no Congregational church. In 1899 steps were taken to convene a meeting of those who desired to see such a church in the area. The result was the formation of POLLOKSHIELDS Church on 6 October 1899. The services were held at first in the Burgh Hall. The first minister was Andrew Hamilton, who was inducted to the pastorate on 13 May 1900. The lovely sanctuary in Fotheringay Road was opened for worship on 18 April 1903. John K. Templeton, the present treasurer of the Congregational Union, is the grandson of John Templeton one of the pioneer members of this church. WOODSIDE* (formerly EASTPARK) Church originated in a secession of members from Cedar Street mission, which was under the direction of Elgin Place Church. They met in Vernon Street, Maryhill, where the church was formed in March 1900. James Baxter one of their number was appointed pastor. In 1928 the Cedar Street mission closed and its premises were thereafter used by the church, which assumed the new designation of Woodside Congregational Church. A. S. Marshall was the first minister of the newly-named church. It ceased to meet in 1946, when the building was sold to the Glasgow Education Authority. A church was formed in SHETTLESTON* on 29 May 1904. It met in Hill Street Hall and afterwards in the Parish Church room. No suitable place of worship was ever procured and apparently the membership never rose above the original forty or so. Lachlan McFadyen was its first and only pastor. The church was dissolved on 28 May 1908. CATHCART (Battlefield) Church was formed in February 1911 with fifty-five members, and designated Battlefield Congregational Church. In April of the following year Daniel McIver was called as first pastor. A hall was adapted as a place of worship in November 1912. During the ministry of William Gray (1918-27) the name of the church was changed to Cathcart Congregational Church. By the nineteen-thirties the original premises were too small for the growing population and a new and larger church was built. This, the present church in Holmlea Road, was opened for public worship in April 1935. In more recent times the church witnessed the long and successful ministry of Thomas Carlyle Murphy, who left a strong fellowship in 1941 to take up the Secretariat of the Congregational Union. BRISBY MEMORIAL Church was formed as an independent congregation under the ministry of John Brisby in 1916. For many years it went under the designation of a 'Christian Union church'. It is now within the fellowship of the Congregational Union of Scotland. MOSSPARK Church was formed in 1929. Thomas S. Loudon became the first pastor in the same year, and through a long and assiduous ministry of twenty-one years built up a strong congregation. KNIGHTSWOOD Church, Glasgow, was formed in 1933 as an extension charge sponsored by the Congregational Union of Scotland. In October of that year a temporary Deacons' Court was formed of thirteen members selected from ten churches in the district. In the same month the present church building was dedicated and Walter Gerrard was inducted as first pastor. Under his guidance the infant church grew vigorous and strong. By 1935 there were 437 members and a Sunday School of 315 with forty-seven teachers. The church became self-supporting in 1934 and by the outbreak of the Second World War the membership roll had risen to 620. The church suffered much during the blitz. Three members were killed, the church building was damaged, 111 householders, making a total of 200 members, had to leave the district. The minister's health was affected by the strain of the war years and in 1945 he resigned. Thomas Mearns succeeded him in the pastorate and during his ministry there was a revival of congregational life especially in the sphere of youth work. In 1950 a memorial hall was built. Under the present pastor, John T. George, the advance has continued, and now with a membership of 655 Knightswood Church has the second largest congregation among the churches of the denomination in Glasgow. CHRISTCHURCH,* Glasgow, was formed in April 1934, when Vera M. M. Kenmure, minister of the Partick Church, and some of the members seceded from that church. The services were held in the Central Halls pending the procuring of a place of worship. The congregation amalgamated with Hillhead Church in 1936, when Mrs. Kenmure became minister of the united charge. PRIESTHILL Church was formed in January 1950 with fifty members, the first of the post-war churches of the denomination. Charles Cammock became the first pastor. The present building was opened in September 1951. DRUMCHAPEL Church was formed in 1953 through the activities of members of the Glasgow District Churches. The new hall-church was dedicated in December 1954. Isabel G. D. Shedden became the first pastor of the charge and was inducted in Drumchapel Parish Church in March 1954. On its first anniversary the church had a membership of 283. The church at EAST KILBRIDE was formed in 1955 and James Dey became the first pastor. The foundation stone of the present church was laid 16 February 1957 and the church dedicated on 12 March 1958.

LANARKSHIRE

ELDERPARK STREET, GOVAN Church was formed in January 1870 of some sixteen members. Robert Simpson became the first minister in the same year. A church was opened at the corner of Windsor Street and Broomloan Road in November 1874. The present church in Elder Park Street was opened for public worship in May 1895. A church in WHITE STREET* originated in the evangelistic labours of Hugh Riddell and was formed in 1865. The church joined the Evangelical Union in 1869, in which year William Reid settled as pastor. A church in JAMES PLACE* was formed in 1897 by members of Evangelical Union churches.

Beyond the Glasgow district the oldest church in Lanarkshire is that in CAMBUSLANG which was formed in 1803. A number of people there who had come under the influence of the Haldane movement communicated in October 1799 with Greville Ewing, 'soliciting him to send some of the young men studying for the ministry under his tuition to preach to them and their neighbours'. They rented a house as a place of meeting. It was opened for worship by Ewing in November

1799. Ten months later they decided to build a chapel, which was opened in the spring of 1801. John Paterson became pastor in July 1803. He was succeeded in 1806 by Alexander Kerr who 'laboured for nineteen years without seeing much fruit'. For a time Kerr eked out his meagre salary by teaching, and part of the chapel was used as a schoolroom. John McRobert who ministered to the congregation from 1838 to 1846 was a man of outstanding personality and preaching powers. He was on terms of intimate friendship with David Livingstone. The latter during his student days used to walk over from Blantyre to Cambuslang on Sunday evenings to help the Congregationalists in their open-air services. The present church building was erected in the early seventies of last century during the ministry of Thomas Brisbane. The present pastor, James K. Smith, who settled in 1948 has, by his assiduous labours, added considerably to the membership. The next church formed was in LARKHALL, in 1804, as the result of the labours of James Haldane, Greville Ewing and others. It met in Wellgate Street. There is no record of any ordained minister over this church until 1822, when Thomas Alexander settled in the pastorate, from which year till 1834 he laboured as pastor of the united churches of Larkhall and Hamilton. The Larkhall church ceased in 1848. For a period of twenty-seven years there was no church of the Congregational order in the town. In the early seventies a few of the inhabitants of Larkhall who had been attracted by the broader theology of the Evangelical Union joined the church of that denomination in Park Road, Hamilton, of which Daniel Craig was minister. The Larkhall members increased in numbers to such an extent that it was decided to form a church in Larkhall. Accordingly services were commenced in 1874 and continued under the oversight of Hugh Riddell, Home Mission agent of the Evangelical Union. A hall, later known as Union Hall, was rented and became the first meeting place of the church which was constituted there in April 1875. The church was admitted to the Evangelical Union in the same year. George Wood was the first pastor. A church in Muir Street was opened for public worship in August 1876.

HAMILTON. The church now designated ST. JAMES' was formed as the result of the labours of James Haldane, Greville Ewing and others in 1807, and John Wilson became its first pastor in June of that year. The original congregation were known as the 'Missionars' and met for worship in an upper room in Back-of-Barns Street. The membership numbered thirty-three. The average Sunday offering amounted to twelve shillings, and Poor Fund collections were three or four shillings weekly. The church soon built for itself a small meeting house in Blackwell's Lane and here it gathered till a new place of worship was erected in Campbell Street in 1841 called Ebenezer Congregational Chapel. The little meeting-place in Blackwell's Lane was known locally as the 'Wee Kirk', and this was the sanctuary which Fergus

Ferguson, senior, knew when in 1834 he left Ralph Wardlaw's church in Glasgow to reside in Hamilton. It was here also that young David Livingstone learnt his Bible lessons. The names of Neil Livingstone and his wife, the missionary's parents, appear on the church membership roll in 1835. One of the early members has put it on record that the Livingstone family who lived at Blantyre used to come regularly to his father's house between the church services. They brought their lunch with them on these occasions and, with characteristic Scottish independence, he tells us, 'Mrs. Livingstone would never accept anything but sufficient boiling water to infuse the tea with which also she came provided'. The minister's salary varied, according to the financial situation, from £70 to £100 a year. No salary was paid to the precentor. John Hyslop, Alex. Gilmour, and Henry Drummond acted in that capacity. The meeting house was lighted with tallow candles, snuffers being in frequent requisition, but as the light was not always of the best, each line of the metrical psalm was frequently read out as the singing proceeded. The name of the tune, such as Caroline, Martyrdom, Coleshill, Bangor or Devizes, was usually announced in a loud voice by the precentor before the singing began. The Wee Kirk with its handful of good men and true was generally first in every forward movement. If it was a collection for missions its contribution was invariably double that of other congregations with much larger memberships. The Total Abstinence Society had its ablest supporters from the Wee Kirk. The parents of James Gilmour of Mongolia became members of the church in 1866. James attended classes in Glasgow University and latterly at the Theological Hall, and was ordained as a missionary to Mongolia in Augustine Church, Edinburgh on 10 February 1870. James Gilmour's two brothers, John and Alexander, were both active members of the church in the early years of the present century. It was not until Adam Dunlop's ministry (1860–65) that David Livingstone's two sisters left the church to suit the convenience of their aged mother who was unable to walk the distance. Hamilton Church separated from the Congregational Union over the 'heresy' of its minister John Kirk, but it never formally joined the Evangelical Union. The separation lasted ten years. It was restored in 1854. In September 1857 the church helped to organise the welcome meeting for David Livingstone held in the Muir Street U.P. Church. During the time the church worshipped in Ebenezer Chapel the following members entered the ministry at home and abroad: Fergus Ferguson, junior, David Ferguson, Alex. Cross, James Frame, Thomas Salmond, John Park, David Livingstone, Charles Livingstone, and James Gilmour. The present church designated St. James', in Auchingramont Road, was opened in December 1873. Hector Ross, the late pastor, was president of the Congregational Union of Scotland in 1954–5. A second church in Hamilton, PARK ROAD, in one sense dates from 1807 when St.

James' Church began, but it was formed in 1854 and 'must be related to the evangelical and prophetic ministry of John Kirk, whose power and personality took a new orientation from 1841 through his association with James Morison'. When Kirk left Ebenezer Chapel for Edinburgh in 1845 he left behind a church severed from the Congregational Union and yet not in association with the Evangelical Union. Not unnaturally some eight years later there was a cleavage in the congregation. Those who clung loyally to John Kirk's teaching, mostly office-bearers, found themselves in a minority, and turned to the Evangelical Union. They were recognised as a church in February 1854. 'The meeting to form the church was held in the parlour of John Naismith's house at Greenside Tannery but presently Logan's Hall ... in Cadzow Street was secured, and later permanent premises were built in Church Street, probably called Zion Congregational Church. Later still these were sold and meetings were held in the Town Hall.' The present church in Park Road was opened for worship in October 1872. The first pastor was James B. Robertson, one of the nine students expelled from the Congregational Theological Academy in 1844. One of the original deacons was Neil Livingstone, the father of David Livingstone. The longest ministry was that of George Bell (1877-1911), who was prominent in the affairs of the Congregational Union. His son is Professor Robert J. T. Bell, distinguished mathematician of Dunedin, New Zealand, an LL.D. of Glasgow University. The most scholarly minister was John Murphy, world-renowned as a writer on anthropology, who became Professor of Comparative Religion in Manchester University. Some of the laymen of Park Road Church have played a prominent part in the life of the denomination. John McBryde, the historian of the Church, is a member of the General and of the College Committee: Lockhart W. Hutson, O.B.E., was chairman of the church Building Committee, and Mrs. A. J. Christie is treasurer of the Women's Union. A body of Old Scots Independents met in Baillie's Lane in AIRDRIE in the first decade of the nineteenth century. A small 'missionary' church was formed there in 1807 which enjoyed the ministrations of Robert Haldane. After that gentleman had sold his estate of Airthrey in Stirlingshire to procure funds for evangelical work in Scotland, he purchased in 1809 a tract of moorland five miles east of Airdrie and upon it built the mansion house of Auchengray. In the offices a little distance from the house he had a chapel constructed where his brother James preached two or three times a week on his visits to Auchengray, and where he himself usually conducted Sunday worship. The pulpit from which the Haldanes used to preach is now in the Museum in Airdrie Public Library. Robert Haldane's biographer tells us that 'on the Lord's Day he was for several years in the habit of going to Airdrie, where there was a church founded on the model of that with which he was connected in Edinburgh. He generally himself delivered an exposition of some part of Scripture.' When Robert Haldane ceased to act as pastor he was succeeded by John Calder, a working weaver, who was in every respect a worthy man and of superior intelligence, being the author of several controversial pamphlets on religious subjects. From 1809 the church appears to have been Baptist in sentiment. In the year 1835 a few earnest men and women, the majority of whom seem to have been members of the Secession Church with some few from the aforementioned Baptist Church, resolved to form a church in accordance with Congregational principles, which they did in July 1836. That church, which is now designated EBENEZER, met first in Painters' Hall, Baillie's Lane, then in Mason's Hall, again in Painters' Hall, and lastly in the church in Broomknoll Street which was opened in 1839 and rebuilt in 1882. For several years the church was supplied by students from the Glasgow Theological Academy. Alexander Cuthbert, 1839-40, was the first ordained minister. In Baillie's Lane the first Sunday School in the district was opened. It was under the ministry of James Taylor, 1840-42, that the church made most headway in these formative years. Many of its young men conducted cottage meetings and street preachings with great zeal. People attended the church from the whole district round about, and before long the church was in the midst of a genuine movement of the Spirit. Great hopes were raised for its future, but in 1842 Taylor resigned the pastorate, and with a large part of the congregation formed the Baptist Church in Airdrie. In the Morisonian movement a division of opinion arose in Ebenezer Church, and in 1845 another contingent of members left and formed the Evangelical Union Church in Graham Street, Airdrie. During the ministry of Alexander Mann, 1896-1905, the membership steadily increased. The church began to take a more active interest in the social welfare of the community. Mann was a powerful opponent of the drink trade and was one of a gathering which met at the home of James Knox (later Sir James Knox) where the Airdrie Lodge of Good Templars was born. In four years it grew to the stature of the premier lodge in the world with a membership of 2,725. Mann was its first chaplain. The name of John Orr will always be associated with Ebenezer Church. His sincerity brought him to the Provost's chair and he was one of the most outstanding men of commerce in the burgh. His name is found from 1910 onwards to the date of his death in 1952 in the records of the Congregational Union of Scotland, mostly as an enthusiastic supporter of the Church Aid Committee. As its chairman he helped to lead to the conception of the Central Fund as a sure basis for Union finance. PARK (Graham Street) Church was formed in November 1845 by members from Ebenezer Church who sympathised with E.U. principles. The church joined the Evangelical Union in 1846. The congregation met from 1845 to 1846 in Abercromby School, High Street; from 1846 to 1848 in the Trades Hall, Bank Street;

from 1848 to 1851 in a hall in Graham Street; and then in a church in Graham Street which was opened for public worship in July 1851. The present church in Park Place was opened in May 1906. COATDYKE Church was formed in 1911 by members who had seceded from an Evangelical Union (continuing) church which met in a hall in Kippen Street. The present church premises in Glencraig Street were erected in 1911. John Edmonston was the first pastor. There was a disastrous split in the congregation, locally known as the 'Coatdyke disruption' during the ministry of R. McRoberts, 1920-25, from which the church seemingly never recovered. Under the leadership of Charles J. A. Innes, 1951-57, the cause considerably revived. A year ago a manse was built entirely by voluntary labour, the work being done almost wholly by church members. Unfortunately, however, the church is situated in an area where many of the houses are scheduled for slum clearance. In 1837 a church was formed in NEW LANARK* as a result of the preaching of students. Patrick Anderson became pastor in April 1838. The church ceased to meet in 1870. The present church in LANARK was formed in February 1847 from a mission in sympathy with E.U. principles. John Inglis who had laboured in the town since 1846 became pastor in 1849. The church met at first in West Port. It was admitted to the Evangelical Union in 1862. In recent years the membership has risen from 150 to 370, due in large measure to the vigorous ministry of Isabel G. D. Shedden, 1949-54. The church in BELLSHILL was formed in October 1841 by members of the church in Hamilton, largely owing to the evangelistic work of Fergus Ferguson (sen.). Ferguson was the first pastor. The congregation met originally in a disused pit and later in a schoolroom. A church was erected in October 1842. The church was admitted to the Congregational Union but severed its connection in 1844. It joined the Evangelical Union in 1854. The church in CARLUKE was formed in October 1846 as a result of revival services held in the district by John Kirk and others. John Hamilton was the first pastor. The church joined the Evangelical Union in 1858. The congregation met first in the Commercial Hall in Kirkton Street, and then above Cringan's workshop in Clyde Street. In August 1851 the first church was opened at the Wee Moss. The present church was opened for public worship in October 1882. The church at SHOTTS was formed in September 1844 in a barn of Stane farm, by Fergus Ferguson (sen.). The original membership was composed of attenders on the ministry of Fergus Ferguson at Bellshill. The church was admitted into the Evangelical Union in 1876. Its first minister was William Bathgate. The original church building at Manse Field was opened in November 1844. The present church became the home of the congregation in September 1908. In COATBRIDGE the church designated BUCHANAN STREET was formed in 1860 in connection with the Evangelical Union, and John Inglis was the first pastor. The church joined the E.U. in the same year. Peter Marshall, Chaplain to the U.S. Senate, whose life work is commemorated in *A Man Called Peter*, was a son of this church. A second church, ALBERT STREET, was constituted in January 1877 from a preaching station opened in August of the previous year by the Western District of the Congregational Union. Many of the original members came from Ebenezer Church, Airdrie. David Beaton was ordained and inducted to the pastorate in March 1877. The present church building was opened in January 1878. Buchanan Street and Albert Street congregations united in 1958 under the ministry of T. Mearns. The church in WISHAW was formed in 1862 as the result of the preaching of Evangelical Unionists in the district and the Revival of 1859 with which the Evangelist E. P. Hammond was prominently identified, and which greatly increased and encouraged the sympathisers with E.U. views. The more immediate origin of the church was a secession of some families from Cambusnethan Free Church who favoured E.U. teaching. 'The occasion of their leaving was the preaching of the minister who decried the gospel preached by the E.U.s as "another gospel", and passed severe strictures upon the broad and full gospel of the "Universalities" by which so many had found peace.' These friends met in Clerk's Hall at the West Cross and other places and were ministered to by preachers supplied by the Evangelical Union. In October 1861 a preaching station was opened by the E.U. Home Mission, and in the spring of the following year it was constituted a church. Robert Inglis Gray became pastor. A church in Young Street was opened for public worship in October 1862. When it was in process of construction, passers-by were filled with wonder to behold on week-evenings within its naked walls, and while it was still unroofed, a little company of men and women, lighted candles in their hands, singing psalms and gospel songs, and raising their voices in prayer. Young Street Church became a centre and scene of sincere religion and consecrated social service for forty-five years. The trust deed of 1862 reminds us of the democratic character of the congregation: the names inscribed upon it are those of manual workers, miners, masons, joiners, and shoemakers. Wishaw Church had always had the total abstinence plank in its terms of membership. The Evangelical Unionists clearly saw the dreadful obstacle drink places in the way of Gospel effort and they eagerly allied themselves with any cause which combated the presence and sad harvest of the public house. When, for example, the Good Templars movement began to take root in Scotland it quietly won the sympathy and devoted support of men like William Halliday, minister of Wishaw E.U. Church, 1867-76. The present imposing church building in Kirk Road was opened in December 1907. At the time of the amalgamation of the two Unions in 1896, Wishaw Church stood apart, believing that the majority churches were by the union surrendering what was distinctive in the E.U. tradition. It was not until 1901 that Wishaw threw in its lot with the united denomination. Throughout its history Wishaw Church has been the nursery and training ground of future ministers. At least twelve of its sons have gone into the Christian ministry at home and abroad. Charles Richardson who is perhaps the greatest figure in Scottish Congregationalism in the present half-century, was a son of Wishaw Church. The church in MOTHERWELL was formed in October 1872 by Fergus Ferguson, senior, from a Home Mission Station established by the Evangelical Union in August of the same year. The newly-formed church met in the Mason's Hall, but a church building in Brandon Street was opened for public worship in 1875. David Greenhill was inducted as first pastor in March 1874. The Church grew and prospered during the long pastorate of John Mackintosh, 1897-1924, and also in the pastorate of Andrew James Forson, 1924-32, a distinguished Editor of *The Scottish Congregationalist*, who in May 1931 was honoured with election to the presidential chair of the Union. It is probable that a Congregational church met in BLANTYRE before 1850 in the Blantyre Works and was 'supplied' from Hamilton. This church ceased to meet. The present church in Blantyre, LIVINGSTONE CENTENARY, was formed in July 1877 by local E.U. churches, after being under the supervision of the Home Mission Committee of the Evangelical Union for a year or so. William Wyllie was its first pastor. A church building was opened for worship in October 1878, in which year the church was admitted into the Evangelical Union. Since 1938 the church has borne its present designation 'Livingstone Centenary E.U. Congregational Church'. The church at UDDINGSTON, which had its origin in Home Mission work supervised by the Evangelical Union, was formed in August 1877. The first pastor was Thomas W. Bowman. The church joined the E.U. in 1879. The present church building was opened for public worship in 1880. Those who are competent to judge have appraised it as one of the most beautiful churches in the neighbourhood. The church in STONEHOUSE was formed in 1894 from members who had seceded from the Hamilton Memorial Free Church because of a disagreement over procedure in the election of a minister. Peter Smith became pastor in the same year. The present church was opened for worship in 1896. The congregation is now at the peak figure of 285. A church was formed in RUTHERGLEN, which came to be known as REGENT STREET* Church, by sympathisers with E.U. principles in 1883. Its first pastor was Robert Brown. The first place of meeting was probably the Masonic Hall in Cathcart Street. In 1888 the congregation moved to a 'tin kirk' situated at the corner of Moray Place and Regent Street. In 1899 differences arose on matters of church polity consequent upon the amalgamation of the Evangelical and Congregational Unions, three years previously, in which Regent Street Church had participated. In May 1901 more than half the membership seceded with the intention of forming another church, which they did in the Harriet Street Hall in June 1901. This is the present RUTHERGLEN CHURCH. Robert Whiteford became pastor in November of that year. Subsequently the congregation worshipped in King Street Hall. In September 1903 a church in Main Street was opened for worship. (The Regent Street Church apparently ceased in 1905.) The Rutherglen congregation moved into the present attractive building in Johnstone Drive in November 1935. STRATHAVEN [West Church] separated from the Church of Scotland and was admitted into the Congregational Union in 1958, when T. Hall Bisset became pastor.

WESTERN COUNTIES

RENFREWSHIRE

The oldest Congregational church in this county is the one in PAISLEY designated SCHOOL WYND. It is claimed by James Ross in his *History of Congregational Independency* (p. 236) that this church dates back to 1795. This claim is also made, I am informed, in Kinniburgh's MS. This early date, however, is based on oral evidence which may or may not be correct. The hymn-book first used by the church bears the date 1796, writes a former pastor in 1848. 'Certain old men' say that it was 'published the year after their formation' (as a church). On this reminiscence rests the claim that the Paisley church is the oldest of the denomination in Scotland. There is no documentary or other historical evidence, to support it. Consequently we must regard this date as an interesting tradition, but as too vague to be accepted with any degree of certainty. Against this early date it has to be borne in mind that in the early years of the Union the Aberdeen and not the Paisley church was officially referred to as the oldest of the Scottish Congregational churches. What seems certain is that some time in the last years of the eighteenth century this church originated in the agitations of the Friends of the People, of whom there were many societies throughout the country. They were composed of men who had been stirred by the events connected with the French Revolution, and who sought political reform. Among those of this class in Paisley it would appear were some who were equally convinced of the necessity of reform in connection with religion, and especially of deliverance from the dominant power of the minister in the Established Church. The liberal views of two successive ministers of the High Church in the town—John Witherspoon and Dr. Snodgrass—'had awakened much attention to the principle of rational freedom'. The original members of School Wynd church used to ascribe the formation of the church to the teachings of these two men. It is interesting to note that

Witherspoon became Principal of Princeton College, New Jersey, U.S.A., in 1768 and was the only clergyman to be one of the signatories of the Declaration of Independence on 4 July 1776. School Wynd Church met at first in a malt barn. The members heard of a Burgher minister, David Stewart Wylie, who sympathised with their views, and after a time they called him to be their pastor. Wylie remained only a short time with them, but during his ministry a chapel to seat 500 was erected. His adoption of Baptist views hurt the new church, for many of the members also became Baptists and withdrew. For some time there was no settled minister but only occasional preachers. The students from Greville Ewing's classes gave frequent 'supply' as did others, both ministers and laymen. One of the students, John Young, accepted the pastorate in 1801, but, becoming like his predecessors, a Baptist, he resigned. In February 1807 George Robertson from Inverkip took up the work and had a happy ministry of eight years. At his induction the membership stood at forty-nine, but each year some twenty new members were added. In October 1850 another church was formed in Paisley as the result of the labours of John Harrison Lochore, a local schoolmaster. The church met in the Exchange rooms, and then in the Trades Hall, New Street, till 1855, when the congregation purchased the old tabernacle in CANAL STREET,* which gave its name to the church. This church united with School Wynd in 1871. The present church building of School Wynd Church was erected in 1887. The church in NEW STREET, Paisley, was formed in September 1845 by a number of people who were in sympathy with the theological position of James Morison. The Church was admitted into the Evangelical Union in 1846. The congregation met at first in the Abercorn Rooms, thereafter in the Exchange Rooms, and the services were conducted for the most part by students of the E.U. Theological Hall. One of these, Alexander M. Wilson, became the first minister of the church in October 1846. In 1847 the congregation began to worship in the historic Old Low Church, associated with the ministry of John Witherspoon, which ultimately it bought in 1849. The church which met in the LIBERAL CLUB HALL* was formed in 1897 by members of E.U. churches. Preaching in the village of INVERKIP* was engaged in by students from Glasgow during the summer of 1800, their expenses being met chiefly by Lady Shaw Stewart of Ardgowan and her daughter Barbara Maxwell of Pollok, later Mrs. Greville Ewing. In November of that year George Robertson, later of Paisley, received an invitation numerously signed by the inhabitants of the village 'to take up his abode and preach statedly among them'. By the appointment of the Society for Propagating the Gospel at Home he went and began services in an unfurnished garret. The following summer Inverkip Tabernacle was built and a church formed. In April 1802 George Robertson was ordained. For five years he laboured in the pastorate with considerable success. He was succeeded by Thomas Low who found conditions hard and difficult. In April 1806 thirty-three members transferred to the newly-formed church at Greenock. The congregation was never very large or flourishing and after some years ceased to meet. In GREENOCK the first Congregational church was the one now designated GEORGE SQUARE. It owed its origin to the interest some in that town had shown in the services held in the church at Inverkip. Similar services they desired to have nearer home, and preaching was begun in 1804. A chapel was erected in St. Michael Street and opened for worship by Greville Ewing in December 1805, when the church appears to have been formed. John Hercus the first ordained pastor began his ministry early in January 1806. The present building in George Square was opened for public worship in September 1840. From its formation the church was foremost in Home Mission work. As early as 1837 it had its Society for Religious Purposes, and for many years the church was associated with the three U.P. Churches in the conduct of the Town Mission in Cartsdyke. In 1852 a Sunday School was started, and later when it was found that many of the scholars had little or no education, week-evening classes were held on two nights a week by young men and women of the church, till the advent of School Boards made such classes unnecessary. It is interesting to read in the church minutes that on 2 December 1868 'the practice of publicly reproving those convicted of unseemly and sinful conduct was given up'. The church in NELSON STREET was formed by seventeen persons in Slater's Schoolroom, Tobago Street, Greenock, in March 1846. It owed its origin mainly to Alexander Muir, an elder expelled from the national church because of his sympathies with the teachings of James Morison. Muir and two other like-minded men had rented the afore-mentioned schoolroom, and in 1845 applied to the Evangelical Union for pulpit supply. In November of that year the request was granted and Greenock was recognised as a preaching station. The church was constituted in the following year. One is impressed by the democratic character of the little congregation; its original members were mostly of the artisan class. The congregation joined the Evangelical Union in 1846. For a meeting place they secured the old Assembly Halls, and in 1847 A. C. Rutherford became the first pastor. He was one of the four ministers suspended from the United Secession Church in 1842-43, who with their few supporters founded the Evangelical Union in the latter year. The Morisonians had to face much criticism and animosity in Greenock. 'Their right to claim to be Christians at all was questioned in some quarters.' The missionary spirit of the members, however, brooked no obstacle. 'In one of the few church documents referring to those times is a description of young mothers, holding an infant in one arm, going about the town distributing the *Daystar* and other publica-tions of the Union.' Gourock and Port Glasgow people were soon drawn to the Church. They were numerous enough to have special elders, residing in these towns, appointed to serve them. In 1849 the congregation purchased the old Independent Chapel in Sir Michael Street where the church met until June 1865, when the present attractive building in Nelson Street was opened for worship. Under the leadership of John Guthrie its second minister, 1851-61, the church was consolidated and through his culture and scholarship 'assumed a new and accepted status, on terms with the older denominations'. The membership was at its height during the ministry of Andrew Ritchie, 1894-1903. During the pastorate of W. F. Riddell, 1904-10, the church had an important place in the life of the town: Riddell was at the forefront in social questions and 'was the one minister in Greenock who could be counted upon to fill the Town Hall on public occasions, no matter what the type of his address'. The ministry of Allan S. Guild which has just terminated greatly enriched the church and maintained its best traditions. In 1871 the EAST Church, St. Lawrence Street, Greenock, was formed by members of George Square Church. The first pastor was George Moir. The church in MEARNS STREET was formed in September 1882 by members of Nelson Street Church. Thomas W. Bowman became the first pastor in 1883, in which year the church joined the Evangelical Union. The congregation met for some time in the Temperance Institute. The present church was opened for public worship in August 1886. MARTYRS' Church, Greenock, was formed in 1898 by John Richardson from a mission in the town. Richardson became the first pastor in 1898, and continued there till 1935. A church was formed in LOCHWINNOCH* about 1805 by members of Glasgow and Paisley Churches. Hugh Fraser was the first pastor and was ordained in 1806. The congregation was never very large and after a few years ceased to meet. The church in BARRHEAD was formed in the Mason Hall, Neilston, in June 1844 by sympathisers with Evangelical Union principles. The original membership roll contained 145 names. Twenty-two of these remained to worship in Neilston, while the others some nine years later built the present church in Arthurlie Street, Barrhead, when people of Newton Mearns, Nitshill, Grahamston as well as the local inhabitants, were being attracted by the new Morisonian teaching. The church was admitted to the Evangelical Union in 1857. The second pastor was Alexander Davidson, father of John Davidson the poet. Alexander Davidson was a man of high character and a preacher of distinction. His salary, we note, was £80 a year—and a free manse. There was a church in GOUROCK* formed in 1879 by members of the U.P. Church there. The first pastor was John M. Sloan, who settled in 1880. The church ceased after the retirement of John C. Nesbitt, its second pastor, in October 1888. The Church in PORT GLASGOW was formed in November 1880 from an E.U. Mission station supported by members of Greenock churches.

X

Its moving spirit was Alexander Davidson the pastor of Nelson Street Church. A. D. Anderson was ordained to the pastoral charge of the church in May 1881. The present church building in Balfour Street was opened for public worship by James Morison in April 1883. A. D. Anderson was an indefatigable worker in the cause of temperance and founded the Blue Ribbon Army in Port Glasgow. His church was frequently referred to as the 'Blue Ribbon Kirk'. Robert A. Taylor the present pastor has led the Port Glasgow church in worship and witness faithfully and well since 1927.

DUNBARTONSHIRE

Of the churches in CLYDEBANK the one designated MORISON MEMORIAL was formed, from mission work promoted by the Evangelical Union, in 1893. The first pastor was Robert McQueen. The church was admitted to the Evangelical Union in 1893. It met first in Wardrop Hall and subsequently in the Conservative Club Rooms. The church was opened in May 1897, and, like its neighbours, suffered structurally from the terrible enemy bombings in the 'forties. A second church, RADNOR PARK, was formed in October 1908.

Occasional preaching was given by Greville Ewing's students in KIRKINTILLOCH* in 1800 and 1801. Hugh Fraser was the first stated preacher, and under his direction a church was formed in 1802. George Greig, who had been assistant to Greville Ewing in Glasgow, was ordained and inducted in June 1804 but left for London two years later. After his departure there was a succession of preachers but no settled pastor. In 1809 the cause became extinct. The handful of members left were unable to support a minister and the chapel had to be sold to pay the debt on it. In June 1839 a church was formed in ALEXANDRIA* from the efforts of the students of the Theological Academy. James Mann became the first pastor in the following year. The church ceased in 1880. An E.U. preaching station was started in Alexandria round about 1861. The present church in DUMBARTON was formed in May 1878 from a preaching station under the supervision of the Evangelical Union. The church met for worship in the Burgh Hall. James Hamilton Paterson was the first pastor. The present church building was opened in December 1882. The congregation joined the Evangelical Union in 1885. The church in HELENSBURGH originated in a visit of two agents of the Society for Propagating the Gospel at Home, who preached there in the summer of 1799. The following year a small group of people who had been meeting together for fellowship and mutual exhortation in the house of William Bruce, one of their company, applied to Greville Ewing of Glasgow for a student preacher, as Helensburgh was destitute of any place of worship. In June of that year one of the two agents aforementioned was sent as pulpit supply. From this time onwards for about two years a preaching station was regularly supplied by students under Ewing's tuition. 'There was no common bond between the worshippers but the Gospel.' The attention of the small but growing congregation was soon turned to the possibility of having some permanent place of worship. Accordingly a 'bare ungainly structure was erected in a field near the line of James Street'. It is said to have been primitive and uncomfortable with seats high and stiff, and the ground unfloored. Its entrance was through undrained land and in wet weather somewhat critical, 'as a row of stepping stones had been laid down along the approach in the crossing of which caution and strict balance were alike essential'. Questions of church government did not at first exercise the minds of the hearers who attended the preaching of the Gospel within these rude walls. Their interest was in the Gospel, not in the organisation of a new denomination. However, as time went on, they were forced to discuss the matter of church polity, as no association can exist long without some form of organisation. Some had a preference for the Original Secession Church; others for the Relief; some favoured the Congregationalists, whose principles were beginning to be understood in Scotland. Protracted meetings were held to decide the issue, and ultimately it was resolved that the matter should be put to the vote. The result gave the Congregationalists a majority. Accordingly about 1804 the preaching station was organised into a Congregational church—the first and for several years, the only church of any kind in Helensburgh. John Edwards was the first pastor. In 1851 the old building was demolished and a new one erected on its site. This building still exists and is used as the church hall. The present attractive sanctuary was built and opened in 1884. The Helensburgh church has had distinguished ministers, among whom we might mention John Arthur, James Troup, William Blair, W. D. Bruce, and Daniel Cook, under whose inspiring leadership the historic church maintained its traditional witness and influence in town and district.

ARGYLL AND BUTE

The pioneers of home missionary enterprise in Argyllshire were Neil Douglas of Dundee and MacNaught of Dumbarton, ministers of the Anti-Burgher Church, who had been sent out by that body to itinerate in the Highlands in July 1797, contemporaneously with James Haldane's evangelistic tour of the north. Their preaching excited great interest, and was blessed to many, but they met with persistent opposition from ministers of the Established Church and the landed proprietors. In 1800 James Haldane and John Campbell visited and preached in the extensive district of Kintyre, and thereafter the Society for Propagating the Gospel at Home decided to send Archibald

McCallum, a native of Kintyre, to itinerate in that district. McCallum had been a student in connection with Greville Ewing's class in Glasgow, and was a man of great piety, zeal, and prudence. His labours as a preacher began in 1800, with the result that in 1802 a church was formed on Congregational principles in KINTYRE* consisting of fifty members, over whom Archibald McCallum was ordained pastor in the same year. In 1806 the number of members had increased to 150. So greatly had the good work begun by McCallum prospered that in a few years there were four churches, the members of which numbered 272, and in connection with which there were twenty-six prayer meetings. But the opposition to the good man and his work was great and persistent. The ministers of the Established Church threatened to send him out of the country, and to deprive all who heard him of their church privileges. Indeed the proprietor of the estate on which many of the members lived was so determined in his opposition that he put it in the option of his tenants either to relinquish all connection with McCallum or leave their farms. They preferred leaving their farms to forsaking their pastor, and in consequence many of them removed to CAMPBELTOWN* and neighbourhood, where a church was formed in 1805, which continued till 1864. Of the churches formed PORT ELLEN,* Islay, had the services of Peter McLaren and James McLean till 1843. PORT CHARLOTTE,* Islay, formed in 1823, was served from that date by Malcolm McLaurin and CLACHAN* by Dugald McGregor till 1848. The church in SKIPNESS* was formed early in the century and George Murray was pastor till his death in 1861. The church in OBAN was formed in 1805 by twenty converts made by the earnest evangelistic efforts of Dugald McEwan and John Reid. There was at first no church building. The services were held either in the open air or at a farmstead in the hills seven or so miles east of the town. The first pastor, Dugald McEwan (1805-7) had his induction service in a field on the south side of the town. His ministry was cut short by a split in the congregation over the baptismal controversy. Many holding Baptist views left and those remaining, being deprived also of Robert Haldane's financial assistance, were unable to support a settled pastor. However, John Campbell, who had been a zealous evangelist in the Breadalbane district, was ordained as pastor in 1811 and remained in that capacity for over forty years. For a long time the church and its minister were greatly obstructed in their good work, 'almost all the Established Church clergy and the gentry using every possible means for rooting out of the country the families and individuals who had embraced Congregational principles. All those who went to hear Campbell were threatened to be deprived of church privileges, and some of the members were deprived of their farms.' One of the landlords sent 'summonses of removal to all the tenants on his estate who gave countenance to the preachers, and one of his men was sent purposely to take down the names of his tenants who were found hearing one of the preachers on the Lord's Day at the village of Muckearn'. Campbell and his brave and loyal followers were warned off almost every piece of land in Oban. One day indeed the proprietor of the land upon which they were meeting 'called out the militia and drove them at the point of the bayonet to the sand below the tide-mark'. Here at 'The Codling Rock' the Congregationalists of Oban held their services. Despite intense opposition and difficulties John Campbell built his first chapel which was opened in 1820. He travelled to Glasgow, Edinburgh, and even to London to raise the necessary funds. In 1880 the old church was demolished and rebuilt. The Oban Church maintained many preaching stations in the neighbourhood, including those at Easedale, Muckearn, Benderloch, and Lismore. Was it prophetic, we wonder, that in February 1954 the first Ecumenical Conference in Oban was held in the Congregational Church? A small church was formed in APPIN* in 1843 from the labours of John Campbell of Oban. It joined with Lismore and ceased in 1875. Archibald Farquharson was ordained pastor of the church in TIREE* in 1835, and remained until his death in 1878. The church ceased to meet early in the present century. The church in DUNOON* was formed in 1899 by some twenty-five members who owing to a dispute had seceded from the U.P. Church. James Baxter Allan became the first pastor in 1900, in which year the church was accepted by the Congregational Union. The congregation met at first in the Burgh Hall. Later they acquired the old Episcopal Chapel. The church ceased in 1917. The church in ARRAN (Sannox) was formed in 1806 after a visit by the Haldanes from Campbeltown. In that year Alexander Mackay was ordained pastor. For sixteen years the congregation met in the homes of the people of North Sannox. A church was built in 1822 which was repaired and renovated in 1937. The second minister, John Blacklock, 1860-78, conducted a theological academy for some years during his pastorate, from which students entered the Presbyterian as well as the Congregational ministries. R. W. Dale sometimes lectured at the academy in the summer months. Blacklock later entered the ministry of the Free Church. The Sannox Church suffered much in the early years by the emigration of many of its members. The pastor for some time had to support himself by teaching, until financial aid was given by the newly-formed Congregational Union of Scotland. The great-grandparents of the present Prime Minister, Mr. Harold Macmillan, were among the early members of Sannox Church. In 1836 a small church was formed in ROTHESAY* as the result of evangelistic labours in the Gaelic language. In the same year a small chapel was opened. Archibald McEwan became pastor in 1837. The number of members never exceeded twenty. On McEwan's death in 1839, Anthony McGill became pastor. The church ceased in 1848. In 1943 the cause was resuscitated for a while.

SOUTHERN COUNTIES

AYRSHIRE

The oldest Congregational church in this county was formed in AYR* in 1804 by the converts of Richard Penman who apparently became the first minister in that year. The church seems to have been a struggling one from the first, and had a chequered history till its dissolution in 1878. WALLACE STREET Church was formed in 1844. It was admitted to the Evangelical Union in the following year. Its first pastor was William Bathgate. The congregation originally met in a house, and subsequently in a public hall. In 1860 it took over the Burgher church. The present church building in Wallace Street was opened for public worship in 1865. The church has had a chequered history. A split in the membership in 1897 resulted in the formation of Morison Church. In 1898 the minister and many of the members joined the U.P. church. The minority began to meet again in April 1900 and were admitted into the Congregational Union as Wallace Street Church in 1905. MORISON Church was formed in the Volunteers' Hall, Newmarket Street, Ayr, in March 1897 by members of Wallace Street Church. Arthur H. McConnachie was inducted as pastor in May 1898. Towards the close of that year the church began to worship in the Masonic Hall, Nile Court. In 1901 it procured the Original Secession Church in George Street where it still meets.

In KILMARNOCK a church was formed in 1825 as the result of John Campbell's evangelistic labours there, when he was a student of the Glasgow Theological Academy. Campbell was ordained to the charge in 1825. The following year Greville Ewing officiated at the opening of a chapel to hold 700 hearers. After a succession of pastors, owing to discouraging circumstances the church ceased to meet about 1866. In 1840 James Morison became minister of the United Secession Church in Clerk's Lane. In June of the following year he was expelled from that denomination for teaching the universal atonement of Christ. All but a few of his congregation left the Secession Church and continued to meet as an Independent church in Clerk's Lane Chapel under Morison's ministry. This church is now known as WINTON PLACE, having moved to its present imposing building in November 1860. In 1895 two memorial windows were installed in memory of James Morison and of elders who had assisted in the formation of the Evangelical Union. In the year following a tablet was placed in the vestibule of the church commemorating Dr. Morison's ministry. The church also houses some Morisonian relics; and the Communion vessels that were used originally in the Anti-Burgher church which transferred from Kilmaurs to Clerk's Lane Chapel, Kilmarnock in 1775 are on view. They remind us of the long and nationally important history of the congregation. During the last half century Winton Place Church has been linked with the life and work of the late David Carruthers, who was a life-long member of the congregation and could trace family associations right back to the beginnings of both the Congregational and Evangelical Unions. Indeed his grandfather, his father and Mr. Carruthers himself were in succession the only three treasurers of the E.U. branch of the Chapel Debt Fund which was later amalgamated with the Congregational Union Fund under David Carruthers's continued treasurership. As the legal adviser of the Union he was a central figure in its life for many years. The Church in STEWARTON owed its formation to the labours of William Cunningham of Lainshaw, patron of the parish, who found himself unable to accept the office of elder because he could not assent to the teaching of the Westminster Confession, especially with regard to the limitation of the Atonement. He was accordingly refused admission to the Sacrament in the Established Church. In February 1827 Cunningham and his followers, who had for some time gathered in Sunday Schools and other meetings for instruction and fellowship, formed an Independent church of which Cunningham was pastor until his death in 1849. He endowed the church. The congregation met in Cunningham's Institute and subsequently purchased the 'Auld Licht' Chapel. The church entered the Evangelical Union in 1873. The church in ARDROSSAN was formed in 1837 from a mission station started in the previous year by the Western Association of Congregational Ministers. Peter Mather, who had assisted in the work prior to the formation of the church, became pastor in October 1838. The congregation met in a small hall at the rear of the site now occupied by the Railway Hotel in Princes Street. When in 1842 accommodation there proved inadequate the church, then the only one in the town, moved to a hall situated in Glasgow Street. In 1860 a church was built in Bute Place. The congregation withdrew from the Congregational Union in 1844 under the influence of the Morisonian Movement, and were admitted to the Evangelical Union in 1894. The present attractive church was dedicated in October 1903. A church was formed in BEITH in July 1839 from a preaching station. James Robertson (1840-42) was its only pastor. In 1861 the Evangelical Union church was formed from a preaching station connected with that body. The congregation joined the E.U. in the following year. Stephen Todd was the first pastor. The church in CUMNOCK owed its origin to a few members of the church in Kilmarnock who, finding the distance to that town too great to travel, began meeting in the house of one of their number. On the 15 November 1838 they formed themselves into a church. They met in a hall of the Black Bull Inn. By 1840 the membership had reached twenty-seven, and James Sime became pastor. In 1847 a building that had formerly been a parish school was bought and converted into a church.

There the congregation worshipped till 1884 when the present beautiful church was erected. CUMNOCK E.U. Church* was formed on 31 August 1884 from a mission begun in April of that year. A church was opened for public worship in July 1886. Peter McLeod became pastor in the following year when the congregation was admitted to the Evangelical Union. The church was closed in 1895. James Keir Hardie was connected with this church, and his daughter who married Emrys Hughes, member of Parliament for south Ayrshire, became Provost of Cumnock. It is tempting to believe that Hardie imbibed some of his social idealism from his association with the E.U. movement. He was the friend of Thomas MacRobert the minister of the E.U. Church in Dreghorn to whom the Labour leader brought his infant daughter to be baptised. When at a later date Hardie stood for a constituency in East London and was dubbed an atheist by some ill-informed newspaper, it was Thomas MacRobert who, at Hardie's request, wrote to the press stating the truth. In January 1887 Keir Hardie started a monthly magazine called the *Miner*, and the first article in it was a short biography of its founder-editor by the pastor of Dreghorn. A well-known and greatly-esteemed Congregational minister remembers as a boy at the Dreghorn Manse looking out of a window and 'seeing a man, evidently dressed for a funeral, with a frock coat on, carrying a silk hat in his hand. Keir Hardie had been at a funeral, wearing a silk hat for the first time in his life. As he was going on to address a Miners' meeting he sent the hat for safe keeping to the manse. It was placed in a wardrobe in the spare bedroom. Shortly afterwards two E.U. students . . . who were conducting a series of Evangelistic meetings in the church were sleeping in the bedroom. One night they went off to bed, but returned to the study with the M.P.'s hat, laid it on the floor upside down and proceeded to put on the hat by putting their heads into it. However, one of them finally toppled over and that finished the hat, for which my father had to pay fifteen shillings. I don't know whether that was why K. H. shocked the House of Commons by attending it in a cap!' It is pleasant to recall that this great humanitarian, the first working man to be sent to Parliament, learnt his democracy under Christ in a Congregational church. The centenary of his birth has recently been commemorated and it is fitting that his name should be inscribed in this book of religious annals, graced with humour and the human touch he so much loved. The church in GALSTON was formed in 1843 by thirty-six members of Kilmarnock E.U. Church. The congregation joined the Evangelical Union in the following year. The first place of meeting was a weaver's shop. The first pastor David Drummond, 1843-46, was inducted to the charge at a service held in a field at the top of Orchard Street. The present church was opened for public worship in May 1845. A church was formed in CATRINE* in 1844 as the result of a movement in favour of E.U.

principles led by Alexander Forsyth, an evangelist. The congregation joined the Evangelical Union in the same year. A church was opened for public worship in July 1851. The church ceased to meet in 1926. A second church, GORDON MEMORIAL, was formed in 1956, of which Charles J. A. Innes became pastor in the following year. The church in KILWINNING was formed in May 1844. It was admitted to the Evangelical Union in the following year. The congregation worshipped in a hall. Robert Hunter was the first pastor. A church was opened for public worship in March 1850. Representatives from DARVEL, ardent disciples of James Morison, were present at the historic meeting held at Clerk's Lane Church, Kilmarnock on 16 May 1843, which inaugurated the Evangelical Union. In 1844 thirty-seven members from Kilmarnock and some others formed a church in Darvel, and in the same year William Landels became its minister. The church worshipped in the old chapel in Ranoldcoup Road. When the pastor demitted the charge in 1846 to become minister of a Baptist congregation in Edinburgh the church was closed. The cause, however, did not die out, for a number of faithful members walked the four miles to the E.U. church in Galston for nearly forty years. From this nucleus the present church in Darvel was formed in March 1884 from a preaching station established in January of that year. It met again in the old chapel and when its first pastor John McIntosh was called in 1885 the congregation numbered about fifty. The present attractive building on a well-chosen site at the centre of the town was opened for public worship in December 1889. A church in DALMELLINGTON* was formed in 1844 on E.U. principles. It joined the Evangelical Union in 1850. It was supplied with preachers by the Home Mission Committee of the Evangelical Union till 1872, and in September of that year Robert Brown became pastor. In the early years of the present century the congregation applied for admission to the U.F. Church. The church in SALTCOATS was formed in September 1859 by members of the church in Ardrossan. The congregation had no minister for several years. It met in the Temperance Hall. The present building was opened for worship in January 1863, in which year the congregation was admitted into the Evangelical Union. The church in DREGHORN was formed in 1864 by supporters of the Evangelical Union from a preaching station established by that body some three years previously. The church joined the Evangelical Union in 1865. Robert Paterson was the first pastor. The congregation met for some years in a shop at the east end of the village that had been adapted as a church. The present building was opened for public worship in 1904. Dreghorn Church in the minds of modern Congregationalists in Scotland is linked with the name of the late Thomas MacRobert who for fifty-seven years faithfully ministered to the needs of the congregation and the community. In 1882, at the commencement of his ministry, the church had a membership of only thirty and was in poor shape. He shepherded the congregation through hard and difficult times and left them in 1940 one of the strongest village causes in the country. His two sons, A. F. and T. M. MacRobert, hold places of high honour in the denomination, one as a much esteemed minister of the gospel, the other as a famous teacher and an authority on the Church's Psalmody. A church was formed in MUIRKIRK as a result of the missionary labours of James Haldane and John Aikman, at the beginning of the nineteenth century. Andrew Rattray appears to have been the first settled pastor, 1805-7. Two cottages converted into a hall served as a place of worship until the middle of the century. The present church was formed in 1854 by sympathisers with the Evangelical Union and among its founder members were many from the older church which seems by this time to have ceased. In 1854 a new church building was erected in Glasgow Road. By 1894 this had proved inadequate to the requirements of the congregation and the present building was erected and opened for public worship in March of that year. Unfortunately, the records of this church up to the year 1878 have been lost and this sad fact accounts for the large hiatus in the list of its ministers included elsewhere in this volume. Though always a struggling cause and never numerically strong, in both its traditions Muirkirk Church has survived for a century and a half as a Congregational witness to Christ and His way of life.

DUMFRIESSHIRE

The church in ANNAN is one of the oldest Congregational churches in Scotland. There is, however, a conflict of opinion as to the date of its formation, for three different dates have been given. Kinniburgh says that 'sometime about the year 1800 a Congregational Church was formed here'. James Ross assigns an earlier date, 1794, 'in which year Andrew Carnson was ordained minister'. He refers to an interesting account of Carnson's settlement which was given in the *Evangelical Magazine* of 1794. This date might be accepted without demur but for a letter in the *Missionary Magazine* (Vol. III, pp. 15-16), which points to a third date. This letter is from J. Robertson, Annan, and is dated 5 December 1798. The writer expresses his pleasure at the forming of the Aberdeen church, and remarks that 'the sentiments of the church at Aberdeen are such as the church here have adopted, of which the writer, though unworthy, has the pastoral care, and which was formed about two years since, in much the same and solemn way in which that at Aberdeen was'. It would appear that Andrew Carnson ministered to a congregation from some time in 1794, but the formal constitution of the church on Congregational lines did not take place till a later date. Andrew Carnson must have been a compelling personality. A native of Londonderry, he became a Congregationalist through the study of the works of John Owen. He commenced his labours in Annan by holding meetings in the open-air, which were well attended. After his removal, there was a succession of ministers of whom little trace can now be found. A church building was erected in Scott Street, which was sold in 1806 to the Burgher Church and ultimately became a Roman Catholic chapel in 1839. The Annan congregation in the early years of the nineteenth century was supported by Lady Glenorchy, who supplied it with preachers. Soon, however, the church got into difficulties and was dissolved, the chapel being disposed of to discharge its debts. The cause was revived in the early 'thirties of the last century and the church was re-formed on 2 March 1837, John Ward becoming pastor in the following year. It met in the Old Academy in the High Street. However, the church was soon dissolved owing to the mismanagement of a case of discipline. In 1842 preaching supply was provided for Annan by the Congregational Union and on 31 October 1843 the present church was formed by thirty persons disjoined from the Congregational churches of Dumfries and Carlisle. Ebenezer Young became pastor in November 1846. The congregation met first in a house in High Street, from 1843 to 1847; then in a church in Greencroft Wynd, from 1847 to 1903; and lastly in the present church in Station Road which was opened for public worship in June 1903. George Kennedy the second pastor resigned in 1890 to form 'Annan Free Congregational Church' of which we have no further information. The Annan church would appear to have flourished best under the ministry of Ebenezer Young, 1846-88. He was a great evangelist and preached in the open air in all the surrounding villages. During the forty and more years of his ministry members from many miles around walked into Annan for the services. During his pastorate no fewer than twenty-five young men went forth from the church to be ministers and evangelists. One of these, John Pillans, was noteworthy. A church was formed in SANQUHAR in 1807 with fifteen members and David Davidson became pastor. For some time the cause had fair success but disputes on the question of Baptism wrecked it about the time Davidson left. Most of the members seceded and formed a Baptist church and the rest were scattered among the various churches in the neighbourhood. The present church in Sanquhar was formed in October 1864 by eighty-nine members, from a preaching station connected with the Evangelical Union established in March of the same year. The membership was composed of people from the other churches who were opposed to the Calvinistic doctrine preached by the ministers. George Gladstone, the orator of the Evangelical Union, became the first pastor in 1865. The present church building was erected in 1864. James Haldane preached in DUMFRIES in the summer of 1801 every Sunday for four months from a tent in a field.

Prior to this a few serious persons had been holding a prayer meeting. During James Haldane's visit the attendances at this gathering greatly increased and the meeting began to be held in a more public manner than formerly. Interest was kept up by visits from Ralph Wardlaw of Glasgow and other preachers. A 'Tabernacle' was built in 1803 by Robert Haldane which was situated on the site of the present Municipal Chambers. It was not until 1805 or 1806 that the church, now known as IRVING STREET was formed. The original members numbered about twenty and William Watson settled as first pastor in 1806. When the Haldane brothers became Baptists the church lost its place of meeting at the Tabernacle, which was sold and used first as the County Court House, and later became the Burgh Town Hall. From 1814 till 1835 the members had no church building of their own and worshipped in a small chapel which they rented. In the latter year, however, the present building in Irving Street was opened. It was greatly enlarged in 1862-64 and partly rebuilt at the turn of the century. Although the church has never had a large membership there has been an almost continuous succession of ministers, nineteen in all, since the first one in 1806. Two of these, Robert Mackintosh and John Murphy, became distinguished professors at Lancashire Independent College, Manchester. In June 1917 a union was effected with Waterloo Place, the other Congregational church then existing in the town. The church in WATERLOO PLACE* had been formed in 1870 by members of Irving Street Church and James Strachan its first pastor was settled in the same year. His long and useful ministry terminated only in 1913. A building was opened for public worship at Whitesands in June 1877. A church in IRISH STREET* was formed from a preaching station in 1862. In that year it was admitted to the Evangelical Union. John Dunlop was its first pastor. The church ceased to meet in 1881. The church in THORNHILL was formed in 1851 from an E.U. preaching station opened two years previously. James Pearson became the first pastor in 1855. The year following the congregation joined the Evangelical Union. The church first gathered in the house of Alexander Grierson, then in the Masonic Hall, and thereafter in the present building, which was opened for public worship in 1873.

KIRKCUDBRIGHTSHIRE

A church was formed in GATEHOUSE-OF-FLEET* in 1806 as the result of the labours of various itinerant preachers. In July 1807 the first pastor, Archibald Miller, was settled. He continued with success for nearly thirty years. The church ceased about 1845. The church in DALBEATTIE was formed in 1866 from a preaching station established three years previously by the Evangelical Union. John Inglis became pastor in the same year. A place of worship was built in 1867 and the congregation joined the Evangelical Union in 1872.

SELKIRK AND PEEBLES

The church in MELROSE* was formed in March 1842 as the result of the labours of Cavers Missioners and later of Ebenezer Young who became the first pastor of the church in June of the same year. The congregation joined the Evangelical Union in 1883. A chapel was opened in September 1842 and a new place of worship in 1878. In October 1844 thirty-four members of the church in Melrose formed the church in GALASHIELS (UNION STREET) in connection with the Evangelical Union, and in the same year James B. Robertson became pastor. A church was opened for public worship in Union Street in July 1846. The present church built on the same site was opened in December 1872. The congregation joined the Evangelical Union in 1864. The church in INNERLEITHEN was formally constituted in 1848 from a preaching station that appears to have existed for some years. William Dobson became pastor. A church was opened for public worship in March 1848. The present church was opened in December 1889. The church in WALKERBURN was formed in 1886 by fifteen members of Innerleithen Church, and two years later Benjamin D. Morris became the first pastor. The congregation met at first in the Good Templar Hall. A church was opened in June 1890. The congregation was admitted to the Congregational Union in 1891. Walkerburn Church united with Innerleithen Church under one pastor in 1956. The church in SELKIRK (Philiphaugh) traces its remote origin to the labours of a small band of earnest evangelists known as Cavers Missioners, who, in the early years of last century 'traversed a wide region, and laboured to much purpose as preachers of a simple gospel'. These men owed their name to the fact that they were employed by James Douglas of Cavers, a man of strong evangelistic sympathies and with an intense interest in the religious welfare of the district. The church was formed in March 1842 of twenty-two members from Melrose Church. At that time the congregation met for worship in Chapel Street Hall. In 1858 Sir John Murray, who had become a Congregationalist, gifted to the church an Episcopal Chapel which he had built on the Philiphaugh Estate. Until 1871 the Selkirk Church had been Congregational, though its sympathies from the first were of a Morisonian character, but in that year the congregation was formally connected with the Evangelical Union. In 1878 there was among the members a difference of opinion regarding Bible instruction in schools which unhappily led to a split in the membership. The seceders formed a second church in May 1878 known as CHAPEL STREET or THOR-NIEHALL, in connection with the Evangelical Union. A new church was opened in June 1885. In 1917 Thorniehall Church, then without a pastor, successfully approached Philiphaugh Church with a view to union under one pastor. This arrangement continued until 1930, when it was decided to use one church building. As the result of a vote Thorniehall was chosen as the place of worship. In 1951 Philiphaugh Church was converted into a hall-cum-church by voluntary labour, and as it now stands near to a new housing site it is hoped it may be utilised in extension work.

ROXBURGHSHIRE

Through the instrumentality of James Douglas of Cavers, Francis Dick, an earnest evangelist, was brought to labour in the district around Cavers in 1823-24. The first result of his work was the formation of a church at DENHOLM* in 1826, consisting of seven members all representative men—one from Jedburgh, two from Hawick, two from Cavers, and two from Denholm itself. For about ten years the church was supplied by Francis Dick and other preachers, but in June 1835 Robert Wilson, a student at the Glasgow Theological Academy, became its first pastor. Soon after the death of its third minister, John McRobert, the church seems to have been dissolved. There was a church in JEDBURGH* formed in 1841 by members of Denholm Church, of which Ebenezer Cornwall became pastor in 1843. The congregation met in the Black Bull Inn. It was admitted to the Evangelical Union in 1875. It ceased as a church in July 1886, and thereafter became a mission station. It was ultimately closed in November 1886. A church at KELSO*, later in connection with the Evangelical Union, was formed in 1841 and joined that body in 1871. It met in the Friends' Meeting House and for many years had no settled minister. John Hunter Rutherford was the first pastor. The church ceased in 1877. In 1798 James Haldane and John Aikman preached in HAWICK to large congregations. Their pulpit was a heap of stones, the debris of the ancient tower of Hawick. From their joint labours as evangelists sprang the first Congregational church in the Borders. It was composed of William Thorburn, William Laidlaw, Peter Taylor, Robert Leithead, David Dick, and some others who separated themselves from their former congregations, not without considerable disapproval, and rented a barn in Backbrae Lane 'for the purpose of mutual edification, religious exercise and worship'. There they gathered, strengthened in their beliefs and principles by the visit of many an itinerant preacher, until in 1804 they built the Tabernacle in the Kirk Wynd, and in November of the following year a church was formally constituted and Charles Gray, a student of Robert Haldane's Academy in Edinburgh, was called to the pastorate. For a time the congregation prospered, although never wealthy and possibly never exceeding 150, which was all the Tabernacle could hold. Then Gray was converted to Baptist views along with the Haldanes themselves 'and the Church was as good as swamped in the immersion of its minister'. The reappearance of Con-

gregationalism in Hawick in the thirties of the nineteenth century was
due to the evangelical zeal of James Douglas of Cavers whose benevolence and Christian philanthropy have already been noticed. In 1823
Douglas offered to provide for a probationer to preach and visit among
the people in the district of Hawick, without interference with the
attendance at the stated services and labours of the settled minister, an
offer which was turned down by the Secession Presbytery of Selkirk.
Thereupon he turned to the Congregational Union of Scotland who
gladly welcomed his assistance in the gospel. In the following year
Francis Dick, a native of Monifieth, came to the district on his first
preaching tour of the south of Scotland. During the summer months
of that and the nineteen succeeding years he laboured earnestly
preaching on Sundays in the Cameronian Chapel at Denholm, and in
the old, deserted Parish Kirk of Cavers, and in the Common Haugh,
Town Hall, and Subscription Rooms, Hawick. 'This undersized stout
gentleman, strongly pitted with smallpox, carrying an equally corpulent
and weatherbeaten green cotton unbrella, and hurrying along the street
on a Sunday evening, with short and rapid step, as if intent on the
performance of some work that did not brook delay, found many honest
and hearty admirers in every congregation, who came to the Subscription Rooms to hear the plain commonsense gospel sermon which Mr.
Dick so earnestly uttered.' As a result of his labours a Congregational
church consisting of fifteen members was formed at No. 3 or No. 5
O'Connell Street in 1836, of which William Munro became pastor in
the following year. This church seems to have ceased about 1878.
Another Congregational church was formed in the town in April 1842
largely as the result of evangelistic services combined with an interest
in the Temperance movement which had begun in the district about
the same time. For a few years this church was under the pastoral care
of William Dobson. It appears to have ceased about 1845. The present
Church in Hawick was formed in connection with the Evangelical
Union in May 1848 by forty-five members of William Munro's church.
Alexander Duff became the first pastor in the year following. The
congregation joined the Evangelical Union in 1859. At first it worshipped in the Subscription Rooms. A church was opened in O'Connell
Street in March 1849. The present building was opened for worship
in August 1894. The church at LANGHOLM was formed as an E.U.
congregation in 1864 as a result of the 1859 Revival, though preaching
by the Evangelical Unionists had been provided since the 'fifties. The
present building was opened for worship in 1870. It is of notable
interest that Robert Borland, author of *Border Raids and Reivers*, was
pastor of this church, 1874-77. In recent years the congregation has
been strengthened by the ministry of Beatrice Bonnar.

The church in NEWCASTLETON was formed in 1849 by a number
of members who had seceded from a U.P. congregation, which had its

roots in the mid-eighteenth century. This group of seceding Presbyterians were attracted by the doctrines of James Morison and formed themselves into a church on the E.U. pattern in the summer of the aforementioned year. The congregation joined the Evangelical Union in 1870. The new church first met for worship in a room in Douglas Square. In 1850 a church building was erected in South Hermitage Street, and in that year William Davidson Black was called to the pastorate. In April 1935 the old U.P. congregation (which since the union with the Church of Scotland in 1929 had been designated the South Church) severed its connection with the Church of Scotland and amalgamated with the E.U. Congregational Church. The premises and Manse of the South Church were used henceforth by the united congregation. The church is largely Presbyterian in its internal constitution.

BERWICKSHIRE

There was a church in the town of BERWICK* in 1806 under the pastoral care of John Dunn who remained until 1809. From that year no record of the church can be found. Another church was formed in October 1848 and was supported by the Congregational Union of Scotland for ten years or so. The first pastor was William Duncan Knowles. A building was opened for public worship in Castlegate in May 1849. The congregation ceased to meet in 1859. In EYEMOUTH there was a church in 1806 under the pastoral care of Mr. Brotherton, but it existed for only a short time. The present church in Eyemouth was formed in 1861 after the 1859-60 revival by friends of the Evangelical Union from a preaching station supervised by that body. Robert Findlay became the first pastor in 1864. The congregation joined the Evangelical Union in 1873. At the time of its foundation Edward Swan, the father of Annie S. Swan the novelist, was an elder of the Eyemouth church. A place of worship was built in 1862-63 on a 'co-operative basis', the fishermen transporting the stones on their boats, and both they and their wives carrying them in creels to the building site. At the time of the Eyemouth disaster of 1881 the church lost at least half of its male membership and took many years to recover. Today it is possibly as strong as ever it was. There appears to have been a church in RESTON* in 1806, to which John Boag ministered for a time. A church was formed in COLDINGHAM* in 1877 by about thirty members of the United Presbyterian Church who with others petitioned unsuccessfully for the use of unfermented wine at the Sacrament. The church met in a dwelling house. The first pastor was George McFarlane. It ceased in 1887.

WIGTOWNSHIRE

The church in GARLIESTON was formed in 1803 as a result of the evangelistic labours of James Haldane and John Aikman during their tour through the south of Scotland in June 1798. On that occasion Haldane visited Galloway House at the invitation of the Earl of Galloway, and in a weaving-shed preached the gospel with great fervour to the people of the village. The earl, doubtless under the influence of the 1799 Act of Assembly, refused a site for a church and subsequently obstructed the building of a place of worship, when a site had been obtained. He refused to allow the congregation to take building stones from his estate. However, the dauntless Congregationalists not to be hindered boated the stones across Wigtown Bay. The earl thereupon relented and granted building materials and a church was erected in 1804. It was constructed for utility and not to satisfy any aesthetic canon. Its floors for the most part were earthen and bare. During Thomas Smith's ministry, 1803-29, an undenominational Sunday School was opened, probably before 1811, the first of its kind in the south of Scotland.

LIST OF MINISTERS

Note.—I had hoped to give in the following list the years of settlement and removal of every pastor, but in many cases this has been found impossible, owing to defective church records, or the absence of any early records at all. In other cases, the correspondence required to supply missing dates, and in some cases defective ones, would have led to undue delay in the publication of this volume. The names of extinct churches are inserted within brackets.

ABERDEEN

ALBION STREET, 1847

James Hall Wilson, 1848-58; John Duncan, 1858-78; George Moir, 1878-85; William Johnston, 1885-92; Robert Matheson Cairney, 1893-1909; James Anderson, 1910-15; Alexander Campbell, 1915-20; Charles Lynch, 1920-23; Thomas Dobson Knox, 1923-25; William Carnson Crawford, 1927-36.

ST. PAUL STREET, 1846

Fergus Ferguson, Sen., 1846-72; Andrew Martin Fairbairn, 1872-77; Alexander Brown, D.D., 1877-1914; Joseph Charles Ormerod, M.A., 1915-20; William Ellis Pearson, M.A., 1920-26; Alan William Stevens, M.A., 1927-37.

Y

ALBION AND ST. PAUL'S, 1938

Mitchell Hughes, 1938-51; David Sutherland, M.A., 1951-.

BELMONT STREET (GEORGE STREET), 1798

William Stephens, 1800-3; John Philip, 1804-19; Alexander Thomson, 1820-53; David Arthur, assistant, 1839-41; colleague, 1841-53; sole pastor, 1853-74; Frederick Sydney Morris, assistant, 1872-73; James Barton Bell, 1874-76; James Stark, D.D., 1877-1905; Henry Alexander Inglis, M.A., colleague, 1902-5, sole pastor, 1905-13; James Francis Shepherd, M.A., 1914-19; James Gilmour Drummond, M.A., 1920-25; William McLeod Girdwood, B.D., 1926-34; Frank Young Leggatt, M.A., 1935-43; James Wood, M.A., 1943-47; Elvet Harry Lewis, 1948-50; Thomas Mearns, M.A., 1950-58; James Russell Shanks, B.SC., 1959-.

[BON-ACCORD, 1897

John Inglis Martin, 1898-99; James Ross, 1900-5; James Stark, D.D., 1905-8; Donald McIntosh, 1909-16; Samuel Ivan Bell, 1917-24; James Hall, B.A., 1925-30; Robert William Dickson, M.A., M.TH., 1930-34; (A. J. Packer—acting pastor, 1934-37)].

[FREDERICK STREET, 1807

David Russell, 1807-9; Richard Penman, Sen., 1815-40; Richard Penman, Jun., co-pastor, 1837-40; David Wallace, 1840-71.]

[DEE STREET, 1860

James Hunter, 1865-82.]

[JOHN STREET, 1863

Alexander Stewart, M.D., LL.D., D.D., 1864-1909; Andrew Leggatt, 1910-13.]

SKENE STREET (BLACKFRIARS STREET), 1820

James Spence, M.A., 1820-35; John Kennedy, M.A., 1836-46; George Thomson, 1846-47; Ninian Wight, 1848-52; John Thomson, 1852-59; Thomas Gilfillan, 1860-71; Joseph Vickery, 1871-82; James Bell, 1882-88; Samuel Darcy Thomas, 1889-93; Edward Branch Mahon, B.A., 1893-99; William Kirk, M.A., 1900-6; Heber Justin Evans, M.A., 1907-8; Thomas Richards, 1908-11; William Dick, M.A., 1912-20; William Kirk, M.A., 1921-37; Donald Marriott Perkins, 1938-45; Robert Howat McMurray Adam, 1946-51; John Beattie Wilson, 1952-.

TRINITY (SHIPROW), 1878

John Duncan, D.D., 1878-1901; Frederick John Japp, assistant, 1895; James Baxter Allan, M.A., B.D., assistant, 1897-1900; James P. Stephenson, assistant, 1900-1; Robert Steel, 1901-6; James Adam, 1907-16; Frederick John Japp, 1916-29; James Kinmond Smith, M.A., 1930-35; Eric Allan Matheson, B.D., 1936-45; Frank Field, 1946-50; John Fullerton, M.A., 1950-58 ; Thomas Duncan, 1958-.

WOODSIDE (PRINTFIELD), 1821

Neil McKechnie, 1821-38; James Byres Laing, M.A., 1840-58; James Strachan, M.A., 1862-69; William Robertson, 1869-70; James Rae,

1870-79; George Saunders, 1879-92; George Coates Milne, 1893-1925; George White, 1926-33; Donald Sutherland Sutherland, 1934-36; David William Thomson, 1936-43; William Russell, M.A., 1943-51; James Gentles Day, M.A., 1951-55; John Innes, 1955-.

MASTRICK, 1953

Andrew Gillespie Jenkins, 1953-56; Robert Howat McMurray Adam, B.D., 1957-.

[ACHARAN (TUAR,) 1802

——Farquharson, 1802-4; Mr. McKillican, 1804.]

ABERFELDY, 1800

(Daniel Dewar, missionary, 1802-4); James Kennedy, 1806-25; Malcolm McLean, 1825-36; John McLaren, 1836-70; James Barton Bell, 1870-74; William Northcott Challice, 1875-81; William Henry Muncaster, M.A., B.D., 1882-84; William Stevenson, 1884-92; David Jenkins Graham, 1893-1911; Robert Matheson Cairney, 1911-13; Ben Sibbald, 1913-16; (James Duff in charge, 1916-19); Allan Stewart Guild, 1919-26; James Pollock Morison, 1926-30; (W. J. Dickson, 1930); James Miller, 1931-36; Duncan McMillan Turner, M.A., 1937-38; Russell Lewis, 1938-47; Robert Rigg, 1947-53; Joseph Pickthall, M.A., B.D., PH.D., 1954-57; Daniel Cook, 1958-.

AIRDRIE

EBENEZER, 1836

Alexander Cuthbert, M.A., 1839-40; James Taylor, 1840-42; James Sime, 1843-46; John Menzies, 1848-51; Supplies, 1852-55; James Innes, 1856-60; William Goldie, 1862-63; Thomas R. Atkinson, M.D., 1864-74; James Buchan, M.A., 1874-85; Joseph Jones, 1885-86; James Bayne, 1887-95; Alexander Mann, 1896-1905; William Riddell Hunter, 1906-10; Joseph Charles Ormerod, M.A., 1911-15; James Gilmour Drummond, M.A., 1915-20; Thomas George Ogilvie, B.D., 1921-43; John Thompson George, 1943-51; William Russell, M.A., 1951-59; Kenneth K. Lodge, 1959-.

COATDYKE, 1911

(John Edmonston, in charge, 1911-14); John Edmonston, 1915-18; (R. Miles in charge, 1918-20); (R. McRoberts in charge, 1920-25); William Ralston, 1925-29; David William Thomson, 1929-32; James Pollock Morison, 1933-36; Leonard Sykes, 1937-44; James Foster, M.A., 1944-50; Charles John Alexander Innes, M.A., 1951-57; Thomas Clifford Kelly, 1958-.

PARK, 1845

(Robert Hunter, 1845-46); David Drummond, 1846-48; (Samuel Chisholm, William Paton, and William Hutchison, 1848-51); Alexander M. Wilson, 1851-69; Adam Scott, 1869-73; James Monie, 1873-78; George Wood, 1878-81; Robert Joseph Kyd, 1881-82; Oliver Dryer, 1883-96; William Finlayson Riddell, 1896-99; James Monie, D.D., 1899-1913; William Orr, 1914-16; (George A. Hardie, 1916-17); David

Mitchell Donald, 1918-21; James Kelt, 1921-29; Thomas Dobson Knox, 1929-33; Hugh Lammie, 1933-41; Robert Howat McMurray Adam, 1941-46; John Hanna, 1946-58; Brian Kingsmore, 1959-.

[ALEXANDRIA, 1839

James Mann, 1840-42; Thomas Miller Reekie, 1847-49; John Douglas, 1859-68; William Mackay, 1868-72; William Dargie, M.A., 1872-75; Ebenezer Marshall Tennant, 1876-79.]

[ALLOA, 1810

William Howden, 1810-14; Alexander Nicol, 1815-21; John Hill, M.A., 1824-29; (William Lyall, supply, 1832-33); Alexander Fraser, M.A., 1834-41; George Simpson Ingram, 1842-44; Alexander Duncanson, 1844-46; (James Bishop Robertson, 1849-50); John Burke, 1850-53.]

ANNAN, c. 1800

Andrew Carnson, 1794- ; after Mr. Carnson there were four or five pastors among whom were John Robertson, Andrew Rattray, and John Boag; The church was re-formed in 1837 and John Ward was pastor from February to November of that year; The church was again re-formed in 1843; Ebenezer Young, 1846-88; George Kennedy, 1889-90; Thomas Johnstone, 1891-95; George Hayton, 1896-1905; Andrew Moffatt, 1905-7; John Miller Wright, 1908-12; George Smissen, 1913-16; James B. Crombie, 1917-23; David Low Neave, 1923-26; James Dobbie, 1927-47; David Mitchell Donald, 1948-53; Redvers J. Samson, 1954-.

[ANSTRUTHER, c. 1800

W. Hastie, 1802-6; T. Japp, 1808-24; John Murdoch, 1830-44; John McDougall, 1844-46; William Jeffrey Craig, 1847-53; George Wisely, 1854-56; Hugh Stewart, 1858-70; John Geddes, 1871-72; James Hamilton Paterson, 1872-78; John Whitson, 1878-90; James Russell, 1891-96; Alexander Macauley, 1900-5; Andrew Noble Scott, 1906-13.]

[APPIN, 1843

Charles Whyte, 1844-54; Henry Whyte, 1855-75.]

ARBROATH

QUEEN STREET, c. 1800

Thomas Smith, 1801-3; Richard Penman, 1803-14; Udny Anderson, 1815-28; John Ramsay, 1838-39; John Strachan Moir, 1840-43; John Gillies, 1848-79; Alexander R. Milne, M.A., 1879-89; James Wylie, 1890-94; John Miller, 1894-1900; George Kydd Cuthbert, 1900-6; James Hume, 1906-24; Thomas Shanks, 1924-29; John Robert Ramsay, 1930-36; Frank Jones, 1936-41; May Findlay, M.A., B.COM., 1942-43; John Thomas Hornsby, M.A., PH.D., 1943-53; William James Gaston, 1956-.

[KEPTIE STREET, 1864

Gilbert Paterson, 1865-73; Robert Snowdown, 1874-80; Daniel Galbraith, 1881-83; Andrew Fergus Ferguson, 1884-88; Robert Rae, 1889-96; Gordon Lee McLachlan, 1896-1900; Andrew Burnet Halliday, 1901-3; William Farries, 1904-6; George Strathearn, 1906-8.]

ARDROSSAN, 1837

Peter Mather, 1838-46; Alexander Cross, 1846-87; Joseph Liddle King, M.A., 1888-92; James M. Cowan, 1893-95; John Masterton, 1897-1901; George Sharpe, 1901-5; John Miller Wright, 1906-8; John Macmillan, M.A., 1908-15; Horace Edward Govan, M.A., 1915-21; James E. Kirkwood, 1921-24; Nathaniel Johnston, 1925-29; James Hamilton, 1930-31; Russell Lewis, 1932-38; Arthur Coulthard, B.A., B.D., 1938-44; Robert Dobbie, M.A., B.D., M.TH., 1944-46; Robert Macmenemy, 1947-53; Jean Innes Thomson, M.A., B.D., 1954-.

ARRAN

SANNOX, 1806

Alexander Mackay, 1806-56; John Blacklock, 1860-78; Allan Cameron McDougall, 1878-1934; Arthur Renwick Wiseman, 1936-46; John Safeley, M.A., PH.D., 1946-47.

[AUCHTERARDER, 1854

John Inglis, 1855-55; Robert Mitchell, 1856-70; James Strachan, 1860-61; Robert Steel, 1864-66; John Miller, 1866-69.]

AVOCH, 1808

Alexander Dewar, 1808-49; James McKinven, 1850-58; David W. Philip, 1858-85; George Moir, 1885-88; Thomas Kerr, 1889-1937; John Lees, M.A., 1938-.

AVONBRIDGE, 1844

Robert Anderson, 1846-51; John Reid, 1855-59; James McNaughton, 1859-63; Peter McNish, 1867-69; (William Crombie in charge, 1878-82); James Rae, 1884-87; Matthew Richmond, 1887-96; John Heggie, 1896-1901; Andrew Scouller, 1901-7; John Robert Ramsay, 1907-9; David Low Neave, 1910-11; George Bell, M.A., 1911-15; Charles Lynch, 1915-20; Thomas Baillie, 1921-25; William Smart Todd, 1925-30; (H. Stoddart, 1931-32); (William Henry S. Webb, as student, 1933-35); Neil MacDougall Robertson, 1936-38; Samuel Jones, 1938-47; James Ralston, 1947-48; Dahlia Mary Simpson Grigor, 1950-55; Donald Sutherland Sutherland, 1955-58; Donald Findlay, 1959-.

AYR, 1804

[Richard Penman, 1804-5; Alexander McLean, 1808-33; Robert Lang, M.A., 1836-37; Henry Lea Berry, M.A., 1839-40; John Smith, 1841-44;

John Hunter, 1845-47; James McConnachie, 1848-50; Thomas Orr, 1852-63; Daniel Jackson, 1865-68; J. M. Metcalfe, 1869-73.]

WALLACE STREET, 1844

William Bathgate, 1847-50; James Virtue, 1857-61; James Bishop Robertson, 1861-65; Robert D. Mitchell, 1866-70; John McIldowie, 1872-76; William Francis Adamson, M.A., 1876-83; Alexander Stewart, M.A., B.D., 1884-98; William George Allan, M.A., B.D., 1905-8; John Robert Ramsay, 1909-12; Robert McQueen, 1913-19; James Cowper McLachlan, M.A., 1920-27; Arthur E. Hayton, 1927-30; J. Morrison, 1932-35; William C. Crawford, 1936-44; May Findlay, M.A., 1944-47; Charles Campbell, student pastor, 1948-49; James Russell Shanks, B.SC., 1950-54; Thomas Duncan, 1955-59; Cecil E. Stewart, 1959-.

MORISON, 1897

Arthur Hamilton McConnachie, 1898-1913; Thomas Carlyle Murphy, M.A., B.D., 1913-16; Isaac Henry Clyde, 1916-19; George B. Piercy, 1919-21; George White, 1921-26; John Coulson Thomson, 1926-31; Robert Grainger Currie, 1931-53; William Craig Cowan, 1954-.

[BALFOUR, 1806

John Campbell, 1806; Thomas McKinnon, 1809.]

[BANFF, 1809

Joseph Gibb, 1809-29; John Murker, M.A., 1833-79; Bailey John Barker, 1879-81; James F. McHardy, 1882-84; William McLean, 1884-86.]

BARRHEAD, 1844

Gilbert McCallum, 1846-52; Alexander Davidson, 1853-60; John Andrew, 1861-66; John Geddes, 1867-70; Alexander McNair, M.A., 1873-78; David Leith, 1879-81; Edward Bruce Kirk, 1883-1915; Thomas Smith Loudon, 1916-29; Arthur Glendinning Reekie, 1930-34; Harry Duncan Bedford, 1935-36; Alexander May, M.A., B.D., 1937-46; John Fullerton, M.A., 1947-50; George Maurice Marks, M.A., 1951-57; Alpine McAlpine Munro, 1957-.

BATHGATE, 1843

Robert Morison, 1843-55; Archibald C. Gray, 1856-60; Andrew Martin Fairbairn, 1860-72; Alexander M. Wilson, 1873-88; Charles Richardson, M.A., 1888-92; William Kirk, M.A., 1892-1900; Christopher Nicholson, 1900-17; David Stoddart, 1918-24; John Short, M.A., PH.D., 1925-30; Joseph Chatfield Alexander, B.A., 1930-38; Charles Sim Duthie, M.A., B.D., 1938-44; William Robertson Milne, 1945-55; Thomas Maxwell, M.A., 1956-.

BEITH, 1839

[James Robertson, 1840-42]; 1861—Stephen Todd, 1862-65; Thomas G. Salmon, 1866-70; John Whitson, 1871-78; Archibald Bowman,

1879-1900; James Wallace, 1901-4; David William Gaylor, 1905-13; David Stoddart, 1913-18; Daniel McIver, 1918-26; John M. Halliday, 1927; Harry Duncan Bedford, 1928-35; George Charles Thomson, 1935-45; Jean Innes Thomson, M.A., B.D., 1946-54; Frank Allan Maxwell, 1954-.

BELLSHILL, 1841

Fergus Ferguson, Sen., 1843-46; (John McDougall, 1846-47); Hugh Riddell, 1847-55; John Inglis, 1856-60; David Drummond, 1860-71; Robert Snowdown, 1872-74; George Wisely, 1874-78; Robert Winchester Jackson, 1879-84; Alexander M. Higgins, 1885-87; Richard William Rowe Trenwith, 1888-1903; John Inglis Martin, 1903-8; Daniel McIver, 1908-12; John Edward Cattral, 1912-18; Joseph Alexander, B.A., 1918-21; George Deans Donald, 1921-24; James Kinmond Smith, M.A., 1925-30; Robert Gibson, 1930-35; Robert McMenemey, 1936-47; Alexander Mackay Ferguson, 1947-54; Herbert Lloyd Monro Cameron, 1955-.

[BERVIE, 1803

Adam Paterson, 1803-6; James Mackenzie, 1806-45.]

[BERWICK-ON-TWEED, c. 1806

John Dunn, 1806-9; 1848—(J. M. W. Boyd, 1846-47); William Duncan Knowles, B.A., 1848-52; George Cowie Morrison, M.A., 1852-55; William Knox, 1855-56; Davidson Black, 1857-58.]

[BIXTER, 1808

James Tulloch, 1808-58; Laurence Fraser, 1859-92.]

[BLACKBURN (LINLITHGOW), 1824

John Hamilton, 1824-28; John Boag, 1829-36; James Taylor, 1839-40; John Boag, 1842-53.]

[BLAIRGOWRIE, 1803

Peter Grant, 1807-17; John Lyall, 1823- ; John Tait, M.A., 1834-67; John E. Dobson, 1867-69; John Miller, 1869-78; Ebenezer Marshall Tennant, 1879-1909; Alexander Campbell, 1910-15; Alfred Wilson, 1916-20.]

BLANTYRE, 1877

William Wyllie, M.A., 1878-87; Robert Paterson, 1887-98; Robert Whiteford, 1898-1901; John Brown, 1902-4; John McMillan, M.A., 1904-8; William Baxter Blackwood, 1909-10; (William Alexander Falconer, in charge, 1916-20); David William Thomson, 1921-29; Thomas Shanks, 1929-34; Edwin A. K. Grant, 1935- ; James Hamilton, 1942-50; John Wilson McMinn, M.A., 1953-57.

[BRECHIN, 1839

Hugh Smith, 1841-42; John Masson, M.A., 1845-48; 1867—(William H. Reid, 1868-69); Alexander Cosser, 1871-75; (Peter McLish, Evangelist, 1877-79); Alexander Mitchell, 1880-1920.]

BROUGHTY FERRY, 1864

James Bailey, 1864-70; Richard Charles Jessop, B.A., 1871-72; Alfred J. Bedells, 1872-75; Edwin Heath, 1876-1902; James Partis Stephenson, 1902-7; Alexander George Mitchell, 1907-19; Thomas Carlyle Murphy, O.B.E., M.A., B.D., 1919-27; Alexander George Bruce Sivewright, M.A., 1928-35; John Gray, M.A., 1935-.

[CALLANDER, 1805

Peter McLaren, 1808-26; Archibald McEwan, 1826-35.]

CAMBUSLANG, 1803

John Paterson, 1803-4; William Craig, 1804-5; Alexander Kerr, 1806-25; David Murdoch, 1829-33; James Geddes, 1833-37; John McRobert, 1838-46; David Drummond, 1847-55; James Pullar, 1857-59; Robert Pirrie, 1859-61; James Virtue, 1862-66; John Johnston, 1866-70; Robert D. Hutchison, 1870-72; Thomas Brisbane, 1872-95; Sydney Thomas Ticker, 1895-1900; Matthew Park Noble, 1901-36; Robert Dobbie, M.A., B.D., 1936-41; Isaac Galloway Pollock, 1942-44; Alexander Mackay Ferguson, 1945-47; James Kinmond Smith, M.A., 1948-58.

[CAMPBELTOWN, 1805

Duncan McPherson, 1805- ; Daniel McKeith, 1829-36; David Webster, 1840-42; Adam G. Forbes, 1842-45; Thomas Lightbody, 1846-48; Donald Galbraith, 1849-60.]

CARLUKE, 1846

John Hamilton, 1846-52; William Jeffrey Craig, 1853-58; David Drummond, 1858-60; James Howie, 1861-63; James Gunn, 1864-66; (Adam Scott, student pastor, 1867-69); James Miller, 1869-74; John Adam, M.A., 1874-86; Gilbert Paterson, 1886-1902; John Miller Wright, 1902-6; William Watson, 1906-15; William Gray, M.A., 1916-18; Donald Grigor, 1919-45; John R. May, M.A., 1945-48; Robert Squince McCulloch, 1948-53; William C. Crawford, 1954-.

[CATRINE, 1844

George Anderson, 1850-51; William Anderson, 1853-54; Robert Hunter, 1854-58; John Reid, 1859-60; John Miller, 1860-61; James Foote, 1863-67; David Greenhill, 1869-74; William Jeffrey Craig, 1875-84; Robert Russell, 1884-91; James Hamilton, 1894-1905; John McLachlan McGauley, M.A., 1905-10; George Arthur Everett Walker,

1912-13; Charles Lynch, 1914-15; John McLachlan McGauley, M.A., 1919-21; Henry Donald, M.A., 1921-22; Gordon Lee McLachlan, 1922-26.]

GORDON MEMORIAL, 1956

Charles J. A. Innes, M.A., 1957-.

[CLELAND, 1903

Robert Montgomery Bright, 1904-6; Andrew Scoullar, 1907-23; James B. Crombie, 1923-30; J. Hamilton, 1932-36.]

CLYDEBANK

MORISON, 1893

Robert McQueen, 1893-1900; Thomas M. McKendrick, 1900-21; Walter Gerrard, 1921-33; Arthur Glendinning Reekie, 1934-43; Robert Sinclair, 1943-46; Angus Hugh MacKinnon, 1947-53; Andrew Workman, 1954-.

RADNOR PARK, 1908

George Deans Donald, 1908-13; John Miller, 1913-22; David McGowan, 1929-44; William Campbell, 1944-47; George Forbes Morgan, 1947-50; Thomas Ballantyne Gordon, 1951-56; Robert McVey, 1958-.

COATBRIDGE

BUCHANAN STREET, 1860

John Inglis, 1860-67; James Foote, 1867-71; John Inglis, 1871-75; Richard Goodwillie, 1875-80; George Peebles, 1882-83; David Hobbes, M.A., 1889-95; Maxwell Robert Kirkpatrick, M.A., 1896-1901; Frederick John Japp, 1902-16; Donald McIntosh, 1916-22; Thomas Templeton, M.A., PH.D., 1922-31; John Smith, 1932-39; David Sutherland, M.A., 1940-51; Andrew Finlayson Tennant, 1952-57.

ALBERT STREET, 1877

David Beaton, 1877-80; James G. Murray, 1881- ; John Jenkins, 1882-86; William Rosling, 1886-89; John Blair, 1889-1937; Frank Allan Maxwell, 1938-44; Francis Ferrier Robertson, 1946-48; Charles Moore, 1951-53; Thomas Irvine Mackay, 1955-57.

BUCHANAN ST. AND ALBERT ST. CHURCHES, united in 1958

Thomas Mearns, M.A. 1958-.

[COUPAR-ANGUS, 1848

James Frame, 1850-54; Robert Wallace, 1855-76; James J. Brown, 1876-80; John D. Brown, 1882-82; David Stevenson McLachlan, M.A., 1883-90; William Tiplady, 1890-91; David Zerubabel H. Forson, 1892-1910; Magnus Sinclair, 1910-17; William Sinclair Rosie, 1917-18; A. W. Groundwater, 1921-52.]

CRIEFF, 1869

William Davidson Black, 1870-75; James Bell, 1876-82; John McGavin Sloan, 1883-83; James F. McHardy, 1884-98; Alexander Robinson, M.A., B.D., 1899-1907; Robert Troup Sivewright, M.A., 1907-14; Walter Lockwood Terrett, 1915-17; Wallace A. McCubbin, A.B., 1919-23; Robert Mitchell Hendry, 1923-25; Thomas G. Taylor, M.A., 1926-29; William F. Riddell, 1930-37; John Strachan, 1938-39; Hassal Hanmer, M.A., B.D., 1939-44; Neil Taylor, 1945-51; Thomas Bell, student-pastor, 1952-54; ordained pastor, 1954-55; Henry Vigors, 1956-.

CRUDEN BAY (PORT ERROL), 1882

John D. Hardie, M.A., 1883-　; Donald McIntosh, 1895-1901; Lachlan McFadyen, 1902-5; Alexander Macauley, 1910-27; John A. Sinclair, 1927-30; David Spence Aitken, 1930-37; Robert Macready Lawson, 1938-46; George Porter, 1947-53; Alexander Taylor, 1954-56; George Kirk, 1956-.

[CULLEN, 1846

Charles A. Piper, 1846-54; David Brown, 1854-62; Charles Hardie Murray, 1867-69; John Taylor, 1872-77.]

CUMNOCK, 1838

James Sime, 1840-42; Peter W. Grant, 1844-53; John McAuslane, 1854-65; Thomas Brisbane, 1866-72; John Murray, 1873-76; Francis Lamb, 1877-81; Andrew Noble Scott, 1882-84; William Matheson, 1884-1913; Mark Newton Robson, 1913-34; James Callander Drife, 1934-50; William McGill Thomson, 1950-54; Matthew Sullivan, B.A., 1955-.

[CUPAR, 1800

Francis Dick, 1802-3; —— McLean, 1804-6; Peter McLaren, 1809.]

DALBEATTIE, 1866

John Inglis, 1866-71; Thomas Darling Hogg, 1872-74; Robert Robertson, 1874-77; John M. Sloan, 1878-80; John Cameron, 1881-92; John Penman, 1892-1900; Jabez Livingston Gower, 1900-8; James Dobbie, 1910-27; Colin Livingston, 1927-30; F. Vivian Berry, 1930-40; Donald Findlay, student pastor, 1940-　; Charles William Turtle, 1944-51; John Cleminson Bell, M.A., 1951-.

DALKEITH

HIGH STREET, c. 1804

Alexander Arthur, 1804-29; Edward Napier, 1831-42; Anthony Thomson Gowan, M.A., 1843-72; Andrew Findlater Simpson, M.A., 1872-93; William Macaulay Russell McAleese, 1894-1920; David Russell Scott, M.A., PH.D., 1922-36; (Frank Field, in charge, 1936-37); William Kitching, 1937-41; James Massie Milne, 1941-47; Thomas Stirling, 1947-51; James Wood, M.A., B.D., 1952-57; Angus Hugh MacKinnon, 1957-.

[CROFT STREET, 1847

John Hamilton, 1855-57; Alexander French, M.A., 1857-59; Supplies, 1859-63; William Dunlop, 1863-66; Nisbet Galloway, 1868-69; Supplies, 1869-70; John Morton, 1870-80; Thomas Henry Walker, 1882-83; Robert D. Mitchell, 1885-1900.]

[DALMELLINGTON, 1844

Robert Brown, 1872-75; Robert Steel, 1875-88; David Z. H. Forson, 1889-92; Andrew Scoullar, 1898-1900.]

DARVEL, [1844

William Landels, 1844-46]; Re-formed 1884—John McIntosh, 1885-97; John Ebenezer Christie, 1898-1925; William B. Stewart, 1926-30; James Oliver, 1931-38; James Milroy, 1938-44; James Miller, 1945-51; Laurence John Matthews, B.A., B.D., 1951-54; James Foster, M.A., 1955-.

[DENHOLM, 1826

Robert Wilson, 1835-43; John Spence, 1844- ; John McRobert, 1846-76.]

[DOUNE, 1843

George Wight, 1843-47; John Craig, 1847-57; David Bisset Mackenzie, 1858-63.]

DREGHORN, 1864

Robert Paterson, 1864-66; Angus McPhee; Richard Goodwillie, 1872-76; George Peebles, 1877-80; John L. Hill, 1881-82; Thomas MacRobert, M.A., 1882-1940; Alexander Fisher MacRobert, B.A., M.A., 1940-50; John W. Hornsby, 1950-51; James Henry Carlin, 1952-59.

DUMBARTON, 1878

James Hamilton Paterson, 1878-86; James Monie, 1886-92; John Wilson Crawford, 1892-1931; David W. Thomson, 1932-36; Alexander G. Jackson, M.A., 1937-42; Thomas Mearns, M.A., 1943-46; John Gardner McIlvean, M.A., 1946-54; Kenneth Kingsley Lodge, 1955-59.

DUMFRIES

IRVING STREET, 1805 or 1806

William Watson, 1806-9; John Dunn, 1809-20; Thomas Young, 1827-33; Robert Machray, M.A., 1835-42; James Cameron, 1843-47; James Mann, 1847-52; Thomas Pullar, 1852-54; Robert Machray, M.A., 1855-69; John Park, 1870-73; H. Campbell, 1873-77; Frederick Binns, 1877-82; William Henry Pulsford, M.A., 1883-90; Robert Mackintosh, M.A., B.D., 1890-94; Wallace Arthur McCubbin, 1894-1900; John Murphy, M.A., B.D., 1901-7; Griffith David Hughes, 1907-10; Alexander Day, 1911-51; Raymond William Fenn, 1951-55; Dahlia Mary Simpson Grigor, 1955-.

[IRISH STREET, 1862

John Dunlop, 1863-65; James McConnachie, 1865-68; Nisbet Gallo-way, 1869-72; William Tiplady, 1876-78.]

WATERLOO PLACE, 1870

James Strachan, M.A., 1870-1913; W. Wilson, 1913-17; united with Irving Street.

[DUNCANSTON, 1808

Donald Morrison, 1808-46; Patrick Morrison, 1846-50; Peter Whyte, 1851-55; Thomas Brisbane, 1856-66; Andrew Findlater Simpson, M.A., 1866-69; James McConnachie, 1869-83; Robert Harvey Smith, M.A., 1883-93; Lawrence Williamson, 1893-1911; thereafter supplied largely by the Rhynie Church.]

DUNDEE

[CASTLE STREET, 1855

Alexander Hannay, 1855-62; David Johnson, 1863-64; George Thomp-son, 1865-67; Francis Clark, 1868-72; James Hunter Crawford, 1873-93; Joseph Vickery, 1893-1913; Robert Troup Sivewright, M.A., 1914-15; James Miller, 1916-17; David Russell Scott, M.A., 1918-20; Andrew Ferguson Simpson, M.A., 1921-30; John Lees, M.A., 1930-37; Harold Haworth, M.A., 1938-45; Alexander May, M.A., B.D., 1946-48; combined with Ward Chapel.]

[LINDSAY STREET, 1840

D. K. Shoebotham, 1840-45; Thomas Reekie, 1845-47; David Cook, 1847-72; John Wallace, 1872-77; William Horne, M.A., 1877-82; S. G. Kelly, B.A., 1883-84; Alfred Gardner, 1884-1913; Henry Gideon Jeffries, 1914-23.]

GILFILLAN MEMORIAL, 1879

David Macrae, 1879-97; Walter Walsh, 1899- ; Adam Hamilton, M.A., 1918-20; George Leslie S. Thompson, M.A., B.D., 1920-26; Harry Andrew, 1928-55; Thomas Jones, 1956-57; Thomas Irvine Mackay, 1958-.

MORISON, 1864

John Cameron, 1866-67; Peter McNish, 1869-77; James Monie, 1878-85; Alexander Denholm, 1886-93; Andrew James Forson, 1893-1904; James W. Hamilton, 1905-18; Andrew Ferguson Simpson, M.A., 1918-21; John McLachlan, McGauley, M.A., 1921-51; John Innes, 1952-55; Gerald Blanchflower Punter, B.A., 1956-.

PANMURE STREET, 1853

Robert Lang, M.A., 1853-72; William Jackson Cox, 1872-95; Thomas Johnstone, 1896-1907; Thomas Templeton, M.A., 1907-22; Henry Alexander Inglis, M.A., 1923-46; John Dick, 1946-.

[PRINCES STREET, 1839

Andrew Russell, M.A., 1840-45; Alexander Hannay, 1846-55; Robert Harvey Smith, M.A., 1856-59; Maurice John Evans, B.A., 1859-63; R. H. Irvine, M.A., 1863-69; George Campbell, 1869-81; John Park Noble, 1881-90; David Barran, 1891-1910; William Selby Stein, M.A., 1911-13; Robert Cowan Richardson, 1914-34; John Wilson Currie, 1934-43; Leonard Sykes, 1944-49; John Coulson Thomson, 1950-57.]

[RUSSELL CHAPEL, 1866

John Masson, 1866-78; Jonathan Roebuck, 1878-92; David Caird, 1892-95; Thomas Templeton, M.A., 1895-1900; William Henry Chesson, 1900-9; John Baxter Allan, M.A., B.D., 1910-18; William Jordan, 1920-25; Charles Florence, 1925-30; Frederic Albert Ore, 1930-41; Henry Martyn Cook, M.A., 1941-43; vacant, 1943-47; Bert Albert Cox, 1948-50.]

TRINITY, 1848

Alexander M. Wilson, 1848-50; Alexander C. Rutherford, 1851-56; Hugh Riddell, 1856-59; William Ross, 1860-61; John Miller, 1861-66; John Andrew, 1866-69; William Hamilton, M.A., 1872-1922; Henry Donald, M.A., 1922-27; John Morton Halliday, 1928-.

WARD CHAPEL, 1810

David Russell, D.D., 1810-48; Robert Lang, M.A., 1849-53; Robert Spence, M.A., 1853-70; Charles Short, M.A., D.D., 1870-92; Kerr C. Anderson, D.D., 1892-1919; William Major Scott, M.A., 1919-22; Thomas Samuel Taylor, M.A., B.LITT., 1923-37; D. Edgar Bowen, M.A., B.D., 1938-44; Harold Thomas Donaldson, M.A., 1945-59.

DUNFERMLINE [1801

Peter Grant, 1801-3, ceased about 1805.]

CANMORE STREET, 1840

George Thomson, 1841-46; Robert Hunter Craig, 1847-49; Alexander McAuslane, 1852-58; John Hutchison, 1859-65; James Mitchell Robbie, 1865-81; Frederick Binns, 1882-89; David L. Ritchie, 1890-96; Alexander McLennan, M.A., 1897-1906; Andrew Ritchie, M.A., 1906-10; Robert Maxwell Moffatt, M.A., 1911-12; W. Selby Stein, M.A., 1913-18; John Safeley, M.A., PH.D., 1919-34; Thomas Aeron Lewis, M.A., 1934-47; Allan Cameron McDougall, M.A., 1948-.

NORTH (BATH STREET), 1851

Robert George Harper, 1853-54; James Frame, 1855-57; Nisbet Galloway, 1862-68; John Adam, M.A., 1868-69; James Foote, 1871-1906; Robert Montgomery Bright, 1906-14; Walter Gerrard, 1914-17; John Miller Wright, 1918-27; Robert Dobbie, M.A., B.D., 1927-36; Peter Peace, 1936-51; Sidney Lawrence, 1952-54; William McGill Thomson, 1954-58; George Gahagan, 1959.

[DUNKELD, 1800

John Campbell, 1801-4; Robert Kinniburgh, 1809-10; John Black, 1813-57.]

[DUNOON, 1899

James Baxter Allan, M.A., B.D., 1900-10; John McLachlan McGauley, M.A., 1910-13; John H. Harvey, 1914-16.]

EAST KILBRIDE, 1955
James Gentles Dey, M.A., 1955-.

EDINBURGH

[ALBANY STREET, 1799, 1808

James Alexander Haldane, 1799-1808; William Stephens (colleague), 1804-6; William Innes, 1808-10; George Payne, M.A., 1812-23; Gilbert Wardlaw, M.A., 1823-30; Henry Wilkes, M.A., 1833-36; Alexander Fraser, 1837-42; John Robertson Campbell, M.A., 1844-55; William Pulsford, D.D., 1856-65; James Cranbrook, 1865-67; John Pulsford, D.D., 1867-84; Alfred J. Basden (assistant and colleague), 1881-82; Andrew B. Morris, 1884-1906; John Murphy, M.A., B.D., 1907-12; George Deans Donald, 1913-21; Horace Edward Govan, M.A., 1921-25; Robert Deans, 1926-31; W. J. Ainslie, 1931-32; Sidney Lawrence (in charge), 1932-38; John S. Guthrie, 1938-45; Neil McDougal Robertson, 1946-54.]

AUGUSTINE, 1802

John Aikman, 1802-34; George Cowie (assistant), 1804-13; John Cleghorn (assistant), 1814-34; John Cleghorn, 1834-43; William Lindsay Alexander, M.A. (colleague), 1835-43; William Lindsay Alexander, M.A., D.D., 1843-77; James Gregory, 1880-95; Alexander Roy Henderson, M.A., 1895-1902; Henry Parnaby, M.A., 1903-11; Arthur Davis Martin, A.T.S., 1912-21; Joseph Pickthall, M.A., B.D., PH.D., 1922-26; Rees Griffiths, M.A., B.D., PH.D., 1927-34; Gordon Kusel Hawes, M.A., B.D., 1935-40; Andrew Graham, M.A. (hon. assistant).

BRISTO PLACE, 1845

John Kirk, D.D., 1845-76; John Mackintosh, 1876-84; Robert Craig, M.A., D.D., 1885-1906; Thomas G. Taylor, M.A., 1907-26; John Thomas Hornsby, M.A., PH.D., 1926-40.

AUGUSTINE-BRISTO, 1941

Andrew Graham, M.A., Interim Minister; Cornelius T. Rae, M.A., B.D., 1941-50; William Benjamin John Martin, 1951-58; Erik R. Routley, M.A., B.D., D.PHIL., 1959-.

HOPE PARK, 1832

Henry Wight, 1832-43; C. H. Bateman, 1843-46; Henry Wight, 1846-60; William Jackson Cox (co-pastor), 1855-60; Edward Price, 1860-62; Ninian Wight, 1864-72; John Wemyss, M.A., 1873-1901; William John Collier, M.A., 1901-4; John Spence, F.R.A.S., 1905-7.

BUCCLEUCH, *c.* 1857

George T. M. Inglis, 1859-65; Robert Paterson, 1866-67; William Adamson, D.D., 1868-95; Robert Rae, 1896-1908.

HOPE PARK AND BUCCLEUCH, 1908

Robert Rae, 1908-26; George Leslie Thompson, M.A., B.D., PH.D., 1926-33; Henry David Gray, B.A., B.D. (Interim), 1933-34; William Henry S. Webb, 1935-39; Thomas Mearns, M.A., 1939-43; Malcolm Mackie, B.A. (Interim), 1943; John Wilson Currie, 1943-54; James Russell Shanks, B.SC., 1954-59.

DALRY, 1872

James Stark, 1872-77; Robert Auchterlonie, 1877-1907; Samuel Jones, 1908-13; William S. Todd, 1914-26; Allan Stewart Guild, 1926-33; John Dick, 1934-40; Robert S. Birch, M.A., PH.D., 1940-42; Harry Escott, M.A., PH.D., 1943-51; William Gilchrist, 1951-.

[DALRY (MURIESTON CRESCENT), 1891

John Kirk, 1891.]

[EAST FOUNTAIN BRIDGE, 1866

William Dunlop, 1866-75; John Kirk, 1875-91; John Muir, 1891-98.]

[RICHMOND PLACE, 1880

Andrew Noble Scott, 1884.]

GRANTON MAINS, 1936

Donald Sutherland Sutherland, 1936-42; Andrew Finlayson Tennant, 1942-44; Gordon Rainey Workman, 1944-50; Bert Albert Cox, 1950-.

KIRK MEMORIAL, 1890

John Adam, M.A., 1891-1906; James Arthur Hadfield, B.A., 1906-14; William Everett Evans, 1914-15; William Watson, 1915-22; John Robert Ramsay, 1923-30; David Gordon Livingston, M.A., 1930-53; Charles Campbell, 1953-54 (student-pastor), ordained pastor, 1954-58; Josiah Buchan, 1958.

MORNINGSIDE, 1887

William Douglas Mackenzie, M.A., 1889-95; David Caird, M.A., 1895-1900; William Morton Barwell, M.A., 1901-11; Harry Moffat Scott, 1912-25; Roderick G. Davies, M.A., 1926-41; Harold Goad Newsham, M.A., 1942-51; Philip Nash Williams, M.A., 1952-.

[NEWINGTON, 1899

Lewis C. Hammond, 1899-1900.]

[PICARDY PLACE, 1897

John Anderson, 1897-98; John Nicol, 1899.]

SAUGHTONHALL, 1929

Andrew Ferguson Simpson, M.A., B.D., 1930-43; Henry Martyn Cook, M.A., 1943-49; Murdo McLennan, 1950-59.

SAUGHTON MAINS, 1951

James Stanley Perkins, M.A., 1951-54; Charles C. Paul, 1954-.

[SYDNEY HALL, c. 1877

Alexander D. Robertson, 1877-97; Supplies, 1897-1900.]

[TRINITY, 1892

Andrew H. M. Sime, 1894-95; Hugh Jenkins, M.A., 1896-98.]

[ELGIN, 1804

William Ballantine, 1804-7; Alexander Stewart, 1807-8; Neil McNeil, 1808-54; George Douglas McGregor (assistant), 1852-53; John Burke (assistant), 1853-54; Archibald Guthrie, 1854-60; William Lothian, 1861-63; James Stark, 1864-72; James Anderson, 1872-78; James Simpson Swan, 1879-93; John Shields, B.A., 1893-1917; J. Cook, M.A., 1917-19; D. Dale, B.A., 1920-26; W. Torrance, 1929-46.]

[ELIE, 1802

J. Gilbert, 1805-8; George Douglas, 1808-12; John Pullar, 1812-29; David Bisset Mackenzie, 1838-49; John Hutchison, 1852-58; David Fox Longwill, M.A., 1859-67; David Johnstone, 1867-70.]

EYEMOUTH

[c. 1806—Mr. Bortherton]. 1861—Robert Findlay, 1864-69; William Wyllie, M.A., 1873-78; Robert Jackson, 1879-86; William Wyllie, M.A., 1887-93; Thomas G. Taylor, M.A., 1894-97; Crystopher Nicholson, 1897-1900; Daniel McIver, 1903-8; Robert S. Birch, 1910-14; David Beale, 1919-21; John H. Smith, 1924-28; Frank Allan Maxwell, 1929-31; W. Brown, 1933-36; Thomas Hall Bisset, 1939-44; David McGowan, 1944-46; J. Massie Milne, 1947-55; Cecil E. Stewart, 1956-59.

FALKIRK

[BANK STREET, 1803

Robert Caldwell, 1803-13; John Edwards, 1813-18; David Bisset Mackenzie, 1822-36; James Mann, 1842-44; William McNab, 1845-45; William Wilson, 1853-57; James McLean, 1859-67; John Anderson, M.A., B.D., 1867-88; John Duthie Buchan, 1888-98.]

[BANK STREET, E.U., 1843

Alexander Cumings Rutherford, 1843-46; Alexander Duncanson (co-pastor), 1846, full pastoral charge, 1847-52.]

TRINITY, 1873

George Bell, M.A., 1874-77; John Spaven, 1878-79; John Morton, 1880-81; John Liddle King, M..A, 1882-84; Robert Winchester Jackson, 1885-96; Alexander Pollock, M.A., 1896-1904; George Scanlan, 1904-16; James Hall, B.A., 1917-25; John Lees, M.A., 1925-30; Alexander Shaw Marshall, 1930-48; Francis Ferrier Robertson, 1948-.

[FALKLAND

(1) 1806—James Garden, 1807-10. (2) 1838—John Elrick, M.A., 1840-42; Hugh Smith, 1842-46; George Greig, 1847-52; John Menzies, 1852-54.]

FORFAR, 1832

William Low, 1837-60; Francis S. Johnstone, 1861-66; John Coyle, 1866-68; Donald L. McCorkindale, 1870-89; William Paterson, 1890- ; Allan S. Guild, 1915-19; Charles Florence, 1921-22; W. Jenkins, 1925-26; Alfred Wilson, 1928-52; Donald Findlay, 1953-59.

[FORRES, 1804

John Martin, 1804-34; Robert Weir, 1837-43; Nisbet Galloway, 1844-47; John Jefferson, 1848-50; William Bathgate, 1851-57; Robert Hunter, 1858-65; Robert Kerr, 1867-71; John Miller, 1874-90; James Neil, 1890-94; Robert L. Hunter, 1895-98; Hugh Elder, 1899-1920; Thomas Shanks, 1921-24; Thomas Baillie, 1925-28; John W. Derry, 1929-36.]

[FOULA, SHETLAND, 1817

Laurence Christie, 1819- ; Laurence Fraser, 1849-55; Robert Georgeson, 1865-80; George Morrison, 1881-94; Stanley Blackwell, A.T.S., 1895-96; Peter Sinclair Brown, 1896-1901; William Robertson, 1902-18.]

FRASERBURGH

[MANSE STREET, 1845

Archibald Duff, 1845-47; Alexander Davidson, 1849-53; Robert Anderson, 1855-56; William Hutchison, 1864-67; James A. Gray, 1868-69; Thomas G. Salmond, 1869-70; John Cameron, 1871-78; Richard W. R. Trenwith, 1879-88; James M. Cowan, 1890-93; Joseph Liddle King, M.A., 1893-95; Alexander Macaulay, 1897-1900; James Stirling, 1900-4; William George Jeffrey, 1905-7; James Wardrop Gillies, 1907-.]

MID STREET, 1803

Udny Anderson, 1803-15; Alexander Begg, M.A., 1819-40; Alexander Munro (assistant); Archibald Duff, 1841-45; Adam G. Forbes, 1945-53; James Sime, 1853-59; James Mitchell Robbie, 1859-65; John Wemyss, M.A., 1866-73; James Hill, M.A., 1873-83; James Stirling, 1884-98; Alfred John Parker, 1900-7; Thomas Johnstone, 1908-37; John Thompson George, 1938-43; Andrew Ferguson Simpson, M.A., B.D., 1943-49; Ronald Newman Sewell, 1950-52; Alpine McAlpine Munro, 1953-57; John Hanna, 1958-.

GALASHIELS

UNION STREET, 1844

James Bishop Robertson, 1844-48; James Howie, 1852-56; Alexander Brown, 1861-77; John Christopher Nesbitt, M.A., 1878-82; William

Z

Francis Adamson, M.A., 1883-1910; Arthur James, 1911-17; Walter Lockwood Terrett, 1918-20; Allan Cameron McDougall, M.A., 1920-25; Andrew Ritchie, M.A., 1925-29; George Kirk, 1929-34; James Sibbald McKay, 1934-38; John Young, M.A., 1939-46; Ronald Newman Sewell, 1947-50; James Milroy, 1951-55; Harold E. Berry, M.A., 1956-.

GALSTON, 1843

David Drummond, 1843-46; James McMillan, 1848-49; —— McPhee, 1849-50; James Pearson (student), 1850-51; James McConnachie, 1851-55; Thomas Suttie, 1861-70; Robert Inglis Gray, 1870-82; David Galbraith, 1883-84; Charles A. Crossthwaite, 1886-88; Robert Steel, 1889-98; James David McCulloch, 1898-1907; David Hobbs, M.A., 1908-10; J. Lyle Rodger, 1910-15; Robert McKinley, M.A., 1915-22; Charles Lynch, 1923-32; John Hanna, 1932-46; Frank Allan Maxwell, 1946-55; William Robertson Milne, 1955-.

GARLIESTON, 1803

Thomas Smith, 1803-29; John Wiseman, 1830-32; Thomas Young, 1832-71; John McAuslane, 1871-77; John Brook, 1878-79; J. H. Johnstone, 1880-83; Alexander Sutherland, 1884-86; Robert Matheson Cairney, 1887-93; James Smith Thomson, 1893-1900; Peter Sinclair Brown, 1901-26; Thomas Boyle Milliken, 1927-33; James Miller, 1932-33; William B. Stewart, 1934-45; Gilbert Graham, 1946-49; James Hall, B.A., 1949-58; W. Beggs Stewart, 1958-.

[GARVALD, 1804

John Dunn, 1804-6; George Forrester, 1806-8.]

[GATEHOUSE-OF-FLEET, 1806

Archibald Miller, 1807-35; Robert Hall, 1840.]

GLASGOW

[BATH STREET, 1850

S. T. Porter, 1849-73.]

BETHANY, 1870

Thomas F. Mathieson, 1871-77; Robert Dey, 1878-80; David E. Irons, M.A., B.D., 1881-1906; Robert Cowan Richardson, 1907-14; David Spence Aitken, 1914-30; David Lowe Neave, 1931-42; Albert Irvine, 1942-44; Anderson Yule, 1945-55; Alexander Taylor, 1956-57; Idris John Vaughan, 1957-.

BRISBY MEMORIAL, 1916

J. M. Brisby, 1916-35; Evan Grant, 1935-42; J. McKenzie, 1942-45; J. Hutchison, 1946-55; James Hamilton, 1955-59.

BROOMHILL (WHITEINCH), 1898

James Bell, 1898-1913; Edward Wales Hirst, M.A., B.SC., 1913-20;

Arthur Temple Cadoux, B.A., D.D., 1920-48; Geraint Vaughan Jones, M.A., B.LITT., 1949-.

CATHCART (BATTLEFIELD), 1911

Daniel McIver, 1912-18; William Gray, M.A., 1918-27; Thomas Carlyle Murphy, O.B.E., M.A., B.D., 1927-41; John Beattie Wilson, 1941-52; John Clark Bateman, 1952-.

[CHRIST CHURCH, 1934

Vera Mary Muir Kenmure, M.A., B.D., 1934-36.]

DALMARNOCK ROAD, 1858

Robert Anderson, 1858-87; John Muir, 1888-91; John Mathieson Forson, 1892-1904; George Hayton, 1905-25; George Forbes Morgan, 1925-44; Andrew Gillespie Jenkins, 1944-50; George Forbes Morgan, 1950-54; Alexander Mackay Ferguson, 1954-59.

DENNISTOUN, 1877

William Arnott, 1877-1921; John Murphy, M.A., B.D., 1921-30; John A. Sinclair, 1930-33; William Robertson Milne, 1934-40; Griffith J. Owens, 1941-45.

WARDLAW, 1857

Gilbert McCallum, 1857-71; Alexander Craib, 1871-81; Enoch Doughty Solomon, 1881-85; Donald McKinnon, 1886-97; William Northcott Challice, 1897-1908; J. Wilson, M.A., 1908-12; J. Hamilton, 1912-13; W. J. Norman, 1913-17; Frederick Walter Tilley, B.D., 1918-26; Percy Stanley Eley, 1927-38; James Oliver, 1938-46.

DENNISTOUN-WARDLAW, 1946

James Oliver, 1946-48; Leonard Sykes, 1949-58; David G. Robinson, B.A., 1958-.

DRUMCHAPEL, 1953

Isabel Gibson Dunlop Shedden, M.A., 1954-.

DUNDAS STREET, 1848

John Guthrie, M.A., 1848-51; James Morison, D.D., 1851-84; Alexander Davidson (colleague), 1860-62; Robert Mitchell (colleague), 1864-68; Ebenezer C. Leal (Colleague), 1869-75; George Gladstone (colleague), 1876-84; George Gladstone, 1884-1910; William Selby Stein, M.A. (assistant), 1908-10; Andrew Ritchie, M.A., 1910-25; James Gilmour Drummond, M.A., D.D., 1925-.

ELGIN PLACE, 1803

Ralph Wardlaw, D.D., 1803-53; S. T. Porter (colleague), 1848-50; Alexander Raleigh, 1855-58; Henry Batchelor, 1859-75; Albert Goodrich, D.D., 1876-90; Timothy Eynon Davies, A.T.S., 1891-96; Ambrose Shepherd, D.D., 1898-1914; Arthur Cooke Hill, D.D., 1915-36; Sidney Maurice Watts, B.D., 1937-42; James Ernest James, 1943-45; Thomas Charles Brimley, 1946-49; Edward James Baker, B.A., 1950-54; Arthur Edward Burgess, 1955-.

[EMMANUEL, 1871

James McLean, 1872-82; William T. Thornton, 1883-85; James Grant, 1885-91; James McLean, 1891-99; James Russell, 1899- ; John Edward Cattral, 1909-12; James Smith Thomson, 1912-.]

FERGUSON MEMORIAL, 1890

Alexander Peat, 1892-93; Thomas Pearson, 1893-97; Robert M. Rollo, 1897-1903; John Robert Ramsay, 1903-5; John George McGarva, 1906; T. McLennan, - ; John Shields, B.A., 1917-26; J. H. Hynd, 1926-28; T. D. Alexander, 1928-34; Robert Lang Telfer, 1935-.

FORSYTH MEMORIAL (GOVANHILL), 1876

Robert Wallace, 1876-88; William Forsyth, 1888-1928; William Ralston, 1929-.

GIFFNOCK (EGLINTON STREET), 1825

Edward Campbell, 1825-36; Peter Mather, 1836-38; David Russell, D.D., 1839-89; James Ross (colleague), 1881-89; James Ross, D.D., 1889-1906; Robert W. Newlands, B.D., 1906-11; William George Jeffrey, 1912-24; William Jordan, 1925-26; Hector Ross, M.A., 1926-33; William Jordan, 1925-26; Hector Ross, M.A., 1926-33; George Kirk, 1934-53; David Clews McArthur, M.B.E., 1954-.

[GREAT HAMILTON STREET, 1849

David Johnstone, 1850-68; John McMunn, B.D., 1868-76; J. B. Johnstone, 1876-79; William Lowe, 1880-86; John Jenkins, 1886-1902; George Watt Smith, M.A., 1904-10; David Hobbs, M.A., 1910-.]

[GUTHRIE MEMORIAL, 1876

William Halliday, 1876-1908; Thomas Halliday, 1908- ; Andrew B. Halliday, 1913-38; William Gilchrist, 1938-51.]

HILLHEAD, 1800

Greville Ewing, D.D., 1800-39; George Greig (assistant), 1800-3; William Henry (assistant), 1804-7; John Morell Mackenzie, M.A. (colleague), 1837-39; Alexander Thomson, M.A., 1842-46; Alexander Fraser, 1847-63; Ralph Wardlaw Thompson, 1865-70; George Stewart, 1871-79; Frederick Smith, 1882-83; Alexander Cowe, M.A., 1884-97; Harry Herbert Snell, B.A., 1898-99; Thomas Templeton, M.A., 1900-7; John Safeley, M.A., 1908-19; (William Blair, in charge, 1920-21); Herbert Henry Summers, M.A., B.SC., 1921-27; Donald McIntosh (in charge), 1928; Percy George Samuel Hopwood, B.D., B.LITT., PH.D., 1929-35; Vera Mary Muir Kenmure, M.A., B.D., 1936-45; Edward James Baker, B.A., 1946-50; Harry Escott, M.A., PH.D., 1951-.

HOOD MEMORIAL, 1843

Robert Simpson, 1844-45; William Bathgate, 1846-47; Nisbet Galloway, 1848-62; Robert Hood, 1862-94; John Albert Lees, 1894-97; Alexander D. Anderson, 1898-1921; James Hamilton, 1921-30; James Hall, B.A., 1930-49; James Foster, M.A., 1950-53; George Cunningham, 1955-57; James Hamilton, 1959-.

KNIGHTSWOOD, 1933

Walter Gerrard, 1933-46; Thomas Mearns, M.A., 1946-50; John Thompson George, 1951-.

LLOYD MORRIS (HUTCHESONTOWN), 1874

Thomas Ruell Atkinson, 1874-76; John McMunn (in charge), 1880-81; H. W. J. Millar (in charge), 1881-83; Thomas Havre, 1883-85; George Coates Milne, 1885-93; Edwin Lloyd Morris, 1894-1929; George Charles Thomson, 1930-35; Charles Cammock, M.A., 1935-45; William Milne Anderson, 1945-53; Leslie Newton, 1955-.

[MONTROSE STREET, 1844

Fergus Ferguson, M.A., D.D., 1845-97; Robert Craig, M.A. (assistant), 1866-78; Charles Richardson, M.A., 1898-1924; Harold Goad Newsham, M.A., 1915-31; Ralph Forman Godly Calder, B.A., B.D., 1933-43; James Stanley Perkins, M.A., 1944-50; Thomas Carlyle Murphy, O.B.E., M.A., B.D., 1951-55.]

MOSSPARK, 1929

Thomas Smith Loudon, 1929-50; Andrew Gillespie Jenkins, 1950-52; Robert Squince McCulloch, 1953-.

[NEW CITY ROAD, 1862

Andrew Paterson, 1862-68; John Douglas, 1868-95; William Smart Todd, 1897-1914; John William Derry, 1914-29; Arthur E. Hayton, 1930-39; William Milne Anderson, 1940-44.]

[NORTH HANOVER STREET (Albion Street), 1834

Thomas Pullar, 1835-43; George S. Ingram, 1844-53; A. G. Forbes (dates unknown); P. Grenville, LL.B., 1866-70; David Ebenezer Irons, M.A., B.D., 1871-72; David Cook, 1872-76.]

[PARKGROVE

P. Grenville, LL.B., 1870-79; David Jamieson, 1880-86.]

PARKHEAD, 1873

David Gardner, 1873-76; John Graham, 1876-1905; George Sharpe, 1905-6; Henry Wallace, 1906-37; James R. McCorkindale, 1937-48; William Robert Nelson Gray, M.A., 1949-.

PARTICK, 1891

James Grant, 1891-1902; Wesley Kelly, 1903-5; Alex. George Bruce Sivewright, M.A., 1906-27; Vera Mary Muir Kenmure, M.A., B.D., 1928-34; James Kinmond Smith, M.A., 1935-41; John Mackie, B.SC., 1941-46; Robert M. Lawson, 1946-51; John Young, M.A., 1952-.

POLLOKSHIELDS, 1899

Andrew Hamilton, M.A., 1900-20; William Grove White, 1921-24; Harry Moffatt Scott, A.T.S., 1925-39; William H. S. Webb, 1939-45; Kenneth Gowan Ogilvie, M.A., 1946-53; Vera Mary Muir Kenmure, M.A., B.D., 1954-.

PRIESTHILL, 1950

Charles Cammock, M.A., 1949-55; J. Ernest Cairnduff, B.A., 1955-.

[SHETTLESTON, 1904

Lachlan McFadyen, 1905-8.]

[SOUTH SIDE (Nelson Street), 1849

Samuel Chisholm, 1851-55; John Andrew, 1855-56; Robert George Harper, 1857-59; Hugh Riddell, 1859-73; William Dunlop, 1875-91; Adam Hamilton, 1912- ; Joseph Chatfield Alexander, B.A., 1921-30; Alpine McAlpine Munro, 1931-34; John Strachan, 1935-38.]

TRINITY, 1862

William Pulsford, D.D., 1864-84; John Hunter, D.D., 1887-1901; Arthur C. Turberville (assistant), 1883; David S. Herd, B.A. (assistant), 1895-97; James Shaw Brown (assistant),   - ; John Hunter, D.D., 1904-13; T. M. Watt, M.A. (assistant), 1911-13; Henry Simpson McLelland, B.A., B.D., F.R.G.S., 1915-56; Clifford Harry Macquire, 1957-.

[WATERLOO STREET (EBENEZER), 1845

William Scott, 1845-77; John Guthrie, M.A., D.D., (hon. pastor), 1877-78; Robert Hislop, 1877-98; William Finlayson Riddell, 1899-1904; James Wallace, 1904-6.]

[WEST CAMPBELL STREET, 1866

John Guthrie, M.A., D.D., 1866-77; John Adam, M.A. (assistant), 1870-74; this church united with Waterloo Street in 1877.]

[WOODSIDE, 1900

James Baxter, 1903-9; David Z. H. Forson, 1910-14; (John Barr, 1917-24); Alexander Shaw Marshall, 1929-30; Anderson Yule (in charge), 1930-36; Anderson Yule (ordained pastor), 1936-39; William Russell, M.A., 1940-43; Sidney Lawrence, 1943-46.]

[GOUROCK, 1879

John McGarva Sloan, 1880-82; John Christopher Nesbitt, M.A., 1883-88.]

GOVAN

ELDERPARK STREET, 1870

Robert Simpson, 1870-87; Daniel McKenzie (colleague), 1876-87; Daniel McKenzie, 1887-91; James Edwards, M.A., B.D., 1892-1906; Peter Smith, 1906-28; Frank Robinson, 1929-36; James Miller, 1936-45; Andrew Finlayson Tennant, 1946-52; James Ralston, 1953-55; Thomas Bell, 1955-.

[JAMES PLACE, 1897

Charles A. Crosthwaite, 1897-98; James C. Neill, 1899-.]

[WHITE STREET (LANGLANDS), 1865

William Reid, 1869-70; George Gladstone, 1871-76; Alexander D. Denholm, 1877-78; Robert Paterson, 1880-84; Ebenezer James E. Boon, 1885-1903; Andrew James Forson, 1904-24; Samuel Ivan Bell, 1924- ; Frank Allan Maxwell, 1931-34; Andrew Gillespie Jenkins, 1942-44; William James Gaston, 1944-48; W. Gray-Brown, B.A., 1949-.]

[GRANGEMOUTH, 1806

William Watson, 1807-22.]

GREENOCK

GEORGE SQUARE, 1805

David Ramsay, 1804-5; John Hercus, 1806-30; Alexander Lyle, 1832-34; Alexander Campbell, M.A., 1836-44; Alexander Raleigh, 1845-48; John Milne Jarvie, 1851-91; Alexander Roy Henderson, M.A., (assistant), 1887-89; Henry William Clark (assistant), 1890-91; William Henry Addicott, 1893-1906; Robert Stell, 1906-32; D. Marlais Davies, 1933-40; Joseph W. Gregory, M.A., 1941-45; David Clews McArthur, M.B.E., 1946-54; Laurence John Matthews, M.A., B.D., 1954-58; Thomas Aeron Lewis, M.B.E., M.A., 1959-.

MEARNS STREET, 1882

Thomas W. Bowman, M.A., PH.D., 1883-89; John Clark Neil, M.A., B.D., 1889-95; Robert Cowan Richardson, 1895-1907; James David McCulloch, 1907-37; Roy Rigg, M.A., 1937-40; William John Johnstone Herron (interim pastor), 1940-42; Thomas Cameron Hamilton, 1946-.

NELSON STREET, 1846

Alexander C. Rutherford, 1847-50; John Guthrie, M.A., 1851-61; Alexander Davidson, 1862-86; W. Richmond Scott, 1887-91; Robert Mitchell, 1892-93; Andrew Ritchie, M.A., 1894-1903; William Finlayson Riddell, 1904-10; Alexander Rowatt Maxwell, 1911-15; James Adam, 1916-23; Arthur Ernest Nicholas, 1923-33; Allan Stewart Guild, 1933-55; Richard Snoddon, 1955-.

EAST (ST. LAWRENCE STREET), 1871

George Moir, 1871-78; Robert Bell, 1878-97; William James Ainslie, M.A., 1897-1903; George Gerrard, 1903-13; David William Gaylor, 1913-27; John William Wright, 1927-42; George Renton Brown, 1942-45; John Young, M.A., 1946-52; Ronald Newman Sewell, 1953-56; Cecil J. Jamison, 1956-.

MARTYRS, 1898

John Richardson, 1899-1935; Thomas Mearns, M.A., student pastor, 1935-39; Ian Bissett, M.A., 1939-46; Supplies, 1946-49; T. B. Gordon, 1949-51; Benjamin Poole, 1951-.

[HADDINGTON, 1804

James Hill, 1804-12; William Ritchie, 1813-29; Robert Ferguson,

1830-31; Andrew Russell, M.A., 1833-40; Thomas D. Thomson, 1841-47; George Wight, 1847-55; Alexander Gosman, 1855-58; William McLellan, 1862-67.]

HAMILTON

ST. JAMES (AUCHINGRAMONT ROAD), 1807

John Wilson, 1807-11; Thomas Alexander, 1822-35; John Moir, 1835-38; John Kirk, 1839-45; John Hart, 1846-50; Patrick Morrison, 1850-53; Thomas Pullar, 1854-58; James Proctor, 1859-60; Adam Dunlop, 1860-65; James Sime, M.A., 1865-68; Daniel Jackson, 1868-85; William Schofield Thomson, 1885-1906; John Albert Lees, 1906-25; Harry Bedford, 1925-28; Thomas Baillie, 1928-48; Hector Ross, M.A., 1948-57; Leonard Sykes, 1958-.

PARK ROAD, 1854

James Bishop Robertson, 1854-59; James Maconochie, 1861-65; Alexander Wilson, 1865-67; John Cameron, 1867-70; Daniel Craig, 1871-74; Alexander Denholm, 1875-77; George Bell, M.A., 1877-1911; John Murphy, M.A., B.D., 1912-21; Charles Florence, 1922-25; David William Gaylor, 1927-39; Douglas Mackenzie Gordon, M.A., 1940-47; John Innes, 1948-52; George Kirk, 1953-56; Stanley A. M. Britton, 1957-.

[HARRAY AND SANDWICK, ORKNEY, 1810, 1812

John Masson, M.A., 1835-45; David Brown, 1846-54; Robert Harvey, 1855-57; Donald L. McCorkindale, 1860-70; William Northcott Challice, 1870-75; William Hill Philip, 1877-81; David Smith, 1882-1900; John Heggie, 1902-4.]

HAWICK

[(1) 1805—Charles Gray, 1805-9.]

[(2) 1836—William Munro, 1837-70; William Lowe Walker, 1873-78.]

[(3) 1842—William Dobson, 1842-45.]

(4) BOURTREE PLACE, 1848

Alexander Duff, 1849-56; James Proctor, 1857-58; Robert Mitchell, 1860-64; David Hislop, B.A., 1864-1902; William James Ainslie, M.A., 1903-21; Aeneas Anderson, 1922-27; Alexander Baxter, 1927-33; John Safeley, M.A., PH.D., 1934-41; G. B. Hewitt, M.A., 1942-49; Henry Martyn Cook, M.A., 1949-.

HELENSBURGH, c. 1804

John Edwards, 1804-8; R. Syme, 1808-15; John Boag and supplies, 1815-23; John Arthur, 1824-66; James Troup, M.A. (colleague), 1858-66; William Milne, 1866-69; James Troup, M.A., 1869-97; William Blair, 1898-1924; David Stoddart, 1924-34; William Davidson Bruce, 1934-44; Daniel Cook, 1944-58; John M. F. Butler, 1959-.

HUNTLY, 1800

George Cowie, 1800-6; Donald Morrison (assistant), 1805-6; Donald Morrison (acting pastor), 1806-8; John Thomas, 1811-12; John Hill,

M.A., 1817-48; Robert Troup, M.A., 1849-77; John Pillans, 1877-91; Thomas Templeton, M.A., 1891-96; William John Collier, M.A., 1896-1901; James Lewis, A.T.S., 1902-16; Magnus Sinclair, 1917-28; John Dick, 1929-34; Alexander Fisher MacRobert, M.A., B.A., 1934-40; David O. Reece, 1940-44; C. P. Laslett, 1945-48; William James Gaston, 1948-51; Peter Peace, 1951-55; and RHYNIE, Andrew Finlayson Tennant, 1957-.

INNERLEITHEN, 1848

William Dobson, 1848-67; Archibald Cree, 1868-76; James Grant, 1877-85; Alexander Mann, 1886-91; John Meldrum Dryerre, 1891-96; Thomas M. McKendrick, 1896-1900; Thomas Smith Loudon, 1904-16; David L. Neave, 1916-23; G. D. Donald, 1924- ; J. Morison, 1930- ; Alexander May, M.A., B.D., 1933-37; A. Ferguson, 1937-45; Arthur G. Reekie, 1945-51; William Muir McPherson, 1952-54.

INNERLEITHEN AND WALKERBURN, 1956

Gordon Rainey Workman, 1956-.

[INSCH, ABERDEENSHIRE, 1874

John Graham, 1874-76; James Murray, 1877-78; Thomas Havre, 1879-83; James Edwards, M.A., B.D., 1884-92; Laurence Williamson, 1893-1911; Charles Derry, 1912- ; J. Morison, 1923-29; James Wyllie, 1929-.]

[INVERKIP (AULD KIRK), c. 1800

George Robertson, 1802-7; Thomas Low, 1808-51.]

[INVERNESS

(1) 1818—James Kennedy, 1825-58.

(2) Church re-formed in 1871; William Milne, 1871-72; John Wright, 1872-75.]

INVERURIE, 1822

William Brown, 1824-29; Alexander Smith, M.A., 1835-39; John Miller, 1843-69; J. B. Johnstone, 1870-76; David Jamieson, 1876-80; John Petrie Wilson, 1880-84; Frederick Alexander Russell, 1885-87; James Wylie, 1887-90; William Rae, 1891-93; John Hardie, M.A., 1893-94; William Muir, 1894-1923; Gordon Lee McLachlan, 1923-26; Robert Gibson, 1926-30; John Young, M.A., 1932-39; Anderson Yule, 1939-45; William Kitching, 1945-50; James Ralston, 1951-53; George Forbes Morgan, 1954-58; William Alastair Tindall, M.A., 1958-.

[KEITH, 1801

Mr. Japp, 1801.]

[KILBARCHAN

D. M. Donald, 1930-37; William West, 1937-39; John Strachan, 1939-42.]

[KILLIN

William Tulloch, 1801-3; John McLaren, 1818-20.]

KILMARNOCK

[(1) 1825—John Campbell, 1825-29; John Hill, M.A., 1829-32; John Ward, 1832-38; John Dickenson, 1838-42; Robert Weir, 1843-48; John Campbell, 1855-59; A. W. Lowe, 1860-62; John C. McIntosh, 1862-66.]

[(2) CLERK'S LANE, 1841
James Morison, 1841-51; William Davidson Black, 1854-56; William Bathgate, 1857-60; Robert Hislop, 1864-77; Robert Borland, 1877-80; James Forrest, M.A., 1881-85.]

(3) WINTON PLACE, 1841 (1860)
William Bathgate, D.D., 1860-79; John Sloan (assistant), 1876-78; Alexander C. Denholm (assistant), 1878-79; Alexander C. Denholm, 1879-86; Alexander McNair, M.A., 1886-1918; Walter MacPherson Cownie, M.A., 1918-23; John Anderson, B.A., PH.D., 1923-38; Alpine M. Munro, 1939-47; Alexander Shaw Marshall, 1948-.

KILSYTH

(1) [1838—Charles A. Piper, 1842-43.]
(2) 1848—John C. Anderson, 1858-59; Josias C. Jago, 1865-69; David Gardner, 1869-73; George Rutherford, 1873-85; James C. Hodge, 1885-92; Matthew Park Noble, 1893-1901; Donald McIntosh, 1901-9; S. J. Bell, 1909-17; William H. Watson, 1917-21; David Beale, 1921-28; James Kelt, 1929-41; John Strachan Hughes, 1942-46; Kenneth Kingsley Lodge, 1947-55; Robert Little, M.A., B.D., 1956-.

KILWINNING, 1844

Robert Hunter, 1846-54; G. Salmond, 1863-66; Alexander Wilson, 1867-70; Richard William R. Trenwith, 1874-79; James Russell, 1882-91; Robert M. Rollo, 1894-97; Andrew Kirk, B.A., 1898-1901; William Watson, 1902-6; Frederick Drennan, 1906-10; John Thomas Hornsby, 1910-17; John Hart, 1918-21; William Falconer, 1921-25 William Cleland Connacher, 1926-53; William Campbell, 1954-.

[KINTYRE, 1802

Archibald McCallum, 1802.]

KIRKCALDY

WEST END, 1800
Archibald Maclae, 1800-11; Robert Aitkenhead, 1811-49; James Mitchell Robbie, 1849-59; R. Cowan, 1859-69; George McHardy, M.A., D.D., 1869-1913; William Paxton (assistant), 1912-13; William James Dickson, 1913-30; W. D. Bruce, 1930-34; Richard Smith, 1935-47; James L. Proudfoot, M.A., B.D., 1947-.

PATHHEAD, 1867

Ebenezer J. E. W. Boon, 1870-85; Robert Jackson, 1886-91; William Wylie, M.A., 1893-1916; John Harvey, 1916-29; Robert Macmenemey, 1930-36; Arthur Morton Price, M.A., B.D., PH.D., 1936-44; Thomas Shanks, 1945-54; Thomas Girvan Watson, 1955-59; Alex. M. Ferguson, 1959-.

[KIRKINTILLOCH, 1802

Hugh Fraser, 1802-4; George Greig, 1804-6.]

[KIRKLISTON, 1803

William Ritchie, 1803-13.]

[KIRRIEMUIR, 1804

D. Dunbar, 1804-8; A. Collins, 1810-24; Robert Machray, M.A., 1825-29.]

KIRKWALL, 1806

John Black, 1806; David Ramsay, 1807-53; George Robertson, 1815-33; Thomas Smith McKean, 1838-41; David Webster, 1842-44; George Smith, 1847-52; James McNaughton, 1852-59; Robert Price, - ; William Northcott Challice, 1868-70; Alexander Smith, 1870-72; Alexander Pirie, 1873-83; James C. Hodge, 1883-85; John Blair, 1886-89; Kenneth McKenzie, 1890-93; John Waugh Chalmers, 1894-95; George Gerrard, 1896-1903; Donald E. McInnes, 1904-5; Robert Rigg, 1905-12; E. Sanderson, 1915-19; J. Thomson, 1920-23; Alfred Wilson, 1924-28; James Ramage McCorkindale, 1929-37; John William Morley, 1938-47; James Ramage McCorkindale, 1948- ; Thomas Ballantyne Gordon, 1956-.

[KNOCKANDO, 1804

John Munro, 1804-53.]

LANARK, 1847

John Inglis, 1849-54; James McDowall, 1856-62; James Davidson, 1863-72; William Annott, 1872-78; William Forsyth, 1878-88; John Wilson Crawford, 1889-92; James Cowper McLachlan, M.A., 1893-98; David Spence Aitken, 1898-1914; J. Lyle Rodger, 1915-18; Harry Marsden, 1919-24; Peter Wylie, 1924-27; James Cowper McLachlan, M.A., 1927-34; Thomas Shanks, 1934-45; William Beggs Stewart, 1945-49; Isabel Gibson Dunlop Shedden, M.A., 1949-54; William Muir McPherson, 1954-58.

LANGHOLM, 1864

James Cron, 1864-65; James M. Campbell, 1866-74; Robert Borland, 1874-77; William Richmond Scott, 1878-87; Andrew Ritchie, M.A., 1888-94; George McKendrick, 1894-1900; Robert McQueen, 1900-13; Richard Smith, 1916-18; William Robertson Milne (in charge),

1920-21; Nathaniel Johnstone, 1922-24; J. C. Drife, 1925-34; William C. Cowan, 1935-40; Beatrice Dunnett Bonnar, B.D., 1941-.

LARKHALL

[(1) 1804—Thomas Alexander, 1822-48.]
(2) 1875—George Wood, 1875-79; Robert Brown, 1878-83; Alexander M. Higgins, 1883-85; James Rae, 1887-1917; John T. Hornsby, 1917-26; David L. Neave, 1926-31; J. Coulson Thomson, 1931-39; Andrew G. Jenkins (student pastor), 1941-42; John Logan, M.A., 1943-45; John Hamilton, 1945-46; Donald Findlay, 1946-53; John Gardner McIlvean, M.A., 1954-.

[LAURENCEKIRK, 1842

David Moir, 1842-45; Adam Stuart Muir, 1846-47; David Webster, 1848-51; Andrew Noble, 1852-71; David Smith, 1872-79; James Tait Scott, 1880-84; William A. Farquhar, 1884-86; William Muir, 1887-94; William L. Walker, 1894-1905; Ebenezer J. Boon, 1905.]

LEITH

CONSTITUTION STREET, 1805

John Pullar, 1805-17; Alexander Christie (colleague); William Henry, 1818-22; George D. Cullen, M.A., 1822-56; Angus Galbraith, 1857-60; William Jackson Cox, 1860-72; George Allen, 1873-87; David Robb, 1887-1919; George B. Shepherd, M.A., B.D., 1920-41; Lenton G. Seager, 1942-47; John William Morley, 1947-.

DUKE STREET, 1844

Ebenezer Kennedy, 1844-51; Joseph Boyle, 1853-62; David Hislop, B.A., 1862-64; Robert Hunter, 1865-78; Alexander McNair, M.A., 1879-86; Alexander Davidson, 1887-91; Charles Richardson, M.A., 1892-98; Hugh Jenkins, M.A., 1898-1908; James Neil, 1908-14; Robert S. Birch, M.A., PH.D., 1914-28; David Beale, 1928-42; Ralph F. G. Calder, B.A., B.D., 1943-47; Walter Laurie Wooding, M.A., B.D., 1948-54; Hamish Smith, 1956-.

LERWICK, 1808

George Reid, 1808-39; William Lawson Brown, M.A., 1840-42; Robert Hunter Craig, 1844-47; John Murdoch, 1848-57; John McKniven, 1858-64; James Troup, M.A., 1865-69; John E. Dobson, 1870-75; John McMunn, 1876-77; William A. Farquhar, 1878-84; Alexander Yeats, 1884-87; John Anderson, M.A., B.D., 1887-93; J. Livingston Gower, 1894-97; Henry Booth Aldridge, 1897-1904; George D. Donald, 1905-8; J. Livingston Gower, 1908-13; John Spence, 1913-15; James Scott, 1915-18; J. C. Drife, 1920-25; T. B. Milliken, 1925-26; D. McKay, 1927-29; A. T. Ritch, 1931-32; James Henry Carlin, 1933-42; John R. May, M.A., 1942-46; William Campbell, 1947-54; Sidney Lawrence, 1954-.

[LETHAM, 1803

William Lindsay, 1803-41; John Masson, 1848-54; Charles A. Piper, 1854-64; George Moir, 1864-86.]

[LEVEN, 1804

John Elder, 1802-34; Ebenezer Cornwall, 1835-43; Boyd Roebuck, 1843-48; James Hamilton, 1848-55; John Sinclair, 1856-60.]

[LINLITHGOW

(1) 1807—Alexander W. Knowles, 1807-49; William Wilson, 1850-53; David Webster, 1853-60; Alexander C. Peacock, 1861-62; James Ross, 1862-64; James Lemon, 1865-67; John Craig, 1867-78; James Rae, 1879-83.]
(2) 1887—John M. Ure, 1890-91; John Cameron, 1892-1907; George Smissen, 1908- ; James Lewis, A.T.S., 1916- ; E. Richards, 1921-.]

[LOCHEE, 1803

Alexander Thomson, 1803-20; James Dalrymple, 1821-26.]

MACDUFF, 1879

George Coates Milne, 1879-85; Matthew Park Noble, 1886-93; Alfred Ernest Garvie, M.A., B.D., 1893-95; Adam Drummond, 1895-1905; James Sandilands, M.B., CH.B., 1905-11; Robert Rigg, 1912-30; James Brand Crombie, 1930-33; Isaac Galloway Pollock, 1933-42; Frederic Albert Ore, 1942-48; James Ralston, 1948-51; Herbert Lloyd Monro Cameron, 1951-55; J. Massie Milne, 1956-.

[MELROSE, 1842

Ebenezer Young, 1842-47; William Crombie, 1851-85; William George Allan, M.A., B.D., 1888-95; Alexander Taylor Hill, 1896-97; James Groat, 1897-98; John Liddle King, M.A., 1898- ; John Jenkins, 1914- ; Walter L. Terrett, 1920-22; William J. Ainslie, M.A., 1922-28; James Irvine Macnair, 1928-30.]

MILLSEAT, 1830

Joseph Morrison, 1831-56; George Saunders, 1857-79; Alexander Francis, 1880-89; William Murray, 1890-1930; Peter Peace, 1930-36; Christopher Philip Laslett, 1937-45; G. C. Thomson, 1945-49; Donald S. Sutherland, 1950-55; James Ralston, 1955-56; Andrew Hutson, 1956-.

MONTROSE

BALTIC STREET, 1800

George Cowie, 1800-5; John Black, 1810-14; George Cowie, 1814-24; John Wilson, 1827-28; Alexander Cuthbert, 1830-33; James Robertson Campbell, M.A., 1835-44; Hugh Hercus, 1844-55; Peter Whyte, 1856-72; Frederick Sidney Morris, 1873-76; James Ross, 1876-81; William Douglas Mackenzie, M.A., 1882-89; Alexander Roy Henderson, M.A.,

1889-95; Alfred Ernest Garvie, M.A., B.D., 1895-1903; David Russell Scott, M.A., 1904-18; William Kirk, M.A., 1919-20; Hector Ross, 1921-26; Aeneas Anderson, 1927-35; Frank Robinson, 1936-46; Douglas McKenzie Gordon, M.A., 1947-.

[JOHN STREET, 1847

Alexander C. Wood, 1847-49; William Davidson Black, 1851-54; William Hutchison, 1854- ; David Hislop, 1858-62; William Halliday, -1866; John Whitson, 1866-67; Robert Paterson, 1867-75; John Robertson, 1876-78; George Wisely, 1879-81; John Baxter, 1881-85; James Cowper McLachlan, M.A., 1885-93; Robert Jackson, 1893-.]

MOTHERWELL, 1872

David Greenhill, 1874-83; William S. Todd, 1884-97; John Mackintosh, 1897-1924; Andrew James Forson, 1924-32; Harry B. Miner, B.D., 1932-35; Frank Field, 1937-46; Frank Robinson, 1946-.

MUIRKIRK

[1805—Andrew Rattray, 1805-7; T. Campbell, 1810- ; John Boag, 1824-29.]

1854—James Munro, 1878-79; John Liddle King, M.A., 1880-82; John Robertson, 1882-83; Alexander Taylor Hill, 1889-90; David Spence Aitken, 1894-98; Thomas Smith Loudon, 1899-1904; James Wardrop Gillies, 1905-6; Thomas Halliday, 1907-8; James Russell, 1908- ; C. Livingston, 1915- ; William Cleland Connacher, 1919-26; W. Jenkins, 1926-29; Alexander James Millar, 1929-32; John Beattie Wilson, 1933-35; Telford, 1937-39; W. C. Littlewood, 1939-42; Arthur Robertson, 1946-51; William Beggs Stewart, 1952-.

MUSSELBURGH

FISHER ROW, 1801

John Watson, 1806-40; Adam Lillie (assistant), 1833-34; Adam S. Forbes (co-pastor), 1840-44; John Mann, 1844-47; Boyd Roebuck, 1848-52; William Ingram, 1852-57; Mr. Lowe, 1857-60; David Johnson, 1861-63; Matthew Simpson, 1863-89; John McMunn, 1890-93; David Farquharson, 1893-1923; Richard Smith, 1923-35; Robert Gibson, 1935-57; Jean B. Robson, M.A., 1957-.

[TOWN HALL, 1885

Alexander D. Anderson, 1887-91; Edward Aston, 1891-92.]

NAIRN, 1806

James Dewar, 1806-43; John Gillies, 1844-47; James Howie, 1847-57; William Ingram, 1858-59; J. B. Johnstone, 1859-70; Robert Dey, 1871-78; Charles Whyte, M.A., 1878-85; William J. Thornton, 1885-90; George C. Martin, M.A., B.D., 1890-95; Frederick John Japp, 1895-1901; George Scanlan, 1902-4; James Ross, 1906-18; Aeneas Anderson, 1918-22; Donald McIntosh, 1922-27; James Stewart, M.A., B.D., 1928-31; J. D. McLean, 1931-35; Aeneas Anderson, 1935-53; Thomas S. Kee, 1954-55; Lenton George Seager, 1955-.

NEWBURGH

[1841—Andrew Yuill, 1841-46; Archibald Russell, 1847-64; James H. Cameron, 1865-71.]
1873—Nisbet Galloway, 1873-77; James Frame, 1877-80; George Wood, 1880-84; Edward Aston, 1884-91; James Monie, 1895-99; John Robert Ramsay, 1899-1903; Andrew Burnett Halliday, 1903-13; J. Miller, 1914-16; J. Harris Smith, 1916-24; S. T. M. Robertson, 1924-27; R. M. Johnstone, 1928-29; T. G. Taylor, 1931-34; John Thompson George, 1935-38; George Renton Brown, 1938-40; D. L. Neave, 1942-50; Andrew Hutson, 1950-56; Alexander Brown Cairns, M.A., 1957-.

NEWCASTLETON, 1849

William Davidson Black, 1850-51; Supplies, 1851-66; Robert Steel, 1866-75; A. Turnbull, 1876-77; Supplies, 1877-82; Peter Andrew, 1882-83; George Davis, 1883-86; William Paterson, 1887-90; John Whitson, 1890-91; John Hunter Craig, 1891-95; James W. Gillies, 1899-1905; George A. E. Walker, 1908-12; T. Enfield Jones, 1912-15; Charles Derry, 1916-23; James Anderson, 1923-26; A. F. White, T. Hall Bisset, Alexander Gemmell (student pastors), 1927-34; Lewis C. Hammond, 1934-39; Alexander R. Sparke, 1929-42; James Henry Carlin, 1942-52; William Kitching, 1953-58; Dennis E. Ferguson (lay pastor), 1959-.

NEW DEER, 1879

James Rae, 1879-1912; Donald Grigor, 1912-19; George Forbes Morgan, 1919-24; A. E. Hayton, 1925-27; A. Richards, 1928-32; Roy Rigg, M.A., 1932-35; John Robert Ramsay, 1936-47; J. M. McIntyre, 1948-50; Charles William Turtle, 1951-.

[NEW LANARK, 1837

Patrick Anderson, M.A., 1838-68; George McHardy, M.A. (colleague), 1865-68; George McHardy, M.A., 1868-69.]

[NEW PITSLIGO, 1861

John Johnston, 1862-66; David J. Gass, 1867-69; Robert Auchterlonie, 1869-74; James Cullen Hodge, 1875-83; James Bayne, 1884-87; Thomas Templeton, M.A., 1887-91; Robert McKinlay, M.A. 1891-1915; W. G. White, 1916-17; David H. Forson, 1917-24.]

NEWPORT, Fife, 1801

Thomas Taylor, 1803-6; Thomas Just, 1806-44; Thomas Just, Jr., 1844-49; Samuel Fairly, 1849-53; Thomas Just, Jr., 1853-67; John Tait, M.A., 1867-78; Robert Allen, 1878-90; T. W. Hodge, B.A., 1891-1900; William Wood, 1900-12; Arthur Bunce, 1913-24; John Albert Lees, 1925-35; Lenton George Seager, 1935-42; A. R. Sparke, 1942-45; Donald Grigor, 1945-52; Aeneas Anderson, 1953-59; Thomas G. Watson, 1959-.

OBAN, 1805

Dugald McEwan, 1805-7; John Campbell, 1810-53; Charles Whyte, 1855-78; John Blacklock, 1878-79; John McNeill, 1879-82; James McLean, 1882-91; Alexander Mann, 1891-96; William Rosling, 1896-1902; Alexander G. B. Sivewright, M.A., 1903-6; Andrew McIntosh, M.A., 1906-9; George Strathearn, 1909-12; R. M. Johnstone, 1913-16; Mr. Edmonston, 1916-19; Mr. Fortescue, 1919-21; D. Gordon Livingston, 1925-30; Charles Cammock, M.A., 1930-35; John Shaw Guthrie, 1936-41; John Fullerton, M.A., 1941-45; John Clark Bateman, 1946-52; Edward George Stout, 1954-58; James Kinmond Smith, M.A. 1959-.

PAISLEY

[CANAL STREET, 1850

John Harrison Lochore, 1850-63; William Elston, 1863-64; Adam Dunlop, 1865-70; this church united with School Wynd Church in 1871.]

[LIBERAL CLUB HALL, 1897

T. C. Mactrusty, 1897-1900.]

NEW STREET, 1845

Alexander M. Wilson, 1846-48; Thomas Elder, William Taylor, John G. Aitchieson (student pastors), 1849-51; Ebenezer Kennedy, 1851-55; George T. M. Inglis, 1856-60; William Park, 1860-65; John Spaven, 1866-70; Alexander Wilson, 1870-1917; James Wallace, 1917-45; J. Logan, M.A., 1945-50; James Gilbert Ritchie Strachan, 1950-.

SCHOOL WYND [founded at the close of the eighteenth century]

John Young, 1801-5; George Robertson, 1807-15; Robert McLachlan, M.A., 1816-45; William Ross, 1846-54; John Renfrew, 1856-66; Andrew Bayne Morris, 1867-70; John McRae Simcock, 1871-80; William Northcott Challice, 1881-97; William James Dickson, 1898-1913; Wallace MacPherson Cownie, M.A., 1913-18; Isaac Henry Clyde, 1919-21; James Rodger McPhail, 1922-43; Thomas Hall Bisset, 1944-58; Sidney Bindeman, 1959-.

PERTH

[CANAL CRESCENT, 1851

John Pillans, 1851-61; Thomas Neave, 1861-65; John Wallace, 1865-72.]

[E.U. CHURCH, 1856

William Adamson, 1857-68; Robert Finlay, 1869-   ; united with Mill Street Church in 1896.]

KINNOULL STREET (formerly MILL STREET), 1798

James Garie, 1798-1801; Robert Little, 1802-6; John Hinmers, 1806-7; William Orme, 1808-24; James Robertson, A.M., 1826-28;

Robert Machray, A.M., 1829-33; James William Massie, 1836-41; Kerr Johnstone, 1842-47; John Low, 1847-49; William Duncan Knowles, B.A., 1851-84; William Charles Willoughby, 1885-87; David Caird, M.A., 1888-92; Robert Finlay, 1896-1918; G. S. Leslie Thompson, B.D., 1918-20; William Hannah Watson, 1921-29; Daniel Cook, 1930-44; Arthur Morton Price, M.A., B.D., PH.D., 1944-.

PETERHEAD, 1823

James Scott, 1823-31; Robert Massie, 1839-42; David Cook, 1845-47; Robert Harvey, 1848-56; William Nicholson, M.A., 1858-59; Robert Harvey Smith, M.A., 1859-67; Alexander Legge, 1868-74; William Cook Russell, M.A., 1875-81; Alexander Gray, 1882-83; John McMunn, 1884-88; Samuel Griffiths, 1889-98; William A. Stark, M.A., 1899-1905; Leyton Richards, M.A., 1906-10; James Gilmour Drummond, M.A., 1911-15; R. W. T. Middleton, B.A., 1915-20; Hassal Hanmer, M.A., B.D., 1920-24; Robert William Dickson, M.A., M.TH., 1924-30; H. Stoddart, 1932-38; Andrew Finlayson Tennant, 1938-42; John Gardner McIlvean, M.A., 1942-46; Richard Smith, 1947-53; Charles Moore, 1953-56; James Brooks, 1957-.

PORT-GLASGOW, 1880

Alexander D. Anderson, 1881-87; Alexander Cossar, 1888-1911; David L. Neave, 1911-16; G. Paterson Graham, 1917-23; John Barr, 1924-27; Robert Arnott Taylor, 1927-.

PORTOBELLO, 1836

James Cameron, 1837-43; Robert Lang, M.A., 1844-49; George Douglas McGregor, 1851-54; George Wight, 1855-57; J. Wilson Coombs, B.A., 1858-60; William Low, 1860-69; John Fordyce, M.A., 1870-72; Robert Auchterlonie, 1874-77; Edward Walker, 1877-78; James Kennedy, M.A., 1878-81; William Hope Davison, M.A., 1882-91; James Kelly, 1892-1917; James Baxter Allan, M.A., B.D., PH.D., 1918-26; William Gray, M.A., 1927-57; Andrew Ferguson Simpson, M.A., B.D., PH.D. (interim), 1958-59.

REAWICK AND SAND, 1835

James Stout, 1842-62; Laurence Fraser, 1855-75; Laurence Williamson, 1876-93; Magnus Sinclair, 1893-1910; William Baxter Blackwood, 1910-13; Charles E. Allan, 1913-42; David Black, 1942-45; Henry Vigors, 1848-50; G. Ramsay, 1952-55; Sidney Lawrence, 1956-.

[RENDALL, 1823

James Russell, 1835-37; David Blellock, 1838-42; Alexander Smith, M.A., 1842-70; Laurence Williamson, 1870-76; Alexander Whyte, 1878-82.]

[RENFREW, 1905

James B. Crombie, 1905-12; J. Stevenson, 1913- .]
AA

RHYNIE, 1804

George Cruickshank, 1804-41; Alexander Nicoll, 1843-78; James Cameron, 1878-80; James Edwards, M.A., B.D., 1881-84; W. Singer, M.A., 1885-86; Alexander Yeats, 1887-96; George Compton Smith, M.A., 1897-1903; Arthur Shand, M.A., 1903-5; William Farries, 1905-15; J. Fraser Ross, 1916-21; Thomas Leslie, 1921-28; Leonard Sykes, 1929-37; Harry Escott, M.A., 1938-43; James G. R. Strachan, 1943-50; William James Gaston, 1951-55; and HUNTLY, Andrew F. Tennant, 1957-.

[ROSYTH

Richard Smith, 1918-20; Alfred Wilson, 1920-23.]

[ROTHESAY, 1836

Archibald McEwan, 1837-39; Anthony McGill, 1843-48; in 1943 the cause was resumed for a while.]

RUTHERGLEN

[1883—Robert Brown, 1883-84; John Clark Neil, M.A., B.D., 1885-89; John Liddle King, M.A., 1889-99; Andrew Noble Scott, 1899-1905.]

JOHNSTONE DRIVE, 1901

Robert Whiteford, 1901-13; John L. King, M.A., 1913-27; William Davidson Bruce, 1927-30; H. P. Bralsford, 1930-33; J. Massie Milne, 1933-41; Donald S. Sutherland, 1942-47; Lenton George Seager, 1947-55; Leonard Hulme Oldfield, B.A., B.D., 1956-.

ST. ANDREWS, 1805

Thomas Paton, 1805-18; William Lothian, 1819-54; John C. McIntosh, 1854-62; James McEwan Stott, M.A., 1864-67; John Currie, 1867-75; Robert Troup, M.A., 1877-95; Alexander G. B. Sivewright, M.A., 1896-1903; David Samson, 1903-7; James Smith Thomson, 1907-12; George Auchterlonie Hardie, 1912-16; Harry Marsden, 1916-19; Harry D. Bedford, 1920-25; James Stewart, M.A., B.D., 1925-28; Hugh Lammie, 1929-33; Helen Elizabeth Woods, J.P., B.D., 1934-59; John Brownlow Geyer, B.A., 1959-.

ST. MONANCE, 1877

John W. Lockie, 1877-1921; Supplies; Kenneth Kingsley Lodge, 1937-47; Arthur Robertson, 1951-.

SALTCOATS, 1859

J. McDowell, 1862-68; Edward B. Kirk, 1879-83; David Greenhill, 1884-1909; John Cleminson Bell, M.A., 1909-51; Cecil James Jamison, 1953-56; Charles Moore, 1956-.

SANQUHAR

[(1) 1807—David Davidson, 1807- .]

(2) 1864—George Gladstone, 1865-71; George Bell, M.A., 1871-74; George Blair, 1876-77; Oliver Dryer, 1878-83; George Davies, 1886-89; John Ebenezer Christie, 1890-98; David William Gaylor, 1898-1905; Mark Newton Robson, 1905-13; Andrew Barclay, 1913-15; J. B. Pollock, 1915-20; David Mitchell Donald, 1920-26; John Barr, 1927-30; A. R. Wiseman, 1932-34; Thomas D. Alexander, 1934-37; Sidney Lawrence, 1938-43; Angus Hugh MacKinnon, 1943-47; Frederic Albert Ore, 1948-56; John Wilson McMinn, M.A., 1957-.

[SAUCHIEBURN (1773) 1809

James McRae, 1809-11; Thomas McKinnon, 1812-54.]

SCALLOWAY, 1840

Adam Gordon, 1840-41; J. Fraser, 1845-47; Nicol Nicolson, 1862-80; John Stirling Miller, 1881-82; Alexander Yeats, 1882-84; John Currie, 1885-1902; Alexander Campbell, 1902-9; Charles E. Allen, 1910-13; John Hart, 1914-17; Edgar Richards, 1919-21; John Arthur, 1921-27; W. L. Telford, 1927-42; Supplies, 1942-48; William McGill Thomson, 1949-50; Supplies, 1950-55.

SELKIRK

PHILIPHAUGH, 1842

John Nichol, 1850-85; William Robertson, 1885-98; Richard D. E. Stevenson, 1898-1903; William Ore, 1904-8; Walter Gerrard, 1908-14; George B. Shepherd, M.A., B.D., 1914-20.

THORNIEHALL (CHAPEL STREET), 1878

John D. Brown, 1879-81; James Frame, 1883-88; William S. Angus, 1889-92; Alexander Pollock, M.A., 1892-96; Winning Russell, 1897-1907; Robert Stein, 1908-10; George Paterson Graham, 1911-16; John Jenkins (in charge), 1917-20; the two churches united in 1920 sharing their places of worship with the same pastor, Richard Smith, 1920-23; G. C. Thomson, 1923-30; it was now decided that Thorniehall Church should be used and designated SELKIRK CONGREGATIONAL CHURCH, Robert Rigg, 1930-47; A. A. M. Thomson, 1948-54; John Wilson Currie, 1954-.

SHAPINSAY, 1852

(Thomas G. Salmon (missioner), 1851-55); Thomas G. Salmon, 1855-59; William Hutchison, 1859-64; William J. Craig, 1865-75; William Tiplady, 1878-90; Alexander Taylor Hill, 1890-96; Matthew Richmond, 1896-98; John Heggie, 1901-2; John Jenkins, 1903-14; Thomas Foster, 1915-23; Joseph Briggs, 1923-27; Peter Peace, 1927-30; Charles Derry, 1930-37; William E. Littlewood, 1937- ; John R. May, M.A., 1939-42; David Black, 1945-47; Henry Vigors, 1950-56.

SHOTTS, 1844

William Bathgate, 1844-46; Peter Mather and Hugh Templeton (supplies), 1846-47; William Hutchison, 1847-49; James Maconochie, 1849-51; Robert Anderson, 1851-55; David Drummond, 1855-56; James Maconochie (recalled), 1857-61; William Reid, 1861-66; John Whitson, 1866-71; David Drummond (recalled), 1871-74; Alexander Cossar, 1875-88; James Neil, 1889-90; Robert Russell, 1890-94; John George McGarva, 1895-1906; Walter Lockwood Terrett, 1907-15; Robert Deans, M.A., 1915-25; James Anderson, 1925-36; Albert Irvine, 1937-42; Nancie Ward, B.A., B.D., 1943-51; George Porter, 1953-.

STEWARTON, 1827

William Cunningham, 1827-49; Robert Smith (assistant), 1843-49; Robert Smith (sole pastor), 1849-72; George Peill, 1872-97; John Albert Lees, 1897-1906; Harry Marsden, 1907-12; John Robert Ramsay, 1912-23; John Coulson Thomson, 1923-26; David Mitchell Donald, 1926-30; Robert Deans, 1931-40; William C. Cowan, 1940-54; Charles Cammock, M.A., 1955-58; William Muir McPherson, 1958-.

[STIRLING, 1804

William Henry, 1807-17; Alexander Marshall, 1825-44; Andrew Russell, M.A., D.D., 1845-59; James R. Ferguson, 1859-64; James Ross, 1864-70; Alexander Nairn, 1871-76; J. Roebuck, 1877-79; William McLellan, 1879-84; William Henry Muncaster, M.A., B.D., 1884-88; William Blair, 1888-97; James Cowper McLachlan, M.A., 1898-1920.]

STONEHOUSE, 1894

Peter Smith, 1894-1906; James Wallace, 1906-17; Walter Gerrard, 1917-22; Robert McKinlay, M.A., PH.D., 1922-32; David C. McArthur, 1933-44; James G. R. Strachan (in charge), 1941-43; James Kinmond Smith, M.A., 1944-48; George Renton Brown, 1948-51; Robert M. Lawson, 1951-.

STRATHAVEN [WEST CHURCH], 1958

T. Hall Bisset, 1958-.

[STUARTFIELD, 1802

James Robertson, 1802-32; Alexander Cuthbert, M.A., 1835-37; Neil McKechnie, 1841-51; Angus Galbraith, 1852-57; J. Ferguson, 1857-59; Angus Galbraith, 1860-66; Thomas Mathieson, 1867-71; William Robertson, 1871-77; William Mathieson, 1878-84; William Murray Reid, 1884-88; James Provan, 1888- ; Walter R. Robinson, 1894-1900.]

[SULLOM (NORTHMAVINE)

John Nicholson, 1841-45; James Fraser, 1847-84; David K. Fisher, 1886-98; Charles Davidson, 1899-1906; Charles Derry, 1906-12; Henry McKinlay, 1912-13; James C. Drife, 1914-20; John Lawrie, 1921-23; Robert Gibson, 1924-36; Charles Derry, 1926-30.]

THORNHILL, 1851

James Pearson, 1855-59; John McIlvean, 1860- ; Alexander Nairn, 1864-67; Robert Inglis Gray, 1867-70; Robert Dingwall Mitchell, 1871-85; James Hume, 1885-92; James Wallace, 1892-1901; Robert Hislop, 1901-19; George Kirk, 1920-23; James Hume, 1924-33; Duncan Macmillan Turner, M.A., 1934-36; David Mitchell Donald, 1937-48; Charles Cullen Paul, 1949-54; Allan S. Guild, 1954-.

THURSO, 1799

William Ballantine, 1799-1801; David Sutherland, Edward Mackay, Walter Balfour, David Black, and others (unordained supplies), 1801-11; James Clark, 1811-13; James Taylor, 1813- ; Alexander Ewing, 1818-33; George Robertson, 1834-48; James Wishart, 1849-54; David Bisset Mackenzie, 1854-57; James Sime, 1858-65; James Virtue, 1866-72; Archibald Prentice, 1874-77; William Lowe Walker, 1877-81; William Stevenson, 1881-84; Wesley Kelly, 1885-1902; John William Derry, 1903-14; A. F. Simpson, M.A., 1914-18; Colin Livingston, 1918-21; J. F. Irvine Fortescue, 1921-23; W. C. Crawford, 1924-27; Gordon Lee Maclachlan, 1927-37; Nancie Ward, B.A., B.D., 1937-43; Donald Findlay, 1943-46; David Black, 1947-51; W. H. Marshall (in charge), 1953-54; Neil Taylor (lay pastor), 1956.

TILLICOULTRY

ANN STREET, 1851

John Whitson and others in charge, 1851-53; George Anderson, 1853-56; John Andrew, 1856-61; James Strachan, 1861-66; Alexander Nairn, 1867-71; James Davidson, 1872-1909; Alexander F. MacRobert, M.A., B.A., 1910-11.

HIGH STREET, 1872

Enoch Doughty Solomon, 1873-81; Arthur Smith, 1882-83; William Conn, 1884-93; Lachlan MacFadyen, 1894-1902; Robert Steen, 1903-7; George Strathearn, 1908-11. The two churches united in 1911 as TILLICOULTRY E.U. CONGREGATIONAL CHURCH (1911), A. F. MacRobert, 1911-29; Charles Florence, 1930-55; Peter Peace, 1956-.

[TIREE

Archibald Farquharson, 1835-78.]

UDDINGSTON, 1877

Thomas W. Bowman, 1878-83; Thomas H. Walker, 1883-1923; George Kirk, 1923-29; A. F. MacRobert, M.A., B.A., 1929-34; John Beattie Wilson, 1935-41; Robert Squince McCulloch, 1942-48; James Oliver, 1948-58; Charles Cammock, M.A., 1958-.

WALKERBURN, 1886

Benjamin D. Morris, 1888-92; James Johnstone, 1892-93; Alfred John Parker, 1894-1900; Donald Grigor, 1900-12; George Gerrard, 1913-15; T. Enfield Jones, 1915-19; Nathaniel Johnstone, 1919-22; Charles

Derry, 1922-26; David McGowan, 1927-29; James Massie Milne, 1930-33; Frank Allan Maxwell, 1934-37; William Campbell, 1938-44; Arthur G. Reekie, 1945-51; Warnock S. Lowry, 1952-55.

WALKERBURN AND INNERLEITHEN, 1956

Gordon Rainey Workman, 1956-.

WALLS, 1812

Alexander Kerr, 1825-36; Peter Paterson, 1837-57; John Craig, 1857-67; Archibald Prentice, 1870-74; Laurence Fraser, 1875-91; Samuel Bond, 1892-98; William Farries, 1899-1902; Walter Floyd Robinson, 1902-6; J. D. Hay, 1907-9; A. W. Groundwater, 1909-21; H. G. Goodwin, 1921- ; A. Richards, 1924-27; A. Henderson, 1930-36; David Black, 1936-42; Henry Vigors (in charge), 1948-50; George Ramsay (in charge), 1952-56; Sidney Lawrence, 1956-.

WESTHILL (SKENE), 1805

John Smith, 1806-35; Anthony Thomson Gowan, M.A., 1836-43; Alexander Munro, 1843-64; John Geddes, 1864-65; Robert Martin, 1869-71; Nisbet Galloway, 1872-73; David Drummond (unordained), 1874; Robert Joseph Kyd, 1879-81; George Wisely, 1881-1900; William Cran, M.A., B.D., 1901-31; Charles Lynch, 1932-44; Charles Francis Graham, 1945-58.

WICK

SHORE LANE, 1799

John Cleghorn, 1799-1813; Robert Caldwell, 1813-34; John Wiseman, 1834-42; G. Macfarlane, 1842-44; James Sime, 1846-53; James Innes, 1854-56; John Currie, 1856-67; William McLellan, 1867-75; David Leith, 1876-79; Adam Dunlop, 1880-87; Sidney Tucker, 1888-95; Alexander McLennan, M.A., 1895-97; David Russell Scott, M.A., 1897-1904; Adam Drummond, 1905-12; John Miller Wright, 1913-18; R. Moffatt Johnston, 1918-28; D. S. Sutherland, 1929-34; David Sutherland, M.A., 1935-39; John Dick, 1940-46; D. S. Sutherland, 1947-50; John M. McIntyre, 1950-54; Frederic Albert Ore, 1956-57; Robert Boyne, 1958-.

[VICTORIA PLACE, 1846

David Drummond, 1843-52; James Marshall, 1853-59; James Strachan, 1860-68; William Hutchison, 1868-73; Gilbert Paterson, 1873-78; Daniel Galbraith, 1880-81; Matthew Richmond, 1882-84; Robert Brown, 1885-92; Arthur McConnachie, 1896-97; Alexander Taylor Hill, 1898-1901.]

WISHAW, 1862

Robert Inglis Gray, 1862-66; William Halliday, 1867-76; Peter McNish, 1877-94; James Adam, 1895-1907; James A. S. Wilson, M.A., B.A., 1907-9; Alexander Pollock, M.A., 1910-36; Griffith J. Owens, 1936-41; William Kitching, 1941-44; Charles Cammock, M.A., 1945-49; Gordon Rainey Workman, 1950-56; Andrew Gillespie Jenkins, 1956-.

[WESTRAY, 1806
William Tulloch, 1806-10.]

LISTS OF OFFICIALS

CHAIRMEN, SECRETARIES, AND TREASURERS OF THE CONGREGATIONAL UNION

Chairmen

Revs. W. L. Alexander, D.D., L.L.D, 1863; R. Spence, M.A., 1864; J. M. Jarvie, 1865; H. Batchelor, 1866; D. Arthur, 1867; A. T. Gowan, D.D., 1868; J. Robbie, 1869; P. Whyte, 1870; W. Pulsford, D.D., 1871; R. Troup, M.A., 1872; W. J. Cox, D.D., 1873; D. Russell, D.D., 1874; G. D. Cullen, M.A., 1875; J. Masson, 1876; N. Wight, 1877; W. D. Knowles, B.A., 1878; J. Tait, M.A., 1879; J. Troup, M.A., 1880; John Pillans, 1881; Edward J. Scott, Esq., 1882; Charles Short, M.A., D.D., 1883; Ebenezer Young, 1884; Albert Goodrich, D.D., 1885; George McHardy, M.A., D.D., 1886; James Ross, D.D., 1887; James Stark, D.D., 1888; Thomas Alexander, Esq., 1889; James Gregory, 1890; J. Duncan, D.D., 1891; John Robertson, Esq., 1892; A. F. Simpson, M.A., 1893; W. Douglas Mackenzie, M.A., D.D., 1894; John Hunter, D.D., 1895; J. R. Sandilands, 1896.

Secretaries

George Payne and John Watson, 1812-16; John Watson, 1816-44; William Swan, 1845-55; Henry Wight, 1856-60; David Russell, 1861-77; James Ross, 1877-83; John Douglas, 1883-91; W. Hope Davison, M.A., 1891-97.

Treasurers

R. Gray, 1812-42; James McLaren, 1842-53; David McLaren, 1854-78; James S. Mack, S.S.C., 1878-91; J. R. Sandilands, 1891-97.

PRESIDENTS, SECRETARIES, AND TREASURERS OF THE EVANGELICAL UNION

Presidents

Revs. Robert Morison, Bathgate, 1843; Alexander C. Rutherford, Falkirk, 1944; James Morison, Kilmarnock, 1845; John Guthrie, M.A., Kendal, 1846; David Drummond, Airdrie, 1847; Alexander M. Wilson, Paisley, 1848; Robert Hunter, Kilwinning, 1849; James Howie, Kelso,

1850; Ebenezer Kennedy, Leith, 1851; John Kirk, Edinburgh, 1852; Fergus Ferguson, jun., Glasgow, 1853; John Guthrie, M.A., Greenock, 1854; Gilbert McCallum, Falkirk, 1855; Nisbet Galloway, Glasgow, 1856; William Bathgate, Kilmarnock, 1857; William Taylor, Kendal, 1858; Fergus Ferguson, sen., Aberdeen, 1859; Joseph Boyle, Leith, 1860; Alexander Davidson, Glasgow, 1861; Hugh Riddell, Glasgow, 1862; James Maconochie, Hamilton, 1863; George Cron, Belfast, 1864; Robert Wallace, Coupar-Angus, 1865; William Adamson, Perth, 1866; Robert Mitchell, Glasgow, 1867; James Morison, D.D., Glasgow, 1868; David Hislop, M.A., Hawick, 1869; John Whitson, Shotts, 1870; Andrew M. Fairbairn, Bathgate, 1871; Fergus Ferguson, sen., Aberdeen, 1872; Alexander Cross, Ardrossan, 1873; George Gladstone, Govan, 1874; Robert Hislop, Kilmarnock, 1875; Robert Craig, M.A., D.D., Glasgow, 1876; William Bathgate, Kilmarnock, 1877; Robert Hunter, Leith, 1878; George Wiseley, Montrose, 1879; Robert Anderson, Glasgow, 1880; John Miller, Forres, 1881; James Davidson, Tillicoultry, 1882; James Foote, Dunfermline, 1883; Fergus Ferguson, M.A., D.D., Glasgow, 1884; Robert D. Mitchell, Dalkeith, 1885; Robert Hood, Glasgow, 1886; Robert Steel, Dalmellington, 1887; Professor Alexander McNair, M.A., Kilmarnock, 1888; James Morison, D.D., Glasgow, 1889; Alexander Stewart, M.D., LL.D., Aberdeen, 1890; William Adamson, D.D., Edinburgh, 1891; John Wilson, Esq., M.P., Glasgow, 1892; Robert Finlay, Perth, 1893; Professor Fergus Ferguson, D.D., Glasgow, 1894; Alexander Brown, Aberdeen, 1895; Professor William Taylor, D.D., 1896.

Secretaries

Robert Hunter, 1843; John Guthrie, 1843-44; A. C. Rutherford, 1844-52; A. M. Wilson, 1852-87; George Gladstone, 1887-97.

Treasurers

William McWhirter, 1843-51; Robert Moyes, 1853-57; Rev. Nisbet Galloway, 1857-62; Rev. John Andrews, 1862-66; William Ridley, 1866-69; Peter Ferguson, 1869-97.

PRESIDENTS, SECRETARIES, AND TREASURERS
OF THE CONGREGATIONAL UNION OF
SCOTLAND

(Comprising the Evangelical Union and Congregational Union as
existing at 1896)

Presidents

William Taylor, D.D., and J. R. Sandilands, 1897; Fergus Ferguson, M.A., D.D., 1897; J. R. Sandilands, 1897-98; James Ross, D.D., 1898-99; George Gladstone, 1899-1900; John Leith, J.P., 1900-1; William Hamilton, M.A., 1901-2; A. E. Garvie, M.A., B.D., D.D., 1902-3; A.

Wilson, 1903-4; R. Auchterlonie, 1940-5; John Orr, J.P. (Glasgow), 1905-6; A. Shepherd, D.D., 1906-7; W. F. Adamson, M.A., 1907-8; A. Gardner, 1908-9; W. Adamson, D.D., 1909-10; A. W. Russell, M.A., M.B., C.M., 1910-11; A. Brown, D.D., 1911-12; J. Macpherson, J.P., 1912-13; W. L. Walker, D.D., 1913-14; A. F. Simpson, M.A., 1914-15; T. H. Walker, 1915-16; C. Richardson, M.A., 1916-17; John Orr, J.P. (Airdrie), 1917-18; T. Templeton, M.A., 1918-19; T. MacRobert, M.A., 1919-20; H. Brown, J.P., 1920-21; Rev. Robert Rae, 1921-22; Rev. A. Ritchie, M.A., 1922-23; Rev. G. C. Milne, 1923-24; Sir Malcolm Campbell, J.P., 1924-25; Rev. James I. Macnair, 1925-26; Rev. A. G. B. Sivewright, M.A., 1926-27; Rev. A. Pollock, M.A., 1927-28; Rev. D. Russell Scott, M.A., PH.D., 1928-29; Rev. J. A. Lees, 1929-30; Rev. R. McKinlay, M.A., PH.D., 1930-31; Rev. A. J. Forson, 1931-32; Rev. H. Moffat Scott, 1932-33; J. Gillies, J.P., 1933-34; Rev. A. C. Hill, D.D., 1934-35; Rev. J. Safeley, M.A., PH.D., 1935-36; Rev. T. Johnstone, 1936-37; Rev. T. S. Taylor, M.A., B.LITT., 1937-38; Rev. J. G. Drummond, M.A., 1938-39; Rev. C. Richardson, M.A., D.D., 1939-40; E. W. Watt, M.A., LL.D., 1940-41; Rev. R. G. Davies, M.A., 1941-42; Rev. D. Grigor, 1942-43; Rev. G. Forbes Morgan, 1943-44; Rev. A. F. Simpson, M.A., B.D., 1944-45; Rev. James M. Calder, 1945-46; Mr. A. E. Walker, 1946-47; Rev. George Kirk, 1947-48; Rev. J. T. Hornsby, M.A., PH.D., 1948-49; Mr. George Blatch, F.I.B., F.R.ECON.S., 1949-50; Rev. Harry Andrew, 1950-51; Rev. Vera M. M. Kenmure, M.A., B.D., 1951-52; Rev. Charles S. Duthie, M.A., D.D., 1952-53; Rev. T. Carlyle Murphy, O.B.E., B.D., 1953-54; Rev. Hector Ross, M.A., 1954-55; Mr. James McLay, 1955-56; Rev. Arthur Morton Price, M.A., B.D., PH.D., 1956-57; Rev. Allan Cameron McDougall, M.A., 1957-58; Rev. Prof. James Wood, M.A., B.D., 1958-59; Miss Catherine M. Robertson, M.A., 1959-60; Rev. Thomas Mearns, M.A., 1960-61.

Secretaries

W. Hope Davison, M.A., and George Gladstone, 1897; W. Hope Davison, M.A., 1897-99; C. Richardson, M.A., 1900-18; A. G. B. Sivewright, M.A., 1918-24; C. Richardson, M.A., D.D., 1924-41; T. Carlyle Murphy, O.B.E., B.D., 1941-51; James M. Calder, 1951-60.

Treasurers

Peter Ferguson and J. R. Sandilands, 1897-1900; David Strathie, C.A., and Dr. A. W. Russell, 1900-9; David Strathie, C.A., 1909-12; George Wolfe, J.P., 1912-24; Henry Brown, J.P., 1924-33; Daniel McLay, 1933-41; George R. Green, M.A., C.A., 1941-55; John K. Templeton, C.A., 1955-60.

Chairmen

Hassal Hanmer, 1946-49; George Kirk, 1949-53; Arthur Morton Price, M.A., B.D., PH.D., 1953-56; George R. Green, M.A., C.A., 1956-57; James L. Proudfoot, 1958-.

BIBLIOGRAPHY

SOCIAL, CULTURAL, AND RELIGIOUS BACKGROUND

BREWSTER, PATRICK. *The Seven Chartist and Military Discourses.* Paisley, 1843.

BROWN, P. HUME. *Scotland: A Short History.* Enlarged edition. Ed. W. H. Meikle. Edinburgh, 1951.

FERGUSON, THOMAS. *The Dawn of Scottish Social Welfare: A survey from medieval times to 1863.* London, 1948.

FERGUSON, THOMAS. *Scottish Social Welfare, 1864-1914.* London, 1958.

FINLAY, IAN, *Scotland.* London, 1945.

FLEMING, J. R. *A History of the Church in Scotland, 1843-1874.* Edinburgh, 1927.

GALT, JOHN. *Annals of the Parish.*

Gazetteer of Scotland. Dundee, 1803.

GRAHAM, H. G. *The Social Life of Scotland in the Eighteenth Century,* 4th edn. 1937.

HALDANE, ELIZABETH S. *The Scotland of our Fathers: A Study of Scottish Life in the Nineteenth Century.* London, 1933.

HENDERSON, H. F. *The Religious Controversies of Scotland.* Edinburgh, 1905.

JOHNSTON, T. *The History of the Working Classes in Scotland.* Glasgow, 1920.

MACINNES, J. *The Evangelical Movement in the Highlands of Scotland, 1688-1800.* Aberdeen, 1951.

MACKAY, JOHN. *The Church in the Highlands.* London, 1914.

MACKINNON, J. *The Social and Industrial History of Scotland from the Union to the present time.* London, 1921.

McLAREN, MORAY. *The Scots.* 1951.

MACLEOD, J. *Scottish Theology in relation to Church History since the Reformation.* Edinburgh, 1943.

MACPHERSON, HECTOR. *The Intellectual Development of Scotland.* London, 1911.

MEIKLE, H. W. *Scotland and the French Revolution.* Glasgow, 1912.

MOWAT, C. L. *Britain between the Wars, 1918-1940.* London, 1955.

MUIR, EDWIN. *Scottish Journey.* London, 1935.

OAKLEY, C. A. *The Second City.* London, 1947.

SPINKS, G. S. (Editor). *Religion in Britain since 1900.* London, 1952.

TAIT, JAMES. *Two Centuries of Border Church Life.* Kelso, 1889.
TREVELYAN, G. M. *English Social History.* Chapter XIV. London, 1944.
WALKER, N. L. (Editor). *Religious Life in Scotland; from the Reformation to the present day.* London, 1888.
WATSON, JOHN. *The Scot of the Eighteenth Century: His Religion and His Life.* London.
WRIGHT, LESLIE C. *Scottish Chartism.* Edinburgh, 1953.

BIOGRAPHIES, MEMOIRS, DIARIES, ETC.

An Account of the Life and Character of Mr. John Glas. Edinburgh, 1813.
ADAMSON, WILLIAM. *The Life of the Rev. Fergus Ferguson.* London, 1900.
ADAMSON, WILLIAM. *The Life of the Rev. James Morison, D.D.* London, 1898.
ALEXANDER, WILLIAM LINDSAY. *Memoirs of the Rev. John Watson.*
ALEXANDER, WILLIAM LINDSAY. *Memoirs of the Life and Writings of Ralph Wardlaw, D.D.* 2nd edn. Edinburgh, 1856.
ALLAN, J. B. *Rev. John Duncan, D.D.: A Memoir.* London, 1919.
BAILLIE, ROBERT. *Letters and Journals.* Ed. Laing. Edinburgh, 1841-42.
BRADLEY, W. L. *P. T. Forsyth: The Man and His Work.* London, 1952.
CALDER, JAMES M. *Scotland's March Past.* London, 1945.
CARLYLE, ALEXANDER. *Autobiography,* 3rd edn. London, 1816.
COCKBURN, HENRY. *Memorials of His Time.* Ed. Edinburgh, 1909.
ESCOTT, HARRY. *Peter Taylor Forsyth: Director of Souls.* London, 1948.
EWING, GREVILLE. *A Memoir of Barbara Ewing.* Glasgow, 1829.
GAMMIE, ALEX. *Preachers I have known.*
GILFILLAN, GEORGE. *Remoter Stars in the Church Sky.*
GILMOUR, DAVID. *Reminiscences of the Pen' Folk,* 2nd edn. Paisley, 1873.
HALDANE, ALEXANDER. *Memoirs of the Lives of Robert Haldane of Airthrey (1764-1842), and of his brother James Alexander Haldane (1768-1851),* 9th edn. Edinburgh.
HOBBS, DAVID. *Robert Hood the Bridgeton Pastor.* Edinburgh, 1894.
HUNTER, LESLIE S. *John Hunter, D.D.: A Life.* London, 1921.
JAFFRAY, ALEXANDER. *Diary.* Spalding Club, Aberdeen, 1856.
KINNIBURGH, ROBERT. *Fathers of Independency in Scotland.* Edinburgh, 1851.
KIRK, HELEN. *Memoirs of Rev. John Kirk, D.D.* Edinburgh, 1888.
The Life and Opinions of Arthur Sneddon of Paisley. 1860.
MACDONALD, GREVILLE. *George Macdonald and his Wife.* London, 1924.
McLAREN, E. T. *Dr. Lindsay Alexander.* London, n.d.

McNair, James I. *Livingstone the Liberator.*

Matheson, J. J. *A Memoir of Greville Ewing.* London, 1847.

Mathews, Basil. *Dr. Ralph Wardlaw Thompson.* London, 1917.

Peel, Albert. *The Congregational Two Hundred, 1530-1948.* London, 1948.

Ross, James. *W. Lindsay Alexander, D.D., LL.D.: His Life and Work.* London, 1887.

Selbie, W. B. *The Life of Andrew Martin Fairbairn.* London, 1914.

Shepherd, Eric. *Ambrose Shepherd, D.D.: A Memoir and Sermons.* London, 1915.

Smeaton, Oliphant. *Principal James Morison. The Man and His Work.* Edinburgh, 1901.

Stark, James. *Memoirs of Rev. James Troup.* Helensburgh, 1897.

Stark, James. *John Murker of Banff.* London, 1887.

Walker, T. H. *Fellow-Labourers: A Ministerial Septuary.* Greenock, 1916.

The Worthies of the Evangelical Union. Glasgow, 1883.

OTHER CHURCHES

BAPTIST CHURCHES

Yuille, George (Editor). *History of the Baptists in Scotland,* 2nd edn. Glasgow, 1926.

THE CHURCH OF SCOTLAND

An Abridgement of the Acts of the General Assembly, 1638-1810. Edinburgh, 1811.

Calderwood, David. *The History of the Kirk of Scotland.* Editor T. Thomson. 8 vols. Wodrow Soc. Edinburgh, 1942-45.

Campbell, Andrew J. *Two Centuries of the Church of Scotland.* Paisley, 1930.

The First Book of Discipline.

Henderson, G. D. *The Church of Scotland: A Short History.* Edinburgh, 1939.

Peterkin, Alexander. *Records of the Kirk of Scotland.* Edinburgh, 1838.

Rainy, Robert. *Three Lectures on the Church of Scotland.* 1872.

The Scots Confession of 1560.

THE RELIEF CHURCH

Struthers, G. *The History of the Rise, Progress, and Principles of the Relief Church, etc.* Glasgow, 1843.

THE SECESSION CHURCH

McKerrow, John. *History of the Secession Church.* Edinburgh, 1839.

ENGLISH CONGREGATIONALISM

DALE, R. W. *History of English Congregationalism.*

DAVIES, HORTON. *The English Free Churches.* 1952.

PEEL, ALBERT. *A Brief History of English Congregationalism.* London, 1953.

PEEL, ALBERT. *These Hundred Years: A History of the Congregational Union of England and Wales, 1831-1931.* London, 1931.

WADDINGTON, J. *Congregational History.* Vol. 2.

SCOTTISH CONGREGATIONALISM

BEREANS

CAMERON, A. C. *The History of Fettercairn.* Paisley, 1899.

PHILIP, ADAM. *The Evangel in Gowrie.*

GLASITES

An Account of the Life and Character of Mr. John Glas. Edinburgh, 1813.

Continuation of Mr. Glas's Narrative. Edinburgh, 1729.

GLAS, JOHN. *Works.* 5 vols. Perth, 1782.

HORNSBY, J. T. *John Glas.* Unpublished thesis, Edinburgh University.

OLD SCOTS INDEPENDENTS

The Case of James Smith, late minister at Newburn, and of Robert Ferrier, late minister at Largo, truly represented and defended. Glasgow, 1816.

McGAVIN, JAMES. *A Concise Abstract of the Faith, Hope, and Practice of the Old Scots Independents.* 1814.

McGAVIN, JAMES. *Historical Sketches of the Old Scots Independents and the Inghamite Churches; with the Correspondence that led to their Union.* Colne, 1814.

THOMPSON, RICHARD W. *Benjamin Ingham . . . and the Inghamites.* Kendal, 1958.

MODERN CONGREGATIONALISM

A. GENERAL LITERATURE

An Account of the Proceedings of the Society for Propagating the Gospel at Home. 1799.

BALLANTYNE, W. *A Treatise on the Elder's Office.*

BROWNE, ROBERT. *A New Year's Gift.* Editor C. Burrage, 1904.

BULLOCH, J. *Centenary Memorial of the First Congregational Church in Aberdeen.* Aberdeen, 1898.

CLARK, HENRY E. (Editor). *Memorials of Elgin Place Congregational Church, Glasgow. A Centenary Volume, 1803-1903.* Glasgow, 1904.

Congregationalism in Scotland with biographic sketches. Dingwall, 1895.

ESCOTT, HARRY. *Beacons of Independency: Religion and Life in Strathbogie and Upper Garioch in the Nineteenth Century.* Huntly, 1940.

The Entire Correspondence between the four Congregational churches in Glasgow and the Congregational churches in Hamilton, Bellshill, Bridgeton, Cambuslang, and Ardrossan on the doctrine of election, etc. Glasgow, 1845.

EWING, GREVILLE. *Animadversions on some passages of a pamphlet entitled Lay-preaching Indefensible on Scripture Principles.* Glasgow, 1800.

EWING, GREVILLE. *Facts and Documents Respecting the Connections which have subsisted between Robert Haldane, Esq. and Greville Ewing.* Glasgow, 1809.

The Expulsion of Nine Students from the Glasgow Theological Academy, etc. Glasgow, 1844.

FERGUSON, FERGUS. *A History of the Evangelical Union.* Glasgow, 1876.

FORSON, A. J. *The Story of our Union.* 1929.

GAMMIE, ALEX. *The Churches of Aberdeen.* Aberdeen, 1909.

Glasgow District Committee Handbook. 1946-47.

HALDANE, JAMES A. *Journal of a Tour through the Northern Counties of Scotland and the Orkney Isles in autumn, 1797.* Edinburgh, 1798.

HALDANE, JAMES A. *The Celebration of the Lord's Supper every Lord's Day by the late Mr. Randal . . . Mr. Glas . . ., to which are subjoined a letter from Mr. Haldane.* Edinburgh, 1802.

HALDANE, JAMES A. *Observations on the Association of Believers; Mutual Exhortation; The Apostolic Mode of teaching; Qualifications and support of Elders; Spiritual gifts, etc.* Edinburgh, 1808.

HALDANE, JAMES A. *Reasons of a change of sentiment on the subject of Baptism. . . .* Edinburgh, 1808.

HALDANE, JAMES A. *Observations on Forbearance.* Edinburgh, 1811.

HALDANE, JAMES A. *Remarks on Mr. Jones's Review of Observations on Forbearance.* Edinburgh, 1812.

HALDANE, JAMES A. *Letters to a Friend containing strictures on a recent publication upon Primitive Christianity. . . .* Edinburgh, 1820.

HALDANE, ROBERT. *Address to the Public concerning Political Opinions and Plans lately adopted to promote Religion in Scotland.* Edinburgh, 1800.

HILL, ROWLAND. *Journal through the North of England and Parts of Scotland. . . .* London, 1799.

HISLOP, DAVID. *Congregationalism in the Border District, 1798-1898.* 1898.

JAMIESON, JOHN. *Remarks on the Rev. Rowland Hill's Journal.* Edinburgh, 1799.

The Jubilee Memorial of the Scottish Congregational Churches. Edinburgh, 1849.

LAING MSS. Edinburgh University. Div. 11, Nos. 500 and 501.

MCHARDY, GEORGE. *Handbook of Congregational Principles.* Edinburgh, 1894.

MURRAY, ABIJAH. *The Story of Augustine Church, 1802-1877.* Edinburgh, 1911.

Pastoral Admonition of the General Assembly. 1799.

PENRY, JOHN. *A Briefe Discovery.*

PHILIP, R. *The Missionary Enterprise of the Rev. J. Campbell.*

Report of the Proceedings of the E.U. at its First Annual Meeting held in Bathgate, June 3-6, 1844.

Reports of the Society for the Propagation of the Gospel at Home.

ROSS, JAMES. *A History of Congregational Independency in Scotland.* Glasgow, 1900.

SANDILANDS, J. R. *Scottish Congregationalism: A Retrospect and a Plea.* Edinburgh, 1896.

SIMPSON, ANDREW FERGUSON. *Congregationalism and the Church.* 1946.

The Story of the Scottish Congregational Theological Hall, 1811-1911. Edinburgh, 1911.

The Story of Ward Chapel: A Hundred years of Congregationalism. Dundee, 1934.

THOMPSON, G. L. S. *The Origins of Congregationalism in Scotland.* Unpublished thesis, Edinburgh University.

TROUP, ROBERT. *The Missionar Kirk of Huntly.* Huntly, 1901.

The Witness of Congregationalism in Scotland. 1933.

B. PAMPHLETS RELATING TO THE UNION OF 1896

Proposed Union between the Congregational Union and Evangelical Union. Explanatory Statement. January 1895.

Supplementary Statement. February 1895.

Proposed Union of the Congregational and Evangelical Unions. The Report of the Dissentient members of the Amalgamation Committee. A Reply. February 1895.

The Facts Bearing on the Proposed Union . . . clearly stated. Edinburgh, 1895.

The Proposed Union of the Congregational Union of Scotland with the Evangelical Union. The Present Situation by James Ross. Edinburgh, 1896.

To the Churches of the Congregational and Evangelical Unions. A Letter. 1896.

Reports of Committees on Union with the Evangelical Union. Glasgow, 1896.

Minutes of the adjourned meeting of the Congregational Union of Scotland and of the Joint-Meeting of said Union with the Evangelical Union of Scotland, held in Glasgow, 1st October 1896.

C. PERIODICAL LITERATURE

Edinburgh Quarterly Magazine. Vols. I and II.

The Missionary Magazine. Vols. I, VIII, and XV.

Records of the Scottish Church History Society, Vol. VI. Glasgow, 1938.

Scottish Congregational Magazine. Vols. I and II.

The Scottish Congregationalist, 1875-1958.

Transactions of the Congregational Historical Society. Vol. XIII, No. 1. September 1937.

Year Books of the Congregational Union of Scotland, 1900-1958.

D. LOCAL CHURCH HISTORIES

Printed

ABERDEEN

Belmont. *Centenary Memorials of the First Congregational Church in Aberdeen.* J. Bulloch. 1898.
Belmont Congregational Church, Aberdeen, Jubilee Celebrations, 1915.
Annals of Belmont Congregational Church, Aberdeen, 1898-1948.

Woodside. *Records of the First Church in Woodside, Aberdeen . . . 1818-1945.*

ABERFELDY. *Brief History of Aberfeldy Congregational Church.*

AIRDRIE

Ebenezer. *Ebenezer Congregational Church, Airdrie, Centenary Souvenir, 1835-1935.*

Park. *Faith's Pilgrimage, 1845-1945. The Story of Park E.U. Congregational Church, Airdrie.*

ARBROATH. *Queen Street Congregational Church, Arbroath, Triple Jubilee Brochure.* 1950

ARDROSSAN. *E.U. Congregational Church, Ardrossan, 1837-1937. Centenary Souvenir.*

BARRHEAD. *E.U. Congregational Church, Barrhead, Centenary Celebrations, 1844-1944.*

BATHGATE. 'E.U. Centenary Celebrations at Bathgate'. *West Lothian Courier,* May 7th 1943.

CARLUKE. *Carluke E.U. Congregational Church. A Historical Sketch. 1846-1946.*

DUNDEE

Princes Street. *Princes Street Congregational Church, Dundee. Commemoration of the Centenary, 1839-1939.*

Ward Chapel. *A Hundred Years of Congregationalism: The Story of Ward Chapel.* 1934.

DUNFERMLINE

Canmore Street. *Canmore Street Congregational Church, Dunfermline, 1840-1940. Commemoration of the Centenary.*

North. *North Congregational Church, Dunfermline, Centenary Brochure, 1851-1951.*

EDINBURGH

Albany Street. *Albany Street Congregational Church, Edinburgh. Centenary, 1808-1908.*
Albany Street Church Manual. 1883.

Augustine. *The Story of Augustine Church, 1802-1877.* 1911.

Augustine-Bristo. *Augustine-Bristo Congregational Church, Triple Jubilee Celebrations, 1802-1952.*

Dalry. *Dalry Congregational Church, Edinburgh, 1872-1932. Diamond Jubilee.*

Hope Park and Buccleuch. *Hope Park and Buccleuch Congregational Church, Edinburgh. Constitution and Rules with historical preface.* 1946.

Morningside. *Morningside Congregational Church, Edinburgh. The Story of Fifty Years, 1887-1937.*

FALKIRK. *History of Trinity E.U. Congregational Church, Falkirk.*

FRASERBURGH. *A Northern Light. The Story of Mid Street Congregational Church in Fraserburgh.* 1947.

GALASHIELS. *Galashiels Congregational Church, 1844-1944, Centenary Brochure.*

GLASGOW

Dundas Street. *Dundas Street Congregational Church Centenary Brochure.* November 1948.

Eglinton Street. *Brief History of Eglinton Street Congregational Church, Glasgow, 1825-1925.*

Elgin Place. *Memorial of Elgin Place Congregational Church, Glasgow. A Centenary Volume, 1803-1903.*
Triple Jubilee Brochure. 1953.

Knightswood. *Knightswood Congregational Church, Twenty-First Anniversary.* 1954.

Lloyd Morris. *Lloyd Morris Congregational Church, Glasgow, Diamond Jubilee, 1879-1939.*

Montrose Street. *Montrose Street E.U. Congregational Church, Centenary.* July 1944.

Nile Street (Hillhead). *List of members of Nile Street Congregational Church, 1854.*
Reports of West Nile Street Chapel. 1857.

Partick. *Partick Congregational Church Diamond Jubilee, 1891-1951.*

GOVAN. *Govan Congregational Church History, 1870-1920.*

BB

GREENOCK

George Square. *History of George Square Congregational Church, Greenock, 1805-1905.* Glasgow, 1906.
Triple Jubilee Brochure, 1955.
Nelson Street. *Nelson Street E.U. Congregational Church, 1846-1946. Centenary Commemoration.*

HAMILTON

Park Road. *Park Road E.U. Congregational Church, Hamilton, Centenary, 1854-1954.*
St. James. *Centenary of St. James Congregational Church, Hamilton, 1807-1907.*

HAWICK. *Hawick Congregational Church Centenary Commemoration, 1848-1948.*

HUNTLY. *The Missionar Kirk of Huntly.* R. Troup. 1901.

KIRKCALDY

West End. *West End Congregational Church, Kirkcaldy. 150th Anniversary.* 1947.

LARKHALL. *Congregational Church, Larkhall, 1875-1925. Jubilee Souvenir.*

LEITH

Duke Street. *Duke Street E.U. Congregational Church, Leith, 1844-1944. A Short History.*

LERWICK. *Congregational Church, Lerwick, Triple Jubilee, 1808-1958. Commemoration Brochure.*

MACDUFF. *Congregational Church, Macduff, Diamond Jubilee, 1879-1939.*

MILLSEAT. *Millseat Congregational Church. A Sketch of its History issued on the occasion of its Centenary.* 1930.

MONTROSE. *Montrose Congregational Church, 1800-1950.*

MOTHERWELL. *Motherwell E.U. Congregational Church Diamond Jubilee, 1872-1932.*

NEWPORT. *Newport Congregational Church Triple Jubilee, 1801-1951. Souvenir Brochure.*

PAISLEY

New Street E.U. Congregational Church Bi-Centenary Souvenir, 1738-1938.
Church and Tabernacle: A Century of Church Life in Paisley. A. B. Carswell. 1914.
Statement of Principles held by the Tabernacle Congregational Church, Paisley. 1860.

PERTH. *Historical Sketch of the Congregational Church, Mill Street, 1794-1885.* William Sievwright.
Perth Congregational Church, 1798-1948.

PORTOBELLO. *Portobello Congregational Church, 1836-1936. Centenary Brochure.*

RHYNIE. *Beacons of Independency.* H. Escott. 1940.

RUTHERGLEN.*Congregational Church, Rutherglen, Jubilee, 1901-1951.*

SHOTTS. *E.U. Congregational Church, Shotts. Short History of the Church.* 1944.

STONEHOUSE. *Stonehouse Congregational Church Diamond Jubilee, 1849-1954.*

WISHAW. *Wishaw E.U. Congregational Church, 1862-1912. History of the Church during the first Fifty years of its existence.* 1912.

In Manuscript

ABERDEEN. Mastrick, Skene Street.

AIRDRIE. Coatdyke.

ANNAN.

AVONBRIDGE.

AYR. Morison.

BATHGATE.

BROUGHTY FERRY.

CAMBUSLANG.

COATBRIDGE. Albert street.

CUMNOCK.

DALKEITH.

DARVEL.

DREGHORN.

DUMFRIES.

DUNDEE. Castle Street, Lindsay Street, Princes Street, Russell Chapel.

EDINBURGH. Granton, Saughtonhall.

EYEMOUTH.

GALSTON.

GARLIESTON.

GLASGOW. Bethany, Broomhill, Cathcart, Christchurch, Dalmarnock, Dennistoun-Wardlaw, Giffnock, Hillhead, Hood Memorial, Parkhead, Trinity.

HELENSBURGH.

KILMARNOCK.

KILSYTH.

KIRKWALL.

LANGHOLM.

LEITH. Constitution Street.

MUSSELBURGH.

NAIRN.

NEWBURGH.

NEWCASTLETON.

OBAN.

PAISLEY. School Wynd.

REAWICK AND SAND.

SALTCOATS.

SANQUHAR.

SCALLOWAY.

SELKIRK.

SHAPINSAY.

STEWARTON.

THORNHILL.

THURSO.

TILLICOULTRY.

UDDINGSTON.

WALLS.

WICK.

SUBJECT INDEX

ACADEMY, Glasgow Theological Greville Ewing's *Memorial* concerning it, beginnings, tutors and curricula, inaugurates a new era in Scottish Congregationalism, appeals to the churches on its behalf, its first class, its students few for lack of funds, its students itinerated during vacations, Gaelic students encouraged by it, Ewing itinerates on its behalf, its success, 90-93

ACADEMY, Robert Haldane's originated by him, Greville Ewing its first tutor, constitution of classes, character of training, removal to Glasgow, Ewing relinquishes his connection with it, 76-81

BAPTISM CONTROVERSY, 83-85, 261, 262, 263, 265, 267, 268, 273, 274, 276, 278, 281, 283, 286, 294, 295, 314, 319, 324, 331, 332, 334

BAPTISTS, Old Scotch, 85

BAXTER TRUST, 220

B.B.C., 206

BEREAN CONGREGATIONS, 96, 267, 272, 273

'BONSKEID', 210

CALVINISM, the revolt from, 107-134

CAMBUSLANG 'WARK', 90

CAVERS MISSIONARS, 334-335

CENTRAL FUND, 185-192

CENTRAL FUND COMMITTEE, 188 f.

CENTRALISATION, the tendency towards, 202-204

CENTRAL PENSION FUND, 213 f., 249 f.

CHAIRMAN OF THE UNION, the new office of, 204, 247

CHAIRMEN OF THE UNION, 377

CHAPLAINS, army, 187, 237; industrial, 247; school, 247; university, 247

CHRISTIAN INSTITUTE, 172 f., 248

Christian News, 132, 165, 169

CHURCH AID COMMITTEE, 186 f., 209

CHURCH EXTENSION, 203, 206, 207 f.

CHURCH EXTENSION COMMITTEE, 207, 230 f.

CHURCH EXTENSION FUND, 229-232

CHURCH OF SCOTLAND, in relation to Congregationalism, cf. Introduction; and seventeenth century re-

ligious Independency, 3-13; and the Glasites, 18-23; and the Old Scots Independents, 24 f.; and the Bereans, 37-41; the growth of Moderatism within it, 46 ff.; its failure to hold the people in the Revolutionary period, 49; its antagonism towards the Haldane movement, 69 f.; Evangelical cells within it, 55; its preaching criticised by the 'missionars', 58 f.; it benefited from the Haldane movement, 60; the Haldanes members of its communion, 67; its persecution of the Haldanes and their colleagues, 68, 265, 324, 325; accuses Rowland Hill and the S.P.G.H. of sedition, 69 f.; its *Pastoral Admonition*, 70 f.; other presbyterian bodies joined it in antagonism, 71 f.; it seeks the support of the government in its attack on the Haldanes, 72; illustrations of its hostility, 73 f; Greville Ewing leaves it, 88 f.; its criticism of Ewing, 90; it passes the Veto Act (1834), 105; its attitude to nineteenth century revivalism, 106; liberal theology movement within it, 138; its later relations with Scottish Congregationalism, 197, 202, 210, 222, 223, 226 f.

COLLEGE COMMITTEE, 219, 221

COLLEGES, Hackney and New, 198; Lancashire Independent, 216; Mansfield, Oxford, 225; Paton, Nottingham, 217; Princeton, U.S.A., 95; Scottish Congregational, 216-221; Western, Bristol, 217; Yorkshire United Independent, Bradford, 217

COMMITTEE FOR WOMEN'S SOCIAL WELFARE, 212, 235

COMMITTEE ON ENGLISH EDUCATION BILL, 198 f.

C.M.S., 212

CONGREGATIONAL UNION OF ENGLAND AND WALES, its relations with Scottish Congregationalism, 198 ff., 223, 225

CONGREGATIONAL UNION OF SCOTLAND, Robert Haldane entertained idea of it, its formation, its necessity, its aims, original membership,

INDEX OF PERSONS

INDEX OF CHURCHES